# THE EMPOWERED SELF

# THE EMPOWERED SELF

*Law and Society
in the Age of Individualism*

THOMAS M. FRANCK

**OXFORD**
UNIVERSITY PRESS

# OXFORD
UNIVERSITY PRESS

Great Clarendon Street, Oxford OX2 6DP

Oxford University Press is a department of the University of Oxford.
It furthers the University's objective of excellence in research, scholarship,
and education by publishing worldwide in

Oxford  New York

Athens  Auckland  Bangkok  Bogotá  Buenos Aires
Cape Town  Chennai  Dar es Salaam  Delhi  Florence  Hong Kong  Istanbul
Karachi  Kolkata  Kuala Lumpur  Madrid  Melbourne  Mexico City  Mumbai
Nairobi  Paris  São Paulo  Singapore  Taipei  Tokyo  Toronto  Warsaw
with associated companies in  Berlin  Ibadan

Oxford is a registered trade mark of Oxford University Press
in the UK and in certain other countries

Published in the United States
by Oxford University Press Inc., New York

British Library Cataloguing in Publication Data

Data available

Library of Congress Cataloging in Publication Data
Franck, Thomas M.
The empowered self: law and society in the age of invidualism/Thomas M. Franck.
p. cm.
1. Individualism.  2. Nationalism.  3. Identity (Pschology).  4. Group identity.
5. Citizenship.  6. Civil rights.  7. Human rights.  I. Title.
JC571.F6423 1999  302.5´4–dc21  99–045677

ISBN 0–19–829841–2

ISBN 0–19–924809–5 (Pbk)

Typeset in Baskerville
by J&L Composition Ltd, Filey, North Yorkshire
Printed in Great Britain
on acid-free paper by
Biddles Ltd, *www.biddles.co.uk*

*Prometheus Unchained*

Prometheus, in Greek cult mythology, is the God who stole fire from Zeus to endow each human with a divine spark. In Aeschylus' version of this tale, as told in *Prometheus Bound*, this theft draws Zeus' darkest ire, causing Prometheus to be chained to a crag in remote Scythia. Prometheus' eventual release may be seen to represent the reconciliation between the will of heaven and newly freed and assertive human beings. That a divine spark endows each person continues to be a powerful underpinning for modern individualism and the cause of human rights

T. M. F.

for

Martin Daly

To do the gentil dedes that he kan
Taak hym for the grettest gentil man

Chaucer, *Canterbury Tales*

# *Acknowledgements*

I wish to thank my friends and colleagues, whose critiques, advice and encouragement have contributed much to the intellectual pleasures that facilitated this audacious foray into the (for me) *terra incognita* of history, philosophy, psychology, sociology, and anthropology. All these expeditions were launched not from just the comfortably familiar but narrow ledge of law, but from the far broader landscapes made accessible by these wise and caring mentors. I wish profoundly to thank—while absolving them of all responsibility for my perambulations— Judge Rosalyn Higgins and Professors Philip Allott, Nathaniel Berman, Jerome Bruner, Michael Glennon, David Kennedy, Will Kymlicka, Ruth Lapidoth, Georg Nolte, David Richards, Oscar Schachter, and Joan Williams. Special appreciation is owed to the anonymous OUP readers who provided six single-spaced pages of invaluable comments and references, recourse to which has taken many well-spent months while also immeasurably enriching the texture of my argument.

Warmly appreciated, too, is the valuable work of a quarter-generation's worth of student research assistants: Jörg Bettendorf, Justin Brookman, John Chung, Paul Hayes, Young Kim, Paul Martin, Timothy Rhodes, Laurie Rosensweig, Deborah Smith, and Jennifer Wheatley.

My research was facilitated by a year as Visiting Fellow at Trinity College, Cambridge, stimulated by the ministrations of its dons and students as also by the dappled leas and rills of that lovely place. I was propelled by the intellectual bustle and thrust of the new Lauterpacht Centre, its guiding light, Professor James Crawford, and its founder, Sir Elihu Lauterpacht. Towards each I feel much fondness and gratitude, as also to my own law faculty which, via the generosity of the Filomen D'Agostino and Max E. Greenberg Research Fund, supported my work through four additional summers.

Special thanks—quite inexpressible after more than thirty years of fruitful and delightful collaboration on books, students, conferences, and, yes, much talk of cabbages and kings—go as always to my esteemed colleague, Rochelle Fenchel.

T. M. F.

*New York University*
*July 1999*

# Contents

# *Abbreviations*

| | |
|---|---|
| ASEAN | Association of South-East Asian Nations |
| CARICOM | Caribbean Community and Common Market |
| CAT | Convention Against Torture |
| CEDAW | Convention on the Elimination of Discrimination Against Women |
| CSCE | Conference on Security and Co-operation in Europe |
| ECOMOG | Economic Community of West African States' Military Organization |
| ECOSOC | Economic and Social Council (also ESC) |
| ECOWAS | Economic Community of West African States |
| EU | European Union |
| GATT | General Agreement on Tariffs and Trade |
| IBRD | International Bank for Reconstruction and Development |
| ICCPR | International Covenant on Civil and Political Rights |
| ICJ | International Court of Justice |
| IDA | International Development Association |
| ILO | International Labour Organization |
| MWC | Migrant Workers Convention |
| NAFTA | North American Free Trade Agreement |
| NATO | North Atlantic Treaty Organization |
| NGO | Non-Government Organization |
| OAS | Organization of American States |
| OAU | Organization of African Unity |
| OSCE | Organization for Security and Co-operation in Europe |
| PCIJ | Permanent Court of International Justice |
| UNTS | United Nations Treaty Series |

# 1
# *Tribe, Nation, State: Traditional Forms of Imposed Identity*

Nationalism appeals to our tribal instincts, to passion and to prejudice, and to our nostalgic desire to be relieved from the strain of individual responsibility which it attempts to replace by a collective or group responsibility.

Karl R. Popper, *The Open Society and its Enemies* (1962), ii. 49

## 1. THE THESIS

Every day seems to bring new evidence demonstrating that the world is in a deep crisis of militant nationalisms. The thesis of this book is that these events, however horrific, disguise a deeper reality: nationalism is in retreat. It no longer enjoys an exclusive licence to define personal identity. For various reasons examined in ensuing chapters, *individualism* has emerged, at the end of the twentieth century, as an increasingly preferred alternative to self-definition imposed by nationalism's genetic and territorial imperatives.

The individualist is an authentically modern phenomenon: a person who sets out to choose the components of his or her own, unique identity. Until the recent past, such self-definition was strictly forbidden: by law, custom, culture, and religion. One was, simply, the sum of where one lived, where one's parents worshipped, and the language one spoke. The blood in one's veins commanded absolutely the cells in one's brain and heart. Even now, for many, personal emancipation from these dictates of one's identity may still be beyond reach. But, change is coming.

This emerging right to individuality evidences more than an incremental change in the way personal identity is being redefined. Nationalists, traditionally, have invented 'alien others' and defined themselves by distinguishing themselves from and against these 'others'. The new individualists of the late twentieth century, however, do *not* identify an alien other; they identify *with* the alien other. In a sense, they see themselves as the alien other, in opposition to the old, territorially determined communal identity. Whereas, for all recorded history, personal identity has been perceived as a dependent consequence of certain independent variables—one's territorial location, ethnie, language, religion, citizenship—it has of late become possible, even legitimate, for individuals to imagine themselves—rather than linguistic groups, nations or states—as society's real building blocks. To the modern individualist, it has become both possible, perhaps even desirable, to be the 'alien' standing just a little apart from the traditional territorial or biogenetic communities and choosing, autonomously, *who to be*.

Can such self-invented alienage be key to a meaningful identity?[1]

The novelist Salman Rushdie has written that he holds 'a migrant's eye view of the world', experiencing 'uprooting, disjuncture and metamorphosis (slow or rapid, painful or pleasurable) that is the migrant condition . . .'. In his writing, he makes clear that he 'celebrates hybridity, impurity, intermingling, the transformation that comes of new and unexpected combinations of human beings, cultures, ideas, politics, movies, songs'. He 'rejoices in mongrelization and fears the absolution of the Pure'.[2]

In Rushdie's case, the prospects of fruitful synthesis, chance meeting, intellectual cross-fertilization, even physical cross-breeding, may have much to do with his personal hegira from Bombay to London. For many persons who have never left 'their Bombay', however, modern technology has now opened wide the possibility of *imagining* a London. In so doing, they may become aliens—virtually—without ever leaving home. Increasingly, persons, especially in developed and rapidly developing lands, have the option to imagine a chosen identity composed of several elements not necessarily prevalent where they live, casting off from historic, genetic, cultural, and geographic moorings.

As we shall see in Chapter 4, the law—national and international—is moving to accommodate this new interest of persons in taking charge of determining who they are. This spreading individuation is bound to reshape the global social environment. As it does, powerful, traditional communitarian voices will be raised in fear and anger, much as they were against Rushdie's 'defection' from his 'origins'. But others, previously silent, will celebrate their emancipation.

The loud voices raised in fear and anger will warn of consequences: rootlessness, banishment from the kraal, if we neglect the old obeisances and obsequies. Like Zeus railing at Prometheus' theft of the divine spark, there are those who abhor this individuation as metaphoric patricide. Yet, the idea of individualism is not necessarily incompatible with chosen affiliations with community, group, nation, or state. It does not necessarily even preclude individuals choosing to be quite ethnic or nationalistic, as Chapter 5 will demonstrate. Still, communitarians and nationalists do tend to perceive individualism as a direct threat, not because it excludes personal commitments to the group, tribe, nation, or state, but because it denies the exclusive and mandatory nature of these commitments, relegating them to the realm of personal choice or taste. To the romantic nationalist, tribalist, or communitarian, such personal choice is

---

[1] For a stimulating discussion of this thesis see Jeremy Waldron, 'Minority Cultures and the Cosmopolitan Alternative,' in *The Rights of Minority Cultures* 93 (Will Kymlicka ed., 1995).

[2] Salman Rushdie, 'In Good Faith,' in *Imaginary Homelands* 393–4 (1991).

simply inadmissible. One's identity is situationally, not personally, determined. To choose for oneself is meaningless, an affront to the very *idea* of identity.

It is against the inadmissibility of personal choice that this book will argue. Chapter 1 will begin by challenging the authenticity of *a priori* claims on our identities made by nations, ethnie, and other exclusive loyalty-systems. It will demonstrate that gene pools, shared myths, and imagined historical and cultural commonalities are too ephemeral to support a determinist view of human identity.

Individualism is a rights-claim that confronts these usurpers of identity. It asserts that we have entered a new era—engineered by modern technology and legitimated by new social attitudes and laws—that empowers each of us to ask who we are and then challenges us to make the answering of that question a central enterprise of our lives.

## 2. WHY WE ASK WHO WE ARE NOW

In the wake of communism's collapse, we find the stability of our identities threatened by the disappearance of key elements of that which traditionally defined who we are.

The collapse of communism has deprived us of our 'alien other' which defined us by that which we were not.

In the ruins of Berlin circa 1945, and more recently of Sarajevo and Kigali, we recoiled at the terrible trail of blood left behind by neo-nationalist rampages. These challenged our previous romantic identification with the nation and the state.

At the same time, there dawns on us a growing awareness of new affinity options, facilitated by the communications revolution and based neither on shared genes nor on territoriality.

One thus senses the coming of a global identity crisis. Increasingly, there contend in our hearts loyalties to family, to ethnie, to nation, to a universal or particularist church, to a transnational corporation or craft guild, perhaps even to institutions based on our common humanity. So it appears that we need to take stock, to redefine ourselves.

The need to rethink one's prior certitudes is never particularly welcome. The challenge to our identities looms as especially daunting when accompanied by the need to rethink so many other aspects of our perceptive sets. Our traditional beliefs pertaining to right and wrong, to gender and sex, to art and representation, to rituals and manners, all seem at once subject to review and redefinition. These are interesting but stressful times.

Gone are most of the certitudes of the past. More important, we are profoundly shaken in our previous confidence that there are *any* defensible certitudes.

To some, this is less cause for anxiety than an exhilarating opportunity to unchain human consciousness, liberate it of old, false certitudes. In *The Order of Things: An Archaeology of the Human Sciences*, Michel Foucault mirthfully draws to our attention a 'certain Chinese encyclopaedia' in which 'animals' are defined as follows:

(a) belonging to the Emperor, (b) embalmed, (c) tame, (d) sucking pigs, (e) sirens, (f) fabulous, (g) stray dogs, (h) included in the present classification, (i) frenzied, (j) innumerable, (k) drawn with a very fine camel hair brush, (l) et cetera, (m) having just broken the water pitcher, (n) that from a long way off look like flies.

This ancient Chinese dictionary definition delights Foucault because it demonstrates the arbitrariness of categorization by which every culture seeks to impose order—to, as he puts it, 'tame the wild profusion of existing things'. He rejoices in the shattering of 'the thought that bears the stamp of our age and our geography' and relishes 'breaking up all the ordered surfaces and all the planes' that support familiar definitions. He wants to 'disturb and threaten with collapse our age-old distinction between the Same and the Other'.[3]

In the turbulent self-deconstructing times following the collapse of the old cold war order, Foucault would have been in his element, for definitional disarray is the order of the day. At the very top of the list of things now needing reconstructive definition is the self.

But such self-redefinition is not just a personal, psychoanalytic task. It is also a social, interpersonal task of the greatest political importance. Definition, by definition, unites and divides; it communicates and alienates; it integrates and disaggregates. When I define myself, I determine the scope, shape and structure of the society in which I seek to live. Aristotle observed that 'by nature man is a political animal' with a 'natural desire for life in society'.[4] Spinoza agreed that 'man is a social animal'.[5] By such enlightening self-definition, Aristotle and Spinoza captured the way many persons think of themselves. But the intellect has other options, as well. Spinoza's definition of humans as sociable beings was written in 1677. In 1690, John Locke proffered an equally famous but very different definition of the self. To Locke, the individual 'in the State of Nature' was a wholly free and separate animal who parted with freedom only for the limited purpose of securing the peaceable enjoyment of property. For that, only, were free and solitary persons 'willing to joyn in Society with others who are already united, or have a mind to unite for the mutual preservation of their Lives, Liberties and Estates . . .'.[6] It is evident that Locke's definition of the

---

[3] Michel Foucault, *The Order of Things: An Archaeology of the Human Sciences* xv (1973).

[4] Aristotle, *Politics*, bk. I, ch. 2.

[5] Benedict (Baruch) Spinoza, *Ethics*, Pt. I, Proposition 35: note (1677) (Everyman ed., A. Boyle trans.).

[6] John Locke, *Two Treatises on Government*, Second Treatise, ch. IX (1690) (P. Laslett ed., 1960).

individual must imply a set of civic and political values quite different from that proposed by Aristotle and Spinoza: another sort of social being altogether.

In the wake of communism's demise, the rise of supranational institutions wielding power above states, and the simultaneous collapse of established states into warring 'nations', tribes, and clans—as in Yugoslavia, Armenia, Afghanistan, Rwanda, Somalia, and so forth—we are practically compelled by the conditions around us to engage with Aristotle, Spinoza, Locke, as also with Freud, Marx, and Habermas, in rethinking our own identities: our values and loyalties.

Where do we begin? Since the Reformation, the Peace of Westphalia, and the writings of Hugo Grotius, there has been an explicit assumption that the international system is an association of sovereign states; that the state is the sole actor in the international order. Vattel was Locke's transnational sibling. The global community, to him, resembled Locke's nation: consisting of solitary actors united only to preserve their property and liberties. In such a community, the individual has meaning solely through association with a state. In the world of states, baptism comes in the form of citizenship or nationality. As Vattel understood it, the 'Law of Nations is the science of the rights which exist between Nations or States, and of the obligations corresponding to these rights'. However, he added, since 'Nations are composed of men who are by nature free and independent, and who before the establishment of civil society lived together in the state of nature, such Nations or sovereign States must be regarded as so many free persons living together in the state of nature'.[7]

But the modern world is *not* simply a world of sovereign states, and the states, engaged in endless negotiations with one another to define their 'rights' and 'duties', often within the context of supranational institutions, do not live in anything resembling a 'state of nature'. Today, this Vattelian set of assumptions has become untenable. States are constrained, in law and practice, by the need to live in a community of states that requires them to act not 'naturally' but predictably: which is to say, normatively. Further, the community of states has created its own infrastructure. New global institutions have appeared that define and give meaning to lives led in their service. In 1993–4, the United Nations deployed 60,000 blue helmets in various peacekeeping and collective security missions, a far larger militia than that of most members of the UN. Yet the UN is not a state, and the soldiers are not nationals of the institution they serve.

At the same time as the UN acquired statelike accoutrements and engaged the loyalty of troops and administrators, existing states fell apart. Rwanda, Mozambique, Haiti, Afghanistan, and Cambodia at various recent times seemed incapable of giving a coherent definition to the identities of those

[7] Vattel, *The Law of Nations. Preliminaries: Idea and General Principles of the Law of Nations* lv–lvi (Joseph Chitty ed., 1834).

who live in their territories. As failed states, they needed to be reconstituted (or redelimited) by the collective action of a quasi-super-sovereign international political and military system. But the rescue by international institutions of failed national ones need not be as dramatic as in Cambodia and Mozambique in the early 1990s. In 1996, almost unobserved, a vice-president of the World Bank in effect took charge of rescuing Pakistan's failing economy.[8] To persons seeking clear and linear relations with the one, exclusive source of their identity, the state has become much less of a sure thing than it was a century ago. The old definitional order thus becomes woefully inadequate. Foucault would have been ecstatic. We are all on notice that the old building blocks of our identity are crumbling.

So *who* (or *what*) are we, now? To define oneself as a Rwandan—or an American—hardly seems to do justice to the external political realities or to the growing complexity of one's subjectively imagined self-definition. The search for new definitions must begin by a sceptical look at the old lexicon. Just as a start can be made towards a realistic definition of 'animals' only after rejecting the ancient Chinese dictionary's categories, so 'humanity' needs to clean out the underbrush of misleading verbiage still flourishing in the garden of our identity.

### 3. THE TRADITIONAL CATEGORIES OF IDENTITY: NATIONS AND STATES

Words categorize, and categories obscure both the interpenetration between the values expressed in words and the dissimilarities within the categories arbitrarily established. Yet classification is essential. In the apt words of the Cambridge University legal philosopher Philip Allott, a 'legal relation is heuristic because it simplifies actual reality for computational purposes. Actual reality, as it presents itself in human consciousness, is infinitely complex, uncertain and dynamic. In order to make legal relations operationally effective, as instruments of social transformation, they must exclude much of actual reality'.[9]

The words *nation* and *nationalism* are prime examples. For centuries, personal identity has been fixed by one overriding fact: one's belonging to an exclusive, special community—the nation—and by nationalism: the sense of personal worth derived from that categorization. Words—the nation, the state, nation-alism—bear heavy historic responsibility for their long-unexamined categor-ization of us. They warrant close scrutiny if we are to decode the origins of our identity and understand why it is in crisis. But such close scrutiny reveals much conceptual confusion. Hobsbawm has warned that the criteria for defining a

---

[8] 'Pakistan Economic Shift,' Int'l Herald Tribune, 8 Nov. 1996, at 6.
[9] Philip Allott, 'The International Court and the Voice of Justice,' in *Fifty Years of the International Court of Justice* 17, 19–20 (Vaughan Lowe & Malgosia Fitzmaurice eds., 1995).

nation '—language, ethnicity or whatever—are themselves fuzzy, shifting and ambiguous, and as useless . . . as cloud-shapes are compared to landmarks. This, of course, makes them unusually convenient for propagandist and pro-grammatic, as distinct from descriptive purposes'.[10]

A useful start at understanding the concept of 'nation' and 'nationalism' is to uncouple that misleading but common categorization of personal identity: the 'nation-state'. To give credence to much modern writing about international relations would lead us to conclude that the real world system is about inter-acting 'nation-states'. But, today, almost no states are nations and hardly any nations are states. Great obfuscation has resulted from this erroneous linkage of the terms 'nation' and 'state', a linkage made popular by Hegel. He deployed the term not primarily to describe, but to prescribe what he believed should be 'the absolute power on earth', one which demanded 'the sacrifice of personal actuality' and 'absolute obedience, renunciation of personal opinions and rea-soning, in fact complete *absence* of mind . . .'.[11]

There are differences, today, about what Hegel meant: whether he idealized a state to which persons were bound by common stratifications, customs, and traditions, as Professor Charles Taylor has concluded,[12] or whether he embraced actual states of kinfolk, based on a common gene-pool. As Dr Z. A. Pelczynski has observed, in Hegel's view, man 'reaches the height of ethical life . . . not as a member of a cosmopolitan civil society . . . but as a member of a specific, individual national community, which forms an independent state and exists to promote a shared conception of the common good'.[13] In any event, by the late eighteenth century, the notion of a German ethno-cultural nation had taken root and begun to shape the vision of a new empire of the Germans.[14]

The world may have been closer to the nation-state ideal a thousand years ago than it is today, when it has become sheer fantasy. States, historically, often came into being as tribes settled down to farm, and, for one reason or another, ceased to rely primarily on marauding and grazing their cattle. 'Over time, their movements became less common because they encountered more and more groups or "peoples" who had already formed settled communities, because they chose to remain and cultivate certain areas, or because feudal obligations tied greater proportions of the population to particular parcels of land.'[15] In Europe between AD 1200 and 1400, it has been estimated, the newly sedentary com-munities congealed as states: *nation*-states. Even so, the pure kinfolk entity proved transient. While the new states relied on arbitrary personal ties of a

[10] E. J. Hobsbawm, *Nations and Nationalism Since 1780* 6 (2nd edn., 1990).

[11] G. W. F. Hegel, *Philosophy of Right* (1821) (T. M. Knox trans., 1952), at 211–12, paras. 328, 331.

[12] Charles Taylor, *Hegel and Modern Society* 132–3 (1979).

[13] Z. A. Pelczynski, *The State and Civil Society* 265–6 (1984).

[14] See Rogers Brubaker, *Nationalism Reframed* 113–14 (1996). See also Karl R. Popper, *The Open Society and its Enemies*, vol. 2, ch. 12, 'Hegel and the New Tribalism' 27–80 (1963 ed.).

[15] David Elkins, *Beyond Sovereignty: Territory and Political Economy in the Twenty-First Century* 22 (1995).

people to a ruler or a feudal hierarchy, these soon began to strike advantageous bargains with ruling families to which they were unrelated by blood and entered into marriages motivated more by desire for political than carnal union. Thus kings and queens came to rule several distinct communities, often made up of persons who were of different stock. Soon the state began to augment and even to displace kinship-based governance. Subjects found themselves increasingly owing loyalty to foreigners: as Russians did to Catherine of Germany and Britons to George of Hannover.

At the same time as the nation ceased to be an exclusive political unit, it began to fade as a discrete bio-genetic entity. Most states were no longer kinship-based, not anymore composed of only one tribe but of several or many peoples who began to conquer, trade, integrate, and intermarry. Just as tribes coalesced to form states, so states gradually became multitribal, fused, even non-tribal. After the American and French revolutions, the territorially and juridically based idea of the state began to replace the bio-genetic and feudal binders at the centre of persons' identities: we became, simply, citizens of a state.

Unlike nations, states are still very real.

In the modern world there are many states. What, and which, they are is well known. It is their flags that flutter ostentatiously around the United Nations compounds in New York, Geneva, Vienna, and Nairobi. This Organization's name, however, aggravates the confusion, for it is *not* an organization of nations but of states, few of which are constituted by any one nation (nor is it often united). A more accurate name might have been the 'United States' but that designation was not available. Moreover, the chosen name was already in common use to identify the states allied against the Axis powers in World War II.[16]

This is no mere nitpick. Only a very few UN members are, indeed, states consisting of a single nation; rather, most members are multinational states. Conversely, most nations are not UN members nor are they states, but, rather, component constituents of member-states. Thus states, for the most part, are not nations but, rather, nation-blenders or nation-complexes.

But *what*, then, are nations? The idea encapsulated by the term 'nation' is complex, fuzzy, and the subject of a vast literature produced by historians, sociologists, anthropologists, philosophers, and psychologists.[17] Professor Hugh Seton-Watson defined a nation as 'a community of people, whose members are bound together by a sense of solidarity, a common culture, a national consciousness'.[18] To this should perhaps be added a sense of common socio-historic destiny. But this is rarely, now, manifest in a discrete political unit. A

---

[16] Somewhat oddly, membership in the United Nations, according to Charter articles 3 and 4, was to consist of states which had either joined the wartime alliance against the Axis or 'other peace-loving states.'

[17] See e.g. John Armstrong, *Nations before Nationalism* (1982); Ernest Gellner, *Nations and Nationalism* (1983); Hobsbawm, *supra* n. 10; Hans Kohn, *The Idea of Nationalism* (1944); Anthony Smith, *The Ethnic Origins of Nations* (1986).　　　　[18] Hugh Seton-Watson, *Nations and States* 1 (1977).

1995 study by a French scholar-diplomat puts it with Gallic wit: a nation 'brings people together not for what they are but for the memory of what they have been'.[19] Undoubtedly, shared historic myths, heroes, and enemies are important ingredients: 'a common history, . . . common misfortunes, and . . . common triumphs.'[20]

The nation, then, is an imaginatively remembered social unit which now rarely takes political form. Only in a few instances does one find a modern nation-state: one people, exclusive and independent. The claim to be a nation-state nowadays is mostly mischievous anthropological nonsense, a fragile illusion, yet one capable of supporting a mighty malice.

Germany, at least until 1945, used to think of itself that way: 'ein Volk' constituting one exclusive citizenry. This kind of identity made almost natural the elision of the 600,000 German Jews. But the notion of Teutonic German-ness prevailing in Hitler's master-race theories itself was an historic travesty and Germanic homogeneity is an ethnographic illusion. The nation-state of Germany, in historic reality, is a conglomeration made up of what, at various times, were quite distinct tribes: Visigoths, Celts, Franks, Saxons, Prussians, Bavarians, Hessians, and others. The German 'nation' is a modern fusion of these, which only very recently established itself as a political entity. Until the end of the nineteenth century, 'Germany' was a loose association of fifteen kingdoms and three city-states. Before they were united under the Prussian spur, they were inclined to think of themselves as quite separate. Indeed, in the nineteenth century, some of them were still at war with Prussia on the side of Austria.

Today, Germany is a state in which a majority of the population do think of themselves as 'German'. Outside Germany, however, there are persons who also regard themselves as German 'nationals' and others who regard themselves vaguely as of the German culture, yet not necessarily even as *Volksgenossen*, 'ethnic Germans'. But there are also ethnic Germans who do not any longer think of themselves as German because other loyalties now predominate in shaping their identities. Austrians, whose country once called itself 'German Austria', have stopped defining themselves as part of a German 'nation', with its irredentist political implications, after the discouraging experiences of the 1938 'anschluss'. Although the Dutch, and Switzerdeutsch of Zurich, also evince no enthusiasm for Germanic political unification, they are quite as German historically, linguistically, and culturally, as many of the 'low' Germans of Germany. Yet this affinity does not translate into a political unity or social identification nor does it permit us to class the Dutch or Swiss as part of the German nation, because that is not how they think of themselves. They do not share a sense of common socio-historically based political destiny with the people of Munich or Bremen. Nor do the ethnically German but French-speaking

---

[19] Jean-Marie Guehenno, *The End of the Nation State* 5 (1995).   [20] Ibid. at 4.

people of Alsace. Indeed, during the German occupation of this region in World
War II there was less collaboration in Alsace-Lorraine than in the 'French' parts
of France. In Germany itself, while many persons perceive themselves exclusively
as Germans, others also think of themselves as Bavarian-Germans or even
Turkish-Germans. And quite a few of the younger generation now have begun
to think of themselves also as Europeans. Two things stand out in this confusion:
*first*, identity has become complex and, *second*, it has become much more *subjective*,
in the sense of reflecting an intensely personal set of choices.

Confusion caused by the elusive concept of 'the nation' is compounded by
introducing that of 'the ethnie' into the lexicon of identity. Professor John
Armstrong defines this 'ethnie' as a social phenomenon that predates nations
and reflects 'group attitudes formed by myth, symbol, communication and a
cluster of associated attitudinal factors . . .'[21] that need not correspond with the
territorial or other material factors that usually are deemed essential to the
concept of a nation. The gustatory habits of Alsace—a preference for chou-
croute (sauerkraut) and sausages—does not make the inhabitants part of the
German nation, and certainly predicates no desire to join the German state; but
does indicate some degree of lingering affinity for aspects of German culture
(although, in this instance, no longer the German language).

Armstrong cites another example, the Arabs of the Middle East, who shared
a sense of common ethnie in the nineteenth century, but no congruent aspiration to nationhood, let alone to statehood. Only when, with the decline of the
Ottoman empire, a powerful sense of Turkish nationality began to replace the
perception of Turkic ethnie, did a sense of the Arab nation, too, begin to make
itself felt.[22]

Today, there are palpable relations between various German-speakers of
Amsterdam, Vienna, Zurich, and Hamburg, as also between Arabic peoples
of Casablanca, Cairo, and Medina, or, for that matter, between the Anglophonic inhabitants of London, Auckland, Toronto, and New York. Yet their
relationship does not quite fit the categories. These are not citizens of a
common state nor do they share a national identity or a common ethnie.
They have some common cultural configuration that is primarily based on
common language. Yet, to the historically trained eye, this contemporary
linguistic affinity, too, is not a natural given. German has evolved through a
synthesis of tribal languages that may have been Visigoth, Prussian, Rhenish,
Alsatian, Westphalian, Hannoverian, Saxon, Bohemian, Frisian, Sorb,
Bavarian, Tyrolean, Celt, Slavic, or Danish. These languages, to the extent
they have survived, even today show differences from one another. German
itself, like almost every living language, is to a degree synthetic: as ephemeral
and deconstructible as the ethnie and the nation.

The same is demonstrable by reference to 'the British' and their English

---

[21] Armstrong, *supra* n. 17, at 9.      [22] Smith, *supra* n. 17, at 143.

language. Although the French may still refer to those across the English Channel, and sometimes also to others across the North Atlantic, as 'les anglo-saxons', that designation, of course, has but passing contemporary relevance to the origins of the inhabitants of England, let alone those of Scotland, Wales, and Northern Ireland. It is not even beyond argument that the real Britons, or Bretons, live in what is now part of France, where they cherish memories of *their* King Arthur and Queen Guinevere, and where Camelot is an historic incident not of England but of Brittany, a French province that bears the ancient name of Courneille (i.e. Cornwall), and where some people still speak, essentially, Welsh. How confusing!

Great Britain, of course, is actually a melting pot, if not quite as evidently so as the United States, Australia, or Canada. For centuries Frisians, Scots, Celts, Picts, Angles, Danes, Saxons, and Normans, and now Afro-Caribbeans and various Asian peoples, have more or less synthesized to create a political community. This community operates primarily as a civil society of recognizably different strands, albeit one that also has nourished some identifiable characteristics: common educational, religious and social institutions; some shared values; similar speech patterns; and, perhaps, a degree of coherence in self-image. But Britain is not really a nation; neither is it an ethnie. Its people speak a tongue that has incorporated elements of Saxon, German, Celtic, Latin, Scots, Pictish, and Norman French. Britain, the quintessential 'Anglo-Saxon' nation, has nothing remotely approximating a uniform 'blood' pedigree;[23] and, of course, some of its constituent components are less genetically merged than others. The Welsh, Scots, Manx, and Channel Islanders, as well as recent immigrants, still retain some fondly backward-looking sense of their 'national' separateness and, in particular instances, of their collective historic grievances. Some may still harbour a forward-looking wish to secede from Great Britain in a quest to regain their separate imagined sociopolitical identities.[24]

England, too, has had a life of the popular imagination that has not wholly merged into 'Britishness'. William Blake, at the beginning of the nineteenth century, imagined the New Jerusalem in England's—not Britain's—'green and pleasant land', evidencing a belief that Christ's feet may have walked 'upon England's mountains green'. And, to friend and foe alike, the English were a formidable nation long after the United Kingdom became a state encompassing it. Schoolchildren still learn that Napoleon Bonaparte, at Rochefort in 1815, said with a mixture of bitterness and awe, 'Wherever wood can swim, there I am sure to find this flag of England.' We know what he meant, although the flag of England is the cross of St George, little used except by Anglican churches. It is all so confusing because the concept of nation is so vague and misleading.

It is nowadays very hard to find pure nation-states, in which the territorial boundaries are precisely co-extant with conformed—that is, predetermined

---

[23] See Seton-Watson, *supra* n. 18, at 22–35.     [24] Linda Colley, *Britons* 5–9 (1992).

genetic, historic, linguistic, and socio-cultural—attributes, rather than subjectively self-determined ones. Iceland appears homogeneous, its tiny population seemingly deriving from Norse–Viking stock, yet it has an early blending of Celtic blood and its people, like most Scandinavians, speak a 'Germanic' language. Tibet might have qualified before its subordination to China and the induced influx of Chinese.[25] Arabia might qualify, but many of its people still think of themselves primarily as members of an Arab world, part of a socio-cultural and historic formation sharing a vague but powerful sense of common destiny, and stretching from the Euphrates to the Atlantic. And many 'Arab' states encompass significant non-Arab minorities such as the Berbers of Algeria. Japan looks like a candidate, but, of course, has its historic and genetic links to China, and its Parliament has recently enacted a law that recognizes the Ainu minority as Japan's 'original' inhabitants.[26] Bhutan and one or two small African countries may still qualify, but the instances are rare, indeed, of states that encompass one nation entirely and exclusively. As Professor Armstrong has indicated, the few examples of relatively pure ethnie that would be capable of constituting a real nation-state—the Magyars of Hungary or the Berbers—are instead merged into states with majorities of quite other identity groups.[27]

Germany and Britain are in no way unusual in being imaginary nations. Throughout the world, despite the power of the nationalist and self-determination movements, there are today almost no 'nations' in the pure ethnic, genetic, or cultural sense. There are, of course, Scottish nationalists; but the 'Scots' in fact are highlanders or lowlanders, a merger of culturally, linguistically, religiously, and historically distinct clans. Even the non-proselytizing Jewish 'nation' is a mixture of European, Middle Eastern, and African genetic stock. Many Jews do perceive themselves as constituting a 'nation' and manifested that perception in creating Israel. Yet in Israel, too, people's varied and mixed ethnic origins are clearly apparent in social and political contexts. The concept of a unique Jewish nation also ignores not only the conversions to Judaism around the Black Sea and in East Africa, but also the historical synthesis of the tribes of Judah and Benjamin that once made up Judaea, and the twelve tribes that constituted ancient Israel before the division of the kingdom. Of course, none of this should lead us to ignore the facts that Israelis do speak a common language and that most share myths of a common history and culture.

Israel demonstrates something else about nationhood. As inhabitants of a Jewish state in a region of Arab states, Israelis also share a common sense of danger, which, in turn, requires a degree of cohesion. Such cohesion probably cannot simply derive from being a civic association of immigrants but, rather, may necessitate emphasizing the nation as the basis of the state. Danger may be

---

[25] 'Until the coming of the Chinese the population was almost entirely Tibetan but today, on Chinese figures, they actually outnumber the indigenous Tibetan population.' *Tibet: the Facts*, Report to the UN of the Tibetan Young Buddhist Association (1990), at 36.

[26] *Int'l Herald Tribune*, 9 May 1997, at 4.        [27] Armstrong, *supra* n. 17, at 47.

one of the historic factors that forge nation-states.[28] Faced with the fall of France and the onslaught of German V-2 rockets in World War II, the British found themselves reacting as a state with at least some of the indices of a nation: a surprising degree of pride in an imagined ethnic and heroic history; and a future destiny rooted in a rediscovered, shared, exclusive national past, when, according to patriotic songs, Britain—not England, or Scotland—'arose from out the azure main', the British—not the Ulster or Welsh—grenadiers were the greatest 'of all the world's great heroes', and Britannia—not Anglia or Scotia—'ruled the waves'. But this ethos prevailed only for a time and only to a degree. With the decline in Britain's fortunes and the dangers to its security after World War II, schismatic internal 'nations' have re-emerged as significant forces for devolution or disintegration and for reinvention of the ethnic self on that increasingly divided, and perhaps disappointed but still sceptred, isle.

Thus, on examination, the picture becomes ever more complex. If almost no 'nation' is pure in the genetic sense of 'common blood', what is it other than a synthesis of earlier, vanished or submerged 'nations' (or 'tribes' or 'clans'), which, in some instances and to some degree, can be deconstructed by forces we barely understand—as recently happened with such vengeful force when the seemingly homogeneous Somali nation (tribe) broke up into murderous 'clans'?

Whatever people may wish to imagine about their past, deconstructing their myths has dangers but also holds some promise. It gives us a closer approximation of who we were, a useful first step in self-definition. When the Romans met their northern neighbours in Gaul, they reported encountering not peoples corresponding with the modern French or Germans, but warring clans. If we can live with the truth about who we were, we may have taken a first step toward discovering a realistic basis for thinking about who we are becoming.

For one thing, we may discover that our identities have been much more mutable than we imagined. Distinctly different tribes or nations, for historic reasons and to different degrees, do sometimes merge their identities and submerge their origins, opting to become partly or entirely assimilated into a larger tribe/nation identity. This happened to the clans of Scotland and an efficient merger of various provincial Germanic and some Frisian elements made plausible the notion of a Dutch identity.[29] China's population has an identity that, to a significant extent, is constituted out of many quite distinct ethnie. In modern times, this process of social merger and synthesis has accelerated through the technological supremacy of the state, with its ability to instil a sense of community among diverse peoples through means that Professor

---

[28] The forging, in the 17th and 18th centuries, of a British nation depended heavily on a ferocious Protestant fear of, and antipathy to, the Catholic Europe dominated by the archenemy: France. Colley, *supra* n. 24, at 17–54.

[29] See Seton-Watson, *supra* n. 18, at 22, 31–5 (Scotland), 61–6 (Holland). Concerning Holland see also Armstrong, *supra* n. 17, at 256–7.

Benedict Anderson has identified as 'census, map and museum'.[30] The extent to which the merger occurs is always a matter of degree and, longitudinally, of time. In the far north-eastern marches of Holland, some Frisians still remain Frisian in language and custom. There is still a South Moluccan identity in Indonesia, but it appears to be fading. Fading, but not necessarily disappearing. Professor Will Kymlicka reminds us that imposed acculturation and assimilation can be counterproductive ways to merge the identities of separate communities within a modern state: that prospects may be better when the state 'affirms rather than denies' the differences among its constituent ethnies.[31]

There are other non-assimilationist forms of mutability. A nation may decide against merging with others but join, instead, in a multinational state based not on a synthesized ethnie but on a compact establishing what Professor Gellner has called a civil society.[32] In Canada, Belgium, Switzerland and India, and increasingly in the United States, some of the citizenry's various genetic, linguistic, historical, and cultural components have endured, yet have permitted the emergence of a state, albeit one without a deeply homogeneous national identity. Even in France, with its emphasis on cultural unity, there is some recognition of the Celtic language of Brittany, which has much in common with Welsh and nothing with French, as well as for the old Latin of the Languedoc. Almost all Sikhs are Indian citizens, but many do not see themselves as Indian in the ethnic or cultural sense. The citizens of India have imagined a shared civil society in a coherent political state, but not necessarily a shared culture, language, religion, or nation. They have nevertheless succeeded in having a state, in part by inventing and defending their civil society, thereby bypassing the assimilationist effort needed to synthesize the fiction of a nation-state.

Such civil society-based states—with their compacts between the constituent ethnie, tribes, and nations generating but little or only partial fusion of identities—may sometimes disintegrate under the pressure of a suddenly resurgent centrifugal tribalism or nationalism. Loss of empire and global economic dominance has contributed to the fragmentation of British identity, with a revival of Scottish, Welsh, and English consciousness. The composite populace may even revert, as in the former Yugoslavia, to ancient hostilities. Then, some missionaries of neo-tribalism, deploying genocide, may even recreate true 'nation-states' by cleansing territory of any lingering traces of multi-ethnicity. Fortunately, this occurs only in the most extreme cases.

If the concept of 'nation' is full of ambiguities and subjectivities, the same is not true of the idea of the state. To appropriate once again a useful definition of Seton-Watson, a 'state is a legal and political organization, with the power to

---

[30] Benedict Anderson, *Imagined Communities* 163 (rev. edn., 1991).
[31] Will Kymlicka, *Multicultural Citizenship* 187 (1995).
[32] Ernest Gellner, *Conditions of Liberty: Civil Society and Its Rivals* (1994).

require obedience and loyalty from its citizens'.[33] The existence of a state is subjective only in the sense that it is recognition of statehood by other states that attests to achievement of the necessary prerequisites: fixed population and boundaries and an effective government which entitles a state to 'the possession of international personality'.[34]

Most modern states, which at first glance might appear to be nation-states, on closer inspection turn out simply to be states that have created the myth of uninationality by the relatively successful fusing of the cultures, myths, and languages of disparate ethnic or national groups. France is the outstanding example of this sort of fusion, having consisted of many quasi-autonomous ethnie that eventually, with some exceptions, submerged their separate cultures to adopt a common French identity. 'Here "ethnic states" were gradually transformed . . . into genuinely "national states" through the unification of the economy, territorial centralization, the provision of equal rights for more and more strata, and the growth of public, mass education systems.'[35] Even so, French unity is tested by Corsican and other local 'nationalisms'.

China is another example of a state consisting of various ethnie that have gradually and consciously been fused into something approximating a nation-state or 'Chung-hua min-tsu'. Nevertheless, historically and to some extent even today China consists of a large number of these distinct ethnic groups, including Mongols and Tibetans, constituting a multi-ethnic country.[36] The present regime has recognized the distinctiveness of some of these groups, even to the extent of creating autonomous regions in which a particular one predominates and where its language is permitted alongside that of the Chinese-speaking majority (the Han tsu). Even among the latter, however, differences in dialect are great: for example, between Mandarin, Wu, Min, and Hakka. On the other hand, some 'national' languages and cultures, of which Manchu is the most important example, have been absorbed almost entirely into the Chinese.

As these instances illustrate, the term nation-state—even when applied to those few instances of states displaying a high degree of apparent homogeneity—is likely to describe what is a relatively recent synthesis, rather than an historic reality. The term is also lexically misleading in implying that the nation always preceded the state. 'There were states long before there were nations,' Seton-Watson reminds us, although 'there are some nations that are much older than most states which exist today.'[37] Ancient Rome was an imperial state consisting primarily of tribes, cities, and geographical areas many of which had not been nations before being absorbed into the empire.

Today, we observe a few more-or-less homogeneous nation-states in Africa.

---

[33] Seton-Watson, *supra* n. 18.

[34] R. Jennings & A. Watts, *Oppenheim's International Law* 330 (9th edn., 1992).

[35] Smith, *supra* n. 17, at 138.

[36] See *China's Inner Asian Frontier*. The Peabody Museum of Archaeology and Ethnology (1979).

[37] Seton-Watson, *supra* n. 18.

Swaziland and Lesotho are the contemporary statist version of tribal 'home-lands', their boundaries deliberately describing the historic territory of a single tribe. Most contemporary African states, however, are extraordinarily multi-tribal. And even those, like Somalia, which appear to have one or two dominant tribes, turn out to be all too easily divisible into rival clans and sub-clans. Indeed, much of the political effort in post-colonial Africa has consisted of deliberately striving to create a sense of 'statehood' among the many tribes and clans constituting the decolonized countries whose inherited boundaries cut across tribal demography, reflecting European convenience more than concern for ethnographic niceties.

Thus, if two words in the lexicon of identity merit linkage, it is not 'nation' and 'state' but, rather, 'nation' and 'tribe'. Nation and tribe, as Seton-Watson points out, are used as separate categories not to classify different social phe-nomena but, essentially, to demarcate a mental boundary between 'my' normal in-group and 'your' exotic out-group.[38] That boundary is pure conceptual fakery and snobbery. Wrong, too, is the popular notion that tribes are smaller kinship groups: there are far more Hausa than Finns, although the latter have a sovereign state (which they share with Swedes and Lapps) and the former do not. The term 'tribe', like the term 'nation', denotes a community of persons conscious of a common ethnic, social, and cultural identity with some, and a corresponding dissociation from all others. 'Tribalism', like 'nationalism', denotes such persons' desire to preserve, enhance and give political content to their perception of group identity. In these definitions of tribe and tribalism, the term 'nation' can readily be substituted. As Seton-Watson points out, those 'who use the word "tribe" of others are usually convinced that they themselves belong to a higher culture and are looking at persons of a lower culture'[39]—a perspective made rather insupportable by Europe's history of twentieth-century 'nationalist' barbarism, which altogether resembles but far exceeds anything done by Hutus and Tutsis, or Somali clans, to the 'alien other'.

There is a further source of confusion.

In common usage, the term 'state' is frequently deployed to connote the sub-unity of a federal state, as in the United States, Australia, India or Germany. These sub-units may have attributes of once-distinct ethnie, tribes, or nations, as in the case of the Quebecois of Canada, the Ashanti of Ghana, the Sikhs of the Punjab, or the Bavarians of Germany. In Germany, historically, the 'Länder' (states) had claim to some identifiably differentiated internal socio-cultural unity and political independence which, today, through constitutional evolution, migration, and cultural homogenization, is no longer attributable to them. In the United States, too, the original confederated 'states' to a degree represented discrete historic social, cultural, legal, and political realities. But, in both

---

[38] Ibid. 5.        [39] Ibid.

Germany and the United States these 'mini-nationalisms' have come to seem more cute than acute.

Nevertheless, the federated 'states' in Germany and of the US such as Bavaria and Virginia now have assumed an entirely new significance. They represent a legal counterposition against the centralization of power and have emerged as political counterweights to balance the authority of the federal governments. Thus have old socio-cultural and ethnic containers been recycled to serve entirely different political uses. In the process, entities like Bavaria, Gujerat, and New Jersey have ceased to function as small nations and become sub-states, or anti-states. These, too, make loyalty claims which, to some degree, are validated by the inhabitants.

Further to compound the definitional confusion, the term 'nation' is now commonly misused, as we have observed, to describe the constituents of international organizations such as the United Nations. This error is much replicated. Most interstatal institutions get the usage wrong, although the Organization of American *States*, by contrast, gets it right. The very term 'inter*national*' misleads: the Iroquois, Maoris, and Magyars may be true nations, but their representatives do not, typically, sit as such around international conference tables. If they appear at all, it is behind nameplates labelled 'USA', 'New Zealand', and 'Hungary'.

Why do we bother with these linguistic and conceptual problems? Terminological definition is to theory-building as ploughing is to agriculture: a rather tedious but necessary prelude to the principal tasks of sowing and harvesting. In order to discuss the task of self-reidentification in the post-cold war world, it is essential to endure some clarification of terminology. The language of our discourse must be capable of denoting and deconstructing the importantly different and often slippery social, cultural, and historic categories relevant to identity. The traditional concepts—ethnie, tribe, nation—are key to understanding how we became what we are and the process by which we might become otherwise.

## 4. THE MANY FACES OF NATIONALISM

In the twentieth century, it is the state that has been predominant in the shaping of personal identity. Nationalism—a person's pride in being a member of an internationally recognized political community—has played a powerful role in defining who we are.

Here, too, one encounters the problem of ambiguity. 'One-line theories of nationalism are as bad as such theories invariably are in social science,'[40]

[40] Charles Taylor, 'Nationalism and Modernity,' in *The Morality of Nationalism* 31 (R. McKim & J. McMahan eds., 1997).

Charles Taylor cautions. Thus, the Bosnian Serbs and the Quebecois do not comfortably share a category, distinguished only by one being more 'extreme' than the other. Indeed, nationalism has many faces. It is even, in some places and times, experienced as pride of citizenship in a civil state rather than a feeling of kinship with a biological or historico-cultural nation. The states that foster passionate myths of nationhood and common blood profess a form of nationalism that has almost nothing in common with nationalism as understood in the modern United States, France, Switzerland, Britain, or India.

A citizenry is quite capable of changing its kind of nationalism, usually as a response to events. This has been demonstrated eloquently, in the 1990s, by the inhabitants of the former Yugoslavia. Over the centuries in America, too, there have been numerous shifts in nationalism's fashion—from emphasis on the melting pot to the gorgeous mosaic and back—and much mutual distrust between those determined to cast an alloyed American nation from the contents of the melting pot and those who would rather celebrate diversity within a conglomerate liberal society.

Those Americans who favour a melting pot—*e pluribus unum*—are engaged in trying to invent a nation-state where there is only a state, with all its disparities, elasticities, and ambiguities. No doubt they regard themselves as nation-builders, but what they espouse is very different from the recently revived kinship-and-blood nationalism of Serbia, on the one hand, or, on the other, the equally robust but very different phenomenon of Swiss nationalism. While the Swiss, famously, share intense feelings of loyalty, common purpose, and pride in legitimate common institutions, they are yet firmly rooted in various different (German, French, Italian, Romanche) languages and cultures, as well as in historically antagonistic religions (Calvinist, Zwinglian, and Roman Catholic). Their federal constitution encourages the differences through an elaborate system of linguistic and political autonomy.[41] There is no discernible melting pot in Switzerland except among the elite. Yet one does not lie by calling the Swiss 'nationalists': they surely do not defer even to the French or the Germans in their passionate adherence to a common identity. It would be quite pointless to describe the Swiss merely as parties to a social contract, or solely as members of a civil society. Yet, Swiss nationalism is not an emanation of Swiss *nationhood*, there being no historic, religio-cultural or linguistic Swiss 'nation' as such.

Thus we confront more linguistic confusion: nationalism, as popularly used, is not simply the passion a person feels for his or her nation, the way tribalism is the passion of persons who value extraordinarily their membership in a tribe. Rather, nationalism may denote the passionate feeling of persons who value inordinately their place in a state in which many ethnie either integrate in a

---

[41] Christopher Hughes, *The Parliament of Switzerland* 1–20 (1962).

melting pot, or form a gorgeous mosaic, or coexist as separate but friendly entities within an invented whole.

The confusion could be allayed by the choice of words that signal these differences. For example, the nationalism persons feel towards a state, especially one which does not pretend exclusively to embody an ethno-historical nation, could more accurately be called 'patriotism'.[42] Then 'nationalism' could be reserved for a person's loyalty to a nation, tribe, or to a true nation-state. But the term 'patriotism' has its own misleading connotation, deriving from 'patria', which suggests common paternity or shared genealogy.

In any event, the usage matters little so long as we are aware that, in discussing nationalism, we may be speaking of quite different, even contradictory phenomena under a misleadingly common rubric. Nationalism can be a force seeking to create a homeland state—Greece, Israel, Armenia—for an existing nation which does not have one. Or it can seek to create a nation for a state which is not one: out of disparate elements within its territorial boundaries. Both modern France and Italy were fashioned in this deliberate way, the state seeking to create a new unity out of historically, culturally, and linguistically diverse elements. India, Indonesia, and most African states are even more recent examples. Such state-created nationalism may be liberal, emphasizing mutual tolerance and accommodating of differences. It may stress civic virtues that rise to the status of a secular nationalist faith. Or the state may cultivate a nationalism that, seeking to form a nation out of disparate elements, may be illiberal: forcefully suppressing cultural, linguistic, religious or other differences to promote conformist values.

Historically, however, the term has a precise etymology, being the invention of the late eighteenth century in response to the specific circumstances of the American and French revolutions. It certainly was not originally a term to describe the patriotic feelings of a single-identity nation, but, rather, the popular political commitment to a specific set of revolutionary ideas that transcended ethnie, culture, history, or nation. When France and the US were inventing themselves as states they were far from imagining themselves as nations in the ethnic–historic–cultural sense. If the vanguard citizenry of revolutionary America and France (or, for that matter, of Italy and Switzerland) could be said to be the originators of nationalism, it must be understood that such usage describes a phenomenon quite different from the values and passions of twentieth-century Germany, or of contemporary Serbs and Hutus. (This schism between the genus nationalism in its eighteenth- and nineteenth-century modes is further examined in Chapter 3.)

This other, modern manifestation of the genus could best be described as

---

[42] For a discussion of the distinction between 'patriotism' and nationalism see Maurizio Viroli, *For Love of Country* (1996) and Yael Tamir, *Liberal Nationalism* (1993). For Hegel's discussion of patriotism see *Hegel's Philosophy of Right* 163–4 (T. M. Knox trans., 1952 edn.).

romantic, or tribalist, nationalism. In sharp contrast to it, the nationalists of eighteenth-century America and France purported to be interested less in common genealogy than in shared *ideas*. Their rationalism was forward-looking, optimistic and centred on philosophical concepts of liberty and equality. They were also frankly mercantilist, keenly interested in bankable results, in passionate pursuit of security, economies of scale, access to resources, and concomitant material rewards. To some extent in revolutionary America, and certainly in revolutionary France, nationalism served to mobilize a redistribution of wealth and power. Indeed, it was this which so frightened Edmund Burke and other British Tories.[43] Unlike the tribal nationalism of a later era, these nationalist revolutionaries were little concerned with myths of their common culture, romantic historical destiny, and purity of blood. To the revolutionaries of France, blood and genealogy were the *enemy*: arbitrary definitional categories which determined who was to be rich and powerful and who was to be impoverished and oppressed. The revolution meant to overthrow, not enthrone, such romantic devilry.

Thus the term 'nationalism' was given one definition in the practice of late eighteenth-century Europe and quite another by the end of the nineteenth century. Both nationalisms made it necessary for persons to define themselves against an imagined 'alien other', but they did so against two very different palimpsests.[44] The enemies of the American and French revolutions were hereditary privilege and autocracy. Some of the late nineteenth- and twentieth-century nationalist movements instead targeted aliens: imported aristocrats, foreigners in control of commerce, enemies massed on the border, an inferior race, a people without a history, heathens and blasphemers, the agents of mongrelization. While eighteenth-century nationalism thus tended towards expansiveness and Messianism, the more darkly romantic modern versions have, instead, embraced xenophobia and racism.

A *fin du siècle* surge of nationalism, and revived ethnic claims to sovereignty, have generated the sorts of problems roiling the Balkans, Africa, and the Middle East. These, in turn, now challenge the viability of the old Vattelian state-system, which still seeks, less and less effectively, to manage global conflict even as it contributes to its own decline.

[43] Edmund Burke, *Thoughts on French Affairs* (1791).

[44] For an examination of the historical record of national identity as an alienation of others, which long antedates twentieth century European nationalism see Smith, *supra* n. 17, pp. 6–18.

# 2

## The Dreary Future of Imposed Identity:
## A World of 2,000 States?

### 1. NATIONALISM AS IDENTITY TODAY

As we observed in the preceding chapter, nationalism has many faces. In the twentieth century's twilight, however, we witness the resurgence of a kind of nationalism that owes more to post-Hegelian romanticism than to eighteenth-century revolutionary republicanism. This outbreak of nation-consciousness increasingly manifests itself in efforts to secede from, or bring about the disintegration of, multinational civil societies and established states. Around us we see people enthusiastically engaged in acting out the worst imaginable definitions of nationalism: in former Soviet states (Kazakhstan, Tajikistan, Armenia, Georgia (Abkhazia), Azerbaijan, etc.); in Slovakia, Croatia, Bosnia, Serbia, and Macedonia; in Somalia, Rwanda, Burundi; and in the Basque region of Spain. On the cusp of the new millennium, the most visible nationalisms seem violent and destructive.

Despite this dark image, distinctions need to be made. For example, not all nationalist movements seek the deconstruction of existing liberal civil societies.[1] The Plaid Cymru party of Wales espouses autonomy and devolution, not a sovereign Welsh state. And not every nationalist movement, whatever its goal, is motivated by the rabid urge to settle old scores.[2] The dark side of nationalism is said to be absent, or less evident, in the ethnic reawakening underway within Quebec, Scotland, Kashmir, the Karen region of Burma, the South Moluccas, East Timor, the Western Sahara, Catalonia, and Corsica. Even in the Basque region of Spain, two of the three nationalist movements do not share the violent agenda of the ETA military force.

Nevertheless, even the least xenophobic of these movements still evince a tendency to disengage, wholly or partially, from the civil societies of multi-ethnic states. Many seek, instead, to institute a form of governance nostalgically embodying a degree of ethno-national exclusivity.

Such a tendency is an odd one in this globalizing era, but it is also understandable. The modern impetus towards trade liberalization has made it much less important to be part of an economy of scale, thereby vitiating one of the factors which, since the industrial revolution, had encouraged different peoples

---

[1] See e.g. Yael Tamir, *Liberal Nationalism* (1993); Will Kymlicka, *Multicultural Citizenship* (1995).
[2] See e.g. Neil McCormick, *Legal Right and Social Democracy* (1982); Rogers Brubaker, *Reframing Nationalism* (1996).

to share markets and find a common *modus vivendi*. To somewhat the same effect, the information and communications revolution has made even very small independent states commercially viable and competitive. Unfettered by traditional constraints, the number of independent states has risen from 74 in 1946 to 193 today. Of these, 35 have populations below 500,000.[3] The liberalization of markets—commercial, informational, service, etc.—paradoxically has facilitated the blossoming of socio-cultural particularism. Groups that previously coexisted pragmatically now feel free to shatter the painstakingly built political mosaics of civil society.

In the age of electronic markets, infonets, collective security, The World Trade Organization, and CNN, this seems, at first, benignly quaint. But it is not. The concept of nationalism, to an astonishing extent, has been hijacked by elements that wish not only to define themselves *against* others, but to eradicate most others from their midst at incalculable cost, not only to themselves and their immediate victims, but to the rest of the world which is forced to pick up the pieces: 6 billion dollars for Bosnia, 2 billion for Somalia, 1 billion for Rwanda: it mounts up!

Worse, this sort of nationalism is training people to deal with all alien others by hating, fearing, and trying to destroy them: not the best survival strategy for the states of a fragile global system. Romantic tribal nationalism has lately proven again its ability—as in Rwanda and in the former Yugoslavia—to resurface after years of seeming quiescence, even harmony, among persons who have worked, lived, and intermarried within a single civil society as patriotic sons and daughters of a secular state.

In the wake of decolonization, the fall of communism, and continued opportunistic oppression of some minorities, some of these nationalist movements are entitled to evoke empathy. As with most pathologies, one can understand how they 'got that way'. Their resurgence is not simply attributable to injustice. In contemporary Canada, French Canadians are not economic or political victims. Despite past discrimination, in the present half-century, French Canadians have had more than their share of top governmental posts and have enjoyed rapid economic development, religious freedom, an unusual degree of confederal political autonomy, and national linguistic parity. In Yugoslavia, despite regional discrepancies, none of the national groups claim to have been subject to systematic exclusion from social and economic advancement in the fifty years following the Second World War. Indeed, the first to secede, the Slovenes, were also the most economically advantaged. Paradoxically, while secessionism may be the ultimate recourse of the disinherited, it is just as often the path chosen by the most well-off who see no reason to share their good fortune with less advantaged neighbours. It seems that some modern nationalist movements

---

[3] *The Economist*, 3 Jan. 1998, at 65.

are responding less to present injustices than to hoary myths of past grandeur, past oppression, or both.

It is all too apparent that this new wave of very old passions could have systemic, as well as humanitarian repercussions. Unchecked, such virulence could lead to an unmanageable world of 2,000 mutually hostile states, each based on what its leaders claim to be the ideal: a pure-blooded, homogeneous nation born to redress and avenge its woeful past.

Dr Boutros Boutros-Ghali, as Secretary-General of the UN, warned of the 'fierce new assertions of nationalism and sovereignty springing up' causing 'the cohesion of States' to be 'threatened by brutal ethnic, religious, social, cultural or linguistic strife'.[4] He has pointed out that the 'United Nations has not closed its door' to new members, but 'if every ethnic, religious or linguistic group claimed statehood, there would be no limit to fragmentation, and peace, security and economic well-being for all would become ever more difficult to achieve'.[5]

Admittedly, the socio-political organization of populations cannot be contrived primarily for the convenience of international civil servants or with an eye to the capacity of international organizations to accommodate new applicants. But convenience is not the problem. The trouble with a future world of 2,000 states is not primarily that it conjures up the diplomatic and managerial nightmare feared by the former Secretary-General but, rather, that it poses more serious political and economic problems.

One such problem arises out of the natural resistance of states to dismemberment. Existing states are most unlikely to yield peacefully to secessionist claims, especially when—as in the case of the Katangese of the Congo (Zaire), the Ibo of Nigeria, and the Chechens of Russia—secession would mean the loss of territory harbouring many of the state's most important resources. They are likely to resist with force the loss of their largest oil fields, best copper mines, sole outlet to the sea, or territorial coherence. It is easy to understand, for example, Canada's concern that secession by Quebec would sever the nation, threatening its contiguity and viability. States challenged in this way tend to fight for their 'territorial integrity', and that, too, is an understandable pathology.

Another problem with the dark version of the nationalist ideal is that its passion to redress past wrongs, whether real or imagined, tends to blind it to new injustices perpetrated in its name. The same Prussian leaders who pursued self-determination for the ethnocultural Germans of Alsace-Lorraine forcefully repressed their own Polish minority when it demanded the same right for itself. Bismarck dismissed the Poles' demand with the remark that they belonged 'to no other state and to no other people than the Prussian, to which I myself belong'.[6]

---

[4] *An Agenda for Peace*, A/47/277 and S/2411, 17 June 1992, para. 11, at 3.
[5] Ibid. para. 17, at 4.
[6] Theodor Schieder, *Das Deutsche Kaiserreich von 1871 als Nationalstaat* 29 (1961); quoted in Rogers Brubaker, *Citizenship and Nationhood in France and Germany* 127 (1992).

Not too surprising, that. Bismarck, even while trying to unite all the Germans, had little choice but to resist efforts to unite all the Poles, for, within Greater Prussia lived many minorities. He knew about the problem of infinite regression. However, even if Bismarck's response is unsurprising in the circumstances, so is the Polish demand. Often, when a people romantically believing itself to be a homogeneous 'nation' creates a new state there is aroused within it a new, hitherto dormant, minority. A newly independent Slovakia turns out to contain a million Hungarians, who are promptly deprived of their language rights. Of the 20 million newly independent Kazakhstanis, 38 per cent are Russians (to 42 per cent Kazakhs).[7] Their rights and status remain precarious. Except when the problem has been addressed by 'ethnic cleansing', the ideal of creating a modern 'nation-state' is likely to be a cruel illusion, even when it is not a recipe for human savagery. If Quebec secedes from Canada, it will become a nation with a large Anglo and Inuit problem. The Grand Council of the Crees, for one, have already made clear their people's intent to secede from any independent Quebec,[8] which would force the latter either to pacify them by radical measures, agree to partition, or develop a Swiss-style confederation of autonomous cantons. None of these options are particularly appealing to either side, but the government of an independent Quebec would probably try to defend its territorial integrity, thus igniting a new conflict. Secessionists who succeed rarely accede to successive secessionists in their midst. And so the circle of anger and violence begins anew.

Still, there is no gainsaying the current power—the surprising fashionableness—of the idea of apartheid just as it is being interred in South Africa. In many parts of the world it has become socially and politically correct to aver that political organization should be based on the principle of 'likes-with-likes': whether 'likes' be defined in linguistic, ethnic, racial, religious, historical, cultural, or other terms, or any combination thereof. It does not seem much to matter to the force of a secessionist claim whether it is based on a demonstrable genetic–cultural–historical reality or, more likely, is pure romantic invention. Rather, the continuing and resurgent power of this tribal nationalism is actually demonstrated by its evident, if paradoxical, success in arousing the passions of people on the basis of commonalities that are invented. The warring Croats, Serbs, and Bosnian Muslims of the former Yugoslavia, after all, are of the same South-Slav ethno-racial origin and speak almost the same language. Yet this in no way diminishes the capacity of ideologically bankrupt but power-hungry politicians to organize a blood-feud among them.

Even among postmodern academics and writers there is a tendency to romanticize the 'authentic' group, to support it against the liberal democratic

---

[7] Patricia Carley, 'Understanding Kazakhstan's Interethnic Relations,' in *Managing Ethnic Tension in the Post-Soviet Space* 3, 4 (Maria Drohobycky ed., 1995).

[8] Grand Council of the Crees (Quebec) and Cree Regional Authority, *Sovereign Injustice* (1995). The demand is for Eeyou Astchee, a Cree state at James Bay.

state and its unifying principle of personal equality. These critics labour 'to unmask the ethnic and moral 'neutrality' of the liberal state as a covert form of coercion'.[9] The underlying idea is that persons should be organized as peoples; and that peoples should have self-governance in accordance with their historic traditions. In the end, we will all be citizens of a state made up exclusively of our kith and kin.

This determinist view is not merely an observation but also a prognosis. If correct, it has exceedingly important implications for those—not least international relations specialists and lawyers—who think about the future organization of humanity's social, cultural, and political life. If it is indeed inevitable that the world is to advance (or regress) to a 2,000-state global system, then that prognosis would have to be taken into account in planning everything: from the regime to save the whale to the system for preserving world peace.

## 2. A WORLD OF 2,000 NATION-STATES

Is this the world we want? Is this the version of self-definition that best suits the temper of the times? It is useful to begin by exploring some of its possible implications.

*First*, it must be recognized that a world of 2,000 nation-states would not be governable by our existing institutional forums and procedural means for reaching agreements. This predictable failure would be a function of proliferating sovereignty's effect on institutions based on the powerful fiction of state equality, creating, in a world of 2,000 sovereigns, an unmanageable dispersal of power.

Some may argue that such a dispersal of power has beneficial potential, whatever its inconveniences. For example, the recent devolution of aspects of governance to the newly empowered regions of Great Britain might reduce the British role as a world power. Whether that is desirable depends in part on one's view of Britain's exercise of its prerogatives: whether this has been on balance benevolent, or not. Others may argue that less hegemony is a good in itself. However, a serious assessment of the probable consequences of a more general power dispersal must also take into account potentially harmful systemic effects.

One predictable effect may be a sharpening of disagreement on global issues. At its present stage of evolution, the international system tends to move discursively towards convergence in two steps. The first step involves the state as mediator between its domestic interest groups, while the second stage consists of negotiations between states whose positions have been configured by the reconciliation of varied domestic concerns. Thus, the American negotiating position

---

[9] Graham Walker, 'The Idea of Nonliberal Constitutionalism,' in *Ethnicity and Group Rights*, 39 *Nomos* 154, 157 (Ian Shapiro & Will Kymlicka eds., 1996).

at global trade conferences tends to be the outcome of convergence between the demands of trade unions, exporters, importers, investors, consumers, environmentalists, farmers, urban dwellers, and various ethnic interests. The US position on global human rights issues is similarly the result of negotiation and compromise at home.

In a world of 2,000 states, this two-step process could give way to a one-step system of interaction between states which, being mainly small and homogeneous, would press views less filtered and little modulated by the exigencies of vibrant domestic diversity. The interstatal negotiations—whether on trade, investment, human rights, environment, or security—might well find convergence more difficult to achieve as the negotiating parties, many of them 'single issue' states, became not only more numerous but also presented obdurate positions in a shriller voice.

If that did not prevent agreement, it would at any rate prolong the search for it. This is likely to redound to the benefit of the privileged few: those best able to bear the cost. 'Only' 150 states were involved in the 1970s and 1980s negotiations leading to the Law of the Sea Treaty (LOS III). Even so, that conference took a decade, followed by a further three-year renegotiation. This later three-year phase, when, at last it succeeded, had introduced a new negotiating strategy. In effect, the search for compromise was moved to a group of some thirty states, convened informally as 'Friends of the UN Secretary-General'. These were able to hammer out agreement on nine remaining problem areas relating to the deep seabed mining regime.[10] There is a lesson here: paradoxically, the more power is fragmented, the more it tends to flow to an elite.

This is already evident, even in existing forums. The UN General Assembly, in which 185 states are represented, increasingly operates with 'informal, open-ended working groups' charged with 'seeking solutions to major problems relating to the efficient working of the Organization'.[11] These *ad hoc* bodies, while theoretically open to the entire membership, actually give preponderant power to those states with large, year-round staffs in New York or Geneva which are able to maintain an effective presence in such groups. Such selective 'participation of the fittest', however productive, illustrates a subtle undermining of sovereign equality that is already evident in the General Assembly. In a conference of 2,000 states, there would probably be a far greater *de facto* transfer of power to the privileged few.

This is not a matter solely of interest to bureaucrats and students of international organizations. It should also be of direct concern to minorities that, seeking a more direct role in shaping their group-destinies, are tempted to demand independence. While a host of small new nation-states might appear to

[10]  1993 UNYB 1150. See also GA Res. 48/28, paras. 4, 5 of 9 December 1993.

[11]  For review of these working groups' activities see *Report of the Secretary-General on the Work of the Organization*, A/50/1, 22 August 1995, at 6, 9.

offer attractive prospects of empowerment, their very smallness and numerousness could lead, instead, to their marginalization.

If global governance is to be reconfigured to empower a select few to make decisions for all, three models appear hypothetically credible: *steering-committees, proconsulates*, and *blocs*.

Utilizing the elected steering committee model, a small group of states representing real power and/or a representative geographic distribution of states and regions would make decisions binding all. Such an arrangement has a certain ring of institutional legitimacy. The Security Council is one example of the genre. It should be noted, however, that the 185 UN members are already demanding a substantial enlargement of the 15-member Council. How large a steering committee would be acceptable to a 2,000-member organization? Would a group of politically acceptable size be small enough and sufficiently cohesive to function? Would it be responsive to the interests of the majority of unrepresented states?

Another model is that of the proconsulates: government by those best positioned by demography, economics, or military muscle to assert power globally or regionally. In recent years, the five permanent members of the Security Council sometimes have behaved in this fashion, exercising hegemonically much of the power which the UN Charter assigns to the Council as a whole. In a world of 2,000 states, some such concentration of authority in the most powerful states might be effective but it is also bound to be unpopular. The legitimacy of decisions made by such proconsuls would be open to persistent and vigorous challenge by the disenfranchised majority of governments and their people.

A third model postulates the gradual merger of 2,000 states into a limited number of regional, or affinity-based, blocs. These, like the European Union (EU), North Atlantic Treaty Organization (NATO), or Association of South East Asian Nations (ASEAN), might seek to integrate key aspects of their foreign relations and international economic policies in accordance with internally negotiated regional modalities. One reason to reserve judgement on this model is that such effective regionalism has proven obdurately elusive even in Europe but certainly in Latin America, Africa, the Middle East, Eastern Europe, and most of Asia.

What each of these models has in common is an effective devaluation of both state sovereignty and the equality of sovereign states, hitherto the sacrosanct coin of the international system. Thus, the rise of the new ethno-nationalisms, raising the prospect of a 2,000-state system, could end up crippling many of those cherished privileges that induced leaders to seek independence in the first place.

*Second*, one must question whether a world of 2,000 states would be more or less peaceful. On the one hand, it can be argued that the existing world of 200 states is itself not very peaceful, and that its penchant for conflict is caused, in measure, by nationalist secessionism and its repression. It would follow every group seeking independence were simply granted it, conflicts would diminish. There is good reason, however, to question this prescription for conflict reduction. The resultant global system is likely to consist of aroused, nationalistic communities, most of which were born in latent or violent conflict with pre-existing states of which they were once an integral part. In such a world one would expect to see the birth of new grudges and of myriad unsatisfied territorial claims, boundary disputes, and irredentist agitations. Even as the 2,000-member community of nation-states becomes less governable, its disputes might proliferate. True, the disputants would tend to be smallish states. However, recent experience has shown that these—*vide* Greece, Turkey and Cyprus or Ecuador and Peru—do generate bitter and militant confrontations.

*Third*, we return to the problem of illiberal nationalism. A world of 2,000 nation-states may not be able to sustain the progress towards democracy and universal human rights that has marked the community of states during the past half-century. Democracy, whether in Switzerland, Upper Volta, or the United States, tends to flourish in diversity precisely because diversity requires mutual respect and accommodation among the variegated constituent interests inhabiting a common political space. The multi-ethnic democratic state is a preparatory school, sensitizing and training those who would participate in the global system: burnishing their capacity for accommodation and skills in negotiating to consensus. While James Madison warned that 'factions' were democracy's principal enemy,[12] he also recognized that democracy's fibre and endurance would derive from its success in balancing these factions. If the multi-nation states break up into their components, there would be less impetus for leaders and people to pursue the balancing of interests, or to cultivate habits of accommodation and self-constraint.

Such an outcome becomes even more probable if, as seems likely, the birth of new nation-states were to occur in traumatizing inter-ethnic conflict giving rise to psychotic state behaviour and a prevalent siege-mentality.

*Fourth*, there is absolutely no reason to take the estimate of 2,000 nation-states as a terminal point in the unravelling of the modern state. If the unravelling process gains further momentum and more particularist groups' aspirations are satisfied, others will discover long-dormant, shared tribal histories and grievances and half-forgotten singularities of language and culture. A logic of fragmentation that yields 2,000 states can as easily justify 4,000 or 10,000. The consequences all point to the enfeeblement of state sovereignty and equality and the flow of power in the direction of the few power-centres that are best able to resist the trend towards nation-states by the successful operation of a

---

[12] *The Federalist* no. 10 (James Madison).

civil society based not on old divisions of race, language, religion, ethnography, or geography but on newer values of civil society and personal freedom.

## 3. THE GLOBAL SYSTEM AS PARADOX

One would expect that the present global system of states would constitute a powerful bulwark against the sort of disintegration envisaged by those who predict a world of 2,000 states. Unfortunately, this is not the case. Rather, it is necessary to concede at once that the international system, as it operates, constitutes a paradox.

On the one hand, to the extent it consists only of governments of states, the global system has a natural and manifest interest in curbing secessionist ambitions. Inevitably, each government sees every other government's secessionist problems as potentially its own. Thus the United Nations, while calling for self-determination, inconsistently has also defended states' territorial integrity,[13] resisting their disaggregation. The Security Council used troops to put down the Katangese independence movement in 1961–2. In the early 1960s, members of the international community did their best to discourage the break-up of Rwanda-Urundi and, more recently, of the Soviet Union and Yugoslavia. Everyone seemed to regret the divorce of Czechs and Slovaks except the Slovaks. The US government, intervening none too subtly in the 1995 Quebec plebiscite, warned voters of adverse economic consequences of choosing independence.

At the same time, however, the structure of the international system rewards inordinately those who reach for the golden apple of independence. No matter how threadbare a potential new state's cultural or historic claim to nationhood, or how much pain a secession may inflict on others, the global system of states is seen to bestow unique and significant privileges on those who succeed in seceding. Only independent states have voice and, with voice, they can expect to be listened to and to be courted. That expectation is a chimera: just ask the UN ambassador of, say, Vanuatu how much influence he or she really wields. But it is not all illusion. For example, the international monetary institutions and bilateral assistance programmes generally proffer help only to a sovereign entity.

And there is a personal dimension. For elites, what greater reward has life to offer than a presidency, a foreign ministry, an ambassadorship? These, however—the diplomatic privileges, the courtesies and curtsies, the inducements and blandishments, the fawning and favours—come only with independence. They come to the Head of State of Swaziland, but not yet to the Premier of Quebec: not until his people secede from Canada. Some elites find these

---

[13] GA Ress. 1614 and 1641.

blandishments irresistible and use their leadership role to stir up the passions that support a national consciousness and an independence movement.

That, of course, is not the sole (or even the primary) motivating factor. Charles Taylor, commenting on the oft-observed fact that nationalist movements, at least at first, tend to be led by elites that have already been co-opted into the ruling circles of the dominant statist culture, attributes their nationalist reawakening, their eventual rejection of co-option, to a pursuit of 'dignity' in the face of non-recognition of their distinct identity and, thus, their sense of self-worth by the homogenizing forces of modernity.[14] The ultimate achievement and recognition of this self-worth, in defiance of modernity's melting-pot, is only bestowed on a group when it succeeds in seceding and compels its acceptance as a sovereign and equal member of the community of states. By its very structure, the Vattelian community of states tempts groups' elites to seek the recognition only sovereignty bestows.

In other words, the international system, which would break down if it had to accommodate 2,000 independent states, itself is so organized as to promote its own collapse by rewarding disintegration of old multinational states and the proliferation of myriad new ones.

What is to be done?

There are remedial steps that might be taken. One is to organize the global community to give voice to affinity groups other than states—for example, the interstate grouping of the aboriginal peoples of the Arctic region. The international system would thereby encourage social aggregation, rather than disaggregation. A related move might introduce into international governance an element of participation by representatives not of governments but of *persons*. That would give some effect, at last, to the opening phrase of the UN Charter: 'We the peoples . . .'. The Parliament of the European Union has demonstrated that when an international institution composed of elected representatives begins to operate, at however modest a level of power, new voices begin to be heard. Transnational political parties become interest-group coalitions that allow minorities to make themselves heard without recourse to secession,[15] usually in productive transnational alliance with similarly situated minorities elsewhere. Another possibility is to give more voice to non-governmental organizations in interstatal forums,[16] a project to be revisited in Chapter 5.

The international system could also be reformed by giving 'voice' to existing substatal political units. Provinces or states which, by the constitution of the

---

[14] Charles Taylor, 'Nationalism and Modernity,' in *The Morality of Nationalism* 31, 44–5 (R. McKim & J. McMahan eds., 1997).

[15] Article 138a of the EC Treaty, a provision first agreed at Maastricht on 7 February 1992, envisages 'political parties at European level' operating in the context of the European Parliament. See Professor Dimitris Th. Tsatsos, MEP, 'European Political Parties? Preliminary reflections on interpreting the Maastricht Treaty article on political parties (Article 138a of the EC Treaty.' Doc. EN\DV\263\263358.

[16] *Report of the Secretary-General on the Work of the Organization*, 1995, *supra* n. 11, at 10. See especially the work of the ECOSOC Working Group on NGO participation. Ibid.

federal system to which they belong, have responsibility for implementing matters of international concern—such as environmental, health, labour or industrial policies and standards—could be accorded voice in the relevant international organizations (such as the United Nations Environment Programme, the World Health and International Labour Organizations, and the World Trade Organization) which formulate global or regional approaches to matters primarily administered by substatal units.

To some extent this is already happening. Substatal governments in federal states increasingly[17] are able and willing to project their interests at the international level, a trend that goes back to the 1970s and 1980s and which reflects the growth of global and regional institutions and norms that affect substatal interests.[18] This 'globalization of localism'[19] is apparent in the emergence as international actors of US and Australian states, Canadian, Belgian, and Chinese provinces, Swiss cantons, German and Austrian länder, Spanish regions, and even Japanese prefectures.[20] Thus, the international system increasingly consists of a 'bewildering network of linkages between those arenas through which actors relate to each other in a variety of ways . . .' and 'policy-makers are required to operate to an increasing extent in a "multilevel" political environment spanning subnational, national and international arenas where the achievement of goods at one level of political activity demands an ability to operate in the other'.[21]

As Professor Seyom Brown has observed,

[i]n some countries where the national government is ineffective in dealing with the concerns of subnational communities and especially where such communities are concentrated in particular provinces or localities, provincial or local governments have been asserting themselves, not only as agencies of advocacy for the cultural and human rights of the aggrieved communities, but increasingly as their economic agents in the global marketplace, negotiating trade and investment arrangements with similar subunits of government in other countries.[22]

The province of Quebec is an example of a substatal unit which, to a significant extent, conducts its own foreign policy, bilateral cultural, environmental and economic relations, and immigration strategy, deploying Agents-General with many of the diplomatic powers of ambassadors. Somewhat the same is true of the other provinces of Canada.[23] Australian states also maintain offices abroad

---

[17] Brian Hocking, *Localizing Foreign Policy* 1 (1993).     [18] Ibid. at 12.

[19] Ivo D. Duchacek, 'Perforated Sovereignties: Towards a Typology of New Actors in International Relations,' in *Federalism in International Relations: The Role of Subnational Units* 8 (Hans J. Michelman & Panayotis Soldatos eds., 1990).

[20] Vincent Cable, 'The Diminished Nation-State: A Study in the Loss of Economic Power: What Future for the State?' *Daedalus*, 22 Mar. 1995, at 23. See also Hocking, *supra* n. 17, at 15.

[21] Hocking, ibid. at 2–3.

[22] Seyom Brown, *New Forces, Old Forces and the Future of World Politics* 237 (1988).

[23] A. Kim Campbell, 'Federalism and International Relations: The Canadian Experience,' 85 Am. Soc'y Int'l L. Proc. 125, 127–8 (1991); James P. McIlroy, 'NAFTA and the Canadian Provinces: Two Ships Passing in the Night?,' 23 Can.-US LJ 431, 433–4 (1997).

headed by Agents-General.[24] In a rather bizarre instance, the Australian state of Queensland, acting on its own, imposed economic sanctions on New Zealand in reprisal for that nation's decision to refuse port access to US nuclear powered vessels.[25] The three provinces of Belgium already participate in the making of treaties that regulate matters within their several jurisdictions.[26] They regularly affect, and may even block, the central authorities' diplomatic initiatives.[27] The revised 1993 Belgian Constitution gives extensive 'voice' to internal regional and community governments. They are entitled to participate both in the domestic and international processes by which treaties are negotiated and decisions are reached. This results in a sort of confederal foreign relations process which accords substatal units a voice virtually equal to that of the Belgian government.[28]

In a few instances, the separate status of substatal units has even been accorded formal recognition by intergovernmental bodies for limited functional purposes. Two British colonies, the Turks and Caicos Islands and the British Virgin Islands, are Associated Members of the Caribbean Community and Common Market (CARICOM). Puerto Rico has been granted observer status at CARICOM and provision has been made in US law for the Commonwealth's accession to the Caribbean Development Bank. Although part of the United States, the Northern Marianas Commonwealth, by its Covenant, may request to participate in 'regional and other international organizations concerned with social, economic, educational, scientific, technical and cultural matters'.[29]

At a less formal level, US states and Canadian provinces have a long tradition of informal cross-boundary working agreements regarding trade, environment, and culture.[30] Under the Vienna Convention and the law of treaties these may

---

[24] John Ravenhill, 'Australia' in *Federalism in International Relations: The Role of Subnational Units, supra* n. 19, at 76, 99.

[25] Hocking, *supra* n. 17, at 67.

[26] See *La Belgique Fédérale et le Droit International*, articles in Revue Belge de Droit International, 1994/1, at 5–365.

[27] In the case of Belgium, dissent by one of the federated entities may cause an abstention on a vote at a diplomatic conference. Charles-Etienne Lagasse, Representation de la Belgique dans les Organisations Internationales, in *La Belgique Fédérale et le Droit International, supra* n. 26, at 147, 153.

[28] For a full discussion see Louis le Hardy de Beaulieu, 'Federalism and International Relations in Belgium: The Reform of 1993–94,' Revue Internationale de Droit Comparé, 3–1994, at 823.

[29] Other British colonies are also CARICOM Observers (The Cayman Islands, Bermuda) as is the Dutch Associated Territory of Aruba. See as to both Puerto Rico and the CNMI: Jon M. Van Dyke, 'The Evolving Legal Relationships between the United States and its Affiliated US-Flag Islands,' 14 U. Harv. L. Rev. 445, 453 (1992). In 1987 the CNMI directed inquiries to the South Pacific Forum Fisheries Agency to determine whether it might be possible to join, but was advised that it could not. Ibid. n. 31. The relevant provision of the CNMI Covenant is: Covenant to Establish a Commonwealth of the Northern Mariana Islands in Political Union with the United States of America, 48 USC §1681 note (1987), reprinted in 15 ILM 651 (1976), §904(c).

[30] R. F. Swanson, *State/Provincial Interaction: A Study of Relations Between US States and Canadian Provinces*, US Department of State 52 (1974). Thus, the Governors of Washington, Alaska, Oregon and California and the Premier of British Columbia in 1989 signed an Oil Spill Memorandum of Cooperation that plans for joint oil spill responses and provides for an Oil Spill Task Force, the

well be binding on the parties, although it remains puzzling as to who those parties are, for purposes of state responsibility. Is it Alberta and Montana, or Canada and the United States? Undeterred by such concerns, however, governments of US states maintain more than 150 offices abroad that promote trade, investment, and tourism, often with the aid of state statutes that enhance their leverage in international relations.[31]

Another instance of the need to address the problem of 'voice' is that of the many indigenous populations—Inuits of Canada, Saami of Norway, Aboriginals of Australia, Sioux of America, and many others—that do not necessarily seek independence but want rights pertaining to land title, education, and other aspects of group autonomy.[32] These topics, of course, are traditionally within the purview of the respective national governments. Nevertheless, increasingly group rights are also being addressed through international institutions such as the Human Rights Committee and UN Human Rights Commission. Understandably, therefore, these indigenous groups have sought both indirect and direct participation in the international processes most relevant to their interests: either individually or in inter-group alliances such as the Unrepresented Nations and Peoples Organization (UNPO) which currently has approximately 50 members,[33] and the Inuit Circumpolar Conference (ICC), founded in 1986 and consisting of indigenes of Alaska, Greenland, Russia and Canada.[34] The

sharing of technology and joint training. Washington State and the Province of British Columbia have concluded an Environmental Cooperation Agreement as have New York and Quebec. In both instances, there are provisions for consultation before the issuance of permits that entail operations which could adversely affect the environment of the other party. In 1993, New York, Vermont and Quebec concluded a Water Quality Agreement pertaining to in-lake phosphorous criteria which establishes limits on eutrophication of joint waters from sources within the jurisdiction of each party. A 1994 agreement between the Governors of California, Baja California Norte and Baja California Sur created a Californias Border Environmental Cooperation Committee which includes not only joint standards and monitoring but also the joint construction of environmentally-protective infra-structural projects. Peter Jennetten, 'State Environmental Agreements with Foreign Powers: The Compact Clause and the Foreign Affairs Power of the States,' 8 Geo. Int'l Envl. L. Rev. 141, 148, 150, 168–9, 170, 171 (1995).

[31] Peter Eisinger, *The Rise of the Entrepreneurial State: State and Local Economic Development Policy in the United States* (1988); Scott R. Fosler, *The New Economic Role of American States: Strategies in a Competitive World Economy* (1988); Earl H. Fry, 'Sovereignty and Federalism: US and Canadian Perspectives,' 20 Can.-US LJ 309 (1994).

[32] See *Traditional Knowledge and Renewable Resource Management in Northern Regions* (Freeman & Carbyn eds., 1988); David S. Case, 'Subsistence and Self-determination: Can Alaska Natives Have a More "Effective Voice"?' 60 U. Colo. L. Rev. 1009 (1989).

[33] See Richard Ehrlich, 'Aiding Groups Within Nations,' Wash. Times, July 1, 1996, at A10. See further Noel Dyck, 'Aboriginal Peoples and Nation States,' in *Indigenous Peoples and the Nation-State* 1 (N. Dyck ed., 1985); Douglas E. Sanders, 'The Indian Lobby and the Canadian Constitution, 1978–82,' in Dyck, ibid. at 151.

[34] See Russel L. Barsh, 'Indigenous People: An Emerging Object of International Law,' 80 Am. J. Int'l L. 369 (1986); Mary E. Turpel, 'Indigenous Peoples' Rights of Political Participation and Self-Determination: Recent International Legal Developments and the Continuing Struggle for Recognition,' 25 Cornell Int'l LJ 579 (1992). Turpel argues that the struggle for participation in international organizations is primarily waged not for independence but for autonomy rights as the preferred form of self-determination. Ibid. at 593–4.

indigenes, whose agenda often asserts a right to be let alone by national governments to run their own affairs, have made common cause in an effort to earn international recognition of their right to participate in international discourses of concern to them. This has led to the 'paradoxical concept of a Fourth World, which purports to unite peoples from many countries who generally have been distinctive in their tendencies toward localism and the micro-scale of their communities and identities'.[35] However small, this aggregation of communal effort has had its successes: for example, in the World Bank's recent insistence that developing states seeking loans for rural development projects first settle indigenous peoples' unsatisfied land claims.[36]

Can the international system take bolder steps to give voice to substatal entities? A project proposed to the UN General Assembly by Liechtenstein[37] envisages the possibility of according semi-autonomous peoples and regions some qualified form of representation in international forums. In the words of Ambassador Claudia Fritsche, many 'conflicts occur because people seeking ways of asserting their distinctive identity find that they have no accepted channel through which their reasonable aspirations may be reasonably expressed . . .'.[38]

Professor David Wippman has advocated a broadening of opportunities for other voices to make themselves heard[39] in at least some forums, for some purposes. 'In particular,' Wippman points out, 'when states experience severe and prolonged intercommunal conflict, the usual assumption that a state constitutes an indivisible legal entity whose voice is expressed in international affairs by the incumbent government becomes untenable. In such cases, each of the contending substate communities should be given a voice in international decision-making . . .'.[40] Indeed, he argues, in giving the dissidents voice the system becomes better able to help deal with the causes of disaffection and to prevent outright secession and its oft-concomitant conflict and chaos.

Such admission of sub-units of states into the global discourse, even provisionally, might directly assuage one of the causes of the demand for independence. As Professor Albert Hirschman has suggested in his study *Exit, Voice and Loyalty*, when it is possible to have voice within an established operational entity, the option of exit may lose its attraction.[41] Taking up this point

---

[35] Dyck, *supra* n. 33, at 6.        [36] Ibid. at 20.

[37] See 'Request for the Inclusion of an Item in the Provisional Agenda of the Forty-Eighth Session: Effective Realization of the Right of Self-Determination Through Autonomy,' UN Doc. A/ 48/147 of 16 July 1993 et. seq. e.g. Statement to the General Assembly of Ambassador Claudia Fritsche, Permanent Representative of Liechtenstein to the UN, GAOR 3d Comm., 50th Sess., 6th mtg., pp. 3–4, UN Doc. A/C.3/50/SR.6 (1995), 11 October, 1995.

[38] Ibid. See also UN Doc. A/50/492 of 2 October 1995 which reports on two conferences held at Princeton University in March and June of 1995 to explore the Liechtenstein initiative.

[39] David Wippman, 'Hearing Voices Within the State: Internal Conflicts and the Claims of Ethno-National Groups,' 27 NYU J. Int'l L. & Pol. 585, 585 (1995).        [40] Ibid. at 588–9.

[41] Albert O. Hirschman, *Exit, Voice and Loyalty* (1970).

and extrapolating it to the international system of states, it has been suggested that secessionist nationalism tends to arise when the cultural and political-economic ambitions of a linguistic, religious, or ethnic group within a multi-national state are thwarted by an authoritarian central government's refusal to permit sufficient subsidiarity.[42]

On the other hand, there is also evidence that, for constituencies offered only a half-filled cup of sovereignty, *l'appetit vient en mangeant*: autonomy evokes a thirst for independence. The failure of the 1867 *Ausgleich* by which the Habsburg emperor Franz Joseph granted 'equality' with Austria to his Hungarian dominion[43] is sometimes cited as an example of this phenomenon.

A proper examination of this hypothetical but potentially important question requires examination of two related variables: *autonomy* and *participation* in international regimes. For some preliminary indications it may be interesting to follow the developments in Nunavut, a predominantly Inuit autonomous territory created in 1999 within the Canadian federation. Will the temptation to become a player in the global system (participation) pull Nunavut from its newly achieved autonomy towards secession and independence? Or will the staid Vattelian system relent, offering the Inuits voice in matters of direct interest to them? And, if so, will that slake or whet their appetite for the 'real thing'? For that matter, how much would the admittance of a new caste of substatal entities aggravate international forums' problems of membership proliferation?

## 4. COUNTER-INDICATIONS: THE EMERGING SELF IN SELF-DETERMINATION

This chapter has addressed the problem of romantic nationalism institutionally, because the global system's rigid Vattelian structure is both threatened by, and yet also contributes to, the problems posed by resurgent nationalism.

This institutional paradox, however, is not the only key to understanding a revival of nationalism at the end of the twentieth century. More fundamentally, that revival is a symptom of an alienation to which modern internationalization is a significant contributor.

The phenomenon of persons rediscovering the deepness of their local roots, in part, is a natural reaction against finding their lives increasingly affected by remote bureaucratic transnational regimes. It is natural that this alienation should engender a nostalgia for older, more compact, accessible and responsive political units within which the individual is accorded greater weight.

Can international institutions legitimize themselves by more democratically connecting to the people whose lives they increasingly affect?

The idea of individual participation in international forums still sounds odd

---

[42] John A. Hall, 'Nationalisms: Classified and Explained,' *Daedalus*, Summer 1993, at 1.
[43] Alan Palmer, *Twilight of the Habsburgs: The Life and Times of Emperor Francis Joseph* 154–9 (1995).

and vaguely subversive because the Vattelian system, for three hundred years, has fostered the conviction that every individual's identity is defined exclusively by his or her relationship with a sovereign state and its government. Citizenship defines the citizen. In international affairs, persons speak only through their state's representatives. However, this has become a less and less plausible arrangement. As Professor David Held has argued, 'Territorial boundaries demarcate the basis on which individuals are included and excluded from participation in decisions affecting their lives (however limited the participation might be), but the outcomes of these decisions most often "stretch" beyond national frontiers. The implications of this are profound . . .'.[44] The existing system of international relations operates on principles that exclude participation by those most affected.

Orthodoxy has it that all persons are indirect participants in the international system through their governments. While this may be true in theory, the theory's validity has always depended on an assumed indifference to the quality of governance in sovereign states: whether the participating regimes are freely elected or totalitarian, whether they accurately represent their citizenry's (diverse) views and values regarding global issues. While such indifference egregiously misrepresents the democratic spirit of the times, the theory of inviolable state sovereignty it reflects remains essentially unexamined. As US Supreme Court Justice Sutherland said in a much-quoted opinion: 'In this vast external realm, with its important, complicated, delicate and manifold problems, the President alone has the power to speak or listen as a representative of the nation.'[45]

This flaw in systemic legitimacy would be even more serious were it not for the opening up, in recent years, of back channels for participation of persons at the widening margins of global governance. The multinational corporation is the best known. Among many others are the transnational media, global religions, as well as the professional, charitable, and service-oriented organizations. These have introduced the voice of individuals and interest-groups into diplomatic negotiations. In humanitarian law-making and human rights, for example, influence is increasingly wielded by activist organizations without frontiers, such as the International Committee of the Red Cross, Amnesty International and the Helsinki Human Rights Watch groups.

This ameliorates, but does not cure, the legitimacy-deficit of Vattelian international governance and the modern alienation that ensues. As international regimes proliferate and expand to meet problems newly perceived as requiring global solutions, this problem of legitimacy, if left unredressed, is likely to engender ever stronger reflexes.[46] David Held has noted that, as regional and

---

[44] David Held, *Democracy and the New International Order* 8 (1993).

[45] *United States v. Curtiss-Wright Export Corp.*, 299 US 304, 319 (1936).

[46] See David Held, *Democracy and the Global Order* (1995); Andrew Linklater, *The Transformation of Political Community* (1998).

global institutions increasingly affect the lives of persons, 'intergovernmental and transnational power structures' must develop their own 'cosmopolitan democratic model' that 'is adapted to the diverse conditions and interconnections of different peoples and nations'.[47]

Once that is generally accepted, the route ahead is fairly well marked. It is hard to envisage any effective remedy that does not entail some form of direct participation by persons in a representative global democratic process: a parliamentary system.

Realistically, such a systemic change, an earthquake in the Vattelian order, would have to take into account the continuing reality of state pre-eminence. One might envisage a reformed UN General Assembly, in which that organ's very limited powers would be exercised by double majority of two chambers: one constituted by diplomats representing states, the other by representatives elected by universal franchise.

This example, only one of many models of reform currently on offer that introduce the idea of direct public participation, has the potential for creating the beginning of global politics. There, factions, minorities, and other affinity groups could make themselves heard *without* secession and the pursuit of sovereignty, choosing instead to aggregate their interests through transnational political parties and coalitions.

While the idea of global politics radically challenges the Vattelian system, it might also rescue it from its increasingly evident entropy. In the words of Philip Allott: 'New conventions of self-determination will have to be established, new rules as to the forming of the reality of the individual human being within the self-forming of the societies to which the individual belongs.'[48]

[47] Held, *supra* n. 44, at 12.
[48] Philip Allott, 'The Nation as Mind Politic,' 24 J. Int'l L. & Pol. 1361, 1397 (1992).

# 3

## A Different Future: Individualism as Identity

There are many countries in our blood, aren't there, but only one person. Would the world be in the mess it is if we were loyal to love and not to countries?

Graham Greene, *Our Man in Havana*

'Patriotism is not enough.'

Edith Cavell (last words, quoted in *The London Times*, 23 October 1915)

### 1. IDENTITY IN THE POST-COLD WAR ERA

In Bosnia, the vaunted ideal—a vibrant state with Muslims, Orthodox, and Catholic citizens living together in a tolerant civil society—has virtually been extinguished by a torrent of blood and tears. In Belgium, itself a less than 200-year-old product of Catholic rebellion against Orange–Protestant Holland, the Catholics of Flemish-speaking Flanders have all but parted ways with the Catholics of French-speaking Wallonia, leaving an ethnically stressed Brussels paradoxically ensconced as capital of a 'United Europe'. What is going on here, or in Somalia, Slovakia, Quebec, and Kazakhstan?

Especially since the end of colonialism and the fall of communism, the question is on everyone's mind. Obviously, states still matter and many persons still regard themselves as loyal citizens of Norway or India. Quite as obviously, however, the priority of the state in the constituting of personal identity is being challenged by the resurgent power of nations, tribes, ethnie, religions, and linguistic groups. These have all re-emerged as contenders for the intense, exclusivist personal loyalties of their members, a contest sometimes leading to the disintegration of long-established states.

This is nothing new; yet there was reason to think that we had finished with this stage of social evolution. But the arguments by which Serb 'leaders' explicated their 1990s Bosnian rampages eerily echoed the rantings of the Nazis as they dismembered Czechoslovakia in 1938 to 'reunite' their Sudeten ethnic kin with the Fatherland.[1] Is it all back, the deterministic rationalizations about the irresistible force of blood's imperatives?

Or are we witnessing only an historic 'blip', a minor detour on the road to a grander, more rational world order, one in which states, far from disintegrating,

---

[1] See Nathaniel Berman, 'Beyond Colonialism and Nationalism? Ethiopia, Czechoslovakia and "Peaceful Change"', 65 Nordic J. Int'l L. 421, 437–45 (1996).

learn to enhance trade, communications, health, human rights, and the environment by creating humanistic transnational and sectoral regimes? Which way is humanity headed: towards a reinvented tribal past, to resurgent militant nationalisms, to universal, democratic civil republicanism, or in the direction of global union? What human factors will prevail to set our course: genetics, language, religion, culture, geography, commerce, or other social imperatives? As we advance through today's crossroads of identity, who will we become?

Each prognosis is supported by fragmentary evidence. Certainly, liberal civil republicanism seems here to stay, a continuing force in shaping personal loyalties and the modern state system. But outbreaks of less enlightened nationalism may keep recurring. Tribal and ethnic affiliation still seem indispensable sources of meaning in the lives of many.[2] At the same time there appears to be a proliferation of personal commitment to universal religions, transnational enterprises, and various professional and human potential-developing networks.

The safest guess may be that, in the future, various localisms, nationalisms, and globalisms will continue to compete—sometimes in conflict, at other times in coexistence, and often within the same breast. This does not mean, however, that the future will be no more than a projection of the present. What may be on the way out is the monopoly that, together, the state, the socio-cultural group, and certain transnational movements and organizations have had on the shaping and determination of human identity. Insinuating itself amongst these is a new but growing consciousness of individual worth, manifesting itself in the claim to personal autonomy and inherent human rights. Among these new claims, the most fundamental—and most astonishing—is the demand selectively to choose the components of one's personal identity. This new individualism challenges the limits on personal self-determination so long imposed by the traditional objects of allegiance.

The individualist challenge actually consists of two related claims: first, that each individual is entitled to choose an identity reflecting personal preference; and, second, that in composing that identity, each may select more than one allegiance.

The second of these is not new. There have been periods and places where persons were allowed to have multiple layers of affiliation. Practical accommodations were reached that allowed loyalty to be allotted among towns, leagues, guilds, dukes, bishops, princes, kings, emperors, and popes. Today, the right to multiple or layered loyalty is still disputed in some conventional communities, but, as will be demonstrated in Chapter 4, it is no longer considered a particularly radical claim.

However, the first claim—to personal freedom in *choosing* one's identity-forming affiliations—is a long leap from more conventional thinking. Because

---

[2] For a discussion of 'ethnie' see Anthony D. Smith, *The Ethnic Origins of Nations* (1986). See also text at note 10 *infra*.

more persons now demand liberty in law and social practice to select their own values and loyalties, this is becoming the age of individualism. What distinguishes modern identity formation is that, for the first time, persons demand the right to compose their own, unique self-definitions. They are beginning to select freely from among competing options in accordance with individual preference. Any prognosis must make allowance for this new factor.

Admittedly, many persons, in various parts of the world, do not now enjoy this right. Even in the developed democracies—and more so in other places—persons' access to the full panoply of self-identifying options is still limited by the practical consequences of economic, cultural, and racial deprivation and stratification. Yet, this study will offer evidence of an emerging global consensus, at least in principle but increasingly also in practice, that these obstacles must be addressed and progressively dismantled, until each person's potential is unhobbled. Revolutionary recent innovations in technology and social consciousness make this a realistic goal.

While this optic does not capture all the complexities and contradictions of the present, it does provide a glimpse of underlying tendencies that the messy surface obscures. Indeed, the purpose of this chapter is to tap and to crack that brittle, encrusted surface through which new tendencies are beginning to spring forth.

Of course, signs of these new tendencies are not universally welcomed. Professor Amitai Etzioni, for one, sees the current pursuit of personal autonomy as contributing to unbridled self-seeking and the decline of community values.[3] He cautions that 'the need for autonomy reflects the animal base of universal human nature'.[4] A different but parallel scepticism is expressed by those who hold that the factors which contributed to the rise of individual rights in the West do not operate in other societies. These arguments are addressed in Chapters 5 and 6. What is clear even to sceptics, however, is that a different contender has entered the arena: a newly powerful force of individualism.

## 2. ONE-SIZE-FITS-ALL IDENTITY

If we are to accept that individuals are now, for the first time, making free, genuine choices in determining their identities, we should do so only on the basis of convincing evidence that the previously ineluctable hold on us of the old deterministic, communally imposed identities—territorial, tribal, ethnic, racial, religious, and linguistic—has begun to loosen.

Evidence, in ensuing chapters, that the traditionally imposed loyalty-referents are losing some of their once-unchallengeable purchase is best appreciated against a sceptical examination of the imposing provenance claimed by the

[3] See e.g. Amitai Etzioni, *The New Golden Rule* (1996).        [4] Ibid. at 169.

entrenched enemies of individualism: their right to be seen as historically validated building blocks of social order. As we began to see in Chapter 1, modern anthropological research and new social attitudes tend to discount those claims. This has not come about, however, without strenuous resistance. For hundreds of years, individuals in organized society were imbued with a sense of 'belonging' that emphasized their subordination to some consecrated authority ordained to rule a natural grouping of loyal subjects. Individuals 'belonged' to a ruler, a state, a group, a religion. Inevitably, this claim by the rulers to persons' axiomatic loyalty provoked conflict: wars of repression against individuals unwilling to accept imposed subordination and wars between various claimants to persons' exclusive loyalty. These external struggles were replicated internally by conflicts in the psyche of individuals torn between contenders for their adherence.

Even with temporary ceasefires, the historic struggle over the identity of persons has been a cosmic one, with little inclination to compromise. To Hegel, the answer was straightforward; persons belong exclusively to their historic nations. These, he wrote, are the only natural building blocks of world society. 'Nations' have a final 'destination—that of forming themselves into states.'[5] Each person is naturally defined by belonging to a 'nation' and each nation is naturally destined to become a state. Such statehood is the perfect, undeconstructible essence of singleness, subsuming all the characteristics of a person or of *mind*. This 'mind, and its actuality, the state, has individuality. . .'—by which Hegel means that it manifests itself 'in sharp distinction from others . . .'. Those wishes, essentially for national belonging, are always to be seen as definitive and exclusive. Those 'who balk [at] the "wishes" of a collection of people . . . have very little knowledge . . . of the feeling of selfhood which a nation possesses in its independence'.[6] This 'selfhood' is entirely collective and not at all individual. Thus, 'the rights and interests of individuals' are, quite simply, to be nullified, absorbed into a communitarian and absolute 'individuality' which is manifest as sovereignty of the state.[7] This 'nation state is mind in its substantive rationality and immediate actuality and is therefore the absolute power on earth'.[8] It exists as consequence of its people's 'sacrifice of property and life, as well as opinion and everything else naturally comprised in the compass of life'.[9]

Especially in the last half century, Hegel's nation-centred analysis has been rejected by most historians, anthropologists, and sociologists. Ernest Gellner has warned that 'we must not accept the myth'[10] which he regards not only as historically false, but also anthropologically absurd and politically disastrous. 'Nations', according to Gellner, 'are not inscribed into the nature of things, they do not constitute a political version of the doctrine of natural kinds. Nor were

---

[5] G. W. F. Hegel, *Lectures on the Philosophy of World History* 134 (H. B. Nisbet trans., 1975).
[6] *Hegel's Philosophy of Right* 208 (T. M. Knox trans., 1952).      [7] Ibid. at 209.
[8] Ibid. at 212.      [9] Ibid. at 209.
[10] Ernest Gellner, *Nations and Nationalism* 49 (1983).

nation-states the manifest ultimate destiny of ethnic or cultural groups.'[11] To this, Professor E. J. Hobsbawm adds: 'Nations, we now know . . . are not as Bagehot thought, as old as history. The modern sense of the word is no older than the eighteenth century.'[12] Both Gellner and Hobsbawm warn us not to accept the provenances of nations but, rather, to see them as invented forgeries to validate entrenched distributions of power.

We are also warned to be wary of evidence that seeks to legitimate nations by celebrating their deep historic roots. On the contrary, as we saw in Chapter 1, most modern usages of the term 'nation' in one way or another falsify history to validate an imposed group-identity, often one with quite shallow roots.

Before nations, there were amorphous cultures, ethnie, but these usually saw no reason to pursue an exclusivist agenda of social organization, let alone to become nation-states. Moreover, these ethnie, with few exceptions, were themselves amalgams of smaller groups.[13] A further, fundamental distortion occurred with the eighteenth-century superimposition of modern nationalism on France. It gave an aura of eternal validity to a happenstance of rulers' whimsical triumphs and defeats, forcibly uniting an amorphous grouping of ethnie and cultures that had coexisted under the French crown.[14] In fact, French revolutionary nationalism, whatever its pretensions, was neither the necessary working out of some metaphysical historic destiny nor, for that matter, did it become the prevalent organizing principle of nations. Rather, the French model is a unique social phenomenon. It created *nationalism* where there had been only feudal fealty and a *nation* where there had been only disparate regional cultures and languages. The French brand of 'nationalism' thus was unique and the French 'nation' was its sturdiest invention. As Gellner puts it, nations are not 'the bricks of which mankind is made up'.[15] Nevertheless, after World War I, a Wilsonian world of self-determining nation-states[16] seemed to acquire some verisimilitude. The era and its ethos encouraged the belief that it was both 'natural' and 'just' for each person to identify exclusively with a 'people' and for as many such 'peoples' as possible to have states of their own.

Self-determination had its day at Versailles. And its sceptics. John Maynard Keynes remarked despairingly that this Wilsonian dogma 'exalts and dignifies the divisions of race and nationality above the bonds of trade and culture, and guarantees frontiers but not happiness'.[17] Yet the concept continues to resonate, even now. In 1975, in the *Western Sahara* Advisory Opinion, the International Court of Justice seemed to acknowledge the supremacy of a people's legal right

---

[11] Ernest Gellner, *Nations and Nationalism* 49 (1983).

[12] E. J. Hobsbawm, *Nations and Nationalism Since 1780* 3 (2nd edn., 1990).

[13] See John A. Armstrong, *Nations Before Nationalism* 4, 284 (1982).

[14] Ibid. at 8–9.          [15] Gellner, *supra* n. 10, at 48.

[16] See Nathaniel Berman, 'Economic Consequences, Nationalist Passions: Keynes, Crisis, Culture and Policy', 10 Am. U. J. Int'l L. & Pol'y 619 (1995).

[17] John Maynard Keynes, 'A Revision of the Treaty', reprinted in 3 *The Collected Writings of John Maynard Keynes* 1, 8 (D. Moggridge ed., 1972).

to self-determination.[18] It gave judicial heft to the United Nations General Assembly's sweeping decolonialization Resolutions 1514 (XV) and 1541 (XV). And it subtly broadened the category of those entitled to statehood from 'a nation' to 'a people'. Needless to say, this did nothing to clarify *who* could be said to constitute 'a people'. The Serbs of Bosnia, while arguably not a 'nation' could still claim to be a 'people'. It also did nothing to resolve the policy objection Lord Keynes had identified almost half a century earlier.

Others have been quite confident about the irrefutable logic of pedigreed nationhood and its entitlements. Hegel was the architrave upholding an exclusively ethnocentric or tribal architecture of personal identity. Immanuel Kant, on the other hand, championed liberal states based on inclusive civil societies, confidently predicting that these were destined, eventually, to become the building blocks of a global democratic confederation. Thomas Jefferson thought so, too. According to the historian Henry Adams,

Jefferson aspired beyond the ambition of nationality, and embraced in his view the whole future of man. That the United States should become a nation like France, England, or Russia, should conquer the world like Rome, or develop a typical race like the Chinese, was no part of his scheme. He wished to begin a new era. Hoping for a time when the world's ruling interests should cease to be local and should become universal; when questions of boundary and nationality should become insignificant; when armies and navies should be reduced to the work of police; and politics should consist only in non-intervention,—he set himself to the task of governing, with this golden age in view.[19]

To men like Kant and Jefferson, all persons were capable of sharing in such a golden age, a 'perpetual peace' (Kant's term), if only the systems of civil government were better attuned to humanity's higher instincts and capable of resisting 'the crimes and follies of Europe . . ., [the] miserable ambitions that had made the Old World a hell, and frustrated the hopes of humanity'.[20] To them, the nation-tribe was a problem, the state a means, and democratic, confederal globalism the solution. To Hegel, on the other hand, the nation-tribe, predestined to be the fundamental unit of power in the world, was the solution, whereas multinational states (like Austro-Hungary) and grander confederations (like the Holy Roman Empire) were an obstacle wrapped in a chimera. The ensuing two centuries have sharpened the confrontations between these differing visions, a confrontation rather obfuscated by both parties having appropriated the term 'nationalism'.

It should be noted, however, that despite their differences there are also important similarities in the world-view of these old contenders. Both kinds of nationalism have persistently claimed to be the right answer for everyone: a

---

[18] Western Sahara, 1975 ICJ Rep. 12, 32–3, 67–8, paras. 57, 161 (Advisory Opinion of Oct. 16).

[19] Henry Adams, 1 *History of the United States, 1801–1809* 101 (Earl V. Harbert ed., 1986).

[20] Ibid.

one-size-fits-all cloak of identity. Both kinds of nationalism have had a global mission. Neither was in the least inclined to accommodate the liberal individualism now emerging in much of the world, challenging all claims by any authority to determine everyone's personal identity.

## 3. THE VALUES UNDERLYING IDENTITY CHOICES

The purpose of this discourse is not to join, let alone resolve, these long-standing still-troublesome perplexities.[21] It is, rather, to put the resultant dilemma in context by examining the unstated values and assumptions that underpin the lexicons of two polar versions of nationalism, and then to think about what, little noted, may already be replacing both: an individualism that empowers each person to define his or her own, unique identity protected by a new regime of national and international laws.

Before examining the emergent challenge of the new, it will help to clarify further the conceptual foundations of the old, a task begun in Chapter 1. Nationalism, as understood by Hegel, is that which motivates the 'nation state', a drive that 'is mind in its substantive rationality and immediate actuality and is therefore the absolute power on earth'.[22] The nationalism that Hegel imagined is the collective consciousness of an affinity group, one placing certain values high on its agenda: shared genealogical origins, language, and historic myths, as well as cultural and, perhaps, religious compatibility. It infers a popular preference for 'likes being with likes', and a high degree of social conformity.

In sharp contrast, the nationalism of a multicultural liberal state—as imagined, for example, by Jefferson—reflects quite different social values: a preference for a vibrant non-statal civil society; accommodation of, and tolerance for, diversity; freedom of conscience; liberty and personal mobility in such matters as career, religion, and social status.

There are currently ample examples of both kinds of nationalisms. The distinction between them, of course, is a matter of degree, which obscures, but never quite obliterates, their historic and profound differences. Those distinctions, moreover, persist despite the evidence that both nationalisms contain elements of the other. For example, the United States, although imbued with classical, liberal Jeffersonian nationalism, may yet deliberately foster myths of a shared 'melting-pot' nationhood that at times resemble the romantic Hegelian version. In pursuit of unity, or economic and political advantage,

---

[21] See e.g. Nathaniel Berman, 'But the Alternative Is Despair: European Nationalism and the Modernist Renewal of International Law,' 106 Harv. L. Rev. 1792 (1993); Nathaniel Berman, 'Modernism, Nationalism, and the Rhetoric of Reconstruction,' 4 Yale JL & Human. 351 (1992); Nathaniel Berman, 'A Perilous Ambivalence: Nationalist Desire, Legal Autonomy, and the Limits of the Interwar Framework,' 33 Harv. Int'l LJ 353 (1992).

[22] G. W. F. Hegel, *Philosophy of Right* 213 (T. M. Knox trans., 1942) (1821).

liberal nationalist states may aggressively invent a nationhood based on imagined (and often demonstrably false) commonalities of history, genetics, religion,
and culture. France, too, from time to time has manifested this tendency to
invent a romantic nationalist imperative for its citizenry. *Le Monde,* in the recent
'Year of Clovis, the first French king', had to remind its readers that the occasion
celebrates a national myth: 'un catéchisme scolaire, d'origine à la fois royaliste
et républicaine, entretient dans notre pays l'image d'une nation intemporelle,
éternelle, préexistant à sa propre histoire.'[23] It pointed out not only the fallacy
of an ancient French nation but also that, whoever this Clovis was, he probably
spoke proto-German, but certainly not proto-French.

On the other hand, even states weened on Hegelian romanticism are also
sometimes astonished at the fragility of their much more deeply imbedded
myths of historic and biological unity. Many Germans, still thinking of themselves as a nation in the tribal–genealogical sense, after the lifting of the iron
curtain were quite surprised by the formidable cultural and socio-political rift
that had been opened by the short and alien division that was imposed on them
in 1945. That fault-line, fostered by only forty-five years of political separation
but perhaps reflecting deeper and older regional, cultural, religious, and social
disparities, has proven more obdurate than East and West Germans had
expected. It has challenged the widespread prognosis, at the fall of the Berlin
wall in 1989, that the whole nation could easily be stitched back together, for
'we are all Germans'.[24]

Hegelian nationalists resemble other romantic tribalists in emphasizing common genes, history, and culture. They endorse the mythology of an ennobling
past that largely determines their peoples' common destiny. The citizens of a
liberal multinational state, instead, tend to share a vision of a glorious self-
invented future: much as nineteenth-century Americans touted their 'manifest
destiny' but not their manifest history. In this they differed from some other
immigrant-settler peoples, the Afrikaners of South Africa and the Jews of Israel,
who perceived themselves as eternal tribes or nations.

These two kinds of nationalism have been described in Chapter 1: the
idealistic eighteenth-century kind, as opposed to the romantic nineteenth-century variety. The differences between them are profound. But they have shared
an overriding common characteristic: both perceive identity as something
defining persons through an independent variable: territorial sovereignty in
the earlier case, history and biogenetics in the later one. They each postulate
a nationalism that firmly anchors persons to a community of institutions and
values. Neither nationalism accommodates the idea that individuals are entirely
free to choose: to compose their identity, detached from history, culture,

---

[23] Suzanne Citron, 'A propos de Clovis', Le Monde, 28 Feb. 1996, at 8.
[24] For an analysis see 'Survey: Germany', The Economist 1–22 (following p. 88), 9–15 Nov. 1996.

language, religion, and territory. Both have traditionally relied on a 'given': a social unity based on deeply rooted things from which we all draw our telos.

In the late twentieth century, however, many of the profound, shaping experiences of one's life tend to be private and personal, rather than collective and vicarious; and values have come to be more widely recognized as—potentially—subjective preferences, rather than genetically, culturally, territorially or socially determined. With recognition of the subjectivity of experiences and values has come the liberation of at least some individuals: not merely to choose between two conventional kinds of nationalism, but to design customized affinities reflecting an eminently personal telos, drawing on individual preferences.

Today, a person's loyalty system is increasingly likely to be a compound of subjectively chosen external references: to family, culture, religion, ideals, institutions, the state, colleagues, and even to humanity. These identity-shaping compounds are complex and dynamic. Obviously, such liberation of the individual has not promised, let alone achieved, a surcease of struggle and conflict. It has, however, transformed the struggle from one between great external social and political forces in which the individual is the passive prize to one in which the individual, although still the prize, has also become an active participant.

Whatever the outcome of these struggles, it tends to shape persons' identity and values. When national or tribal values predominate, a person's identity is formed primarily by historical considerations: common myths, past glories or defeats, injustices suffered or overcome, shared grievances nourished and burnished. Community preferences become the individual's compass. Common language, culture, genealogy, and religion tend to project the romanticized past onto each person's expectations of the future. Persons defined in this way are likely to want to live among others of the same kind: to eat the food, listen to the music, and dance to the rhythms beloved by ancestors and neighbours. Nostalgia is romantic nationalism's soft side.

Persons imbued primarily with liberal nationalist values, in contrast, tend not to have this same reverence for the past, but do exalt their society's common aspirations for the future. Although shared values are an important ingredient in their patriotism, multi-ethnic states like the United States or India are likely to focus on the strengths of diversity and to make a virtue of necessity by stressing the importance of shared civic values and a vibrant civil society.

Both a nation-tribe and a civil society organized as a multi-ethnic state can run amok with jingoism, but the sources of their respective jingoisms are different. Romantic nationalisms tend towards ethnic or racial xenophobia (Hitler's Germany, Hirohito's Japan), while civil societies such as Napoleonic France or modern America are more likely to pursue, at times aggressively, their globalizing ideals and mercantilist aspirations.

The sinews of a civil society are often thought to be less tensile than those of a romantically imagined nation-state or tribe. The civil society's optimism about its citizens' common future is more contingent and less rooted than is the pride of a tribe or nation based on a gloriously remembered past. Nevertheless, statist identity, based on the vision of a shining future or manifest destiny, may emerge to bind the civil society into a cohesive force. This happened during the Industrial Revolution in Britain, the French Revolution, and the Italian *Risorgimento*. Something like it may even have happened in Tito's Yugoslavia. Sometimes, as in Britain, this statist civil awakening occurs in connection with technological innovations that generate, and ultimately may satisfy, a revolution of social expectations. At other times, a state is called into being at the behest of charismatic leaders—Napoleon, Bismarck, Garibaldi—who succeed in forging a diverse rabble into a questing citizenry by iron will or iron wheels. Such forging may go on until the state becomes a nation: as when the Jewish tribes wandered the Sinai until they cohered as a militant nation-state, albeit one later to split again into tribes. Or it may not happen at all, leaving a civil state that, in the worst examples, is no more than the merest hollow political forum for constituent factions and classes waging civil war by other means.

We speak deliberately of *forging* a nation, but, as with all else about the terminology of personal identity, this usage is not free of controversy. Nations, in the Hegelian and tribal sense, usually pretend to be genetically or ethnically validated manifestations of historical social forces. They do not perceive themselves as being forged out of anything but, rather, as being the true primary elements of history.[25] Not so the state based on civil society, which rarely claims to be a state of nature but perceives itself as self-constructed by persons bound together by artifice—a written constitution, common political institutions, negotiated frontiers—and by some shared ideals.

All belief in humanity's 'state of nature' is pure historical conjecture. Yet it may quite accurately reveal profound personal values of the believer. Myth-tellers seem to have settled on several universal stories. One school, personified by John Locke, speaks of a humanity composed of solitary persons who, in a state of nature, joined together for certain contracted purposes, such as security, division of labour and economies of scale.[26] A second school, exemplified by Aristotle, tells of persons' natural desire for life in society, 'even when they have no need to seek each other's help'.[27] While both these stories of persons' nature emphasize society as an emanation of individual associational choices, a third kind of story—as in Genesis—features a different origin of persons' socialization, one that emphasizes the power of concentric circles of familial and genetic kinship. In this version of 'natural' identity, the commonalities—language,

---

[25] See Stephan Hobe, 'Statehood at the End of the 20th Century—The Model of the "Open State": a German Perspective', 2 Austrian Rev. Int'l & Eur. L. 127, 129–31 (1997).

[26] John Locke, 'Second Treatise,' ch. IX, in *Two Treatises of Government*, para. 124 (Peter Laslett ed., 2nd edn., 1960) (1690).

[27] Aristotle, *Politics, Books III & IV*, bk. III, pt. 6 (Richard Robinson trans., 1995).

culture, religion, and values—are mandated by genetics and geography, but not at all by personal choice.

Historians and social scientists tend nowadays to discount the myths on which these several competing stories are based.[28] They find them valuable not as accounts of our identities' origins but, rather, as evidence of the preferences of those who tell and retell the myths. Thus, of more interest than the myths themselves is their epistemology: the investigation of why some persons prefer one myth of personal identity that portrays the individual in isolation as 'natural', while others choose one of the archetypal myths. Of interest, too, is the choice *among* archetypal myths: why, for example, some choose the story of Adam and Eve, which proposes the 'natural' commonality of a bonded all-embracing humanity, while others prefer the less universalized archetypes embodied, for example, in the Norse saga. The Adam and Eve story, adumbrated in the tale of Abel and Cain and of Jacob and Esau, accounts for *nations* as an aberrational aftermath of ego—'the fall of man'—while much folklore takes a far more benevolent, proud view of the origins of particular ethnie and nations.

There is still another story: the modern liberal myth relating mankind's linear upward evolution from isolated clans to ever more embracing, inclusive communities, culminating in the inevitable reunion of the family of Adam and Eve, a working out of the common strands of everyone's humanity. This modernist–humanist myth presupposes an upward trajectory, a kind of universal Pilgrim's Progress. It perceives nations, tribes, states, and other forms of identity based on groups as mere transitory phases in an amiable but inexorable progression from the primitive clan to the federation of humankind. Immanuel Kant and Clarence K. Streit,[29] each at quite different times, visualized such a progression and, in 1965, Robert Hutchins's Center for the Study of Democratic Institutions published a proposed global constitution.[30]

The liberal-modernist perception of human sociopolitical convergence is also a myth, however, one expressing the myth-teller's social values, but neither literally nor historically accurate. There is little socio-political evidence to demonstrate any ineluctable pull, over time, toward ever-broader convergence. The multinational states formed after World War I have disintegrated with the end of the Cold War, just as the earlier empires gave way to the Reformation or the nationalist aftermath of the French Revolution. Today, a less confident view of history's irresistible march to ever-widening circles of association appears warranted. It may be that groups form, join or even integrate with others, and then, under certain circumstances, part. Neither union nor dissolution seems quite so self-evidently 'natural' or inevitable in the cacophony of today's world. As

---

[28] John A. Hall, 'Nationalism: Classified and Explained', *Daedalus* 1, 4 (Summer 1993); see, e.g., Liah Greenfeld, *Nationalism: Five Roads to Modernity* (1992).

[29] Clarence K. Streit, *Union Now* (1939).

[30] See 'World Government Movements', in 23 *Encyclopaedia Britannica* 679 (1973 edn.).

Professor Linda Colley has observed, '[H]istorically speaking, most nations have always been culturally and ethnically diverse, problematic, protean and artificial constructs that take shape very quickly and come apart just as fast . . .'.[31]

A possible condition making for dissolution is the failure of the association's inceptive dream that spiritual and material rewards would flow from the enlarged political space.[32] Even that, however, is conjecture. It is certainly not today demonstrable that prosperity correlates with the size of the political unit. Luxembourg, with a population of 400,000, has the world's highest per capita Gross Domestic Product.[33] Economies of scale nowadays are achieved as well by functional trading arrangements and open markets as by clever political unifications. We do know that there is no evidence to support the claim of any particular political configuration—the multinational state, the nation-state, the city-state, or any other—to be the 'natural' order of things, to reflect historic destiny or to be the key to human progress. Rather, what appears to be operating is a continual ebb and flow of differing, little-understood mini-imperatives that at various times and circumstances rearrange the values and self-image of persons and thereby provoke revision of the boundaries of political communities.

4. THE EBB AND FLOW OF AFFINITY: SOME HYPOTHESES

These are times when nations and romantic nationalism almost do seem to be *the* jagged building blocks of society and history. Such a determinist prognosis, however, runs aground on an obdurate fact that makes the current neo-tribal revival even more astonishing. This is, after all, also the era of enlightened *internationalism*. Even as Serbs, Bosnians, Tamils, and Chechens fight to the death (primarily the death of others, of course) for the right to unite 'likes with likes' and to sever their political links with the 'alien others', it becomes apparent that their sought-after independence is a chimera in yet another sense. Not only is there virtually no such thing as a real 'nation', but there is also no such thing as real 'independence'. Even the best-established states can daily be observed yielding more and more of their sovereignty to regional and global systems of governance.

They do this not necessarily out of an evolving sense of human kinship but in recognition of functional necessity. Even the newly cleansed ethnic nations of the former Yugoslavia undoubtedly will one day find themselves scrambling to surrender chunks of their precious sovereignty to the European Union, which

---

[31] Linda Colley, *Britons* 5 (1992).

[32] The British imperial and mercantilist expansion of the 18th and 19th centuries promoted the sense of a nation. Professor Colley has noted that this evidenced 'one of the best and most compelling reasons for loyalty. Quite simply, it paid'. Ibid. at 56.

[33] *The Economist*, 3 Jan. 1998, at 66.

strives to manage coherently such 'sovereign' prerogatives as migration, credit, trade and competition policy, human rights, as well as aspects of foreign relations. Without membership in multistate systems, such new nation-states as Serbia, Croatia, and Georgia could soon find themselves becoming tribal theme parks, selling quaint sweetmeats and T-shirts as their foreign trade and industry atrophy. Moreover, for their defence, they are also likely to want to join the North Atlantic Treaty Organization or some other regional military superestablishment. What is currently being witnessed, therefore, is not an irresistible centrifugal trend to a world of rampant ethno-nationalism, nor, for that matter, to rampant centripetal globalism, but to cross-currents of both tendencies.

Professor Ronald Inglehart, after an extensive empirical study, concluded that

[d]uring the past few decades, economic, technological, and sociopolitical changes have been transforming the cultures of advanced industrial societies in profoundly important ways. . . . One could go so far as to say that throughout advanced industrial society, what people want out of life is changing . . . [and] the prevailing worldview in these societies is being transformed.[34]

Inglehart was able to demonstrate a gradual, but widespread, decline in intense feelings of national pride among western Europeans between 1970 and 1985, even while 'about half the public in the European Community as a whole . . . "often" or "sometimes" thought of themselves as citizens of Europe'.[35] The sharpest decline in national pride, however, was found in Belgium where, after the revival of intense Flemish and Walloon separatism, 'the collapse of a spirit of national unity in the 1970's helped account for the distinctive Belgian malaise we have witnessed'.[36] That malaise is apparent in a drop from 70 to 26 per cent of Belgians holding themselves out as 'very proud' of being Belgian during the fifteen years studied.[37] It seems, however, that some of this displaced pride migrated to buttress a militant Flemish or Walloon identity, while some also evolved into a European self-definition, especially in Brussels.

Belgium is an aggravated but not unique example. The likely prognosis is that there is unlikely to be a single trend anywhere. Instead, we now have a dynamic dialectic in which countervailing tendencies contend and coexist. This, too, is not historically unprecedented, nor need it be unmanageable. Gellner points out that, on the one hand, there have always been

city states, tribal segments, peasant communes and so forth, running their own affairs . . . and on the other, large territories controlled by a concentration of force at one point. A very characteristic political form is, of course, one which fuses these two principles: a central dominant authority co-exists with semi-autonomous local units.[38]

---

[34] Ronald Inglehart, *Culture Shift in Advanced Industrial Society* 3 (1990).
[35] Ibid. at 411.     [36] Ibid. at 410.     [37] Ibid. at 411, table 12–9.
[38] Gellner, *supra* n. 10, at 13. As to territorial localism and other variants on federalism see Oscar Schachter, 'Micronationalism and Secession', in *Recht Zwischen Umbruch und Bewahrung' Völkerrecht, Europarecht, Staatsrecht. Festschrift für Rudolf Bernhardt* 179 (1995).

The modern manifestation of such fusion is the European Union's policy of subsidiarity, which seeks to reinforce the governance role of towns, counties and intra- and interstatal regional authorities. Its effect is to diversify the objects of personal loyalty. This phenomenon bears out Hobsbawm's observation that 'we cannot assume that for most people national identification—when it exists—excludes or is always or ever superior to, the remainder of the set of identifications which constitute the social being'.[39] Some of these identifications may be subnational or substatist, while others will transcend those units of governance. To quote, again, Linda Colley: 'Identities are not like hats. Human beings can and do put on several at a time.'[40]

## 5. MULTIVARIEGATED IDENTITY AND LOYALTY

When communities of persons find themselves—their identities—pushed toward integration into larger communities and simultaneously feel a powerful pull toward self-definition in terms of smaller communities of 'likes', the consequence may, but certainly need not, be a kind of collective schizophrenia and loss of centred identity. The very same circumstances can also be liberating, generating a bracing, creative accommodation of multiple loyalties, a sense of belonging to concentric circles of identity and community. Human beings for millennia have defined themselves in terms of loyalty to more than one system of social and political organization: as subjects of the emperor or king; communicants of a transnational church; members of a family, clan, and nation; and perhaps members of an artisan or professional guild or of a secret order or society. Historically, the eternal question—who am I?—has more often than not been answered in terms of multiple external references, to each of which loyalty was felt to be owed. In the eighteenth century, 'I' could have been a Magyar, a Hungarian, a subject of the Habsburg emperor, a burgher of Szeged, a Calvinist, a Freemason, a member of the printers' guild and a paterfamilias of the extended Nagy clan.

This complex system of personal affinities would have been supported by a mixture of nature and nurture. For example, 'I' would see myself as both the subject of my temporal liege lord and a sheep of my spiritual pastor: first, because that appeared to be the 'natural' order of things, and, second, because both my liege lord and my pastor feed and protect me, respectively, in body and soul, in the here and the hereafter.

Throughout history, loyalty systems have been rigidly enforced by nature and nurture: by social habits that were falsely legitimated by Rousseau as being rooted in 'the nature of things' and reinforced by the ruling classes extending or withholding services and benefits. Nature and nurture continue today to be the

---

[39] Hobsbawm, *supra* n. 12, at 11.    [40] Colley, *supra* n. 31, at 6.

active ingredients in communitarian loyalty formation. To understand the dynamic forces creating the dominant loyalties, in any era, it is necessary to examine this prevailing pull of nature and nurture. Nature and nurture, when they operate effectively, buttress the status quo of the belief system.

Even so, loyalties have also evolved. This evolution has taken two directions. There have been transformations, first, in the roster of acceptable references or objects of loyalty; and, second, in the popular perceptions of the process of loyalty formation itself.

## 6. LOYALTY REFERENTS

Historically, humans have defined themselves in terms of loyalty to a person or persons (the emperor, king, prince, or pope) and to an institution or institutions (empire, state, nation, church, transnational orders, guilds, or organizations).

In the West, this has meant, for much of the time, that loyalty was owed, first, to a Roman emperor and empire and, later, to a Germanic successor, the Holy Roman emperor and empire. Both the Roman and the Holy Roman empires, as well as the Ottoman and Muscovite dynasties, usually accommodated a substantial degree of local autonomy to princes, tribes, nations, or religious minorities, which consequently coexisted with imperium as subsidiary loyalty references.

Second, for most of Western history, loyalty was also due to the pope in Rome and 'his' church, or to the Orthodox church and its patriarch in Constantinople, or to other 'Western' religious institutions. Most persons had little difficulty accommodating such disparate loyalties even when, as happened frequently, the loyalty referents were not fully aligned and became dangerously tangled.

During the sixteenth and seventeenth centuries, a new loyalty object began to contend for popular acceptance: the *state*. 'State', however, described neither an empire nor a nationality, but a territory 'owned' by a king or queen. It became the ascendant form of post-Westphalian political organization except in a few surviving empires and the exceptional civic republics like Geneva and the towns of the Hanseatic League. With the Congress of Vienna, the triumph of the state became indisputable and the Treaty of Versailles swept away the last remnants of the old personified continental empires.

During the early statist period, loyalty was still owed by the subject not to the state but, personally, to its monarch. That monarch, by the seventeenth century, had created a claim to fealty by defeating the claims of neighbouring rival princes, and by undermining and overcoming the claims of emperor and pope. The ruler, particularly in post-Reformation Europe, won the right to demand the exclusive loyalty of his or her subjects: for each subject, one liege. In Northern Europe and Britain, this same sort of allegiance was imposed by the Reformation on the national churches which became instruments of the state. The previously common accommodation of multiple loyalties thus generally ceased in late Tudor England, Scandinavia, and also, for all practical purposes, in the Sun King's France, when the state became sovereign and the sovereign came to personify the state.

Within the newly personalized states or fiefdoms, the individual's loyalty to the sovereign was highly personal and real, not, as later, symbolic of a communal 'national' identity. In much of Western and Central Europe there was little sense of community between ruler and ruled, or even among the ruled. The sovereign and the elite surrounding the sceptre may have spoken Latin, French, or German, whereas the populace spoke Gaelic, Czech, or Magyar. In France, for example, most people spoke the dialects of Brittany, Normandy, or the langue d'Oc, while the court and the surrounding Île-de-France spoke French. The subject's loyalty was law-based and religiously enforced, a duty, not a blossoming of common culture or affinity.

The answer to the question—who am I?—in these circumstances had become simpler than in the days of empire and universal church: I am the vassal of my king or queen, a subject of the sovereign's state. Yet nationalism, let alone ethnic or racial solidarity, played little, if any, part in this loyalty system, based as it was on an exclusive, personalized subordination of the person to the state sovereign. 'I' was identified by my personal duty-and-reward relation to the royal government, not by any consociation with my neighbours. I did not perceive myself as a denizen of a *gemeinschaft*. My personal liege, the king, was almost certainly of an ethnie unrelated to mine except in the remotest sense, what with an Austrian on the throne of Spain, a Frenchman wearing the Crown of Sweden and a German wielding the sceptre of Britain.

In the remaining empires of this period—the Habsburg and Ottoman, in particular—there was also little sense of *national* cohesion, although the system tolerated and encouraged some degree of self-rule by its component minority ethnie. These ethnie, however, did not think of themselves as nations. For example, Professor Bernard Lewis reports that, until

the nineteenth century the Turks thought of themselves primarily as Muslims; their loyalty belonged, on different levels, to Islam and to the Ottoman house and state. The language a man spoke, the territory he inhabited, the race from which he claimed descent, might be of personal, sentimental or social significance. . . . [But] the very concept of a Turkish nationality was submerged—and this despite the survival of the Turkish language and the existence of what was in fact though not in theory a Turkish state. . . . The Turkish national idea, in the modern sense, [only] first appears in the mid-nineteenth century.[41]

When nationalism at last attracted the Turks, it drew its impetus, as did parallel developments in the Austrian and Hungarian parts of the Habsburg

---

[41] Bernard Lewis, *The Emergence of Modern Turkey* 2 (1961).

Empire, from the French Revolution. But it drew its romantic ideological inspiration from Germany. The alien other was conceived in genetic–ethnic mythology. 'Even today, [in] . . . the secular Republic,' Lewis notes, 'a non-Muslim in Turkey may be called a Turkish citizen, but never a Turk.'[42]

Two late eighteenth-century revolutions—the American and the French—ended the personalization of loyalty. After 1789, it became possible to answer the question—who am I?—by reference to a radically new concept of loyalty: I am an American or French *citizen*. Citizenship repealed the idea of the person as a *subject*, rejected the idea of personalized sovereignty and substituted the notions of equality, fraternity, and liberty. The state itself became the invented nation: not the nation of consanguinity but a nation of common ideals, institutions and rights. Thus, a Citizen Paine could claim the nationalities of Britain, the United States, and France;[43] the Marquis de Lafayette could become, in effect, an American revolutionary; Montesquieu could be co-opted to inspire the cause of both revolutions; and the Dutchman Hugo de Groot could appear in Paris as the ambassador of Sweden.

The move in terminology from *subject* to *citizen* denotes a tectonic shift in the loyalty system, creating for the first time, at least since the early Athenian and Roman republics, a theory of horizontal, as opposed to vertical, loyalty. Loyalty, hereafter, was to be owed by the people to each other, conjoined in liberty, equality, and fraternity to constitute a new sovereign: the 'nation'. In this usage, it is clear, *nation* meant something entirely different from its later romantic usage. It also meant something different from the earlier notion of a tribal community unified by common genealogy.

Both in the United States of 1776 and in the France of 1789, the term *nation* was used to mean nothing more or less than the *citizenry*. The 'one nation' that was the United States consisted of territory, citizens, and formally shared ideals of liberty and equality, at least for free white men. A decade later, a somewhat similarly transformed polity emerged on the sovereign territory of the deposed French king. It, too, was defined by a common bond of mutual loyalty uniting the citizenry and ideals of liberty, equality, and fraternity. In both instances, this new nationality was based on shared republican ideals and not on the commonality of blood or a shared history and culture. Even though the common republican ideals were to be implemented within a defined territory, they were thought to have the universal validity guardedly claimed for them by Immanuel Kant.

That sort of late eighteenth-century idea of community was far removed from the personalized fealty to monarchs that had preceded it, and even further from the later nineteenth- and twentieth-century loyalties to blood, language, and culture.

---

[42] Bernard Lewis, *The Emergence of Modern Turkey* 2 (1961) at 15.
[43] See John Keane, *Tom Paine: A Political Life* 267–454 (1995).

The French state that emerged in 1789 was not even remotely related, conceptually, to the German state created and led, a century later, by Prussia. French nationalism, at its origin, was primarily a political and intellectual phenomenon, not an ethnic or racial one. It created what, today, we think of as a civil society in a nonsectarian, multinational state. The point of the revolution was to take the state away from the sovereign and create a new community of shared republicanism. To support this new state, its government deliberately set about spreading a national language, culture, and identity; but while these augmented the state, they were not its formative reasons.

Creating these commonalities was no mean task. In 1789, fewer than half the citizens of France actually spoke French and only about one in ten spoke it 'correctly', as a first language.[44] The task of the new French republic was to use the opening created by a new regime of liberty and equal opportunity to entice the citizenry into new national schools, libraries, and museums that would dazzle them—Burgundians, Haut Savoyards, Basques, and Bretons—with the beauties and benefits of acquiring the patina of French language and culture hitherto common primarily in the Île-de-France. Hobsbawm tells us:

To be precise, the advance guard of middle-class nationalism fought its battle along the line which marked the educational progress of large numbers of 'new men' into areas hitherto occupied by a small elite. The progress of schools and universities measures that of nationalism, just as schools and especially universities became its most conscious champions.[45]

This was nationalism created top-down. *Top* in this context signifies a new and much broader-based elite of officials, professionals, educators, and intellectuals: their attributes often combined in a single 'Renaissance' person. They invented the community that was the French Republic. To this end, they also invented myths, but these were, at least at first, relatively benign and outward looking. Almost a century later, Massimo d'Azeglio, the former prime minister of Piedmont, is said to have observed after the reunification: 'We have made Italy: now we have to make Italians.'[46] By a difficult political decision, the Tuscan dialect of Dante and Boccaccio was chosen as the national language over Veneziano, the language of trade, music, and art. Consciously, deliberately the socio-political communities of modern America, France, and Italy were invented to instil a sense of unity based on common loyalty to the quasi-democratic, republican institutions of the state. It is in those three countries, rather than in Germany, that Kant's republican prescriptions[47] were put into

---

[44] Hobsbawm, *supra* n. 12, at 60.

[45] E. J. Hobsbawm, *The Age of Revolution: 1789–1848* 166 (1962).

[46] *Quoted in* Hugh Seton-Watson, *Nations and States* 107 (1977) and in Benedetto Croce, *A History of Italy 1871–1915* 97 (Cecila M. Adyl trans., 1929).

[47] Immanuel Kant, 'On Perpetual Peace,' in Kant's *Political Writings* 105 (Hans Reiss ed., 1970) (1795).

practice to invent—top-down—a liberal nationalism as loyalty reference for the citizenry of new republics. Nationalism was not the reason these states came to exist. Nationalism was a necessary condition for transforming the pre-existing oligarchic states into the revolutionary demos whose new equality of rights and entitlements could be actualized only if the citizenry were made to share a bonding, equalizing language, education, and culture.

In America, however, the further influence of John Locke could be seen in defining the nation. Emphasizing values conspicuously absent from revolutionary France, Locke's American disciples insisted that the power of government and the sway of majorities be limited. By negotiating tangible institutional and legal barriers to centralized majoritarian tyranny, the established Anglicans of Virginia, the Puritans of Massachusetts, the Quakers of Pennsylvania, and the disestablishmentarians of Rhode Island were persuaded to act on Lockean principles. They agreed to preserve the powerful autonomy of their several states, recognized property rights as the requisite of personal liberty, and sharply limited the powers of the federal government. What resulted was a state of states, but it, too, was united by a common loyalty to values, principles, and an optimistic materialism that was to be instilled in all persons within the geographic confines of this new state. Here, too, the decapitation of personal sovereignty had led to the invention of a fair substitute: the sovereignty of immutable citizens' rights.

The nationalism of 1776 and 1789, in sum, was political, territorial, and inclusionary, even though it was also in a special sense xenophobic. Its underlying, unifying principles were not thought to be unique to one people but, rather, of universal applicability, deriving their logic from a new myth of a 'common sense' or 'understanding' that was implicit in the 'nature of mankind'. These principles were creative both in inventing a community where there had been none and in basing that community on a horizontally egalitarian loyalty system, rather than a vertical, hierarchic one. To the extent it defined itself through enmity to an alien other, that other was not the British (in the case of revolutionary America) or Germans (in the case of revolutionary France). On the contrary, America had strong Whig allies in Britain and the French Revolution found enthusiastic echoes in Frankfurt. The alien other, certainly at first, was not a foreign nation, ethnie or culture, but monarchy, hereditary privilege, oppression, and inequality of opportunity: the transnational forces ranged against the American and, far more, the French Revolutions.

If this sort of self-identification constituted an imaginative leap from that of the people in Tudor, Stuart, and even early Hannoverian England or Bourbon France, it was an even farther one to the twentieth-century nationalisms of Hitler's Germany or the Serbs of Bosnia. Buried deep beneath the later-conceived, illiberal, romantic contemporary usage of the term *nationalism* there lie profoundly different, distinctly antithetical antecedents and values.

In the nineteenth and early twentieth centuries, the terms *nation* and *nationalism* took on new definitions first assigned them in the eighteenth century by

Johann Gottfried Herder, the German romanticist who popularized the idea of the German *Volk*. In the words of Professor Hans Kohn:

> Its roots seemed to reach into the dark soil of primitive times and to have grown through thousands of hidden channels of unconscious development, not in the bright light of rational political ends, but in the mysterious womb of the people, deemed to be so much nearer to the forces of nature.[48]

Like Jean-Jacques Rousseau, Herder stressed the purity of the instinctive, natural person over the rational, deductive one, thereby creating (if unintentionally) the elevation of the group over the individual and of blood and genes over the intellect. *Nature* took on quite a different meaning when used in this pantheistic way to glorify cultural primitivism and blood origins, as opposed to the earlier deductive usage of the term to assert the natural rights of individuals to life, liberty, and the pursuit of happiness.

Herder's ideas did not attain much currency until more than a century after his death. Even then, they were more distorted than applied in the unpropitious circumstances of the political collapse of the defeated German, Austro-Hungarian, Russian, and Ottoman Empires.[49] The failure of those crumbling, decadent regimes to provide nurture to their peoples, together with the inspiration of the French and Russian regicide, unleashed a frantic effort to uncover in nature a new reference to which loyalty could be directed in the hope of thus achieving the hitherto unrealized expectation of psychic and material rewards.

This late nineteenth- and twentieth-century romantic nationalism and its tribal definition of the nation are once again everywhere evident at the end of the second millennium. When we now speak of the nation, we must do so in the realization that it is the German romantic, not the American or French liberal-rationalist, idea that appears almost to have carried the day, both lexically and politically. No amount of demythologization of ethnic theories of pure nations prevents some of the world's peoples seeking to organize around febrile Fichtean myths of consanguinity. In popular parlance, America is only a state, Germany a nation (which also, after a hiatus, was able to regain statehood). But, it is said, whatever fragmentation and suppression the German nation-state may have endured after its defeat in 1945, its people never for a moment ceased to think of themselves as a nation. The powerful pull of loyalty exerted by that ultimate referent, the imagined nation, demonstrates how, even in the age of science, a loyalty system based on romantic myths of shared history and kinship may still have a capacity to endure—despite its surprisingly deep

---

[48] Hans Kohn, *The Idea of Nationalism: A Study of Its Origins and Background* 331 (1944).

[49] For example, the governing Turkish Republic People's Party Programme of 1935 proclaimed: 'The Fatherland is the sacred country within our present political boundaries where the Turkish nation lives with its ancient and illustrious history, and with its past glories still living in the depths of its soil.' Lewis, *supra* n. 41, at 317.

east–west fissures—that could well be the envy even of a state with the most enlightened civil society and patriotic citizenry.

In the twentieth century, tenacious loyalty to tribe and the kinship-based nation has clearly re-emerged as a social force. This phenomenon has had to be accommodated in the vocabulary of identity definition. It deserves a term that does not cause it to be confused with loyalty to a liberal civil society or with patriotism directed at a multi-ethnic secular state. It should be called 'romantic' or 'tribal' nationalism.

Whatever it is called, the phenomenon's resurgence in the 1990s should not confuse us into believing that it has the field to itself, having triumphed over other currently prevalent loyalty systems. There continue, for one, to be manifestations of an older, more cosmopolitan nationalism. Professor Neil MacCormick, a lifelong Scottish Nationalist, has been outspoken in criticizing the view that the loyalty-claim exerted by the nation 'necessarily and absolutely overrides every other possible claim on an individual—whether of family, of religious commitment, of friendship, of political loyalty, of professional or scholarly ideals, of solidarity with workmates, of personal conscience'. He calls this 'a morally intolerable claim. If nationalism implies ascribing that sort of absolutist, overriding force to the claims of "the nation," then it is indeed a morally intolerable philosophy'.[50] According to this contemporary political philosopher, we err 'in confusing the nineteenth-century Hegelian conception of nation and nationalism with the concept itself'.[51] He and similar-minded, nuanced nationalists seek clearly to distance themselves from these others, championing, instead, the ideals of civil society and constitutional democracy.

At the beginning of the third millennium, however, both kinds of nationalism are being challenged by another kind of self-identification, a new notion of community. Transnational loyalties are reappearing and multiple loyalties are once again being tolerated. To the traditional transnational references such as churches, 'the working class', or the 'invisible college of international lawyers' (the guild) are being added such newcomers as the transnational corporation, transnational political parties, and supernational political institutions. Other evidence of this post-nationalist phenomenon can be seen in French, British, Italians, and Danes voting to elect members of the European Parliament, or take property and human rights claims against their own governments to the European Court of Human Rights, or carry their European passports across unguarded national frontiers. In the words of Hedley Bull, in the twentieth century,

there has been a retreat from the confident assertions, made in the age of Vattel, that the members of international society were states and nations, towards the ambiguity and imprecision on this point that characterized the era of Grotius. The state as a bearer of rights and duties, legal and moral, in international society today is widely thought to be

---

[50] Neil MacCormick, *Legal Right and Social Democracy* 253 (1982).        [51] Ibid. at 257.

joined by international organizations, by non-state groups of various kinds operating across frontiers, and—as implied by the Nuremberg and Tokyo War Crimes Tribunals, and by the Universal Declaration of Human Rights—by individuals.[52]

This new layered loyalty directed by persons to multiple loyalty references is not confined to the unification movement in Europe. Something comparable is evident in the sight of troops, police, and election monitors from a dozen states of North and South America recently patrolling Haiti's, Nicaragua's, and El Salvador's stumbling efforts to conform to agreed hemispheric standards of democracy. A new ethos is expected of the six thousand civil servants of the United Nations who, by Article 100 of the UN Charter, are required to give primary loyalty to the United Nations system.[53] The thousands of UN blue helmets, or NATO troops, recently deployed in various areas of conflict are national contingents, but they operated under the UN Secretary-General's authority. Daily they manifest the potential and the perils of layered loyalty. Increasingly, individuals from many states and ethnie are seeking and receiving spiritual and material nurture from transnational sources; and this is causing them to redefine themselves by reference to a more complex loyalty system.

## 7. EXCLUSIVE/INCLUSIVE LOYALTY COMPACTS

What does this latest transformation of loyalty patterns portend? Are we on the verge of a new stage of human evolution in which loyalty to the state is transformed into a higher loyalty to humanity, symbolized by global (or regional) institutions of government, commerce, education, and communications?

There is some evidence that we are. Global communications, the emergence of English as a worldwide lingua franca, the personal career mobility and information networks created by transnational corporations, the common humanitarian endeavours of global organizations (e.g., peacekeeping, malaria eradication, ozone-layer protection), and the codification of universal codes of rights and duties are nurturing some persons' fledgling identification with a common humanity. This emergence of transnational loyalty references is as functionally inevitable today as was the eighteenth-century emergence of liberal states in direct response to the dictates of industrial revolution and competitive overseas expansion. Now, as then, new challenges and new sources of nurture evoke new social and attitudinal formations. In many areas of endeavour—

---

[52] Hedley Bull, *The Anarchical Society—a Study of Order in World Politics* 39 (1977).

[53] In the *Bernadotte* case, the International Court of Justice recognized that the United Nations must have legal standing to pursue claims on behalf of its Secretariat's personnel, so that individual civil servants will not need to look to their states of citizenship for protection of their interests. Reparation for injuries suffered in the service of the United Nations, 1949 ICJ Rep. 174 (Advisory Opinion of 11 Apr.).

commerce, defence, environmental protection, health, entertainment, education—human needs and wants cannot any longer be satisfied by, or in, the state alone. Increasingly, as human nurturing is provided by transnational institutions, some flow of personal loyalty in that direction will also come to seem 'natural'.[54] Adam and Eve will be rediscovered and the sin of a humanity divided will be redeemed. Well, maybe.

Whatever its prospects now, the current development of transnational cultures, politics, and loyalties has long been foreseen by prescient observers of social evolution. Kant, writing in late eighteenth-century Prussia, foresaw a universal world order based on law in a cosmopolitan federation of liberal states.[55] He rejoiced in the coming of the *Weltbürger*—citizens of the world—and railed against 'the demand of fools in Germany for national pride'.[56]

Kant's disciple Friedrich Schiller (1759–1805) dramatized his mentor's idea of *Weltbürgertum* (world citizenry), adding *allgemeine Menschenliebe* (general love of humanity) as the personal loyalty appropriate to post-Enlightenment civilization.[57] This is restated with great passion in Schiller's 'Ode to Joy', which, set to music by Beethoven in his Ninth Symphony, has now emerged from the concert hall to become the European national anthem. That such passionate longing for a new universalist loyalty to world citizenry and institutions, united in pursuit of liberty and freedom, should have been the central intellectual pursuit of eighteenth-century Germany's greatest philosopher and leading playwright starkly indicates the provenance of the idea of the long-awaited global loyalty system. Truly remarkable is only the costly and prolonged delay in giving the idea any political impetus.

What is novel, then, is not the idea of *Weltbürgertum* itself, which is hardly new. Rather, it is the dawning of a notion that identity, whatever its manifestation, is a *personal* attribute—whether it be global solidarity, xenophobic tribalism, enlightened liberal nationalism, or whatever; and that an individual's identity is increasingly self-chosen, rather than imposed by accident of birth or some liege-lords' fiat. New is the dawning of a spirit of individual assertiveness: a refusal to accept, as absolutely determinative, the identities traditionally handed out to persons by those claiming to be ordained by God, history, or the law to tell us who we are.

---

[54] This transformation is demonstrated statistically and analysed persuasively in Inglehart, *supra* n. 34.    [55] See Kohn, *supra* n. 48, at 395–402.

[56] Ibid. at 401 n. 136 (citing Kant's *Handschriftlicher Nachlass, no. 1099*, at 489). See also Friedrich Meinecke, *Weltbürgertum und Nationalstaat*, 1907 (Hans Herzfeld ed., 1962).

[57] Kohn, ibid. at 405 (citing 2 J. Minor, *Schiller: Sein Leben und seine Werke* 568 (Berlin, Weidmann 1890); and 2 *Schiller's Complete Works* 340 (C. J. Hempel ed., Philadelphia, Kohler 1870)).

# 4

## Citizenship: An Instance of Identity as a Personal Act of Self-Determination

Have you, in the course of your professional or social activities ever undertaken actions which violate the basic rules pertaining to human rights, especially those set out in the international treaty on Civil and Political Rights of December 19, 1966 or the Universal Declaration of Human Rights of December 10, 1948?

> Questionnaire for applicants seeking employment
> in the German Civil Service, 1995

### 1. MULTIPLE LOYALTY REFERENCES

Presumably the intent of the German Civil Service questionnaire is to place candidates on notice that, if they are to compete for state jobs, candidates must demonstrate their adherence not only to German but also to international human rights law. It is no longer enough to be a loyal German, it seems to announce, one must also be a loyal citizen of the international community.

Undoubtedly, new multilayered loyalty references are emerging, perceived both as natural and as nurturing. Yet it would be premature to conclude that Kant's vision of *Weltbürgertum* has at last been implemented. Such a facile judgement would fail to take into account countervailing evidence: particularly the resurgence of rampant tribal nationalisms in African–Asian lands and eastern Europe after decolonization and the fall of communism. To celebrate the triumph of Kantian humanism would be to ignore the continuing vitality of the still-powerful, still-entrenched state system. In the words of Hedley Bull, '[I]t would be going beyond the evidence to conclude that 'groups other than the state' have made such inroads on the sovereignty of states that the states system is now giving way. . .'.[1] Today, even more than in Kant's Prussia, it is primarily the state that collects taxes, provides education, licenses the professions, regulates commerce, polices the streets, and cares for the sick and hungry. Loyalty to the nurturing state is still an eminently logical fact of life, still considered 'natural' except in those instances where the state fails to deliver.

A balanced view of tendencies at the end of the twentieth century reveals that powerful centripetal and centrifugal loyalties coexist with resilient statist patriotism. In this era, loyalty is likely to be perceived as less like a dollar to be bet on

---

[1] Hedley Bull, *The Anarchical Society—a Study of Order in World Politics* 275 (1977).

one's favourite racehorse, than a handful of birdseed to be distributed among several feeding stations. Thus, one may be, to some degree, loyal to a state, as well as to an ethnic group, race, religion, city, business firm or professional association, and family. One may also feel loyalty to secret associations such as the Masons or Opus Dei, as well as to local or transnational ideological formations such as the 'Third International', Islamicism, and Christian Democracy. Some may even experience affinity with the United Nations, the International Red Cross, Amnesty International, or the Greenpeace movement. Even the Mafia and Islamic Jihad have their transnational networks.

Multiple loyalty, in itself, is not especially remarkable. As we have seen, it has been the rule rather than the exception in Western civilization. Each of the great empires tolerated it to some degree. Bull terms this 'a structure of overlapping authorities and criss-crossing loyalties'.[2] What *is* remarkable is the extent to which a person's loyalty system today, for the first time in history, has become a matter of *personal choice*. In the early Mediterranean imperium, as also in the more recent Ottoman and Hapsburg empires, multiple loyalty references were imposed on persons by virtue of who they were and where they lived. They were not freely chosen.

In the Roman Empire, self-governance by Hellenic, Levantine, Ptolemaic, and Jewish communities was not merely tolerated but encouraged. The Ottoman Empire conceded virtual self-rule not only to the pasha of Egypt but also to the Jewish, Armenian, Greek, Maronite, and other *millets*: communities largely autonomous in law and religious matters.[3] The Holy Roman Empire, in its later days, became a confederation of kingdoms and principalities. The Austro-Hungarian Empire demanded each subject's loyalty to the emperor, but permitted almost complete devolution of political power to governments in Vienna, Prague, and Budapest, as well as a degree of autonomy in other Balkan dependencies. Except in recent times, loyalty to the church of Rome or of Constantinople, or to the Islamic community,[4] would have exerted at least as powerful a pull on most persons in Europe, North Africa, and the Near East as any claim exerted by secular authorities. These various loyalties quite 'naturally' coexisted within each person's identity.

Except after the latter part of the eighteenth century, it was normal for persons thus to define themselves by multiple loyalties: the seventeenth-century Munich householder was a Bavarian loyal to his king, but he was also a subject of the Holy Roman emperor, a faithful communicant of the church of Rome,

---

[2]  Hedley Bull, *The Anarchical Society — a Study of Order in World Politics* 255 (1977).

[3]  'Besides the *Harbi* or infidel beyond the frontier, there was also the *Zimoui* . . . the protected non-Muslim subject of the Muslim state, whose position was determined by the *dhimma*, or pact, between his community, called *millet*, and the dominant community of Islam.' Bernard Lewis, *The Emergence of Modern Turkey* 322–3 (1961).

[4]  For example, Lewis tells us that '[a]mong the different peoples who embraced Islam none went farther in sinking their separate identity in the Islamic community than the Turks'. Ibid. at 323.

and someone who might dimly identify with 'the Germanic peoples'. Only rarely did this multiplicity pose a quandary, and ordinarily only as regards the loyalty of an unfortunate member of the elite who, like Lord Chancellor Sir Thomas More of England, had to choose personally between King Henry VIII and the Bishop of Rome at a moment when they were on collision course. Normally, the need to make such difficult choices was obviated by external realities: persons' loyalty was, quite simply, dictated by where they lived, what religion their liege lord practised, the language their family spoke at home, the education they had received, the career they followed—and all these usually stood in a hierarchic harmony, a harmony achieved by the utter surrender of free will to these sorts of independent external variables that determined one's personal identity.

## 2. MULTIPLE CITIZENSHIP

In the latter half of the twentieth century, an unprecedented claim to free will is being made by more and more citizens: the right to create their own identities on the basis of personal choice and commitment. This claim to self-designed identity—to personal self-determination—is manifest in a series of more specific claims: to choose one's own nationality or nationalities, as well as trans-nation affinities, to select one's preferred name and that of one's children, to follow, or not, any religion as a matter of personal conscience, to pursue a chosen occupation, and even to select one's sex or gender. How these aspects of personal identity came to be the subject of individual claims, rather than of social assignment, will be the subject of ensuing chapters of this study.

This chapter will concern itself with citizenship and will focus, in particular, on individuals' claims to dual (or even multiple) nationality as one reflection of a personal choice regarding loyalty and identity.[5] (As is evident from this paragraph, the terms 'citizenship' and 'nationality' will be used interchangeably as designating the legal relationship of rights and obligations existing in domestic and international law between person and state.[6]) Moreover, this chapter will merely note, but not analyse in detail, the *lex specialis* of the European Union.

---

[5] For a detailed survey see Ruth Donner, *The Regulation of Nationality in International Law* (2nd edn., 1994).

[6] Although 'citizenship' is now the more precise legal term, it is not the only one in use. Thus, Article 15 of the Declaration on Human Rights of 10 December 1948, for example, states the principle that everyone has a right to a nationality of which no one shall 'be arbitrarily deprived'. See, similarly, Article 8 of the Maastricht Treaty establishing the citizenship of the European Union, which states: 'Every person holding the nationality of a Member State shall be a citizen of the Union.' It is true, however, that 'nationality' and 'citizenship' were not always coterminous, as in the distinction between a 'British subject', a 'British Protected Person', and a 'British citizen' in the days of empire. In the Roman Empire, citizenship was extended to many nationalities other than the Roman. See Elizabeth Meehan, *Citizenship and the European Community* 1–10 (1993).

There, a status is emerging, sometimes called 'intercitoyenneté', that permits a citizen of one member state to acquire many of the same affects as if he or she were also a citizen of all of the members, including the right to run for office and to vote in local elections and to have professional qualifications in one country recognized by each of the others (the 'right of establishment').[7] As Professor D'Oliveira has observed, 'If possession of one Member State nationality opens up the other Member States, and provides one with the same rights and duties as [are] normally connected with the possession of each other

[7] Article 8 of the Maastricht accord provides:

1. Citizenship of the Union is hereby established. Every person holding the nationality of a Member State shall be a citizen of the Union.

2. Citizens of the Union shall enjoy the rights conferred by this Treaty and shall be subject to the duties imposed thereby.

Article 8(a) further states:

1. Every citizen of the Union shall have the right to move and reside freely within the territory of the Member States, subject to the limitations and conditions laid down in this Treaty and by the measures adopted to give it effect.

2. The Council may adopt provisions with a view to facilitating the exercise of the rights referred to in paragraph 1; save as otherwise provided in this Treaty, the Council shall act unanimously on a proposal from the Commission and after obtaining the assent of the European Parliament.

Article 8b

1. Every citizen of the Union residing in a Member State of which he is not a national shall have the right to vote and to stand as a candidate at municipal elections in the Member State in which he resides, under the same conditions as nationals of that State. This right shall be exercised subject to detailed arrangements to be adopted before 31 December 1994 by the Council, acting unanimously on a proposal from the Commission and after consulting the European Parliament; these arrangements may provide for derogations where warranted by problems specific to a Member State.

2. Without prejudice to Article 138(3) and to the provisions adopted for its implementation, every citizen of the Union residing in a Member State of which he is not a national shall have the right to vote and to stand as a candidate in elections to the European Parliament in the Member State in which he resides, under the same conditions as nationals of that State. This right shall be exercised subject to detailed arrangements to be adopted before 31 December 1993 by the Council, acting unanimously on a proposal from the Commission and after consulting the European Parliament; these arrangements may provide for derogations where warranted by problems specific to a Member State.

Article 8c

Every citizen of the Union shall, in the territory of a third country in which the Member State of which he is a national is not represented, be entitled to protection by the diplomatic or consular authorities of any Member State, on the same conditions as the nationals of that State. Before 31 December 1993, Member States shall establish the necessary rules among themselves and start the international negotiations required to secure this protection.

Article 8d

Every citizen of the Union shall have the right to petition the European Parliament in accordance with Article 138d.

Every citizen of the Union may apply to the Ombudsman established in accordance with Article 138e.

nationality, then one is virtually a polypatride or multinational!'[8] This phenomenon is here worth noting primarily as an incomparably developed instance of what, elsewhere, is at most a tendency and, in some places, only the vague aspiration of a few.

Nevertheless, tendencies are important for their (admittedly fallible) predictive value, and for what they indicate about other aspects of the societies in which they occur. The response of a legal system to a citizen's claim to 'dual nationality' thus is an excellent indicator of that society's tolerance not merely for multiple loyalty but for the more general right of individuals to choose their affiliations and design their identities. In many countries, most notably the United States, this response has shifted radically in recent years, and tells us much about our changing selves.

Since the end of the Cold War, the official US attitude toward citizenship has undergone a remarkable—even if little-remarked[9]—transition. This transition merits brief recapitulation. In the nineteenth and much of the twentieth centuries, dual nationality was regarded as abnormal and undesirable, as well as a conceptual oxymoron. Citizenship was regarded as the validation of a person's identity which, in turn, manifested membership in a community of persons constituted by a common loyalty to a single sovereign or republic. Professor Ruth Donner has noted that as 'a corollary of this identification of the citizen with his State it was permissible for an individual to have one, and only one, nationality. This has also been explained as the impossibility for an individual to owe allegiance to two sovereigns at once'.[10] The 1907 Expatriation Act provided in section 2 that 'any American citizen shall be deemed to have expatriated himself when he has been naturalized in any foreign state in conformity with its laws, or when he has taken an oath of allegiance to any foreign state'.[11] This clause enunciated the preference of Congress, paraphrased in 1953 by Judge Kirkland in *Gaudio v. Dulles*,[12] 'that the plague of "dual nationality" be eliminated to every degree possible'.[13] 'Dual nationals' as then understood were not primarily persons who had opted for more than one citizenship but, rather, the victims of a clash between unreconciled legal systems which, usually to the unfortunate person's detriment, caused them to be regarded by several states as the exclusive subject of each, thus bearing concomitant and often irreconcilable obligations.

At the Hague Conference called in 1930 to negotiate a uniform convention

[8] Hans U. J. D'Oliveira, 'Plural Nationality and the European Union' 17, Conference on Plural Nationality: Changing Attitudes, European Univ. Inst., Fiesole (1992).
[9] But see H. Ansgar Kelly, *Dual Nationality, the Myth of Election, and a Kinder, Gentler State Department*, 23 U. Miami Inter-Am. L. Rev. 421 (1991–2); T. Alexander Aleinikoff, *Theories of Loss of Citizenship*, 84 Mich. L. Rev. 1471 (1986); Marian Nash (Leich), Contemporary Practice of the United States Relating to International Law, 87 Am. J. Int'l L. 598 (1993); Peter J. Spiro, 'Dual Nationality and the Meaning of Citizenship', 46 Emory LJ 1411 (1997). [10] Donner, *supra* n. 5, at 18–19.
[11] Act of 2 March 1907, ch. 2534, §2, 34 Stat. 1228 (1907) (repealed 1940).
[12] *Gaudio v. Dulles*, 110 F.Supp. 706 (DC Cir. 1953). [13] Ibid. at 709.

on nationality, the US put forward a proposal, which, if adopted, would have required dual nationals, on reaching the age of 23, to renounce one or the other citizenship or else be 'conclusively presumed to have elected the nationality' of habitual residence 'and to have renounced the nationality of the other State of which he was a national'.[14] It failed to be adopted, but the 'plague of dual nationality' was soon again attacked by a 1940 US statute, which provided for withdrawal of citizenship from anyone taking an oath or making an affirmation of allegiance to a foreign state, serving in its armed forces, or voting in its elections.[15] The International Court, in a 1955 decision,[16] also tried its hand at curbing the 'plague' by deciding that 'a concordance must exist' between a state and its citizens, so that 'the legal bond of nationality accord with the individual's genuine connection with the State which assumes the defence of its citizens by means of protection as against other States'.[17] The effect was to make it more difficult for individuals to claim the nationality and protection of more than one state.

Despite these efforts to contain the 'plague', the US Supreme Court, in the 1952 *Kawakita* case,[18] permitted the conviction for treason and sentencing to death of an American-born national who, in 1939 at the age of 18, had gone to Japan on a US passport but, on the declaration of war, had registered as a Japanese citizen, obtained a Japanese passport and served as a government interpreter in camps for American prisoners of war. To be guilty of treason against America, Kawakita had first to be found to have retained his US citizenship, despite his several voluntary acts which, under US law, should have been deemed an effective renunciation. However, writing for the majority, Justice William O. Douglas held that the 'concept of dual nationality recognizes that a person may have and exercise rights of nationality in two countries and be subject to the responsibilities of both'.[19]

*Kawakita* was atypical, driven, as it undoubtedly was, by the still-unspent passions of the war. In 1958 the Supreme Court returned to its traditional point of view, deciding in *Perez v. Brownell*,[20] that citizenship had been lost by a US-born person who had voted in a Mexican election. Only nine years later, however, the same court overturned *Perez*. In *Afroyim v. Rusk*,[21] it held unconstitutional any presumption of intent to renounce US citizenship based solely on

---

[14] Minutes of the First Committee, 2 *League of Nations, Acts of the Conference on the Codification of International Law*, League of Nations Doc. C.351(a).M.145(a).1930.V, Ann. II, at 295 (1930), reprinted in 3 *League of Nations Conference for the Codification of International Law* 1175 (Shabtai Rosenne ed., 1975). The United States did not sign the Convention, which gave states even broader latitude to denationalize those of their citizens claiming dual nationality. Convention on the Conflict of Nationality Laws, 12 Apr. 1930, Art. 6, 179 LNTS 91, 101.

[15] Nationality Act of 1940, ch. 876, 54 Stat. 1137, 1168, sec. 401.

[16] *Nottebohm Case (second phase), Judgment of April 6th, 1955*, 1955 ICJ Rep. 4.        [17] Ibid. at 23.

[18] *Kawakita v. United States*, 343 US 717 (1952).

[19] Ibid. at 723. President Eisenhower commuted the sentence to life imprisonment and President Kennedy commuted that sentence to deportation to Japan. Kelly, *supra* n. 9, at 431.

[20] *Perez v. Brownell*, 356 US 44 (1958).        [21] *Afroyim v. Rusk*, 387 US 253 (1967).

voting in a foreign election. Similar presumptions pertaining to most other acts were held unconstitutional in the 1980 *Terrazas* case, which imposed on the Government the onus of proving a person's intent to surrender US citizenship.[22] Such an intent could no longer be implied from the mere commission of one of the statutorily enumerated expatriating acts.

With these cases in mind, Congress in 1986 repealed parts of the statutory provisions,[23] and added the key requirement that loss of citizenship may occur only on the citizen's 'voluntarily performing any of the [enumerated] acts with the intention of relinquishing United States nationality'.[24] With that, the onus shifted to the Government—or whichever party wished to argue that US citizenship had been lost—to demonstrate that a designated act had been performed both voluntarily and with the specific intent to renounce citizenship. At the same time, the designated acts were pared down to seven activities, including obtaining a second citizenship, swearing allegiance to a foreign state, serving in the armed forces of a foreign hostile state or as an officer, or 'accepting, serving in or performing the duties of any office . . . of a foreign government'.[25] Voting in a foreign election was deleted from the list, perhaps in part because, in Italy, after the Second World War, large-scale participation in its elections by US citizens of Italian origin had been deemed significant in saving that nation from communism.

Following the 1986 amendments, the State Department Board of Appellate Review began holding that the mere taking of a second citizenship would no longer constitute sufficient evidence of intent to renounce US nationality.[26] By 1990, the State Department publicly accepted the 'premise that United States nationals intend to keep their US nationality when they obtain the nationality of another state, make a pro forma declaration of allegiance to another state, or accept a non-policy level position in another state'.[27] While the Department did not actually endorse dual nationality 'as a matter of policy because of the problems which it may cause',[28] the remaining statutory 'acts of expatriation' are now at most potential grounds for loss of US citizenship and only as to persons with demonstrable intent to renounce it, an extraordinarily difficult

[22] *Vance v. Terrazas*, 444 US 252 (1980).

[23] Act of 14 Nov. 1986, §18, 100 Stat. 3655, 3658 (codified as amended in 8 USC. §1481 (1988)).

[24] 8 USC. §1481(a).     [25] Ibid.

[26] *In re* J.J.S., Bd. App. Rev. (17 Dec. 1987); and *In re* E.J.P., Bd. App. Rev. (12 Oct. 1987), cited in 4 Charles Gordon & E. Gittel Gordon, *Immigration and Naturalization Law* at n.55e.1 (Supp. 1989, 1990, 1991). See also *In re* CMS, Dec. no. 90–12, Bd. App. Rev. (5 July 1990), in 67 Interpreter Releases 789, 799 (23 July 1990).

[27] Telegram issued by James Baker, Secretary of State, to all diplomatic and consular posts, US Dep't of State, unclas. no. 121, 931, §5 (16 Apr. 1990), cited in Kelly, *supra* n. 9, at 444 n. 127.

[28] *US Dep't State, Dual Nationality* (rev. edn., 1992), reprinted in 87 Am. J. Int'l L. 602, 603 (1993). See also *US Dep't State, Advice About Possible Loss of US Citizenship and Dual Nationality* (rev. edn., 1992), reprinted in 87 Am. J. Int'l L. 599 [hereinafter *Loss of Citizenship*]. The quoted provisions are unchanged from those in the 1990 editions of both pamphlets, reprinted in Kelly, *supra* n. 9, at 457, 460.

onus for the Government to discharge. The Department now admits that no such intent is to be presumed from such acts as being naturalized in a foreign country, taking a routine foreign oath of allegiance, or even accepting non-policy-level employment with a foreign government.[29]

Even those few remaining limits are not much enforced. US citizens, in the period following the collapse of communism, frequently returned to their state of birth or patrimony to assume senior policy posts without loss of citizenship. Milan Panic, a Serb-born naturalized US citizen, served as Prime Minister of Yugoslavia in 1992, after receiving assurances from the Department of State that this would not jeopardize his US citizenship.[30] Raffi Hovannisian became Foreign Minister of Armenia, stating publicly: 'I certainly do not renounce my American citizenship,'[31] and that was that. Muhamed Sacirbey, Foreign Minister of Bosnia in 1995–6, is an American citizen and dual national.[32] The chief of the Estonian army in 1991–5 also was an American, Aleksander Einseln.[33] Several dual-national Americans have served at the United Nations as ambassadors of their other country of citizenship. This is not an exclusively American phenomenon. Bruce Daniels, a US citizen naturalized in Canada and teaching at the University of Winnipeg, in 1995 declared himself a candidate for the Democratic presidential nomination without apparent fear either of denaturalization by Canada or disqualification by the United States.[34]

The move by the United States to permit its citizens to have more than one passport—freely to design their own identities from among multiple components—is one small indicator of what may be a profound transformation not so much of personal identities themselves as of the way identities are perceived. While some Hutu may define themselves exclusively, virulently, in terms of the tribal identity imposed on them by blood and culture, many more of the world's population are being allowed to define themselves not in accordance with inherited or mandated identities, but in liberated pursuit of personal interests and preferences. As the case of Bruce Daniels hints, the US shift toward acceptance of multinationality is mirrored by Canada. Although the applicable law had stated that a 'Canadian citizen who . . . acquires the nationality or citizenship of a country other than Canada, thereupon ceases to be a Canadian citizen',[35] it was amended in 1976[36] to restrict such a loss of citizenship to cases where the citizen makes application for permission to renounce and that permission is granted by a citizenship judge.[37] Rather more benevolently

---

[29] *Loss of Citizenship*, ibid., 87 Am. J. Int'l L. at 600.     [30] Spiro, *supra* n. 9, at 1455.

[31] Martin Chazonov, 'Job Springs from Ethnic Roots', LA Times, 3 Nov. 1991, at 8, quoted in Kelly, *supra* n. 9, at 447.     [32] NY Times, 5 June 1995, at A5.

[33] NY Times, 4 Dec. 1995, at A6.     [34] NY Times, 26 Nov. 1995, §6 (Magazine), at 49.

[35] R.S.C., ch. C-19, §15(1) (1970).

[36] Citizenship Act, 1976, ch. 108, sec. 1, R.S.C., ch. C-29 (1985).

[37] Ibid., §9(1). See also Citizenship and Immigration Canada, *Dual Citizenship* (1991).

than the Department of State, the Canadian Government points out that, for 'some people, dual citizenship . . . may . . . enhance their feeling of belonging, because they have strong personal ties to more than one country',[38] while also cautioning that the status may also entail certain hazards.

Other states have also changed their laws to accommodate duality. In the Dominican Republic's 1996 presidential elections, many US citizens of Dominican origin returned to cast their votes in accordance with a political reform establishing their right to dual nationality.[39] If present plans favoured by both national parties succeed, Dominican law will soon permit these dual nationals to vote abroad, giving New York the second largest pool of urban voters in future Dominican elections.[40] Indeed, one of these parties campaigned on a platform that called for establishing a 'Ministry of the Diaspora', while the other pledged 'to amend the Constitution to allow the election of congressional deputies specifically to represent Dominicans resident abroad'.[41] If adopted, this would go even further than Israel's Law of Return[42] which extends virtually automatic citizenship to any Jew resettling in Israel from abroad. In 1996, Colombia, too, amended its constitution to permit nationals who acquire foreign nationality to retain their Colombian citizenship, run for office, and vote in Colombian elections at consulates where they reside.[43]

Mexico, like almost all of Latin America, traditionally required its citizens to renounce any foreign nationality. Now, however, its Government, with immigration to the United States in mind, is campaigning for a change in its constitution that would permit them to hold dual nationality.[44] In December 1996, by a vote of 405–1, the Mexican Chamber of Deputies approved a law that allows this for an estimated six million Mexicans living abroad and permits them also to retain property and other rights in their country of origin that are reserved by law for Mexicans only.[45] Ecuador, the Dominican Republic, and Colombia have already adopted versions of this change.[46] New Zealand now permits dual nationality unless, in a specific instance, this 'is not conducive to the public good'[47]—a ministerial determination that is not exercised in practice[48] and, in any event, would probably be subject to some degree of judicial scrutiny. While Australian law as legislated in 1948 appears to withdraw citizenship from any Australian who 'does any act or thing: (a) the sole or dominant purpose of which; and (b) the effect of which; is to acquire the nationality or

---

[38] *Dual Citizenship*, ibid. at 2.     [39] NY Times, 29 June 1996, at 21.
[40] Ibid.     [41] Ibid.
[42] 4 Laws of the State of Israel 114 (1950) (as amended), reprinted in W. Mallison & S. Mallison, *An International Analysis of the Major United Nations Resolutions covering the Palestine Question* 403, UN Sales no. EYE.I.19 (1979).     [43] NY Times, 30 Dec. 1996, at B4.
[44] Sam Dillon, 'Mexico Woos US Mexicans, Proposing Dual Nationality', NY Times, 10 Dec. 1995, §1, at 16.
[45] 'Mexico Passes Law of Dual Citizenship,' NY Times, 12 Dec. 1996, at A7.     [46] Ibid.
[47] Citizenship Act, no. 61, 1977, 31 RSNZ 45 (1993).     [48] Kelly, *supra* n. 9, at 451.

citizenship of a foreign country', a recent case has interpreted this provision not to apply to an Australian of partly Swiss origin who applied to the Swiss Government for recognition of her *jus sanguinis* status as a Swiss citizen. It thereby opened the door to recognition of dual nationality.[49] The court held that, to lose Australian citizenship, her motive must have been to acquire Swiss citizenship, rather than to obtain recognition of an already existing status of foreign nationality.[50]

Britain,[51] Switzerland,[52] Portugal,[53] France,[54] and the new Russian Federation[55] all permit their citizens to acquire dual nationality. The French Civil Code formerly provided that any adult who voluntarily accepted another nationality would automatically forfeit French citizenship, but this provision was amended in 1973 so that now 'any adult, habitually residing abroad, who voluntarily accepts another nationality will only lose the French nationality if he expressly so declares'.[56] Such a declaration must be made formally at a French embassy or consulate.[57] German citizens must get permission to retain their citizenship if they wish to assume a further nationality.[58] This permission is granted or refused by the applicant's state, rather than by the federal authorities, owing to Germany's tradition of local autonomy in matters of nationality. There is therefore some variation as to the ease with which such permission is secured, with Bavaria being the least accommodating in practice.[59] German law does not, however, permit an immigrant to acquire German nationality without renouncing his or her prior citizenship, although the Social Democrats, returned to power at the end of 1998, did promise to legislate a right of

---

[49] Minister for Immigration, Local Government and Ethnic Affairs v. Gugerli, 36 FCR 68 (1992) (admin. app.) (regarding Australian Citizenship Act 1948 §17(1)).           [50] Ibid. at 72–3.

[51] British Nationality and Status of Aliens Act, 1943, 6 & 7 Geo. VI, ch. 14 (Eng.).

[52] See 2 Charles Cheney Hyde, *International Law* 1153 (2nd rev. edn., 1947).

[53] See Rui Manuel Moura Ramos, 'Nationalité, Plurinationalité et Supranationalité en Droit Portugais' 22 (1995) (unpublished manuscript, on file with author).

[54] Code Civil, Art. 21 (Code civil de la nationalité).

[55] Constitution of the Russian Federation, 1993, arts. 62(1) and (2).

[56] The prohibition was in Law of 19 Oct. 1945, Code civil de la nationalité, titre IV: De la perte et de la déchéance de la nationalité française, ch. 1, Art. 87. The amendment to this prohibition, Law no. 73–42 of 9 Jan. 1973, is now in Code civil de la nationalité, titre IV, ch. 1: De la perte de la nationalité française, Art. 87.

[57] Andrew Stewart & Siegfried Kurz, 'Dual Nationality: Êtes-vous français?', Army Law. 3, 4 (Mar. 1991). See also Simone Tan, 'Dual Nationality in France and the United States', 15 Hastings Int'l & Comp. L. Rev. 447 (1992).

[58] *Grundgesetz* (Basic Law), Art. 116(1) (FRG); Reichs- und Staatsangehörigkeitsgesetz [RuStaG] §17 (1913); RuStaG §25, para. 2 (1977). See also Hyde, *supra* n. 52, at 1154.

[59] Interview with German Foreign Ministry legal officer (6 Mar. 1996).

immigrants to dual nationality.[60] Austrian law in these respects is similar to that of Germany.[61]

Ireland, on the other hand, permits a person to retain Irish nationality if the acquisition of a foreign nationality occurred 'without any voluntary act on his part'.[62] This includes children of Irish parents born abroad. As between Britain and Ireland, there is also a statutory basis for mutually according full citizenship rights to nationals taking up residence in the territory of the other party.[63] Thus, Irish citizens in Britain may vote and sit in Parliament.[64] The Irish Constitution was changed in 1984 to permit Britons living in the Republic to vote in elections to the lower house of the Irish national Parliament.[65] Portugal and Brazil have a comparable relationship.[66] Dual nationals of Algeria and France—of whom there are many hundreds of thousands—were permitted by treaty to opt for national service in the military of either country.[67]

Spain, too, has special duality options tenable in its former colonies. In recent years, as a result of many bilateral treaties with Latin American states, dual nationality is actually encouraged. For example, the Agreement on Dual Nationality between the Dominican Republic and Spain affirms, in the preamble, that the parties desire to strengthen 'the links between their two countries and [make] it easier for their nationals to become Spanish or Dominican, as the case may be, while retaining their original nationality . . .'.[68] Similar treaties have been concluded between Spain and Paraguay, Peru, Chile, Bolivia, Guatemala, Ecuador, Costa Rica, Honduras, Argentina, and Colombia.[69] As a result of a 1978 Spanish constitutional provision regarding enumerated states that 'have had or have a particular relationship with Spain' (article 11.3.I), Spanish citizens, in those states, may become naturalized without losing their

---

[60] RuStaG §3 (1913). This is in contrast to French law, which does not require renunciation of prior nationality as a requirement for naturalization in France. See William Rogers Brubaker, *Citizenship and Nationhood in France and Germany* 144–7, 173–4 (1992). The commitment of Germany's Social Democrats to facilitate a right of dual nationality for immigrants is discussed in Roger Cohen, 'Germany's Shift Eastward Helped Schröder Win', N.Y. Times, 29 Sept. 1998, at A1 and A6 at A6. But see 'In Reversal, Germany Drops Dual Nationality Plan for Foreigners,' NY Times, 25 Feb. 1999, at A6.

[61] Staatsbürgerschaftsgesetz 1965, sec. III, Verlust der Staatsbürgerschaft, §28(1) and (2), 1985 Bundesgesetzblatt 2390 (Aus.).

[62] Rep. of Ireland, Nationality and Citizenship Act, no. 26, §24 (1956).

[63] Ibid. §26(1).

[64] Representation of the People Act, 1983, §1(1)(b)(ii); and British Nationality Act, 1981, §52(6), sched. 7. See 4(2) *Halsbury's Laws of England* 76, para. 65 (4th edn., reissued 1992).

[65] Ninth Amendment of the Constitution Act, 1984. The Electoral (Amendment) Act, 1985, provided for the extension of this right reciprocally to citizens of other European Community countries resident in Ireland.

[66] Maura Ramos, *supra* n. 53.

[67] Brubaker, *supra* n. 60, at 145 (citing *La Nationalité Française: Textes et documents* 278 (La Documentation française, 1985)). Approximately a quarter of the persons of Algerian–French dual nationality living in France appear to choose service in the Algerian forces. Ibid.

[68] 724 UNTS 17, signed at Santo Domingo on 15 Mar. 1968 and entered into force 22 Jan. 1969. See Donner, *supra* n. 5, at 203. [69] Cited in Donner, ibid. at 203–4.

Spanish nationality.[70] Aside from these cases, the Spanish Civil Code[71] does contemplate the loss of Spanish nationality when a citizen acquires the nationality of another state. But here, too, there is a large exception, for the Code 'permits the retention of the Spanish nationality when the person involved justifies that he acquired the foreign nationality by reason of emigration. From then on this person will be considered by the Spanish legal system as a unilateral double national'.[72] In practice, the only requirement is that the Spanish emigrant 'justifies the fact of this emigration, and that he declares before the competent authority (usually the consul) that he wants to retain his Spanish nationality'.[73] In other words, 'Spanish law does not contemplate nationality as an exclusive link to one State. Rather, Spanish law promotes or permits situations of double nationality intended by the law.' Thus, 'Spanish law utilizes double nationality . . . as a means to strengthen ties with States with a close relationship to Spain' and also more generally 'as a means to protect the Spanish emigrants' after their departure.[74]

Where, as in parts of the former Soviet Union, special circumstances generate resistance to dual nationality, the constitutional recognition of the special 'national' status of ethnic minorities—a sort of quasi-dual nationality—has become the focus of international efforts to achieve compliance with human rights standards.[75] Dual nationality, in effect, has become one way to establish special status and group rights for minorities within a state, especially in instances where the minority's realistic fears can best be allayed by allowing them to retain a citizenship link with an external 'protector' in addition to citizenship in their state of domicile.

In sum, most Western European states, as well as Canada, New Zealand, and the United States, now permit multiple nationality, which is symbolic of a new tolerance for an individual's 'layered' loyalty and identity. A similar permissiveness is making inroads in Latin Americans' previously exclusivist communitarian attitudes. This does not mean that dual nationality is universally applauded. However, even where attitudes have been wholly negative, they appear to be changing and these changes respond to a change in political attitudes and social values. One example of this change is the Council of Europe's 1963 Strasbourg Convention on the Reduction of Cases of Multiple Nationality and Military Obligations in Cases of Multiple Nationality. It was recently amended by a

---

[70] These are: the Spanish-American states, Andorra, the Philippines, Equatorial Guinea, Portugal and the states which have mutual double nationality treaties with Spain. Civil Code of Spain, Art. 23(IV). In the case of the double nationality treaties, the double nationals have an 'active nationality' in the state that is the 'centre of their lives' and a 'dormant nationality' in the other for purposes of Private International Law.          [71] Article 23(I).

[72] Article 23.I.2 of the Civil Code. The quote is from Miguel Virgós Soriano, 'Nationality and Double Nationality Principles in Spanish Private International Law System', in *Nation und Staat im Internationalem Privatrecht* 237, 244 (E. Jayme & H.-P. Mansel eds., 1990).          [73] Ibid. at 245.

[74] Ibid. at 257–8.

[75] Gidon Gottlieb, 'Nations Without States,' For. Aff. 108–10 (May/June 1994).

protocol that repeals earlier prohibitions and, instead, establishes a list of circumstances in which the national law may permit duality.[76] An even more recent European Convention on Nationality explicitly leaves states the option to recognize dual nationality and establish the terms on which it may be acquired, but provides that dual nationals 'shall have . . . the same rights and duties as other nationals . . .'.[77]

As we have seen, a relaxed attitude to layered loyalty is not new, but when such layering occurred in the past it was *imposed* by the state, not *chosen* by the individual person. Today, there is a conscious shift in attitude, reflected in evolving citizenship law, that makes it acceptable, betimes even admirable, for the individual (or, for that matter, the corporation) to design a complex identity expressive of values and preferences transcending monolithic loyalty to only one political or ethnic community.

This change in the way multiple citizenship is perceived by persons and by governments reflects a more general acknowledgement of changes in patterns of personal affiliation in an era of great mobility and ever-widening communications. As Professor George Fletcher has observed, 'We typically find ourselves in a set of intersecting circles of loyalty commitment. In the United States and indeed in virtually every modern culture, we are . . . caught in the intersection of at least a half-dozen circles of loyal attachment.'[78] That this is normal—and that it may even be useful to the national interest to mitigate the simplistically stark boundaries between unilinear loyalty systems—is being recognized in various legal systems' search for a new accommodation with the recently evolving concepts of personal identity.

International law, too, while normally deferring to national law in matters of nationality, has become more accommodating of dual citizenship. While the 1955 *Nottebohm* case still favoured without qualification a principle of one 'effective nationality' over duality,[79] this preference is being rethought. For example, in 1981, the Iran–United States Claims Tribunal confirmed that dual nationals could make claims, provided their dominant and effective nationality was not that of the respondent state.[80] The European Court of Justice has

---

[76] Second Protocol amending the Convention on the Reduction of Cases of Multiple Nationality and Military Obligations in Cases of Multiple Nationality, 2 Nov. 1993, paras. 5–7, amending Art. 1, Eur. TS no. 149. The Protocol amends Eur. TS no. 43, 5 June 1963.

[77] Council of Europe: European Convention on Nationality, ET Ser./166, 37 ILM 44 (1998), art. 17(1), done on 6 Nov. 1997. [78] George P. Fletcher, *Loyalty* 155 (1993).

[79] Judgement of 6 April 1955, 1955 ICJ Rep. 4.

[80] *Islamic Republic of Iran v. United States* (Case A/18), 5 Iran–US Cl. Trib. Rep. 251 (1984). Moreover, the United Nations Compensation Commission, the body which collects, assesses and provides compensation for claims against Iraq stemming from its invasion of Kuwait, permits states to present the claims of residents who are not their nationals, including stateless persons. John R. Crook, 'The United Nations Compensation Commission—A New Structure to Enforce State Responsibility', 87 Am. J. Int'l L. 144, 149–50 (1993).

recently decided to give full effect to a person's several nationalities.[81] In the specific instance, the Court held that 'the EEC Treaty prohibits a Member State from refusing to recognize the status as a national of another Member State of a person . . . merely on the ground that he possesses simultaneously the nationality of a non-member country and that country was the place of his habitual residence . . .'.[82]

### 3. AUTONOMY VERSUS ANOMIE

This suggests that at least some states are, indeed, moving in the direction of permitting individuals to exercise a greater degree of personal autonomy in designing their identity. It is not necessarily a concomitant of such a development—as is sometimes feared—that persons are becoming more self-sufficient, individualistic, or atomistic in relation to others. The need for community appears to be as strong as ever, even among those who carry more than one passport. The trend toward self-identification does suggest, however, that some significant and growing part of humanity is seeking community with others based on commonalities that are neither genetic nor territorial, and that this community may increasingly take the form of intersecting, or concentric, circles of affinity.

True, the expanding right to such personal and complex self-determination has not so far affected equally all parts of the world, leading to the common criticism that the phenomenon is essentially a 'Western' one: an issue examined in Chapter 6. Another criticism of any generalization concerning personal autonomy is that the phenomenon, in practice, is less a general trend than a privilege currently exercised primarily by professional, commercial, or intellectual elites. This may be true, but the privileged, while still small in number, also wield disproportionate influence on the way society and identity are structured and defined and the direction in which they evolve. And, with economic, social, and cultural development and globalization, the circles of the privileged are likely to widen. There is virtually no evidence that those already educationally and technologically empowered to make self-identifying choices now seek to hinder the spread of that capability to others still denied it. On the contrary, the prevalence of a near-missionary desire on the part of elites to widen distribution of the tools of individual empowerment is surely driven not only by a widespread liberal egalitarian morality but also by the prerequisites of economic expansion in this era of high technology and sophisticated labour. In Western societies, for example, computer ownership and the ability to use it has become

---

[81] *Micheletti and Others*, Case C-369/90, Reports of Cases before the Court of Justice and the Court of First Instance, 1992-7, Sec. I, p. 4239 at 4242.          [82] Ibid. at 4252.

almost as common as radio and television, and is likely to become an increasingly important factor in individual emancipation.

Already states see public uses for their citizens' layered loyalties. In an increasingly interdependent world, these personal ties often are eagerly exploited by foreign offices, businesses, educational institutions, churches, and the communications industry. The fact that, in 1996, the Foreign Minister of Bosnia also happened to be an American citizen, if it raised eyebrows, did so in subtle appreciation of its potentially beneficial implications. Citizen Paine redux! But whereas Paine was an exceptional phenomenon—an eighteenth-century man with three valid citizenships[83]—the multiple national today is becoming quite ordinary. Even where formal citizenship is not involved, there may be multiple loyalty: it is no longer considered derisory for American citizens to be involved in representing and promoting before Congress or the State Department the parochial interests of Ireland, Israel, or South Africa as states to which, in addition to their loyalty to America, they feel a special attachment.

Transnational corporations, too, openly distribute their loyalty among the various countries in which they strive to operate as good citizens. To help them, the states in which they are incorporated, headquartered, or owned usually adopt laws that accommodate such multiple loyalty, for example, not only by encouraging Rupert Murdoch to change—or add to—his citizenships to suit his worldwide business convenience, but by seeking to create rules to mitigate conflict between various state regulatory and taxation regimes.

What is new about all this, in sum, is not the re-emergence—and tolerance—of multiple loyalty references, but the acceptance of a right of persons (and other entities, including transnational corporations) to compose their own identity by constructing the complex of loyalty references that best manifest *who they want to be.* In that sense, we may already have entered an era of freely imagined identities, one in which personal choice is no longer circumscribed by accidents or manipulations of genetics, class, place, or history. Many individuals, in these circumstances, may still opt to attribute their legal and social identity to some single, 'natural' objective imperative: their parents' religion, their place of birth, their social or professional caste. But, increasingly, they are no longer required by law to do so. Instead, by national and international normative usage, they are being freed to design their own identities. It is an awesome responsibility, the ultimate freedom, and symptomatic of a promising reconfiguration of the dynamics of the international system.

---

[83] Paine had, betimes, English, American and French citizenship and, after the Polish revolution of 1791, considered also applying for Polish citizenship. John Keane, *Tom Paine: A Political Life* 446 (1995).

# 5

## Community Based on Personal Autonomy

> He who is unable to live in society, or who has no need because he is
> sufficient for himself, must be either a beast or a god.
>
> Aristotle, *Politics*, Bk. I, ch. 2

> I am not an Athenian or a Greek, but a citizen of the world.
>
> Socrates, from Plutarch, *Of Banishment*

> Human individuality presupposes social existence.
>
> Neil MacCormick, *Legal Right and Social Democracy* 251 (1982)

### 1. FROM TRADITIONAL COMMUNITY TO PERSONAL AUTONOMY

At least since the end of the eighteenth century, with the American and French
Revolutions, the ascendant idea in history has been that of civil society and the
state. Identity is stamped on each person by their community; and, in much of
the world, for two hundred years or more, that defining community has been
the state. The Kantian concept of human communities—states—organizing
and conditioning the identity,[1] loyalty, and industry of free and equal citizens
around notions of 'republican' governance[2] has outlasted the later corporatist
and Trotskyite alternatives, some of which had imagined that the state could
eventually be dismantled in favour of other transnational social structures.

As we have observed in Chapter 3, the modern state was imbued by two quite
different ideas about identity. Eighteenth-century liberal nationalism was vitally
different from later xenophobic,[3] fascist–romantic nationalism. Yet both shared
a vision of the state as *the* central reference of every person's identity, loyalty, and
enterprise. Just as passionate citizenship and loyalty defined every American at

---

[1]  By identity I mean each person's answer in associational terms to the question 'Who am I?': an
answer, as Locke has pointed out, conditioned by consciousness and memory. John Locke, *Essays
Concerning Human Understanding*, Bk. 2, Ch. 27, para. 10 'of Identity and Diversity' at 333–5 (23rd
edn., 1817).

[2]  Immanuel Kant, *Perpetual Peace*, in *Kant's Political Writings* (H. Reiss ed., H. Nisbit transl., 1970).

[3]  Discussing the European state as community during the Victorian era, one observer remarks:
'By gathering up communities of insiders, they revealed—only too often invented—a world of
strangers beyond the pale, individuals and classes, races and nations, it was perfectly proper to
contradict, patronize, ridicule, bully, exploit or exterminate.' Peter Gay, *The Cultivation of Hatred* 35–6
(1993). This Victorian sense of community was constructed of a xenophobia that 'constituted
licenses to unleash feelings of aggression . . .'. Ibid. at 36. Gay points out, however, that the
Victorian decades also saw the flowering of social conscience and 'the stern call for self-control,
especially among the respectable middling orders of society . . .'. Ibid. at 37.

Thomas Jefferson's time, these statist values also defined the new citizens of Bismarck's Germany or Kwame Nkrumah's mid-twentieth-century Ghana.

In the nineteenth and twentieth centuries, the model of the state as exclusive socio-political organizing principle was widely touted and adopted: whether the state was a democratic republic, a liberal monarchy or one of the many prevalent forms of mobilizational authoritarianism. It became increasingly true during these two 'statist' centuries that the state was becoming the defining 'we'—the *communitas*—of most persons. This was so whether the state was more or less a melting pot of ethnies, like France, the US, and Great Britain, or a self-proclaimed nation-state like Germany or Japan. It was true whether the state was seen as a building block in a quasi-federalist ideal structure of humanity (Kant) or as ultimate ethnocentric end in itself (Hegel).

These disparate nationalisms, despite their bitter rivalry, succeeded in forging a new human identity. In the place of the previous 'basic social unit of the peasant village . . . [the] large peer groups and extended families'[4] tied by bonds of indenture and fealty to a remote feudal hierarchy, there emerged, at first tentatively after the Peace of Westphalia, then passionately after the French revolution, a new person: the citizen. These citizens increasingly were emboldened to assert their membership in a new community of equals occupying, and totally refurbishing, the space of the dead feudal sovereign.

With the end of feudalism and the emergence of the nationalist state, entire populations were emancipated to join in the great collective patriotic passions of citizenry: both the good and the bad. Where there had been only the idiosyncratic strategies, grudges, and vendettas of kings and princes, there now emerged the vibrant animosities of 'the people', much of it directed to the 'alien other', whether in their midst or at their borders.[5] As collective animosities became popularized, civilization entered the dangerous age of modern, romantic, statist nationalism. The 'we', wherever state nationalism triumphed, became uniquely and exclusively a community of citizens whose antipathy towards the alien other was no longer mitigated by even the most obvious transnational affinities of genealogy, culture, religion, geography, or mercantile interest, let alone humanist fraternalism.

This repression of human commonalities, this statist fear of the alien other, continued its hold on a large part of Western culture until quite recently and its passions continue to smoulder even now. It was a moving force in dictating a vindictive peace after the First World War. And it promoted community-based common visions of the good that deplored and repressed difference and dissent. This phenomenon was by no means unique to Nazi Germany, where it was to reach its modern apogee. Lecturing at the University of Virginia in 1933, T. S.

---

[4] Ronald William Dworkin, *The Rise of the Imperial Self* 114 (1996).

[5] Peter Gay credits not Darwin but his predecessor, the English philosopher Herbert Spencer, for the ideas celebrating the triumphant aggressor explicit in his phrase, coined in 1862, 'the survival of the fittest.' Gay, *supra* n. 3, at 41. He also notes Spencer's repudiation of its implications. Ibid. at 44–5.

Eliot seems to have created no particular stir with his prescription for fostering the 'society we desire':

The population should be homogeneous; where two or more cultures exist in the same place they are likely either to be fiercely self-conscious or both to become adulterate. What is still more important is unity of religious background; and reasons of race and religion combine to make any number of free-thinking Jews undesirable. . . . And a spirit of excessive tolerance is to be deprecated.[6]

As Peter Gay has sadly commented: 'Nothing seems more natural than the ease with which humans claim superiority over a collective other. It is an immensely serviceable alibi for aggression, solidifying the bracing sense of one's merits—or assuaging the secret fear of one's imperfections.'[7]

Dissenters' views were readily discounted not by rebutting their substance but by appealing to each community's paranoid populism. We have not yet seen the end of this era. The press controlled by the military junta of Burma, for example, recently dismissed Aung San Suu Kyi, the Nobel prizewinning leader of Burma's pro-democracy movement, as a 'fifth columnist' and 'a stooge of the imperialists' backing that charge by noting that she has been 'tainted by marriage of a British scholar Michael Aris'.[8] In the ruling circles of Singapore, the demand for multi-party democracy is frequently rebuffed as an un-Asian and neo-imperialistic toadying to inappropriate Western values.[9] Unwittingly, the tone of today's residual xenophobic discourse is itself bizarrely 'Western', echoing British politics' earlier preoccupation with 'pope-ish' plots and, more recently, the US Congress' investigations of 'un-American' activities.

Nevertheless, there is something vaguely archaic and musty about Eliot's ruminations, or the fulminations of Burma's SLORC junta autocrats; they are nowadays of interest, primarily, as odd remainders and reminders of a style of thinking widely believed to be dying, its bathos wrapped in nostalgia, of interest only for being so exotic to the prevailing modern culture. Of course, one still finds anti-immigrant resentment and violence in many places, even in liberal democracies: particularly, but not exclusively, in places with high rates of unemployment. Eastern Germany, Belgium, France, Austria, and California are recent examples of societies where the 'alien other' remains a popular target. Nevertheless, there are signs of an evolutionary change. To fear and loathe an 'alien other', people must perceive a bright line between 'us' and 'them'. That perception, and the stereotypes that facilitate it, may be losing their grip. Professor Peter J. Spiro has recently observed that it

is becoming increasingly difficult to use the word 'we' in the context of international affairs. Until recently, it was assumed to denote those who shared the speaker's affiliation

---

[6] T. S. Eliot, *After Strange Gods: A Primer of Modern History* 19–20 (1934) (the Page–Barber Lectures).

[7] Gay, *supra* n. 3, at 68.        [8] NY Times, 22 July 1996, at A7.

[9] The best statements favouring such an 'Asian' way are found in Kishore Mahbubani, *Can Asians Think?* 37–94 (1998).

with a particular nation-state. But in the post-cold war context, such affiliation no longer necessarily defines the interests or even allegiances of the individual at the international level. Dramatically multiplied transnational contacts at all levels of society have not only resulted in a greater awareness of the global context, but have also created new commonalities of identity that cut across national borders and challenge governments at the level of individual loyalties.[10]

Thus, various loyalties now emerge to compete with loyalty to the state. Persons increasingly act in social and political solidarity with others on the basis of autonomous—in the sense of non-exogenous or non-preordained—commitment to causes that transcend state lines. To put this another way, many individuals now tend to define themselves and affiliate with others on the basis of dependent variables (such as their economic self interest) rather than being governed by independent variables (such as their race). 'Environmentalists, human rights activists, women, children, animal rights advocates, consumers, the disabled, gays and indigenous peoples have all gone international . . .'[11] and, for that matter, so have mafiosi, drug smugglers, and terrorists.

The emergent communities, the new 'we', are not immune to malevolence or paranoia, but they are different in that they do not seek an exclusive franchise. They do not conform to the romantic nationalist creed: 'one land, one leader, one people.' Each member of these new affinity-based communities feels free to compose—and periodically to revise—a personal portfolio of variegated personal commitments, which is precisely the opposite of what Mr Eliot thought 'desirable' in 1933. As Professor David Elkins points out,

Technological developments—especially in areas of electronics and telecommunications—have shifted the balance away from purely territorial political forms to a greater role for non-territorial organizations and identities. . . . This logic opens up . . . new dimensions of democracy and citizenship, enhanced forms of community, a reconciliation between individual and group needs, and more flexible and focused types of government which offer more choices to citizens than simply which elite will govern them.[12]

To some extent, this formation of affinity-based transnational communities is not really new. Religions—Catholic, Protestant, and Jewish—long created a sense of adherence that crossed European and Latin American political and geographic boundaries, as Islam has transcended the boundaries of North Africa, the Near East, and Central as well as South-East Asia. So, to an extent, did the old feudal monarchies, binding Hungarian peasants (more or less) to the Austrian emperor or Jewish Millets to the Ottoman Porte. There were guilds and Masonic orders before the modern state. In that sense, the very modern post-nationalist sensibility of Article 8 of the recent Treaty of Maastricht could

---

[10] Peter J. Spiro, 'New Global Communities: Nongovernmental Organizations in International Decision-Making Institutions', 18 The Washington Quarterly 45 (Winter 1995).     [11] Ibid.

[12] David J. Elkins, *Beyond Sovereignty: Territory and Political Economy in the Twenty-First Century* 7 (1995).

be traced back to the aspirations of the Concert of Europe, to Metternich and the Congress of Vienna. Article 8 envisages a new transnational European identity, proclaiming that:

Citizenship of the Union is hereby established. Every person holding the nationality of a Member State shall be a citizen of the Union . . .

What is important about this provision is not the as-yet meagre substantive rights that are embodied in the new European citizenship, but the very publicly audible admission by the Union's member-states that its citizens may be parties to *multiple demoi*: that the nationals of one demos (the state) may also, concurrently, be the citizens of another (the Union) without truly devaluing either. The practical consequences of this are everywhere apparent. Thus, in modern German politics it would now be considered bizarre to seek political advantage by labelling an opponent — Chancellor Schröder, for example — as 'pro-British' or 'pro-European'. A hundred years ago, however, this would have been the most damaging shibboleth one could have directed at a German leader. Once people accept the notion of multiple *demoi*, the 'alien other' is harder to identify.

The public accommodation of multiple *demoi* is 'new', however, only in the context of the last two hundred years of European history. Only in this transitory nationalist period did the concept of multiple personal loyalties become anathema to the state and dangerous to the individual. Personal transnational ties that, in the Middle Ages, had raised scarcely an eyebrow, became highly suspect in the nineteenth and twentieth centuries. Even in multicultural America, to become the first Catholic President, John F. Kennedy had to make absolutely clear that he would take no cues from the Pope.[13] Communists, everywhere, were seen as agents of the Soviet Union. In the past two centuries, dual or bifurcated loyalty became an odious identity with serious political, and sometimes legal, consequences. It was not so in 1634, when Hugo Grotius, a loyal Dutchman, accepted the Swedish ambassadorship to France. It may not be so, again. For now, as Spiro points out, the sense of personal identity — the definition of the 'we' — is once again becoming complex, and this is occurring in the context of a growing tolerance towards personal loyalties that are variegated, layered and even transnational.

In the preceding chapter it was argued that a possible measure of this toleration may be the extent to which governments — at least in the West — are permitting citizens to acquire multiple nationality.[14] As they do, states begin to see distinct advantages to some citizens serving as diplomatic, cultural or commercial bridges between themselves and others.[15] As noted in the preceding

---

[13] Lawrence H. Fuchs, *John F. Kennedy and American Catholicism* 172 (1967).

[14] This development is surveyed in Thomas M. Franck, 'Clan and Superclan: Loyalty, Identity and Community in Law and Practice', 90 Am. J. Int'l L. 359, 378–82 (1996).

[15] See e.g. the remarkable endorsement of dual nationality by Citizenship and Immigration Canada, *Dual Citizenship*, at 2 (1991).

chapter, it is now permissible and socially acceptable for citizens of most Western states to hold more than one nationality and even carry several passports.[16] It is becoming common knowledge that this may, but need not, signify kaleidoscopic identity. Some Americans of Irish descent may harbour nostalgia for the Old Country, but others have been known to recover their ancestral citizenship mainly to gain access to the shorter 'European Union' line at continental passport control stations, or to give their children a shot at someday working in Milan or Paris.

In a sense, this 'new' toleration is a reversion to the spirit of an age before the rise of modern nationalism. However, what distinguishes this latest turn from the earlier accommodations made by Holy Roman, Ottoman, and Austro-Hungarian empires to their subjects' complex affiliations and multivariegated personal loyalties is that, this time around, the state seems ready to tolerate not merely multiplicity as such, but autonomous *individual choice* of identities. That, up to 1918, one might have been a passionate Hungarian and also a subject of that paradoxical relic of pre-romantic cosmopolitan nationalism, the Austrian emperor, was a happenstance of birth, place, and history. That, in 1996, Bruce Daniels, born in the United States but naturalized in Canada and teaching in Winnipeg, should have had the right to declare himself a candidate for the US presidency, carries quite another message.[17] It speaks of a new tolerance—in both of Daniels' countries—for *autonomous* personal choice in the formation of identity.

This deference to expressions of personal autonomy may be less a deliberate change of national strategy than an increasingly widespread legal and socio-political accommodation to what is happening to societies: a tectonic shift, elaborated in Chapter 8, towards acceptance of personal autonomy and individual self-determination, manifest in law as a right to authentic personhood. Or the new personal freedom may simply reflect the less central role that citizenship in general now plays in personal identity formation. Both these hypotheses are plausible interpretations of states' greater willingness to accommodate its citizens' preferences, not least in opting for dual or multiple nationality.

The same may be said of corporations, whose identity is also becoming harder to define. A company founded in Dallas, Texas (Texas Instruments), is now the largest Japanese manufacturer and exporter of microchips to the US. For the most part, states lately, rather than fight for exclusive jurisdiction, seek to accommodate the evident transnational identity of such corporations.[18] Increasingly, certain kinds of entities—deliverers of information and services on the Internet or from satellites—in practice have become 'citizens' of every-

---

[16] See e.g. Rui Manuel Moura Ramos, 'Nationalité, Plurinationalité et Supranationalité en Droit Portugais', 97 (1995) (unpublished manuscript, on file with author).
[17] The candidacy of Bruce Daniels is discussed in *The New York Times*, Magazine, 26 Nov. 1995, at 49. See also discussion in Ch. 4, *supra*. [18] Elkins, *supra* n. 12, at 11.

where, or nowhere, with complex identities, multiple loyalties, and layered responsibilities.

Choosing the components of one's identity, one's loyalty references and circles of affinity, has become the central project of one's life: that is, if one chooses personal autonomy. The idea of 'personal autonomy', and its rapid popularization after World War II, will be a recurrent theme of this study. The etymology of the term 'autonomy' helps to explain the usage: *auto* (self) and *nomos* (rule or law). While 'autonomy' has many meanings and, thus, can confuse as well as inform, the usage in this study is quite clear. Personal autonomy means the law-given, socially accommodated right of each person to make moral, social, and political choices, particularly those that define the self.[19] In modern liberal democracies, much of the business of law has consisted of arranging accommodations and drawing reasonable lines between enlarging circumferences of overlapping personal autonomy. For example: I exercise my personal autonomy when I indicate in my will that I wish to be cremated and where the ashes are to be scattered. In many states, individuals used not to have this prerogative. My lawyer tells me, however, that, while this is, indeed, my right, it is not within the ambit of my legally protected personal autonomy to include also a provision prohibiting a memorial service, since to do so would curtail others' personal autonomy to assemble in exercise of their right to free self-expression.

A brief note of caution may here be in order. Autonomy is also frequently used to denote the rights of minorities to self-governing legal subsidiarity within a state.[20] This form of autonomy may be expressed territorially as in, for example, the special status of the *Cotûme de Paris'* civil code in the province of Quebec, or in the legally protected prerogatives of Russians in the Trans-Dniester region of Moldova.[21] It may be recognized by a US Supreme Court decision[22] that Oklahoma has no right to impose a tax on the sale of gasoline inside 'Indian country' as defined by a federal government treaty[23] which 'guarantees the Tribe and its members that "no Territory or State shall ever have a right to pass laws for the government of" the Chickasaw Nation . . .'.[24] Or it may be manifest in a separate legal system applicable to various religious minorities living anywhere in a non-sectarian state. An example is the multiple laws of marriage and divorce applicable to the cultural or ethnic communities of

---

[19] See James E. Fleming, 'Securing Deliberative Autonomy', 48 Stanford L. Rev. 1, 30–1 (1995).

[20] See Ruth Lapidoth, *Autonomy: Flexible Solutions to Ethnic Conflicts* 10, 12–23, 50–8 (1997).

[21] For examples, see *Models of Autonomy* (Yoram Dinstein ed., 1981); Lapidoth, ibid.

[22] *Oklahoma Tax Commission v. Chickasaw Nation*, 115 S.Ct. 2214 (1995).

[23] Article IV of 7 Stat. 333–4.

[24] *Oklahoma Tax Commission v. Chickasaw Nation*, *supra* n. 22, at 2217–18. The Court held that ' "[A]bsent cession of jurisdiction or other federal statutes permitting it" we have held, a State is without power to tax reservation lands and reservation Indians.' *County of Yakima v. Confederated Tribes and Bands of Yakima Nation*, 502 US 251, 258; 112 S.Ct. 683, 688 (1992).

Kenya.[25] In this study, such phenomena are discussed under the rubric of 'group rights' in significant distinction from the issues pertaining to the personal rights of individuals. Although the term 'autonomy' is used ubiquitously, it is important to distinguish its usage in reference to *individualism* from its denoting of *group rights* because these, using a superficially similar vocabulary, are often in opposition to one another (*see* Chapter 9).

## 2. PERSONAL AUTONOMY'S CRITICS

Not everyone unstintingly welcomes the new trend to personal autonomy. Professor Albert O. Hirschman notes that values of individualism that serve a society well at one stage of its development—when personal freedoms generate cultural and economic growth—may be an embarrassment later, when the communitarian values of a caring society need greater emphasis. Thus, the 'institutions of a welfare state draw on a solidarity ethos that is likely to stand in considerable tension to the liberal tradition. . . . This does not mean that a consensus on welfare provisions cannot eventually be found or engineered, or that it is better for a country lacking both individual liberties and welfare state provisions to move directly to the welfare state without first establishing individual liberties. There is, nevertheless, value in appreciating the peculiar difficulties some countries are likely to experience in negotiating certain transitions or sequences'.[26] As an example, he points to France's introduction of unprecedented universal male suffrage in 1793 and 1848, which may have been a principal cause for its (by Western European standards) extraordinary delay—until 1944—in extending the franchise to women.[27]

The need to reinvigorate the political community is stressed by social commentators who deplore what they perceive as a loss of individuals' centredness in their traditional milieu. Professor Amitai Etzioni, for example, calls for the 'regeneration of American society' and insists that this 'requires that the members of the society come together to commit themselves to a core of shared values' and that they 'find ways to embody these in the members' daily conduct and in social formations such as the family and the schools'.[28] He sees 'the centrifugal effects of global economic forces' as challenging 'communitarian progress' and 'the social order, especially its moral foundations'.[29] Worse, he tells us, 'individualists strenuously oppose the concept of a good society' and

---

[25] Y. P. Ghai & Patrick McAusland, *Public Law and Political Change in Kenya* 376 (1970); Eugen Cotran, *Kenya, The Law of Succession* (II) 1–168 (1969); Eugen Cotran, The Law of Marriage and Divorce (I) (1968); Tudor Jackson, *The Law of Kenya: an Introduction* 17–19 (1970); Republic of Kenya, Report of the Commission on the Law of Marriage and Divorce 4–7, 21–9 (1968).
[26] Albert O. Hirschman, *A Propensity to Self-Subversion* 52 (1995).     [27] Ibid. at 54–5.
[28] Amitai Etzioni, *The New Golden Rule: Community and Morality in a Democratic Society* 80 (1996).
[29] Ibid.

'republican virtues'.[30] As evidence of individualism run amok, Etzioni cites 'the [traffic] gridlock in Washington, D.C.' that reflects 'among other things, profound value differences' and erosion of the sense of community by unbridled individualism.[31]

The dangers of uncaring liberal individualism are stressed even more strongly in Professor Michael J. Sandel's *Democracy's Discontents*.[32] He describes the ascendance, more generally, of liberal accommodation of individual rights in the US *polis*, and deplores its excesses as having undermined the republican civic virtues that support the sense of an American community. In his view, an emphasis, by law and by personal inclination, on personal entitlements has eroded the community's coherence: the notion of a common 'good' and the selfless civic virtues that advance it. Addressing himself to the American situation, he juxtaposes two theories competing within the American intellectual and political arenas: *liberalism* (which regards individuals as the building blocks of society and the holders of basic rights) and *civic republicanism* (which regards the community as the basis of society and the repository of basic rights).[33] According to Sandel, the emphasis, in recent years, on individualist-liberalism, has neutered the state, elevated individual rights above the common good, and thereby has eroded the sense of community which alone makes possible a politic in which the individual is socialized to support policies that redound not necessarily to his or her personal gain but also, or even instead, to the good of the community.

That plaint, of course, is not one originating solely in our own individualist era with its admittedly unprecedented emphasis on personal rights and freedoms. Peter Gay, in his study, *The Cultivation of Hatred*, cites numerous instances, from Victorian times, of the intellectual defence of the prevalent culture of flogging precisely on the ground that the practice inculcates social and moral conditioning in an era of rampant individualism and self-expression. In 1867, the Boston School Committee firmly rejected a petition—signed, among others, by Harvard President Thomas Hill and the poet Henry Wadsworth Longfellow—calling for the abolition of corporal punishment in education. In so doing, the Board employed venerable Benthamite terms beloved by civic republicans, proclaiming that '"the greatest good of the greatest number" demands, that the Board should continue to authorize the exercise' of corporal punishment, albeit 'under proper restrictions'.[34] Gay also cites the address, in 1876, of the German educator, Julius Beeger, condemning the 'silken' Zeitgeist, which had generated a 'modern mollycoddling' and 'effeminization' of students and, thereby, of the public, producing the 'moral anemia that was paralyzing the seriousness of justice and the arm of authority'.[35]

---

[30] Amitai Etzioni, ibid. at 85.      [31] Ibid. at 87.
[32] Michael J. Sandel, *Democracy's Discontents*, 1996.      [33] Ibid. at 13–90.
[34] Gay, *supra* n. 3, at 186.      [35] Ibid. at 187.

While governments have always demanded strong means to subdue the disruptive individualist—the Bible gives ample authority for flogging and stoning—such repression now tends to encounter public resistance. In the modern climate of social and political democracy, it has become more difficult to assert a plenary right to draw the line against dissonant individuals in the name of social order and community values.[36] As Sandel recognizes, in the US such resistance is built into the constitutional framework of a nation that mandates the separation of powers and distributes—and thereby deliberately complicates exercise of—the power to decide when individual autonomy must yield to the needs of communitarian social order.

3. FROM PERSONAL AUTONOMY TO NEW COMMUNITY

The American constitution's judicial interpreters have been right in responding sceptically to the siren call of 'republican virtues'. There is evidence throughout history and from many societies that the claim to enforce community values has often been brandished by political and religious oligarchies to impose their personal preferences and secure their own primacy, always in the name of social cohesion and preserving the moral order. At the end of the twentieth century, especially in the West, claims to advance republican virtues—the common good—no longer are automatically accepted by a docile population. Instead, they become the subject of open, public discourse in the political and judicial arenas. Decisions about what persons may believe, read, profess, and do, once the unchallengeable prerogative of the king or cardinal, are nowadays made by voters, legislators, judges, and—most radical departure of all—by individuals deciding such matters in a reserved personal space free of external regulation.

This decentralization of the power to regulate individual conduct has occurred primarily where vibrantly free national economies have begun to satisfy the people's basic needs. Demonstrably, persons in these advanced societies are responding to the phenomenon of plenitude by changing their outlook: shifting, in the words of Ronald Inglehart, 'away from "Materialist" concerns about economic and physical security, towards a greater emphasis on freedom, self-expression, and the quality of life, or "Postmaterialist" values'. That shift has strengthened claims of individual self-determination against claims of government to enforce communitarian order for the common good. Empirical evidence gathered by Inglehart about the 'formative socialization' of

[36] Before the emergence of autonomy, especially in the form of voting rights for the middle class male, it was accepted dogma of governance 'that constituted authority alone understands, and alone acts to realize, the true needs of society. Almost by definition, kings—or, in republics, magistrates—serve their state; factions only serve themselves. Hence, down to the eighteenth century—and into the nineteenth—opposition implied intrigues, conspiracies, even the threat of insurrection. [It was] cast in the lurid light of selfishness or treason.' Ibid. at 215.

contemporary young Europeans shows a marked contrast between them and the less well-off previous generation, with the former tending 'to value relatively high levels of freedom and self-expression' leading to 'a shift towards new value priorities'.[37] A similar trend seems underway in rapidly developing nations from Mexico to China, with a concomitant shift of emphasis from security to liberty, from ethnic, racial, and geographically based social solidarity to personal autonomy.

This evolution in personal priorities from preoccupation with economic gain to a new emphasis on personal expressive freedom is still resisted by some governments. Ranged against those governments, however, in addition to some of their own citizen-activists, are the inexorable realities of modern communications technology and a significant host of global legal and institutional developments advancing under the rubric of human rights.[38] This development is the subject of chapters 8 and 10.

But the vigorous contemporary trend towards individual rights does not necessarily discount republican civic virtues or turn a deaf ear to communitarian responsibilities. Although in extreme form, individualism may lead to alienation and social irresponsibility, the mainstream has not run this course. Nevertheless, many still believe that achieving a balance between personal autonomy and civic virtue necessarily is a zero-sum game. Professor Sandel, for one, views liberal tolerance of personal autonomy as having tended towards outright repudiation of the republican virtues of a caring society. This view is expressed more emphatically and with less nuancing by Lee Kwan Yew, the long-time political and philosophical leader of Singapore. Both deplore what they see as modern individualism's threat to communitarian responsibility. But, then, so in their time did Roman emperors, medieval kings, and Victorian prime ministers. They, too, complained of the breakdown of community values and a loss of respect for the civic virtues. Indeed, some of them had far better cause to complain, faced, in turn, by Visigoths, Christians, shakers, lollards, pirates, brigands, and anarchists: opponents bent on destroying the state or replacing it with radically different modes of authority. Of course, the fact that warnings of this sort are not new does not prove that they are entirely without foundation. Even Lee Kwan Yew's concerns are sensitive to Singapore's quite recent history of anarchic civil disorder.

Still, there is also much tilting at windmills. The contemporary liberalism that Sandel fears is not bent on the eradication of civic virtue or the traditional community. Modern individual autonomy claims arise not primarily out of the deconstructive opposition to community but, rather, from the desire of

---

[37] Paul R. Abramson & Ronald Inglehart, *Value Change in Global Perspective* 1 (1995).

[38] International Covenant on Civil and Political Rights, 999 UNTS 171 (entered into force 1976); European Convention for the Protection of Human Rights and Fundamental Freedoms, 213 UNTS 221 (entered into force 1953); American Convention on Human Rights, 1144 UNTS 123 (entered into force 18 July 1978).

individuals to utilize intellectual and technological innovation to supplement their continued affiliation with a genetically or territorially determined community by taking advantage of their options to make choices which, even when made in accordance with individual self-expression, usually are still powerfully affiliative. To the extent this new freedom of affiliation threatens the pre-eminence of the state, it does so only because it has become apparent that traditional territorial communities are incapable, alone, of resolving many of the more obdurate issues facing humanity. Addressing these successfully necessitates new associational frameworks within which to work out, on a larger scale, effective new policies and strategies.

Whether this working out occurs in the North American Free Trade Area, the UN Security Council, the World Bank, the International Chamber of Commerce or the International Red Cross, there already exists today a mixed public and private skein of transnational governance. Important decisions are referred to the hundreds of institutions, organs, and agents of that governance in what is a highly decentralized system. The process of postmaterialist resocialization thus has produced, alongside a global emphasis on personal autonomy, a new receptivity for interdependence and its institutional manifestations, even as existing territorially based civic communities are revealed as inadequate, by themselves, to resolve some of the most pressing global problems.

In other words, the rights-seeking individual at the end of the twentieth century is less likely to be an anarchist than a 'new communitarian' seeking additional fora of association, in more functionally effective affinities. There is no reason to fear this. Rather, it is altogether useful that individuals should choose to identify with, and seek to participate in, the new transnational regimes and networks, creating popular interest factions that seek to advance the cause of these fledgling centres of power while, reciprocally, also subjecting them to the discursive obligations of community and imposing a level of accountability that is essential to their legitimacy. One example is the many national United Nations Associations which seek to educate electorates and legislators, advocating support and understanding for UN activities while also engaging representatives of various international agencies in policy discourse and interrogation. Another example is the International Committee of the Red Cross and the many national Red Cross and Red Crescent organizations that help develop and implement humanitarian law while they seek to prevent and ameliorate humanitarian disasters.

In particular, the new transnational organizations, both intergovernmental and nongovernmental, need the legitimization that derives from open discourse with their constituents, which is not easily achieved in the absence of a democratic political process, something all the new transnationals still lack. Absent a global parliament, people's interests in intergovernmental operations are represented primarily by diplomats, most of whom, at best, inadequately represent the diverse interests of their citizenry. To address this 'legitimacy deficit' (see

Chapter 2) many non-governmental organizations (NGOs) have sprung up across state boundaries. These appear to be becoming purposeful and expert participants in the intergovernmental diplomatic process by which new policies are formulated, implemented and enforced. At the other end of their operational spectrum, many of these voluntary associations rally individuals to influence the domestic politics that affect global and national agendas: a development welcomed by thoughtful governments and international organizations because 'international institutions that do not allow for the participation of significant non-national voices may suffer a perception of procedural illegitimacy'.[39]

These 'networks of interdependence'[40] engage globally or regionally in policy-making and operations, pursuing values, interests, and specialized capabilities of an often global membership. According to Professor Harold Jacobson, they come to the fore 'when states appear to be inadequate frameworks for achieving values that are actively sought or when the fates of peoples in various states are closely linked through many interconnections'.[41] According to Hazel Henderson, 'Citizen movements and people's associations of all kinds cover the whole range of human concerns—from service clubs, self-help and spiritual groups, to chambers of commerce and professional associations of teachers, doctors, farmers, scientists, musicians and artists—all sharing some concern for human society that crosses national borders. The rise of such organizations [is] one of the most striking phenomena of the 20th century . . . '.[42]

There has been a spectacular increase in the number and size of NGOs in recent years. Whereas it is reported that there were five NGOs in 1850 and 176 in 1909,[43] the 1985–6 Yearbook of International Organizations lists some 18,000 of them. The 1993 UN Human Development Report describes an explosion of participatory movements of nongovernmental organizations. '. . . people's participation', the report finds, 'is becoming the central issue of our time'.[44] For example, in 1992 there were between 1,500 and 2,000 American medical professionals engaged in various disaster areas around the world.[45] Alone, one medical NGO, *Médecins Sans Frontières*, accounts for more than 5,000 doctors and nurses, volunteers recruited from several dozen countries, serving in over 80 states. A different instance of the proliferation of transnational factions is the International Confederation of Free Trade Unions (ICFTU), which has 127 affiliated members in 136 countries. Founded in 1949, with headquarters in Brussels, it seeks to promote democratic trade unionism

---

[39] Spiro, 'New Global Communities,' *supra* n. 10, at 53.
[40] Harold K. Jacobson, *Networks of Interdependence: International Organizations and the Global Political System* 10 (1984).                    [41] Ibid. at 14.
[42] Hazel Henderson, 'Social Innovation and Citizen Movements,' *Futures* 322 (Apr. 1993).
[43] Elise Boulding, *Building a Global Civic Culture* 35 (1988).
[44] UNDP Human Development Report, 1 (1993).
[45] E. Venant, 'Call to Duty', LA Times, 6 Jan. 1992, at E1.

worldwide and to fight for workers' rights in an era of global trade pacts.[46] In 1997–8, for example, it helped mediate the massive strike actions crippling the Korean economy.

Most NGOs, unlike *Medicins* and ICFTU, are not involved in direct action or in political activity (although about 1,000 of them have obtained consultative status with the United Nations[47]). Still, the

> social groups of which nongovernmental organizations are formal expressions constitute the infrastructure of a political system; they give it form and cohesiveness. Though they may not engage in political activities, the possibility always exists that they might; therefore if the nongovernmental organizations are of relatively substantial size, political decision makers are likely to take their anticipated reactions into account in making decisions. Thus their very existence can have political effects.[48]

It appears that we are witnessing the gradual emergence of a civil society not circumscribed by national boundaries.[49] One example is the effective network of national and transnational citizens' groups concerned with preservation of the environment. This 'global faction' has already demonstrated its ability to transform both the international and national discourse, placing 'sustainable' development high on the agenda. NGOs have also affected the discursive process itself. The participation of non-governmental advocates for human rights and the environment in intergovernmental negotiations on trade and development is but one of many recent instances of NGO's prevailing in their insistence on new subject-matter linkages.

Such transformation of the modalities of global and regional discourse should be recognized as another 'up' side of the 'downward' trend perceived by Professor Sandel. We are seeing what Professor Weiler calls 'the privileging of the individual' and the growing 'ability of the individual to rise above his or her national closet'.[50] However, for such rising to occur, Weiler cautions, the state must move in the direction deplored by Sandel, it must cease 'to make such a deep claim on the soul of the individual, reminiscent of the days when Christianity was a condition of full membership of civic society and of full citizenship rights . . .'.[51] This 'does not require a denigration of the virtues of national-ity—the belongingness, the social cohesion, the cultural and human richness which may be found' in the national community.[52] It does require that the national ethos be based on autonomous choice and that it accommodate the inevitable reality of at least some individuals choosing layered identities constructed out of multiple, freely selected loyalties and belonging to concentric or interlocking circles of mainly non-territorial affinities. Because states are now

---

[46] 'Union Body to Fight for Workers' Rights in Trade Pacts', Reuters, 14 June 1996.
[47] Jacobson, *supra* n. 40, at 10.     [48] Ibid.
[49] See Jessica T. Mathews, 'Power Shift: The Rise of Global Civil Society', 76 For. Aff. 50 (1997).
[50] J. H. H. Weiler, 'Does Europe Need a Constitution? Demos, Telos and the German Maastricht Decision', 1 Eur. LJ 219, 250 (1995).     [51] Ibid. at 251.
[52] Ibid.

more willing to tolerate (and, perhaps, even to encourage) their citizens' autonomous pursuit of such multiple affinities, some elements of a global civil society
are emerging: a society with its own civic virtues and, quite as important, with
the capacity to increase the legitimacy of the international regimes with which
they engage.

What Professor Sandel has failed to acknowledge is that liberalization—he
perceives it as the breakdown—of the American sense of civic virtue has not
simply left a void. It has also created an opening: one facilitating not, as he
fears, personal alienation, catatonia, hedonism, and nihilism, but instead, new
opportunities for the formation of communities of shared interest. To the extent
such opportunities are seized, the relation of the person to the state need not be
threatened. Layered identity need not displace conventional state-centred
loyalty, nor must it necessarily lead persons, in composing their personal
identities, to abjure older national civic virtues. It may, however, cause at least
some of us to supplement more traditional loyalties with ones less conventional,
but perhaps more currently relevant.

Of course, such non-territorial communities are neither inherently more nor
less virtuous and socially responsible than the traditional territorially bound
community that is the state. A person's non-territorial affinities might reflect
narrow self-interest, or new values and ideals, or some of each. The important
thing is that persons are naturally and freely choosing to join with other
autonomous but similarly minded individuals, even across national frontiers,
in pursuing values and goals through an activism directed both at national and
international problems, often through support for the goals and means of newly
established institutions. One example is the informal global network that has
emerged in support of national and international efforts to abolish the death
penalty.

Individual values in this individualist era, while autonomously chosen in
emancipated acts of personal self-determination, need not be molecular but,
in most instances, will correspond to values pursued by many others. It could as
well be called the era of a 'new communitarianism'. Its precepts are likely to be
formulated and pursued in interactive global networking. The sense of community once fostered by town meetings and chats across white picket fences
increasingly are being facilitated by discourse on the Internet or in co-operative
efforts on behalf of Amnesty International, Human Rights Watch committees,
or the World Wildlife Fund.

This, too, is not an entirely new development. Already in seventeenth- and
eighteenth-century Europe, composers such as Handel, Bach, and Purcell, in
places quite remote from one another, were aware of each other's activities,
corresponded, and not infrequently espoused common objectives across far
greater divides than any we encounter in the age of computer networks.
'Networked', too, were sixteenth-century theologians like Calvin and Knox.
Now, however, technological progress, especially in communications, has made

it eminently possible for many new kinds of communities to form far beyond the old constraints of geography and sovereignty. The amazing expansion and specialization of knowledge has made inevitable a new kind of bonding between kinfolk of the mind, the intellect supplementing if not supplanting more traditional bonds of blood, land, faith, and language. Indeed, the specialized lingua franca, now commonly spoken in the discourse of scientists, business leaders, and lawyers, has taken its place, alongside territorial vernaculars, as generator of 'linguistic' community.

Thus the contemporary emergence of what Sandel criticizes as the liberal, procedurally neutral, and value-free state may simply be the less significant aspect of a larger development: the growing acquiescence of the state in transnational interest-formation. Far from being neutral, states are declaring themselves in favour of—and a few against—a new freedom of individuals everywhere to join in inventing and propagating new common values through a process of interpersonal and interfactional discourse and professional or socio-political activism that parallels and intersects with more traditional intergovernmental diplomacy.[53]

What is happening is a social convergence facilitated not by invading armies or concordats, but by the communications and information revolutions. As Elkins observes, one 'would expect, specifically, that kindred feelings based on territorial boundaries . . . should assume a *relatively* lower priority when other interests of a non-territorial sort satisfy basic needs and feelings of a community'.[54] Moreover, persons who previously were essentially isolated and alienated within territorially bounded communities—for example, the ten lonely fans of sixteenth-century Gregorian chant living in North Dakota—are now empowered by the revolution in communications technology to join a world-wide 'virtual community' of persons who share their interest and, in a new solidarity, propagate, and facilitate everyone's access to, their esoteric art.

Howard Rheingold has defined and described such 'virtual communities' as 'social aggregations that emerge . . . when enough people carry on . . . public discussions long enough, with sufficient human feeling, to form webs of personal relationships in cyberspace'.[55] He notes that 'It's a bit like a neighbourhood pub or coffee shop. It's a little like a salon, where I can participate in a hundred ongoing conversations with people who don't care what I look like or sound like, but who do care how I think and communicate. . . . I believe [virtual communities] are in part a response to the hunger for community that has followed the disintegration of traditional communities around the world.'[56] He observes that virtual communities resemble the 'imagined communities' studied by Benedict

---

[53] For a discussion of substatal actors as participants in the global legal discourse see Peter J. Spiro, 'The States and Immigration,' 35 Va. J. Int'l L. 121, 174–8 (1994).

[54] Elkins, *supra* n. 12, at 57.

[55] Howard Rheingold, *The Virtual Community: Homesteading on the Electronic Frontier* 5 (1993).

[56] Ibid. at 62.

Anderson, which came into existence because of shared interests, experiences and knowledge of people brought together in a common enterprise.[57]

That may be a partial explanation. Probably a more important contributing factor, however, is the explosion of scientific and other data which promotes, on the one hand, specialization and differentiation of persons and, on the other, the necessity for global networking to produce, manage, exchange, and distribute information in such a way as to involve far-flung participants. According to Rheingold, the 'development of communications technologies has vastly transformed the capacity of global society to build coalitions and networks'.[58] These 'global networks', facilitated by computer mediated communications (CMCs), have broadened the range of options, allowing individuals 'to customize . . . social contacts from fragmented communities'.[59] In this way, CMCs 'foster community, or at least a sense of community, among its users'.[60] In Jessica Mathews' words, the 'most powerful engine of change in the relative decline of states and the rise of nonstate actors is the computer and telecommunications revolution, whose deep political and social consequences have been almost completely ignored'.[61]

The prefatory words 'virtual' or 'emerging' in connection with these new communities suggests to some persons that they are, in some way, not as 'natural' as the territorially 'bundled' communities of yore. Professor Elkins has responded that this reaction reflects the power of that to which we have grown accustomed. Many of us accept as 'natural' anything the origins of which we have forgotten.[62] But, as we noted in chapters 1 and 3, states, too, are not 'natural' in any strict historic or sociological sense. The territorial states which have long dominated personal identity are mostly invented constructs of shifting boundaries and populations. Even older communities, the nations, also were 'unnatural' conveniences invented by ancient ethnie, tribes, and clans. One would have to go far back into European prehistory to discover a 'natural' socio-political formation against which to contrast as 'unnatural' the communities currently evolving in response to new challenges and opportunities.

This does not protect newly imagined communities from being regarded askance by previously imagined ones. It must be expected that the state, or at least some states, will seek a defence against the growing power of the internet and of other CMCs that are learning to bypass controls on the flow of information. Some governments will try to staunch what they perceive as a drain on citizens' loyalty. In South Korea, a 'new' democracy, it has been illegal to tune to North Korean radio or television. Not surprisingly, when in June 1996 a Canadian university student put some North Korean writings on his Home

---

[57] Howard Rheingold, ibid. at 64.

[58] Ibid. at 64–5.        [59] Steven G. Jones, *CyberSociety* 16 (1995).

[60] Ibid. at 18. See also E. Soja, *Postmodern Geographies: The Reassertion of Space in Critical Social Theory* (1989).                                                    [61] Mathews, *supra* n. 49, at 51.

[62] Elkins, *supra* n. 12, at 169.

Page of the World Wide Web, the government in Seoul ordered computer service providers to block its citizens' access to the web site.[63] Germany has extended to the internet its criminal statutes on terrorism and pornography, with penalties not only for originators but also providers. So far, as the failure of the first two prosecutions have demonstrated, enforcement of such laws encounters difficult obstacles in the courts.[64]

In more authoritarian societies, restrictions on access are likely to become more severe as use spreads beyond tiny elites. Iran has made efforts to impose a 'cyberspace curtain', making its Ministry of Posts and Telecommunications the sole provider of access to the internet and banning web sites deemed religiously, politically, or socially offensive to the established communal order. However, even Iranian government officials responsible for enforcement have admitted that '[u]ltimately we know we can't control it mechanically—that we will have to control it spiritually'.[65] It remains to be seen whether public demand, the economic imperatives for keeping abreast of the global information revolution, and the growing capacity of new communications technology to evade censorship will overcome efforts to stifle access in the name of preserving governments' ideas of community values.

These developments presage not the wrongly feared atomization of global society but, rather, progressive—in Elkins' phrase—'unbundling' of those communities that had previously been dictated by kinship and territoriality. And with that have come new communitarianisms: 'the multiplication of social, economic, and political organizations independent of the nation-state and associated with the multiple ways in which each individual chooses to be identified, sorted, targeted and appreciated.'[66] Not incidentally, encouragement to the formation of new communities will not only help to prevent, on the one hand, the dangers of rising personal anomie but also, on the other, the homogenization of cultures in the era of globalization. By allowing idiosyncratic individualists to affiliate in mutual support across traditional divides—the world's champions of Gregorian chants, for one—new technologies help prevent the global homogenization of tastes and values.

In effect, then, such decline as may be observable in civic republicanism and communitarian commitment may simply be the obverse side of the emergence of new 'layers' of association, the formation of many new civil societies cohering around civic virtues (and, alas but of course, also some vices) in response to new and larger common problems and priorities. What is filling the void created by

<hr/>

[63] NY Times, 10 July 1996, at A3.

[64] Charges brought against Angela Marquardt, a leftist thereafter elected to the Federal Parliament, and Felix Somm, accused of child pornography, have not, as of writing, been successful in closing down offending websites or in obtaining convictions. Time Int'l, 14 July 1997, at 30.

[65] Neil MacFarquhar, 'As Western Surf Beckons, Teheran Readies a Cyberspace Curtain' (NY Times Service), Int'l Herald Tribune, 9 Oct. 1996, at 7.     [66] Elkins, *supra* n. 12, at 63.

any decline in traditional communitarianism is not anomie but many new networks of consociational responsibility.

The decline of the state's claim on citizens' exclusive loyalty thus promises to create a roster of personal affiliative options from which persons will make their individual choices. This vista of new opportunities is welcomed by those who understand that 'supranationalism and nationalism are not truly oppositional'[67] and that multiplicity of personal loyalty 'is not meant to eliminate the national state but to create a regime which seeks to tame the national interest with a new discipline'.[68]

Thus perceived, there is little reason to fear the emergence of a modern sense of community based on personal choices made autonomously by those constituting new circles of affinity.[69] Of course 'autonomy' is a relative term when applied to the choices made by individuals all of whom—and all of whose choices—are to some degree historically and culturally conditioned. Since Freud, it has become more difficult to sustain absolute notions about autonomy, individual choice, will, responsibility, and rationality since it is now widely asserted that 'we do not control our own lives in the most fundamental sense'.[70]

Even with that Freudian caveat, however, it is clear that a substantial personal autonomy is both possible and in the future increasingly feasible. Sensibly, the state—the hitherto exclusive repository of collective personal identity—is learning to adjust to a new era in which it coexists with other, individually chosen, foci of personal loyalty and commitment. In the new era there will be few persons who altogether shun commitment. As Aristotle indicates in the quote heading this chapter, only a beast or god has no need of society. Rather, commitments, the bonds of community, will be more valid and stronger, as St Thomas observed about conversions to Christianity, for being emanations of free will.[71]

---

[67] Weiler, *supra* n. 50, at 244.          [68] Ibid. at 249.

[69] This would be equally true of a community constituted exclusively by persons who valued above all else, or even to the exclusion of all competing factors, the particular genetic, cultural, linguistic and religious aspect of their identity. Such a community, so long as it did not preclude persons, who, although sharing the same genes, culture, language, or religion, freely choose to affiliate with communities based on other affinities. Such a voluntarist ethno-cultural demos could choose to coexist with other demoi of which membership is based on shared civic and political values rather than ethno-cultural ones. In practice, however, the nation-based ethno-culturally exclusive community rarely adopts a benevolent live-and-let-live attitude to those of its members who choose another affiliation or towards other affinity groups. It tends to resist especially the notion of individual multi-loyalty, perhaps, as Professor Weiler has suggested, it 'rests . . . in a normative view which wants national self-identity—identified with the State and its organs—to rest very deep in the soul, in a place which hitherto was occupied by religion' ibid. at 255. It may be ventured, however, that the momentum of the modern age is not with such an absolutist quasi-theological view of the state (nor, for that matter, of religion itself).

[70] Nancy Julia Chodorow, 'Towards a Relational Individualism: the Mediation of Self Through Psychoanalysis,' in *Reconstructing Individualism* 197 (Thomas C. Heller, Morton Sosna, & David E. Wellberg eds., 1986).

[71] *Summa Theologiae*, vol. 57, Pt. 3, Question 68, Art. 7 (James J. Cunningham OP trans., 1975).

4. THE LANGUAGE AND CULTURE PROBLEM

It may be argued that the new communities lack the underpinning of common history, culture, and language that bind together the more traditional affiliations. In the absence of a real common language, members of the new communities are unlikely to be able to conduct the sort of vigorous discourse that could be expected to yield agreed values, priorities, policies, and norms. In the absence of a cohesive common culture there will not be agreed values and priorities.

This concern was evident in the *Maastricht* decision of the German Federal Constitutional Court which was asked to rule on the constitutionality of the Maastricht treaty's delegation of further state powers to the European Union. Of especial interest is the opinion of Justice Dieter Grimm, who cautioned against the agreement's implied notion of an emerging European political community. He argued that the 'absence of a European communications system, due chiefly to language diversity, has the consequence that for the foreseeable future there will be neither a European public nor a European political discourse. . . . The European level of politics lacks a matching public'.[72] Without a common language, Grimm wrote, the discourse necessary to the legitimate formation of common values and goals cannot take place. A European authority exercising power without being rooted in a common discursive political tradition cannot be democratic and thus cannot constitute an accountable locus for policy formation or execution. A 'society that wants to constitute itself as a political unit . . . requires a collective identity'.[73]

Grimm's concern that a political society cannot function without a common language and culture has deep historic roots. During the French Revolution, Barère, leader of the Jacobin 'linguistic terror',[74] argued that diversity of tongues in France was a vestige of the king's deliberate policy of divide and rule. 'Citizens,' he proclaimed, 'the language of a free people must be one and the same for all. . . . Let us thus give to the citizens the instrument of public thought, the surest revolutionary agent, the same language.'[75] Without a common language, there could be no republic.[76]

Somewhat the same theme is sounded nowadays by those who seek a constitutional amendment to make English the official language of the United States.[77]

---

[72] Dieter Grimm, 'Does Europe Need a Constitution?', 1 Eur. LJ 282, 296 (1995).

[73] Ibid. at 297.

[74] The phrase is used in Leila Sadat Wexler, 'Official English, Nationalism and Linguistic Terror: A French Lesson', 71 Wash. L. Rev. 285 (1996).

[75] La Rapport Barère, Rapport du Comité de Salut Public sur les Idiomes, Archives Parlementaires, 1re série, T. LXXXIII, séance du 8 pluviôse an II, no. 18, at 713–17. (Paris, Ed. CNRS, 1961) quoted in Wexler, ibid. at 303.

[76] It is interesting to note that, nonetheless, French was not officially designated the official language by the French constitution until 1994 by the 'loi Toubon.' Constitutional Law no. 92.554 of 25 June 1992, Jour. Off. 26 June 1992, at 8406. See also Wexler, ibid. at 317 ff.

[77] This movement is discussed in Wexler, ibid. at 330–69.

n, however, specifically denies that the prerequisite he has in mind is a homogeneous 'Volksgemeinschaft' or ethnic community. He argues, instead, that 'all that is necessary is for the society to have formed an awareness of belonging together that can support majority decisions and solidarity efforts, and for it to have the capacity to communicate about its goals and problems discursively'.[78] But even that much cultural, social, and linguistic unity, Grimm concludes, Europe does not yet have. If Grimm is right about Europe, the same concern, compounded many times, would apply to any regimes of global governance.

The political philosopher Jurgen Habermas, however, has taken issue with Grimm. He replies that any society—except those few seeking cohesion in the 'volk-ish' principle of the classic Hegelian 'nation-state'—is at best an amalgam: not some pre-existing 'primordial substrate but rather an intersubjectively shared context of possible understanding'.[79] In his view, successful institution-building may itself lead to, rather than be the prerequisite for, interactive community and common ways of thinking and acting.

Evidence that Habermas may be right comes, in fact, from Barère's linguistic revolution. In France, it was the Terror's strategy first to create public institutions of education, law-making, and governance, in the knowledge that these would entice people to adopt the common language. Habermas points out that common language evolves as much out of the growth of common institutions— today, television and movies, schools and universities, transactional fora of science and business, easy and cheap travel, and intergovernmental and non-governmental organizations—as the other way around. Habermas' point is that there is a circular, mutually reinforcing flow between the 'institutionalization of citizens' communication' and the growth of communications itself. He thus argues that the existence of a shared sense of social community does not constitute the *a priori* precondition for establishing transnational institutions from which joint values, policies, and actions emanate.[80]

The vibrant communal political life of Switzerland clearly rebuts the extreme assertion that lack of common language inevitably obviates socio-political discourse and shared civic culture. But the language problem, in any event, appears to be solving itself. As Habermas points out, '[e]ven the requirement of a common language—English as a second first language—ought not to be insurmountable with the existing level of formal schooling'.[81] Indeed, the potential of English as at least the 'first second language' is already statistically demonstrable: while there are currently only 350 million persons who speak it as their mother-tongue, for more than 1,400,000,000 persons it is an 'official language', giving it global currency.[82]

---

[78] Grimm, *supra* n. 72, at 297.

[79] Jurgen Habermas, 'Remarks on Dieter Grimm's "Does Europe Need a Constitution?"', 1 Eur. LJ 303, 305 (1995). [80] Ibid. at 306–7.

[81] Ibid. at 307.

[82] David Crystal, *The Cambridge Encyclopedia of Language* 287 (1987).

What Habermas says about institutions preceding socio-cultural integration is an extrapolation from that which has already occurred among persons of many nations voluntarily affiliating with worldwide scientific, cultural, commercial, pedagogic, religious, and other activities. These have already gone some distance towards establishing their particular professional cultures with their common technical lingoes, as well as shared values and priorities.

English would merely be the most recent international second language. Before it, there were French, Latin, and classical Greek. The language barrier, as a factor dividing communities, has been much exaggerated. In the past, absence of a common language did not so much curtail communications between states as *within* them. The ruling classes of Europe spoke Latin, classical Greek, or French to each other, with an occasional lapse into English or German. The Indian elite spoke English. It was the masses who, speaking only Czech, Breton, Macedonian, Tamil, or any of hundreds of other dialects and 'national' tongues, were effectively excluded from the inner circles of power and influence. That, however, was the by-product of social and educational policies that barred the masses from far more than the language-skills of the power-elite. As such deliberate policies of stratification are overcome, so will be the language handicap of the citizenry.

At the end of the twentieth century, in the developed and the rapidly developing nations, ever wider circles of the public have both the ability and valid reasons to communicate beyond the territorial bounds of the state they inhabit; and now, for the first time on a massive scale, they also have the technological means to do so. This societal reconfiguration can be slowed, but will not be stopped, by language barriers. As Benedict Anderson has pointed out, what makes the rise of new 'communities' possible is the 'half-fortuitous, but explosive, interaction between a system of production and productive relations (capitalism), a technology of communications (print), the fatality of human linguistic diversity'. By 'fatality' Anderson means that while language differences can divide, '[p]articular languages can die or be wiped out'.[83] Currently, more than 6,000 languages are spoken in the world, but linguists report that within a generation, at least half of these will disappear.[84] Such natural death of tongues saddens romantic nationalists but gladdens the hearts of scientists, teachers, professionals, politicians, even philosophers, who value the growing ability to communicate and exchange ideas within a widening ambit of peers. The loss of Eyak or Ubykh is not a tragedy comparable to the death of the last condor or panda.

In his study of new 'communities' Anderson was focusing on the phenomenon of decolonized states inventing themselves out of a synthesis of many 'nations'.

---

[83] Benedict Anderson, *Imagined Communities* 42–3 (rev. edn., 1991).
[84] NY Times, 4 Dec. 1997, at A4. See also Paul Lewis, 'Thousands of Languages are Endangered', NY Times, 15 Aug. 1998, at B1.

However, in recent years some of the same forces he detected are also shaping new transnational affinity groups: thus, Anderson's bonding-factors—capitalism and the print media—have evolved into the modern transnational economy and the proliferation of electronic communications.

What appears to be happening in this new age of emergent individual rights and reconfiguration of loyalty systems is best explained in terms of what Professor Alexander Wendt has called a 'sociology of international community'.[85] In his search for an explanatory theory of 'collective identity formation' he found that 'through repeated acts of reciprocal cooperation, actors form mutual expectations that enable them to continue cooperating'. Moreover, 'if we treat identities and interests as always in process during interaction, then we can see how an evolution of cooperation might lead to an evolution of community'.[86] In other words, while orthodox explanations of co-operative behaviour tend to proceed from the assumption of a pre-existing community of shared loyalties and common identity, it is at least as plausible to see (as Wendt and Anderson do) actual co-operative practices as the progenitor of a gradually emerging discursive vocabulary, agreed principles and norms, common loyalty, shared identity, and, at last, a culture of community: what Professor Robert Keohane has called 'epistemic communities'.[87]

## 5. WHAT IS EMERGING: POST POST-MODERNITY

As Joseph Weiler has indicated, the rise of a global culture grounded in the idea of individual autonomy need not destroy traditional communitarian values. Many persons now free to choose among (or renounce) religions may still exercise their new freedom to identify with the faith of their fathers. Or they may adopt the faith of a spouse, or one more congenial than either of these, or they may renounce a commitment of faith in favour of an organized rationalist agnosticism or atheism. More persons will probably identify, in part, with several creeds, or adhere to an organized religion but not necessarily to all its tenets.

So, too, with nationalism. Most persons have now won the right to emigrate and change their nationality. The European Union's 'right of establishment' may become just one instance of this freedom to choose and to move. Persons

---

[85] Alexander Wendt, 'Collective Identity Formation and the International State', 88 Am. Pol. Sci. Rev. 384 (1994).

[86] Ibid. at 390. Although Wendt is speaking, here, of the formation of a global community of socialized states, his observation is equally applicable to the formation of transnational non-governmental interest groups or factions which could be seen as the building blocs of a genuine international community or demos. See also Thomas M. Franck & Edward Weisband, *Word Politics* 129–47 (1972).

[87] See *Knowledge, Power and International Policy Coordination*, 46 Int'l Org., Issue no. 1 (Peter M. Haas ed., 1992).

can opt to be citizens of more than one country. As we have seen, the laws of many states already accommodate, rather than prohibit, dual or multiple nationality.[88] And, moreover, the traditionally strong ties between nationality and habitual residence are almost everywhere loosening.[89]

There may also be an increasingly relaxed attitude, manifest in more accommodating laws, towards the requisites and symbols of patriotism.[90] Not long ago, in Britain and much of the empire, concerts, plays, and even movies invariably concluded with the playing of the national anthem, lustily or desultorily sung by an audience standing at attention. No more.

The pledging of allegiance and singing of anthems may, or may not, become more heartfelt as they cease to be mandatory. Probably, even in a society of genuinely autonomous persons, many will still choose to identify with their territorial community as single-mindedly and tenaciously as did their parents. Those who choose in future to identify exclusively in terms of these older communitarian values and institutions based on traditional territorial, ethnic, tribal, linguistic, and religious elements will still differ from their parents, in that they will make that choice in the face of, and after freely contemplating, other options.

Some among those who do choose among the other options may evince a preference for autonomy as solitude: less peer-group socialization, less government, less sharing, less hectoring by religious, cultural or industrial establishments. Most, however, will simply reflect new interactive interests, affinities, and values.

What is emerging, then, is a global system increasingly characterized by overlapping communities and multivariegated personal loyalties yielding more complex personal identities. This, in itself, is not historically unprecedented. As Harold Jacobson has observed, 'Medieval Europe had many political units and there was considerable interaction among them, but authority patterns were arranged in a series of overlapping layers. Both the pope and the emperor claimed universal authority in certain spheres; and local princes and feudal lords exercised authority in their own domains; and some towns gained virtual autonomy.'[91] This condition of layered loyalties and identities continued until the emergence of the state system after the Peace of Westphalia, which simplified matters by imposing on most persons in Europe an exclusive identity determined by political ties to a sovereign. That identity, conditioned by allegiance to the sovereign, was deemed to take priority over other lingering ties of language, culture and religion. After the French Revolution, this perso-

---

[88] For a discussion of this point see Ch. 4, *supra*.

[89] *The Nottebohm case*, Judgment, 1955 ICJ Rep. 4.

[90] See e.g. the greater constitutional tolerance in US law for refusals to salute the flag, recite the pledge of allegiance and even for flag burning. *Texas v. Johnson*, 491 US 397 (1989) (flag burning); *West Va. State Bd. of Educ. v. Barnette*, 319 US 624 (1943) (refusal to salute the flag).

[91] Jacobson, *supra* n. 40, at 13.

nalized loyalty was replaced by citizenship as the new communitarian identity. With that transformation came a new social force: nationalism.

That force is losing its once-exclusive hold. While still powerful in some places, it is now actively challenged by the claim of a growing number of individuals to invent their own identity.

Now, at the cusp of the twenty-first century, the realities of social interaction, conflict resolution, economic, scientific, and cultural development, and ecological and resource management have combined with various facets of the communications revolution to point us towards the infrastructure of a global civil society. That society features growing, interactive transnational factions, passionate global value-and-policy discourses, and emerging public and private transactional networks: in short, a community of communities is emerging in which, for the first time, individuals are comparatively free to choose the multiple components of their identities and to choose their affinities. As if computerized personal identities can be constituted by adding or deleting almost at will. Thus, 'one might say that an individual in the unbundled world consists of the intersection of multiple communities'[92] even as the world becomes an interactive system in which powerful new communities join states as the principal participants in the processes for making law, developing wealth, controlling crime, and providing health and recreation.

That liberation has begun, but it does not yet engage the majority of the world's people. It may never do so, leaving the world half-determinist and half-autonomous. The direction, however, is towards an eventual outcome in which the dynamism of growing individual freedom engulfs the lingering static forces that confine personal choice by mandating racial, cultural, national, linguistic, and religious particularity. What will then have been wrought is not necessarily world government—some aspects of which, by necessity, are already in place—but, rather, a liberal global neo-community, a civil society based on socially and legally protected individualism.

[92] Elkins, *supra* n. 12, at 180.

# 6

## Freedom of Conscience: A 'Western' Value?

No one must be disturbed because of his opinions, even in religious matters, provided their expression does not trouble the public order established by law.

*Declaration of the Rights of Man and of the Citizen*, Art. 10 Paris, 26 August
1789

### 1. THE AUTONOMOUS CONSCIENCE

A necessary component—perhaps the *sine qua non*—of the new order previewed in Chapter 5 is flexibility on the part of states towards their citizens' increasing desire to design their own identities and to bond with various layers of affinity-based—but non-traditional—community. The precondition for realizing that self-expression is a willingness of states (as well as religions and tribes) to respect individualism, conceding to persons the right to make key decisions regarding identity and to express that right in a broad range of political, cultural, social, and moral choices, including the right of exit.

Is it likely that such recognition of individualism will become the global norm? Is it realistic to expect states and cultures to accommodate so high a degree of personal self-determination? Will established communitarian institutions and societies accede to a global realignment of personal affiliations, bending the old and still-powerful geographic, genetic, and denominational boundaries? We do not know. What is evident is that 500 years ago, throughout the world, persons had very little freedom to choose their nationality, religion, profession, place of residence, and the other aspects of their individual identity. Today, a formal accommodation by the state to personal individuation is no longer a dream. It is not even exceptional, although this transformation of expectations is not invariably evident in state practice.

### 2. THE POSTWAR EMPOWERING OF INDIVIDUAL CONSCIENCE

Such a change has not been gathering momentum, these past fifty years, without incurring some backlash. In Chapter 5, we noted the reaction of some American communitarians, who fear the breakdown of the civic republican spirit. An even stronger reaction has come from some in the non-Western world. As Professor Onuma of Tokyo University has pointed out, to many the 'discourse on human rights is part of the Westcentric intellectual discourse that dominates the entire world. This . . . is foreign to many developing nations because of their diverse civilizational backgrounds' and engenders 'a strong resentment against the political, economic and military hegemony, as well as the imperial and colonial history of Western powers and Japan'.[1] This view is echoed in the West. 'Globalization of law', writes Edinburgh Professor C. M. G. Himsworth, 'becomes, in this respect, merely the Americanization of law' since the 'process of harmonization [is] dominated by the United States.'[2] The object of this chapter is to consider assertions such as those of Onuma and Himsworth that the post-1945 international regime of personal rights is an instrument of Western hegemony.

More specific charges of Western hegemonization are levelled by Professor Makau wa Mutua, who focuses on freedom of religion as a threat to traditional communitarian values and institutions. He sees the impact of free evangelistic advocacy in Africa by the 'messianic faiths' of Christianity and Islam as 'a phenomenon akin to cultural genocide': a 'delegitimization [of African traditions that] can easily lead to the collapse of social norms and cultural identities'.[3] While Mutua does not deplore freedom of conscience *per se*, he sees the messianic faiths exploiting the free market through their dominant fiscal resources and superior educational and medical services and he favours legal protection for embattled traditional indigenous faiths.

The trend is the other way, towards universal protection of religious freedom. The principal international legal guarantee of conscientious liberty is set out in article 18(1) of the 1966 International Covenant on Civil and Political Rights (CCPR),[4] which has been ratified by almost all states of the global system. It also (article 27) prohibits inequality or discrimination based on religion. Despite the near-universal accession of states to the CCPR, some authorities still urged that this global rights approach be replaced, or at least nuanced, by something more sensitive to cultural relativism.[5]

Especially controversial has been the monitoring of entitlements established by the ICCPR, a task the Convention assigns to an elected Human Rights Committee of independent experts. The Committee's work has offended some governments that had regarded their adherence to the Covenant as purely

[1] Onuma Yasuaki, 'In Quest of Intercivilizational Human Rights', Occasional Paper no. 2, at 1, The Asia Foundation, 1996.

[2] C. M. G. Himsworth, 'In a State No Longer: the End of Constitutionalism?' [1996] Pub. L. 639 at 646.

[3] Makau wa Mutua, 'Limitations on Religious Rights: Problematizing Religious Freedom in the African Context', in *Religious Human Rights in Global Perspective* 417–18 (J. D. van der Vyver & J. Wittle, Jr. eds., 1996).                              [4] 999 UNTS 171, 6 ILM 368 (1967).

[5] Martti Koskenniemi, 'The Police in the Temple, Order, Justice and the UN: A Dialectical View', 6 Eur. J. Int'l L. 325 (1995); Ferdinand Teson, 'International Human Rights and Cultural Relativity', 25 Va. J. Int'l L. 869 (1985); Anne F. Bayefsky, 'Cultural Sovereignty, Relativism and International Human Rights', 9 Ratio Juris 42 (1996); Dianne Otto, 'Rethinking the Universality of Human Rights', 29 Col. H.Rts. Rev. 1 (1997).

formal. Inevitably, they were unpleasantly surprised by the Committee's 1993 consensus report interpreting the Covenant's article 18. This declared that the 'right to freedom of thought, conscience and religion (which includes the freedom to hold beliefs) . . . encompasses freedom of thought on all matters, personal conviction and the commitment to religion or belief, whether manifested individually or in community with others' and that 'this provision cannot be derogated from, even in time of public emergency . . .'.[6] Freedom of conscience, the experts said, includes the right to choose one's religious leaders and teachers[7] and 'the right to replace one's current religion or belief with another or to adopt atheistic views . . .'.[8] It also precludes all discrimination in government service or access to education, based on religious tests.[9] Such expansive interpretation of the ICCPR text cannot have been welcomed in some governing circles, where those freedoms are regarded as the subversive influence of America, the devil, or both.

Nevertheless, freedom of conscience is fast becoming an irresistible claim in national and international forums. The European Court of Human Rights, in 1999—in a decision that scarcely raised an eyebrow in Europe—held that three persons elected to San Marino's General Grand Council could not be required by law to take the traditional oath on the 'Holy Gospels' as a prerequisite to taking the seats to which they had been elected. The Court rejected San Marino's argument that the ancient oath merely manifested 'the need to preserve public order, in the form of social cohesion and the citizens' trust in their traditional institutions'. It averred, instead, that freedom of religion is 'one of the foundations of a "democratic society" . . . It is, in its religious dimension, one of the most vital elements that go to make up the identity of believers and their conception of life, but it is also a precious asset for atheists, agnostics, skeptics and the unconcerned. The pluralism indissociable from a democratic society, which has been dearly won over the centuries, depends on it . . .'.[10] Thus, they held, the oath violates article 9 of the European Convention. The Court succinctly admonished the respondent state, holding that 'it would be contradictory to make the exercise of a mandate intended to represent different views of society within Parliament subject to a prior declaration of commitment to a particular set of beliefs'.[11]

---

[6] Report of the Human Rights Committee, A/48/40 (Pt. I), 7 October 1993, General Comment no. 22(48) (art. 18), Annex VI, at 208.          [7] Ibid. at 208.

[8] Ibid. at 208–9.          [9] Ibid. at 210.

[10] European Court of Human Rights: *Buscarini and Others v. San Marino*, applic. no. 24645/94, judgement of 18 Feb. 1999, para. 34. 2 International Law in Brief, no. 3, at 4 (March 1999).

[11] Ibid., paras. 36, 39.

3. ORIGINS, FORCES, AND FACTORS

The idea of free exercise of individual conscience, of course, did not originate with the Covenant and the struggle for implementation is not unique to the Human Rights Committee. These are but one manifestation of a very long chapter in the history of ideas. Progress, as one might expect, has been uneven: remarkable in some places, not much evident in others. The record yields both cause for rejoicing and despair.

But it also yields something else. By studying the progress made towards full implementation of aspects of the principle of individual autonomy we can glimpse some elements of its dynamic: the forces that propel it forward. This, in turn, may help us to judge whether that dynamic, in those societies where it is most developed, is likely to support a more universal prognosis applicable also to those—mostly non-Western—regimes and societies where the principle has lagged, been resisted, or declared inapplicable.

It is primarily to this end that the history of the struggle for freedom of conscience offers rewards. Of the various indicators of individual autonomy, freedom of conscience is probably the most fervently desired by individuals and certainly has been the most strenuously resisted by authorities. The forces for emancipation and for repression, moreover, are not always easy to classify. Historically, the state's resistance to individual nonconformity, in many instances, has been re-enforced by an established church. Yet religion has also played a role in emancipating, as well as suppressing, the autonomous personal conscience. St Paul and St Thomas Aquinas both argued from within the Christian tradition that free will is the necessary precondition for an act of genuine faith.[12] Aquinas, in particular, preached that the individual is endowed with right reason, the key to personal salvation.[13] In sixteenth-century England, '[r]eligious salvation itself changed from a collective to a more individual matter'.[14] At least some of the Protestant reformers seemed to embrace the notion that the Christian faith, in the words of King Edward VI's 1549 Anglican Book of Common Prayer, 'is a relygion to serve God, not in bondage of the figure or shadowe; but in the freedom of spirit . . .'.

This emphasis on personal belief rather than on formal ceremony, of course, did not guarantee freedom of conscience but it did emphasize the inauthenticity of coerced communitarian conformity. This led in time to the 'secularization of

---

[12] St Thomas Aquinas 'resists the forced conversion of Jews and pagans,' in David A. J. Richards, *Toleration and the Constitution* 88 (1986) citing Thomas Aquinas, *Summae Theologiae* 2a 2ae.10, 8, at 61–5.

[13] For the better known contrary tendency in the Christian–Roman Church tradition see St Augustine (Bishop of Hippo Regius in the fourth to fifth centuries, who originated the powerful theory of persecution of dissenters, the schismatic Donatists, in particular), *Letters*, vol. 1, at 187, 203, 368 (Wilfrid Parsons, trans., 1951).

[14] C. John Sommerville, *The Secularization of Early Modern England* 129 (1992).

personhood and association'.[15] And as 'social relations were secularized the sanctity of society was replaced by the sacredness of the individual'.[16] The individual began to emerge from the common mass. In the eighteenth century the British philosophers Locke and Bayle insisted that the independent conscience is 'expressive of an ethical God's imagine in us' and thus independently worthy of the utmost protection from external interference.[17] They advanced the autonomy-enhancing proposition that all expressions of reason proceed from the divine spark that ignites our humanity.

John Locke's *Letters Concerning Toleration*[18] established this essentially religious basis for freedom of conscience: 'The toleration of those that differ from others in matters of religion is so agreeable to the Gospel of Jesus Christ, and to the genuine reason of mankind,' he wrote, 'that it seems monstrous for men to be so blind as not to perceive the necessity and advantage of it in so clear a light.'

Locke's ideas inspired American colonists, and especially its intellectual leaders, Thomas Jefferson and James Madison, to provide in their new federal framework a specific guarantee that state coercion could no longer be applied to the design of religious worship or to secure persons' attendance at specified religious services.[19] With the ratification, in 1791, of the first amendment to the US Constitution, the federal government was enjoined from making any law 'respecting an establishment of religion, or prohibiting the free exercise thereof . . .'.

This constitutional innovation has 'two prongs',[20] one guaranteeing free exercise of conscience and the other prohibiting the establishment of a state religion. The free exercise clause has the longer political history. Its origins are traceable to the British Toleration Act of 1689,[21] which exempted most nonconformists from the penalties of certain laws such as those pertaining to seditious libel, so long as their dissent did not extend beyond what the Act allowed. Thus laymen, if they swore allegiance to the king and renounced transubstantiation, were pretty much free to worship as they pleased, in the more liberal spirit that had followed the overthrow of the last of the Stuarts and the ascent of a comparatively tolerant House of Orange.

They were free, however, not as of right but as of the king's grace, and his majesty's tolerance had its limits.[22] By 1697, King William had wearied of religious controversy, and ordered that his criminal courts and sheriffs execute 'all laws against laymen who scandalized or disturbed the peace of the realm by their religious opinions'.[23] In the Old Bailey in 1698, Susan Fowls was convicted of blasphemy and was pilloried, fined, and jailed for having 'passed the bounds of decency by cursing the Lord's Prayer and verbally abusing Christ'.[24] As the

---

[15] Ibid.     [16] Ibid. at 143.     [17] Richards, *supra* n. 12, at 119.
[18] See Letters 1–4: *The Works of John Locke*, vol. 6, at 1–574 (Thomas Davison, 1823).
[19] Richards, *supra* n. 12, at 111.     [20] Ibid.     [21] 1 Will. and Mar. Cap. 18, 1689.
[22] See, generally, W. K. Jordan, *The Development of Religious Toleration in England*, 4 vols. (1932–40); Leonard W. Levy, *Blasphemy* 226 (1993).     [23] Levy, ibid. at 235.
[24] Ibid.

beneficiaries of the new toleration were soon to learn, it was one thing for the state to accommodate private nonconformity but quite another to endure public criticism of the orthodox beliefs that, it was commonly understood, enshrined the values and preserved the peace of society.

The other prong of the American Constitution's First Amendment, prohibiting the 'establishment of religion', had different origins. Even Britain's Glorious Revolution of 1688 had retained the Anglican establishment in modified form, and none of the writings of John Locke actually argued for the disestablishment of the Church of England. Rather, the second prong's origins are to be sought elsewhere: in the founding of Rhode Island colony on the hewn granite of Roger Williams' disestablishmentarian principles.[25]

Disestablishment, the severance of historically rooted alliance between church and state, is a more radical proposition than is mere toleration. Williams was the foremost seventeenth-century advocate of complete religious freedom, but he had scant regard for mere toleration. While he wrote that there 'is no sin ordinarily greater against God then to use violence against the Consciences of men', he deplored toleration as exemplified by the Toleration Act, for it pretended to give by law that to which all were inherently entitled as creatures of God. In the words of an admiring nineteenth-century European scholar, the theories of

freedom in Church and State, taught in the schools of philosophy in Europe were [in Rhode Island] brought into practice in the government of a small community. It was prophesied that the democratic attempts to obtain universal suffrage, a general elective franchise, annual parliaments, entire religious freedom, and the Miltonic schism, would be of short duration. But these institutions have not only maintained themselves here, but have spread over the whole union. They have superseded the autocratic commencements of Carolina and New York, the high church party of Virginia, the theocracy in Massachusetts, and the monarchy throughout America; they have given laws to one quarter of the globe, and, dreaded for their moral influence, they stand in the background of every democratic struggle in Europe.[26]

Particularly potent was Williams' integration of religious and political liberty. 'Where civil liberty is entire,' he wrote, 'it includes liberty of conscience, and where liberty of conscience is entire, it includes civil liberty.'[27] These views were advanced by Jefferson and Madison in their advocacy of the Virginia Bill for Religious Freedom, in 1786, which disestablished the Anglican church. The

---

[25] Roger Williams, *The Essential Rights and Liberties of Protestants, A Seasonable Plea for the Liberty of Conscience and the Right of private Judgment, In Matters of Religion, Without any Control from Human Authority* (1744); Roger Williams, *The Bloody Tenet, of Persecution for Cause of Conscience* (1644), reprinted in *The Founders' Constitution*, vol. 5, at 48–9 (excerpts) (P. Kurland & R. Lerner eds., 1987). See also James E. Ernst, *The Political Thought of Roger Williams* (1929).

[26] Ernst, ibid. at 1, citing Gervinius, *Introduction to the History of the Nineteenth Century* 65, in turn quoted in Narragansett Club Publications, vol. I, Introd., at 3.

[27] Ernst, ibid. at 203. No citation is given.

Virginia law, and the First Amendment, each went a long step beyond the English Toleration Act of 1689, enforcing a clean break between political authority and all institutionalized religions. In his plea for legal disestablishment in Virginia, Jefferson argued against 'the impious presumption of legislators and rulers, civil as well as ecclesiastical, who, being themselves but fallible and uninspired men, have assumed dominion over the faith of others, setting up their own opinions and modes of thinking, as the only true and infallible, and as such, endeavouring to impose them on others, hath established and maintained false religions over the greatest part of the world and through all time'. He added that 'our civil rights have no dependence on our religious opinions, any more than on our opinions in physicks or geometry . . .'.[28]

These ideas of toleration and disestablishment may be said to have a Western provenance, if by that one means, in a narrow chronological sense, that they first found general political acceptance in societies spread around the North Atlantic littoral. But the same could be said of gravity, or Mendel's Law, neither of which are today thought to be particularly 'Western'. Locke, Williams, and Jefferson may have been products of the Western European Enlightenment, but the ideas they espoused were as eagerly embraced several centuries later by Jawaharlal Nehru, who regarded them as essential principles upon which to found an independent non-sectarian India.[29] They were influential, too, on the thinking of Nelson Mandela, as evidenced by the constitution for a new Republic of South Africa adopted in 1996.[30] This is not to deny the evident fact that, towards the end of the second millennium, much of the world is still being governed by a political establishment that includes a designated church and its ecclesiastical hierarchy.[31] But the momentum, however long it takes to develop and despite episodic backsliding, is with toleration and disestablishment.

The First Amendment's two ideas—toleration and disestablishment—even if still not universally emulated, have both reflected and enhanced a powerful transformation underway in human teleology.

What has created this momentum? The intellectual power of its advocates, perhaps, but also the more general transformation of belief-systems first in Western, and more recently in some non-Western, societies. This enlightenment has altered the balance between belief and doubt, faith and scepticism, tilting it radically in favour of the latter. It was brought about not primarily by theologians but by biologists, chemists, physicists, astronomers, industrialists, and mathematicians. When the spirit of sceptical inquiry reached theology, social and political philosophy, and sociology, then, there too, human reason was elevated above divine revelation. 'Beyond any reasonable doubt nearly all

---

[28] Thomas Jefferson, A Bill for Establishing Religious Freedom, 12 June 1979, in 1 Kurland & Lerner, eds., *supra* n. 25, at 77.    [29] The Constitution of India §25 (1950 as amended).
[30] Constitution of the Republic of South Africa §§9(3), 15 (1996).
[31] David Ziskind, Labor Provisions in Constitutions of Europe, 6 Comp. Lab. L. 311, 374 (1984). Examples include England, Greece, much of Scandinavia and of the Islamic world.

America's Founders qualify on this score,' Professor John Murrin has observed. 'Jefferson and Adams certainly fit that description, Madison . . . seemed much more comfortable with nature's supreme being than with God's revelation by the 1780's. He looked increasingly to history, not the Bible, for political guidance. James Wilson also believed that the Bible usefully reinforced moral precepts that we learned through our moral sense and reason, not the other way around.' In effect, the Founders 'took Protestant private judgement a step beyond earlier eras and used it to evaluate the plausibility of Scripture itself. . . . They flatly rejected miracles' and 'Jefferson advised his nephew [that] one should read the Bible as one would any other book, accepting what is edifying and rejecting what is fantastic . . .' including, in particular, as he advised Adams, 'the fable' of the Virgin birth. In drafting the Constitution, the large majority of Founders refused to invoke God or providence, choosing instead to construct 'a machine that would go by itself'.[32]

The cause of rationalism and scepticism was taken up a decade later by the French Revolution and, later, by Karl Marx.[33] The 'Three Revolutions' permanently undermined the previously prevalent conviction that religion must play a leading role in governance. They rejected the widespread belief that establishment of religion validated and legitimated communitarian values. In the nineteenth century it gradually became thinkable, at least in Western nations, that the role of governments should be limited to the defence and protection of property—seen by Locke as the essential basis of individual liberty—and to the provision of other essential social services. The rest, it became commonplace to assert, should be left to the individual. Jefferson put it in this pithy phrase: 'it does me no injury for my neighbour to say there are twenty gods, or no god. It neither picks my pocket nor breaks my leg.'[34] The state thus ought not to enforce any view, or even multiple views, of religion or of morality, insofar as private beliefs posed no threat to the private beliefs and property of others. In Madison's more elegant formulation, the government had no calling to deny 'equal freedom to those whose minds have not yet yielded to the evidence which has convinced us'.[35]

Despite these triumphantly optimistic early American libertarian views, the 200-year-long struggle for unfettered self-expression in matters of conscience

---

[32] John M. Murrin, 'Religion and Politics in America from the First Settlements to the Civil War', in *Religion and American Politics* 19, 32 (Mark A. Noll ed., 1990).

[33] To Marx, 'the existence of religion is the existence of a defect' and 'the source of this defect can only be sought in the nature of the state itself'. Karl Marx, *Selected Writings*, 'On the Jewish Question' 8 (David McLellan ed., 1977). Nevertheless, Marx did not at first advocate abolition, but freedom, of religion. In 1870, during the Paris commune, he wrote: 'the pay of the priest, instead of being extorted by the tax gatherer, should only depend on the spontaneous action of the parishioners' religious instincts.' Marx, 'The Civil War in France', in Marx & Engels, *Selected Works*, vol. 1, at 525 (1955).

[34] Thomas Jefferson, *Notes on the State of Virginia* 159 (William Peden ed., 1955).

[35] James Madison, *Memorial and Remonstrance Against Religious Assessment*, in *The Mind of the Founder: Sources of the Political Thought of James Madison* 9 (rev. edn., Marvin Meyers ed., 1981).

has never quite ended. The French Revolution's *Declaration*, cited at the beginning of this chapter, more restates than concludes the struggle, for it leaves undecided who should declare whether any particular free expression really does 'trouble the public order established by law'. Even in the US, the outcome of this struggle has never been completely certain. To this day the conflict continues, now waged primarily between mainstream churches that favour freedom of conscience and the vociferous right-wing fringes that still favour a 'dictatorship of religious values . . .'.[36] Nevertheless, in America the trend seems clear and the febrile fringe has had little success in exchanging its passions for the hard currency of laws and institutions. The Constitution and its judicial interpreters have erected considerable obstacles against enforced conformity and, today, even in many American churches there is a humanist tendency to translate God into a shared morality which religious leaders have sought to shape by preaching and teaching, but which, ultimately, is the discursively derived sum of temporal personal beliefs. The emphasis of much religion in the time of free conscience thus is increasingly on influencing but not coercing 'the individual's system of values'.[37]

Professor David Richards rightly summarizes the majority's belief: if we are to have 'any rights, we must have this right, the inalienable right to conscience'.[38] In that view, a free marketplace of ideas is as intellectually optimal for moral and social development as a free economic market is for economic growth.

## 4. THE OPPOSITION TO FREEDOM OF CONSCIENCE

Against the advocates of freedom of conscience stands, and has long stood, an equally diverse array that sees it as no more 'natural' or legally desirable that each person should be entitled to design a personal belief system than to determine whether to steal bread or cross the street at the red light. These opponents can be seen as every bit as embedded in 'Western' thought and culture as are the progenitors of toleration. The reasons they advance against free and unfettered exercise of conscience, moreover, are just as varied as those for toleration. They include the following:

1. Conscience (or 'inner light') can become perverted and those so afflicted lack the rationality essential to freedom. When that happens, the paternal society must intervene, as it would with other delusional persons, to protect them from the consequences of their own self-destructive wilfulness. This was the anti-toleration position taken late in life by St Augustine towards Donatist

---

[36] E. J. Dionne, Jr., 'Religion and Politics,' NY Times, 15 Sept. 1987, at A19.
[37] Robert Wuthnow, '*Quid Obscurum*: The Changing Terrain of Church-State Relations,' in Mark A. Noll, ed., *supra* n. 32, at 337, 347.  [38] Richards, *supra* n. 12, at 85–102.

and other heretics. That line of thought led, eventually, to the excesses of the Spanish Inquisition.[39] It also inspired Calvin to burn Michael Servetus and other Protestant heretics. It may have its modern analogue in the death sentence (fatwah) imposed on the author Salman Rushdie by the Ayatollah Khomeini,[40] or the 1996 decision by Egypt's Court of Cassation to divorce a happily married couple because the husband, Professor Nasr Abu Zeid, was held to have deviated, in his writings, from orthodox Koranic exegesis.[41]

2. Religious truth is revealed institutionally and is worked out through institutional traditions. The validity of these beliefs no more depends on individual assent than do other accepted social conventions such as the alphabet, the numerical system, the calendar, or rules of etiquette. The individual, although possessing free will, has an obligation to accept these traditions. To function in society, persons must repress doubt and accept on faith that which is traditional and, thus, true: at least true for those within the system in which the institutions and traditions operate. This, approximately, is the position regarding doctrine currently taken by the Catholic hierarchy and, to some extent, also by some other 'established' churches of Western and Orthodox Christianity, as well as by mainstream Islam.

3. A society, to function as a community, needs certain common values, beliefs, and ceremonies of rededication. These unite it, give it a sense of common purpose and support a system of restraint on otherwise unbridled individualistic self-seeking. The 'truth' of these values, beliefs, and ceremonies, while unknowable in any epistemological sense, is adequately demonstrable in utilitarian terms through evidence of the society's right-functioning. That this belief-system thus is only contingently justified need not make its guardians less zealous in demanding individual conformity with the common conscience of the community. In the West, this line of justification is usually employed by secular 'religions', including extreme nationalisms, and by 'scientific' Marxism–Leninism.[42] (In Chapter 5 we saw a secular faith in common values espoused by such non-Marxist communitarians as Professors

---

[39] St Augustine, *Letters, supra* n. 13. Richards, *supra* n. 12, at 87–8. See also Peter Brown, *Religion and Society in the Age of St. Augustine* 260–78 (1972).

[40] See M. M. Slaughter, 'The Salman Rushdie Affair: Apostasy, Honor, and Freedom of Speech', 79 Va. L. Rev. 153, 154 (1993).

[41] Professor Nasr Abu Zeid and his wife, Ibtihal Younis, also a Professor, were ordered to separate because of the husband's unbelief. Both had fled to The Netherlands, where his life was believed to be in jeopardy. The decision was publicly and vehemently opposed by leaders of Egypt's Organization for Human Rights as highly destructive of that nation's emerging civil society. NY Times, 6 Aug. 1996, at A6. It was subsequently suspended by Egypt's highest court. NY Times, 20 Dec. 1996, at A17. *See discussion*: J. Miller, 'New Tack for Egypt's Islamic Militants: Imposing Divorce,' NY Times, 28 Dec. 1996, at 22.

[42] Paul Mojzes, *Religious Liberty in Eastern Europe and the USSR: Before and After the Great Transformation* 38–48 (1992). According to Lenin, from the perspective of the state, religion ought to be a private affair but from the perspective of the Party, religion must be fought. V. Lenin, 'To the Rural Poor,' *Collected Works*, vol. 6, at 402 (1972).

Etzioni and Sandel.) What distinguishes 'secular' and essentially non-deistic religions from agnostic humanism is the high value the former place on conformity and their rejection of the latter's subjectivism and individual choice. In the case of Marxist–Leninist doctrine, for example, the rejection of religion as dangerous 'opium of the masses'—a term frequently borrowed from Marx by Lenin (who rendered it 'opium *for* the masses')[43]—was to lead not to liberal heterodoxy but to the establishment of a new orthodoxy in the form of credal 'scientific materialism'.[44]

These three rationalia for suppressing freedom of conscience, although also prevalent in some non-Western societies, remain part of the discourse in even the most liberal Western communities, where they have a long provenance and some continuing contemporary purchase. That does not make intolerance and conformity any more a Western idea (or a non-Western one) than is conscientious freedom.

Non-Western intolerance is not a peculiarly Islamic phenomenon, but elements of all three conceptual bases for denying freedom of individual conscience are evident in contemporary Islamicism. During the United Nations' debate on the Declaration of Human Rights, the Saudi Arabian delegate, Ambassador Baroody, called attention to the fact that 'the declaration was based largely on Western patterns of culture, which were frequently at variance with the pattern of culture of Eastern States'.[45] In particular, he sought to delete from the Declaration any reference to the right of individuals to change religious beliefs.[46] In this he was supported by Iraq[47] and Syria[48] but not by Lebanon,[49] Turkey,[50] and Egypt. In the event, the Saudi amendment failed to be adopted by 27 votes to 5, with 12 abstentions.[51]

In explaining Pakistan's ambiguity, its delegate, Sir Zafrullah Khan, admitted that 'the problem . . . involved the honour of Islam'. He added, however, that 'the Moslem religion had unequivocally proclaimed the right to freedom of conscience and had declared itself against any kind of compulsion in matters of faith or religious practice'.[52] Ambassador Khan quoted the Koran: 'Let he who chooses to believe, believe, and he who chooses to disbelieve, disbelieve.'[53] Egypt's representative, although having voted against the Saudi initiative, nevertheless expressed concern that the Declaration's provision on freedom and tolerance, in permitting autonomous exercise of individual conscience might also seem to license the activities of aggressive Western Christian

---

[43] Mojzes, ibid. at 41–2.    [44] Ibid. at 44.

[45] Official Record of the UN General Assembly, 3rd Sess., 1948–9, 3rd Cttee, Part II, at 49.

[46] Ibid. at 391, 396.    [47] Ibid. at 402.    [48] Ibid. at 403.

[49] Ibid. at 399.    [50] Ibid. at 397.

[51] Ibid. at 406. The negative votes were cast by Afghanistan, Iraq, Pakistan, Saudi Arabia, and Syria.

[52] Ibid., 182nd Plenary Mtg., 10 Dec. 1948, at 891.    [53] Ibid. at 890.

missionaries in seeking converts in Islamic countries.[54] He warned that Egypt had not intended to affirm a legal right to preach error.

It continues to be difficult to reconcile the burgeoning canon of human rights law with the values of self-described 'communitarian' religions like Islam, which insist that individuals are defined by their adherence to the community and not vice versa. Human rights, on the other hand, tend to elevate individual claims over communitarian values, including some that are cherished by tendencies within the Roman Catholic and Islamic faiths. Papal displeasure with global efforts to enunciate and implement women's reproductive autonomy[55] parallels Islamic interest in protecting its societies from non-Islamic missionaries. While the Koran may extend some tolerance to submissive Christians and Jews—'People of the Book'[56]—it is less accommodating to heathen 'People of the Fire',[57] and not at all to those who would openly practise or propagate rival faiths in Islam's bosom. 'Oh you who believe,' it warns, 'take not in except your own kind; for [the unbelievers] will spare nothing to corrupt you. They wish for your destruction. The aspersions of their mouths [against you] have already been manifest and what is yet hidden in their bosoms is worse still . . . '.[58]

Thus, Saudi Arabia, citing its religious obligations, has steadfastly refused to accept not only the UN's Human Rights Declaration, but the International Covenant on Civil and Political Rights.[59] Islamic states also played a leading role in changing the draft text of the General Assembly's more recent UN Declaration on the Elimination of All Forms of Intolerance and of Discrimination Based on Religion or Belief.[60] Deleted were provisions that recognized 'the right to choose, manifest and change one's religion or belief'.[61] The Saudis have also refused to accede to the Convention on the Elimination of All Forms of Discrimination Against Women (CEDAW),[62] to which there are currently more than 150 state parties. Egypt and some other Islamic countries, having adhered, entered reservations to the effect that they are 'willing to comply with the content of this article, provided that such compliance does not run counter to the Islamic Sharia'.[63] This lawyerly formula reflects the dilemma of some Muslim states caught between demands for strict and traditional interpretation

---

[54] Ibid., 183rd Plenary Mtg., 10 Dec. 1948, at 913.

[55] B. Crossette, 'Vatican Drops Fight Against UN Population Document', NY Times, 10 Sept. 1994, at 5.                                                      [56] Holy Koran, 5: 12–18.

[57] Ibid. at 9: 3–4 and 9: 113.          [58] Ibid. at 3: 118–19.

[59] International Covenant on Civil and Political Rights [hereafter ICCPR], 99 UNTS 171, 16 Dec. 1966. Saudi Arabia is not a party.

[60] GA Res. 36/55, GAOR, 36 Sess. Supp. no. 51 at 171, UN Doc. A/36/51 (1981).

[61] 1981 UNYB 880.

[62] 1249 UNTS 13. Entered into force on 3 Sept. 1981.

[63] See Declaration and Reservations to CEDAW, reprinted in Multilateral Treaties Deposited with the Secretary General, at 169 (1995) (St/Leg/Ser.E/14). See also the ratification of Iraq, ibid. at 171; Kuwait, ibid.; and Libya, ibid. at 172.

of their theological canon and a desire to avoid outright confrontation with widely recognized human rights principles.

Because it seeks to protect communitarian cohesion around the True Word of the Prophet, Saudi law firmly 'indicates a legal preference for Islamic doctrine, customs, and values as well as for persons of Islamic faith'.[64] 'Islam', literally, means 'submission'. While contemporary Islam has many faces, they appear to have in common an intense focus on the law, based on the *Koran*, supplemented by the *Sunna* or practices and sayings of the prophet, which expresses the essence of the *ummah* or community. So strong is this bond that, to an extent, it 'replaces other boundaries of corporate identity such as family, tribe and nation'.[65] It especially is intended to preclude any sense of a personal, autonomous identity. While there is room for case-by-case interpretation of doctrine and by the leading collections of tradition such as the *Bukhari*, that interpretative function is vested in those communally authorized and certainly not in the individual person. In cases of doubt, one may consult the legal interpreter of one's choice, but no person may make the call on his or her own.[66]

The effect is to subordinate to an essentially codified way of life what, in one stream of Christian tradition, is the individual's inherent and divine capacity for 'right reason'. The Ayatollah Khomeini's fatwah ordering the death of novelist Salman Rushdie for his 'blasphemy' in *The Satanic Verses*, has been displayed as an example of this Islamic ethos. As Professor M. M. Slaughter has explained,

Whereas the Western liberal tradition places priority on individual autonomy, the Islamic tradition presents a communitarian view in which the concept of the self is realized collectively in the community of Islam and is defined through traditions and concepts of honor. The concept of the autonomous self requires the free speech principle; the socially situated self of Islamic society necessarily rejects free speech in favour of prohibitions against insult and defamation.[67]

For that reason, the Ayatollah's fatwah ordered the death not only of Rushdie but also of his publishers, calling 'on all zealous Muslims to execute them quickly, wherever they may be found' as penalty for blaspheming against the 'Muslim sanctities'.[68]

How profound a challenge are authoritarian religions to the liberal and individualistic conscience?[69] There can be little doubt that they offer a starkly different vision of personal identity. In Islam, Slaughter contends, 'there is no

---

[64] Note: 'Kiss of Death: Application of Title VII's Prohibition Against Religious Discrimination in the Kingdom of Saudi Arabia', Brigham Young U.L. Rev. 399, 408 (1994).

[65] Slaughter, *supra* n. 40, at 173.

[66] Majid Khadduri & Herbert J. Liebesny, eds., 1 *Law in the Middle East* 72–6 (1955).

[67] Slaughter, *supra* n. 40, at 155.

[68] Daniel Pipes, *The Rushdie Affair: The Novel, the Ayatollah, and the West* 27 (1990). The Japanese translator of the book was indeed murdered and an attempt was made on the life of the Italian translator. Slaughter, ibid. at 160–1.

[69] Slaughter, *supra* n. 40, at 189 and authorities cited therein.

*a priori* self as such, but only self as expressed in, and realized through consti-
tutive attachments and relations'.[70] Samuel P. Huntington has concluded that
this creates a wide and essentially unbridgeable chasm between a West devoted
to individual values arrived at through personal choice and the rest of the
world, in which these values are either reviled or relegated to a minor place.
He starkly contrasts Western individualism with an irreconcilably distinct
collectivism elsewhere, thereby endorsing the view that 'the values that are
most important in the West are least important worldwide'.[71] Thus, he sees
an inherent, absolutely fundamental distinction between the Western liberal
tradition of personal autonomy, democracy, the rule of law, religious freedom,
and toleration on the one hand and the rest of the world's regard for social
cohesion and conformity to community values.

Huntington also rejects the theory that all societies are at different places, but
moving in the same direction, on a common road. He doubts that 'modernization' of non-Western societies will have any significant effect on their values.
'Modernization and economic development,' he claims, 'neither require nor
produce cultural westernization. To the contrary, they promote a resurgence of,
and renewed commitment to, indigenous cultures.'[72] These 'indigenous cultures'—individualism and democracy in the West and communitarian authoritarianism elsewhere—are immutable and irreconcilable, making an historic
confrontation almost inevitable.

But is East really East and West really West? How immutable and irreconcilable are these cultures? The question, to be answered seriously, must be understood to have both latitudinal and longitudinal aspects. Latitudinally, a credible
answer requires a careful comparison of the competing tendencies across the
spectrum of contemporary societies, both Eastern and Western, and also within
those societies. What, for example, is one to make of Israel, an essentially
Western, modern, urbanized, and industrialized society, yet one in which only
orthodox rabbis may perform legally sanctioned Jewish marriages?[73] Does the
law reflect Israel's deeply embedded community values, or only some far less-
authentic happenstance of its political culture? As one examines individual
nations—Western and non-Western—the binary categorization begins to fall
apart and the reality does not appear to be nearly as simple and schematic as
Huntington proposes.

Longitudinally, a credible answer requires an examination of the provenance
of modern Western tolerance, its respect for individual conscience and values.
How long has Western culture been identified with democracy, toleration, and

---

[70] Ibid.
[71] Samuel P. Huntington, 'The West: Unique, Not Universal', 75 *Foreign Affairs*, no. 6, at 28, 33–5
and accompanying notes (1996).                                        [72] Ibid. at 37.
[73] See H. Shapiro, 'A Wedding Ceremony for the Tel Aviv Yuppie', The Jerusalem Post, 26 Aug.
1994, at 8B.

respect for individual human rights? A clear-eyed examination of the record will show that, a few centuries ago, we were all—as it were—Islamic fundamentalists.

## 5. THE LATITUDINAL EVIDENCE

Let us focus first, however, on the latitudinal aspect. Here, Huntington's evidence supporting the cultural collision theory is far from convincing. For example, most Americans and many other 'Westerners' probably not only do not oppose, but actually share with non-Western societies a commitment to community-based values and identity. As indicated in Chapter 5, the difference between 'liberal' and 'communitarian' societies is less evident in the value each places on community than in the extent to which the individual is free to self-determine his or her affiliative choices and concomitant values. Liberal communities do exist in profusion. What most distinguishes them from more traditional communitarian societies is that they tend to be voluntary associations, their membership not exclusively predetermined by fixed historic, cultural, national or religious tradition. It might therefore be more accurate to speak less of Western individualism, than of Western 'communities constituted by free choice', in explaining alleged differences between East and West.

This does not eliminate the differences between Western and other cultures, but it describes them more accurately. It also softens the differences, revealing them to be matters of degree, emphasis, or shading. In traditional communitarian society, what is valued is social order and fixed role-assignment. Virtue consists of living up to the demands imposed by one's assigned role in the community.[74] The social and educational institutions of traditional communitarian societies are deemed to have an obligation not to inform at random or encourage intellectual questioning but to inculcate in accordance with 'fundamental goals for the protection, restoration and improvement of public order . . .'.[75] What Professor Frances Foster has called 'the Parental Theory' of socialization is employed 'to remedy . . . popular naivete and inexperience with an information policy that is protective and educational. As a protective measure, the parental theory categorically rejects the notion of a free market of competing ideas. It views such a scheme as detrimental to the interests of both individuals and society.'[76]

However, even in the most individuated Western societies there are today still remnants of a lively culture of enforced social coherence and not inconsiderable

---

[74] See, e.g. Alasdair MacIntyre, *After Virtue: A Study in Moral Theory* 190–209 (1981). See also the discussion of the views of Michael J. Sandel in Ch. 5, *supra*.

[75] W. Michael Reisman, 'Institutions and Practices for Restoring and Maintaining Public Order', 6 Duke J. Comp. & Int'l L. 175, 179–80 (1995).

[76] Frances H. Foster, 'Information and the Problem of Democracy: The Russian Experience', 45 Am. J. Comp. L. 243, 265–6 (1996).

social pressures to conform. The minority of extremely orthodox Jews in Israel, a relatively 'Western' state, have long used their balance of power in Parliament to impose elements of their communitarian sabbatical theology on the largely non-observant majority. Even lunatic-fringe 'freemen' in Montana, while asserting their extreme autonomy against all organized government, huddle in tight little social and military formations. And, in America, as in other democracies, there are parents whose parentalism extends to demanding the teaching of what they regard as fundamental orthodoxies. They oppose the teaching of evolution in school, seek to ban books and films, and ostracize people for being 'different'. Among the 'liberated' young, too, there are obvious peer-pressures to conform to the latest styles in language, deportment, culture, and taste. Thus induced conformity is not exotic in Western society, sometimes as the result of policy and often as a consequence of mere myopia. As an example of the latter, very little effort is made in Western educational institutions to offer a range of cultural, religious, or social options beyond the prevailing norms and values of the dominant society, especially during students' formative years.

Moreover, fanaticism, including death threats against those who offend extreme religious sensibilities, are not uniquely problems of Islam. Fanatical fundamentalism is a force in all five major religions—Buddhism, Christianity, Hinduism, Islam, and Judaism—and, across denominations, it pursues some strikingly similar objectives: particularly the subordination of women.[77] For example, in the United States, anti-abortion radicals have resorted to murder to 'save the lives' of the unborn. No religion or community has a monopoly of fanatics. In Israel, numerous death threats were made against judges of the Supreme Court after they unanimously acquitted John Demjanjuk of being Treblinka concentration camp's 'Ivan the Terrible'.[78] What is seen in the West as Islamic extremism is more often the doings of fanatical fringes, although, exceptionally, in the cases of Iran and Afghanistan, the fringe did succeed, for a time, in becoming the government.

Despite commonalities, there are distinctions to be made between so-called individualistic and communitarian societies. One of these is how they react to religious apostasy: individual exit from the community's prevailing religion and entry into a different set of beliefs. In individualistic, democratic communities, persons encounter few hurdles in disaffiliating. In traditional communitarian societies, on the contrary, it may be possible, even easy, for an outsider to enter the faith, but almost impossible to exit. Jane Kramer has aptly referred to Islam as 'a one-way door, because you can enter Islam easily but can never leave it'.[79]

---

[77] Courtney W. Howland, 'The Challenge of Religious Fundamentalism to the Liberty and Equality Rights of Women: An Analysis Under the United Nations Charter', 35 Col. J. Transnat'l L. 271 (1997).

[78] A. LaGuardia, 'Nazi Death Camp Guard's not Ivan the Terrible', The Daily Telegraph (London), 30 July 1993, at 8.

[79] Jane Kramer, 'Letter from Europe', The New Yorker, 14 Jan. 1991, at 60, 71.

Even this, however, is effectively true of only *some* Islamic societies. The more moderate, while still regarding exit as sinful, would leave punishment to God.

Most Muslims do regard apostasy as an insult to the Islamic community and to God and there is little Islamic counterpart to the tendency of Americans to go denomination-shopping. In the United States, even though a majority of persons still regard themselves as believers, 'sociologists of religion say denominational loyalty has deteriorated markedly since the 1960s. In its place has grown a spiritual searching that can lead people far beyond the faith into which they were born'.[80]

It appears that there *are* distinctions between such traditional communitarian societies as are found in the Islamic world and the more individualistic societies characteristic of the West, but that these are matters of degree, of a spectrum rather than simply of polarities. Thus, in the West, when very conservative Muslims seek to put their beliefs in practice, they, like Christians in Muslim countries, may encounter problems with the law. A recent example is the arrest and criminal indictment of two Iraqi men in their thirties, who had married the 13- and 14-year-old daughters of Iraqi refugees, residents of Ohio, in strict accordance with Islamic tradition. The grooms were charged with rape and the women's parents with child abuse and contributing to the delinquency of minors.[81]

What seems to be occurring, here, is a series of skirmishes where cultures overlap, not titanic clashes of civilizations. Also evident is a gradual accrual of common ground, despite resistance from a wide variety of Western and Eastern fundamentalists, nationalists, and anti-globalists. An example of common ground was provided recently by a court in Pakistan's rigorously traditional society, which held that fathers do not any longer have the right to control their daughters' choice of spouses. A three-judge bench of the Lahore High Court decided by 2 to 1 that a marriage of an adult without the traditional prior permission of a *wali* (guardian) is not invalid in Islamic law.[82] That decision has since been judicially emulated in other instances of 'love marriage'.[83] As Ann Elizabeth Mayer more generally points out, 'Muslims have taken many differing positions on human rights, including the unqualified endorsement of international human rights as fully compatible with their culture and religion.'[84] She points out that human rights constitute but one institutional cluster adopted and adapted by Islamic societies from the West, the state itself being another Westernism. It thus cannot be said that contemporary Islamic thought remains impervious to the assimilation of new, non-Islamic ideas and their adaption to

---

[80] Gustav Niebuhr, 'For 360 Years, a Church that Endures', NY Times, 7 Apr. 1996, at 12. But that phenomenon is much less apparent in other 'Western' nations, where church adherence, however nominal, has remained consistent even as actual belief in doctrine has withered away.

[81] NY Times, 2 Dec. 1996, at A10.        [82] The Scotsman, 11 Mar. 1997, at 10.

[83] 'Disputed Marriage Validated in Pakistan', NY Times, 19 Feb. 1999, at A10.

[84] Ann Elizabeth Mayer, *Islam and Human Rights* 9 (3rd edn., 1999).

the faith. Neither can it be argued, Mayer insists, that this assimilation has been anything but 'freely chosen' by Islam.[85] On the contrary, in the voluntary ratification of the new global human rights canon, the record of such Muslim states as Algeria, Egypt, Iran, Iraq, Jordan, Mali, Morocco, Niger, Syria, and Tunisia compares favourably with that of the United States.[86] While ratification of treaties does not necessarily bespeak actual compliance with their obligations, the fact of ratification at least indicates that the ratifying governments do not fear that the legal principles are incompatible with the faith of Islam, or that they are perceived by Islamic peoples as 'principles that belong uniquely to the West'—whatever their historic origins.[87]

That there is such convergence is not the relaxed view taken by Huntington. It matters whether his theory of a profound East–West fault-line is sufficiently sustained by evidence because, on the basis of it, he predicts the coming of a decisive conflict between the West and East, one exceeding in virulence the now-exhausted confrontation between capitalism and communism.[88] He expects the more traditional conflagrations between states and ideologies to be replaced by clashes between 'civilizations'. These will pit against one another the cultural and religious traditions of Western Christianity, Eastern Christianity, Islam, Buddhism, Hinduism, as well as other Chinese and Japanese beliefs. 'The next world war,' he predicts, 'if there is one, will be a war between civilizations.'[89] He adds that on 'both sides the interaction between Islam and the West is seen as a clash of civilizations', and cites the Indian Muslim author M. J. Akbar and the scholar Professor Bernard Lewis for the prediction that Islamic nations from the Maghreb to Indonesia will confront the Christian West for control of a new world order.[90]

To sustain such a cataclysmic hypothesis, however, the latitudinal evidence is remarkably selective and incomplete. A problem with Huntington's prediction is that it is based on a lack of attention to the divisions within Islam itself. There are the intra-Islamic military conflicts: Iran–Iraq, Iraq–Kuwait, the Afghan civil war between rival fundamentalists and the Algerian war between modernists and Islamicists. There are Islam's theological divisions between Sunni, Shia, and Ishmaili. There is the increasing convergence of interest between the West and at least some Islamic states: Bosnia, Turkey, Albania, Egypt, the Federated Gulf States, Qatar, Indonesia, Jordan, Malaysia, Morocco, and Tunisia. Within Islam, as within Western societies, differences of degree tend to be greater than similarities of kind.[91]

Various religious authorities within Islam take radically different positions, not least in matters pertaining to the rights of individuals. For example, when an Egyptian court, at the instance of religious zealots, ruled in 1995 that the

---

[85] Ibid. at 10.      [86] Ibid. at 11.      [87] Ibid. at 41.
[88] Samuel Huntington, 'The Clash of Civilizations?', 72 For. Affairs, no. 3, at 22 (1993).
[89] Ibid. at 39.      [90] Ibid. at 32.
[91] See Fuad Ajami, 'The Summoning', 72 For. Affairs, no. 4, at 2 (1993).

aforementioned Cairo literary scholar, Professor Nasr Abu Zeid, would have to divorce his spouse, an Egyptian art historian, because his writings were heretical, the ruling was stayed in 1996 by a higher tribunal. Then, when traditionalists brought fifty similar actions against other Muslim intellectuals, the Egyptian Parliament approved a law banning all such private third-party suits based on alleged violations of religious law.[92] The incident illustrates the need to recognize that Islam speaks with more than a single voice. 'I am a Muslim,' Professor Abu Zeid declared, 'it is the militants who are . . . hijacking Islam.'[93]

Similar differences between factions is also evident in the *Satanic Verses* incident. The Shiite fatwah issued by Khomeini against the author of the *Satanic Verses* was countered by a rival Sunni fatwah by Dr Tantawi, the mufti or official expounder of Islamic law and Grand Sheikh of Cairo's Al-Azhar University, the leading Islamic institution of higher learning. This second fatwah, while also condemning the blasphemous portions of *Verses*, annulled the death sentence because such a penalty may only be imposed after a trial with full due process in which the accused's motive is carefully examined, a trial Rushdie did not have. Dr Tantawi also questioned the application of Islamic law to the author, on the ground that he lives outside the Islamic community.[94]

As many writers have made clear, Islam has many interpretative tendencies. It is also worth noting that throughout much of the Islamic world, the state—an institution copied not from the Koran but rather, in self-defence, from the West—has begun to exercise powers formerly allocated to religious leaders. Even in Saudi Arabia '[s]tate jurisdiction now regulates societal areas that were formerly controlled by the religious sphere, and the ulama have become state administrators whose dogma and activities are supportive of the political leadership'.[95] Such a nationalization of religious power brings to mind the developments in post-Reformation countries in Europe—England, Scandinavia, and Prussia, in particular—where the subordination of religious authority to the state, however harsh its initial consequences, in historical retrospect can be seen as a first step on the road to toleration. Moreover, it is usually—now as then—in the state's perceived interest to curb religious excesses when these interfere with economic development. In late 1996, for example, the Federation of Malaysia's Prime Minister, Mahathir bin Mohamad, threatened to suspend the Islamicist government of the federated state of Kelantan. By this manoeuvre, he forced that local government to abandon proposed laws mandating stoning to death for adultery, amputation of hands for theft, and forty strokes of the cane for consumption of alcohol. Although formally acting to protect the federal government's sole prerogatives in matters of criminal law, and despite the fact that Islam is Malaysia's official religion, Mahathir said that modern

---

[92] NY Times, 20 Dec. 1996, at A5; 28 Dec. 1996, at 22.     [93] 28 Dec. 1996, ibid.
[94] Karim Abrawi, 'Letter from Cairo', The Guardian, 3 Mar. 1989, at 26.
[95] Ayman Al-Yassini, *Religion and State in the Kingdom of Saudi Arabia* 135 (1985).

Muslims must be prepared to reinterpret the Koran and sayings of the Prophet Mohammed. 'Only when Islam is interpreted so as to be relevant in a world which is so different from what it was 1,400 years ago', he said, 'can Islam be regarded as a religion for all ages.'[96]

Even in theocratic Iran, Abdolkarim Soroush, a leading religious intellectual and university lecturer, lately has called for curbing the predominance of the clergy in politics and greater adherence to democracy and human rights, which he deems compatible with the Iranian revolutionary Islamic tradition.[97] In his publicly expressed view, Islam is 'not necessarily antithetical to Western values'[98] and 'democracy, freedom of expression, and sustained intercultural relations are the best guarantors of religion'.[99]

This same point is made in very practical terms by a 1996 manual prepared for the Sisterhood is Global Institute [SIGI] by Mahnaz Afkhami and Haleh Vaziri,[100] which openly addresses 'the tension between individual freedom and communal authority'.[101] It examines the canon of modern human rights instruments and compares it to Islamic law of the Koran, as well as the traditions of sayings by the Prophet Muhammad (Hadith). It fervently denies 'that the universalist human rights discourse is an imposition of Western values on a multitude of diverse societies'[102] and prepares Islamic women to assert their rights and oppose extremism. Women are responding. Thousands of them marched in Ankara in 1997 to protest any attempt by fundamentalists to reintroduce Sharia law into the secular Turkish legal system. They carried banners proclaiming: 'Women's Rights are Human Rights.'[103]

Such views are gaining ground, according to Radhika Coomaraswamy, the UN Special Rapporteur on Violence Against Women. While women face deeply ingrained social constraints in much of the non-Western world, their cause is being abetted by new codes of universal rights, particularly the 1979 Convention on the Elimination of All Forms of Discrimination Against Women (CEDAW),[104] which firmly reject communal and religious norms that subordinate women. In Coomaraswamy's view, CEDAW obliges 'the state to correct any inconsistency between international human rights law and the religious and

---

[96] Michael Richardson, 'Malaysia Moves to Rein in Radical Islamic Fundamentalism', Int'l Herald Tribune, 9 Oct. 1996, at 4.

[97] Valla Vakili, 'Debating Religion and Politics in Iran: the Political Thought of Abdolkarim Soroush', Occ. Paper #2, Council on For. Rels., p. 7 (1996) (introd. James Piscatori & Riva Richmond). [98] Ibid. at 5.

[99] Ibid. at 8.

[100] M. Afkhami & H. Vaziri, *Claiming Our Rights: A Manual for Women's Human Rights Education in Muslim Societies* (1996). [101] Ibid. at iii.

[102] Ibid. at xii.

[103] S. Kinzer, 'Turkish Women Protest the Koranic Law', Int'l Herald Tribune, 17 Feb. 1997, at 9.

[104] Convention on the Elimination of All Forms of Discrimination Against Women. Adopted 18 Dec. 1979, entered into force 3 Sept. 1981, 1249 UNTS 14. As of 1996, 121 nations have ratified the Convention, many with extensive reservations.

customary law operating within its territory'.[105] This primacy precludes female genital mutilation, Sharia-type legal punishments (flogging, stoning, amputations) as well as laws restricting women's rights regarding marriage, divorce, maintenance, and the custody of children. She rejects the argument that such universal rights are, somehow, Western and thus inappropriate to women elsewhere, or that they undermine 'cultural pluralism'. On the contrary, she states, '[c]ultural diversity should be celebrated only if those enjoying their cultural attributes are doing so voluntarily. By protecting choice, voluntariness and the integrity of female decision-making, we may be able to reconcile the dilemma between cultural diversity and the need for the protection of women's human rights.'[106]

The Muslim world's modernizers today openly support a lessening of compulsory uniformity in matters of belief, seeing this as a prerequisite for their society's social and economic advancement. While conceding that the retention of the ban on apostasy 'appears to be an anachronism in the laws of modern nation states', they point out that the death penalty for it already 'has been abandoned in most contemporary [Muslim] penal codes'.[107] According to Mayer, the 'principle of tolerance of religious difference, which figures prominently in the Islamic value system and tradition, supports the notion that religious adherence should be left a matter of conscience. Liberal Muslims note that there is no verse in the Qur'an that stipulates any earthly penalty for apostasy and . . . that the Prophet never killed anyone merely for apostasy'.[108] In the Human Rights Committee, its Islamic members have been among the most outspoken in rejecting the notion of incompatibility between Muslim law and the global law of the human rights treaty system.[109] Women, throughout the Islamic world, are strengthening the incremental advance of global standards, always taking into account the specific contexts within which they apply.

A close examination of disparate tendencies in the Islamic world does not support the hyperbole of 'wars of civilization'. To the extent some Islamic states still reject, in practice if not in legal theory, important aspects of the new global human rights canon, they are not manifesting Islamic values. Rather, they are merely another instance of an autocratic (and male) ruling class seeking to perpetuate itself. Islamic societies are not unique, either, in manifesting a certain resentment of the West and what is seen as its cultural imperialism. That these considerations have shaped the responses of some Islamic societies does not demonstrate that these anti-human rights positions are founded on Islam. On the contrary, Mayer says, their 'Islamic pedigrees are dubious' and

---

[105] Radhika Coomaraswamy, *Reinventing International Law: Women's Rights as Human Rights in the International Community* 23 (1997).   [106] Ibid. at 25.

[107] Ann Elizabeth Mayer, 'Universal Versus Islamic Human Rights: a Clash of Cultures or a Clash with a Construct?', 15 Mich. J. Int'l L. 307, 322 (1994).   [108] Ibid. at 157–8.

[109] Interviews with Members of the ICCPR Human Rights Committee, January to June 1997.

their resistance does 'not represent the result of rigorous, scholarly analyses of the Islamic sources or a coherent approach to Islamic jurisprudence. Instead [their opposition seems] largely shaped by their conservative authors' negative reactions to the model of freedom in Western societies and the scope of rights protection afforded by the International Bill of Human Rights'.[110]

Such opposition by conservative authoritarian and communitarian forces within Islamic societies is by no means unique. It is easy to find the same reservation and resistance in Western societies' response to the challenge of modern individualism. There may, indeed, be a great divide, but it is not one that sustains a superficial correlation between contemporary societal views regarding freedom and those based on perceptions of God's will, for the latter sustains many different views on the former. Professor Huntington's prognosis takes Islam's most radically fundamentalist strain to be its mainstream. It is not. Instead of a clash, we are much more likely to see a continuing competition, one as much occurring within, as much as between, societies. That competition is between forces championing the paramountcy of communitarian social rights and those advocating individual autonomy.

The same scepticism should greet the claim that Asian values are incompatible with modern human rights. Professor William Theodore De Bary has pointed out that the Universal Declaration of Human Rights was written with the full participation of Chinese Confucians and 'gained subsequent adherence to it of countries sharing Confucian cultures. There is no basis for asserting any inherent incompatibility between Confucianism and the human rights to which most nations subscribe'.[111] Nor is there a profound schism between Confucian and Western culture: the 'person as understood by Confucianism in the context of human relationships is no less entitled to respect than the individual in Western human rights concepts. Thus the dichotomy between "individual" versus "community" rights is inapplicable and misleading in this case'.[112]

As with Islam, or, for that matter, the West, disagreements between individualism and communitarianism do have roots in societies' history, economic development, urbanization, industrialization, and, of course, their politics. Each people has its own story, but the ingredients of those stories tend to vary in matters of degree and of timing rather than in kind.

---

[110] Mayer, *supra* n. 84, at 191.
[111] William Theodore De Bary, *Asian Values and Human Rights: a Confucian Communitarian Perspective* 155 (1998).                                                                              [112] Ibid. at 156.

6. THE LONGITUDINAL EVIDENCE OF HISTORY

## (a) The Special Case of England

Huntington's 'clash of civilizations' theory misassumes that Islam and other non-western systems are accurately represented by their most radically conservative manifestations. This false assumption undermines his prognosis. More damaging to that prognosis, however, is his further assumption that the West's liberalism and tolerance manifests its occidental culture. Even a cursory investigation of 'Western' history can readily demonstrate that individual autonomy in general, and freedom of conscience in particular, are no more indigenous to the West than to the East. Rather, they are the recently hard-won and imperfectly realized culmination of long struggle.

That struggle was waged against entrenched forces of political and theological orthodoxy bent on enforcing communitarian conformity. Much as in some non-Western societies today, Western leaders long sought to repress the individual conscience—and particularly its public expression—in the name of protecting social cohesion and stability. Even the historic French *Declaration* of 1789, quoted at the beginning of this chapter, contains precisely the self-serving caveat in favour of 'public order' that is always cited by authority to justify the repression of nonconformity. Eventually, gradually, in the West, those zealously enforcing conformity yielded to reason, but only when overpowered by political, economic, and social forces they could no longer control. And they yielded only quite recently.

There is no reason to believe that the underlying emancipating forces—urbanization, industrialization, advances in transportation and communications, medical and other scientific discoveries, a revolution in information storage, distribution, and retrieval—are indigenous to Western society and cannot affect other societies as they have our own. On the contrary, one must assume them to be independent variables which, when they come to the fore anywhere, in the right conjunction of circumstances, will tilt the balance in favour of more individual autonomy and freedoms.

Although we cannot prove this hypothesis about the future, we can challenge countervailing hypotheses built on a falsely imagined past. Thus, Huntington's predictions of a great chasm between inherently irreconcilable civilizations is undermined by evidence that contemporary communitarian conformist societies look very much as did our own only a few years ago.

Consider England, today. It is the cradle of parliament and of the rule of law; it is also the place Salman Rushdie resides. Unlike Iran, England has not issued a writ authorizing Rushdie's murder for blasphemy. On the contrary, it has spent millions of pounds protecting the writer against potential enforcers of the Iranian Mullahs' death decree. Clearly, Iran and England are different, even profoundly so, when it comes to respect for religious dissent. But England, in fact, today still has a common law offence of blasphemy,[113] although not, of course, one imposing the death penalty on violators. Indeed, English Muslims sought to invoke it, by initiating legal proceedings to compel the Crown to prosecute the errant author. The High Court, instead of holding that the law of blasphemy had fallen into desuetude, ruled that, while it continued to be in effect, it prohibited only blasphemy against the Church of England![114]

Even a cursory study of English—or, indeed, Western European—history makes modern Islamicist passions seem quite familiar, its excesses not very exotic.[115] While English blasphemy law may by now be a rather toothless tiger,

---

[113] See *Regina v. Lemon* [1979] 2 WLR 282.

[114] *Regina v. Chief Metropolitan Stipendiary Magistrate, Ex parte Choudhury* [1991] 1 QB 429, 447.

[115] English attitudes to blasphemy and heresy have their roots elsewhere in the West, particularly in ancient Greece, Palestine, and Rome. In none of these was there much to distinguish the values of those societies from those of contemporary instances of communitarian intolerance. Alcibiades, one of the commanders of the Athenian army, was condemned to death for impiety, in 415 BC, while fighting Sparta (Levy, *supra* n. 22, at 5). Aristotle was convicted of the same offence a century later (ibid. at 7). According to the Old Testament, a person 'who blasphemes the name of the Lord shall be put to death; all the congregation shall stone him . . .' (Leviticus, 24: 16). If liberal democratic autonomy and conscientious liberty are peculiarly Western blossoms, they surely were not planted by our mother Athens or father Jerusalem. Toleration was not a sentiment familiar anywhere in Europe before the sixteenth century, certainly not to the Roman Catholic hierarchy or to the Christian monarchies of Europe. By unrelenting persecution, 'the Church attained and long kept its catholicity. Its monopoly as the only recognized and established religion was built on murder as well as on the exclusivity of its control of salvation' (Levy, ibid. at 46). Punishment for heresy and blasphemy was seen by both church and state as therapeutic: it propitiated God, averted the divine wrath directed against societies tolerant of impure beliefs, vindicated the witness of true believers, and reaffirmed 'communal norms' (ibid. at 3). The more severe the punishment of blasphemy and heresy, the better, because toleration of conscientious dissent, everyone knew, 'endangers the unity of society' and 'failure to punish the blasphemer might lead to public disturbances' (ibid). Flogging and stoning became the lesser penalties for conscientious dissent in the Judeo-Christian tradition, with death the more common remedy. Heresy became the charge levelled against obdurate objectors to the Christian creed formulated by the Council of Nicea in AD 325, or to the Trinitarian theology confirmed by the Council of Chalcedon in AD 451. It largely replaced blasphemy as the charge brought against conscientious dissent.

The tolerance of the Eastern Church was no greater than that of Rome. In the Orthodox Christian Church's Byzantine realm, Emperor Justinian's new codex, the Corpus Juris Civilis, in 529 made provision for putting blasphemers to death, since 'failure to do so tended to cause famine, earthquake and pestilence' (ibid. at 50). The repression of dissent mandated by the Justinian Code was endorsed by Charlemagne and his successors upon the founding of the Holy Roman Empire in AD 800 (ibid.).

St Augustine, citing his favourite text ('compel them to come in': Luke 14: 16–23), advocated death for heretics, but was careful to insist that the state, and not the church, be the one to carry it out. While this kept the ecclesiastical hand technically unbloodied, it linked it firmly to that of the temporal power, assuring that for at least 1200 years such views as those advanced by Roger Williams and Thomas Jefferson would be expressed openly only on pain of burning, hanging, ripping out of tongues, gouging out of eyes, cutting off of ears or lips, or various creative combinations of these typically 'Western' answers to the free thinkers' provocations. Levy gives an excruciatingly detailed account of this history (ibid. at 46–462). According to St Thomas Aquinas, heretics 'by right . . . can be put to death and despoiled of their possessions by the secular [authorities], even if they do not corrupt others, for they are blasphemers against God, because they observe a false faith. Thus they can be justly punished more than those accused of high treason' (ibid. at 51–2 and accompanying citations). The Reformation in Europe did little to introduce greater tolerance.

such laws were of great consequence until quite recently. All through the religiously turbulent seventeenth century, English law continuously treated all blasphemy as a form of sedition, rather as does Islamic law today. The English common law, according to Blackstone, punished 'blasphemy against the Almighty, by denying his being or providence; or by contumelious reproaches of our saviour Christ. Whither also may be referred all profane scoffing at the holy scripture, or exposing it to contempt and ridicule. . . . [F]or Christianity is part of the laws of England'.[116] The criminalization of conscientious dissent was seen by the Church of England, after its historic but socially and politically divisive break with Rome, as a weapon against those who would foment civil insurrection. Chief Justice Hale, in the 1676 *Taylor's Case*, held that 'Christianity is parcel of the laws of England' and that statements attacking it or Christ tended 'to dissolve all those obligations whereby civil societies are preserved'.[117]

This was hardly a new perspective. Pre-Reformation and post-Reformation England, in that sense, were indistinguishable. England's breach with Rome had done nothing to mitigate its established church's virulent intolerance. Anglicans and Roman Catholics vied to stamp each other out during the reigns of Henry VIII, Edward VI, and Mary I. Indeed, Henry VIII's Act of the Six Articles imposed criminal penalties, including being roasted alive,[118] on anyone denying such key doctrines as transubstantiation.[119] A few years later, under Edward, it became almost as dangerous to espouse transubstantiation as it had been to deny it. Then, Queen Mary made it once more very unhealthy to deny its validity. The people fully empathized with the anonymous doggerel attributed to one clergyman of the period:

> And this law, I will maintain,
> Unto my dying day, sir,
> That whatever king shall reign,
> I will be the Vicar of Bray, sir!

The vicar could retain his sinecure, however, only by paying closest attention to constantly shifting doctrinal fashion, always enforced by draconian laws and the full power of the state.

One thus speaks at some peril about any Western tradition of respect for individualism. There was no trace of it in Tudor England. The first hundred years after the establishment of the Church of England were fraught with civil war, regicide, and large-scale executions, all the products of religious zealotry.

---

Calvin, in the sixteenth century, burned dissidents in Geneva and Luther called for the burning of synagogues and for cutting out the tongues of Jewish blasphemers (ibid. at 60–1).

[116] 4 W. Blackstone, *Commentaries*, at 59 (1809).

[117] Taylor's Case, 86 ER 189 (KB 1676). The defendant had called Christ a 'whore-master' and 'bastard' among other things.

[118] Levy, *supra* n. 22, at 82–4 and accompanying citations.

[119] Statute 31 Henry VIII, c.14 (1539). See David Feldman, *Civil Liberties and Human Rights in England and Wales* 686–7 (1993).

Even during the last four years of the brief restoration of Catholicism under Mary (1553–8), 273 subjects were burned for heresy, including four bishops and an archbishop.[120]

Only in the late sixteenth century did the prolonged excesses of intolerance very gradually begin to tire the ruling classes. First came the respite from religious dogmatism during the long reign of Elizabeth I, beginning in 1558. It is said that she 'did not share the uncompromising zeal of either Catholic or Protestant'. Whether or not Elizabeth actually said that all difference between Christians 'is a dispute over trifles', clearly '[e]xcessive doctrinal enthusiasm wearied and annoyed her'.[121] During her reign, although formal public adherence to the established church was certainly still required, the Queen's minister, Lord Cecil, convinced her that, while the Crown could not concede liberty of worship, it at least might concede liberty of private conscience.[122] As is so often the case, institutionalized hypocrisy proceeded—and to some extent disguised—profound changes in society, its social values and political institutions. Laws compelling conformity were not repealed but tended not to be vigorously enforced.

Actual public dissent, however, was another matter. For some time it continued to be severely repressed not only in England but almost everywhere in Europe, not least where the Reformation was underway. The burning—in Geneva in 1553—of the anti-Trinitarian, Michael Servetus, on the order of John Calvin, at last aroused enough repulsion to engender Europe's first serious debate on toleration.[123] That debate resounded also in England, where ascendant Presbyterianism—the Calvinist system imported through Scotland by John Knox—although the chief rival to the established Church of England, enthusiastically shared its intolerance of personal religious freedom.

That conscientious dissent from the doctrines of established Christianity could corrode the bonds of civil society remained a deeply held view in England, as elsewhere in Europe, well into the nineteenth and early twentieth centuries. Typical of its resilience among the English faithful was a 'Letter to the Parishioners of Great Yarmouth by their Minister' written in 1847. It vehemently opposed a petition to parliament, then being circulated, that had argued 'in favour of the Removal of Jewish Disabilities'. The petition sought to make Jews eligible for election or appointment to parliament. 'My dear friends,' wrote the Yarmouth divine,

I cannot express to you the pain of my heart to see you petitioning for the abrogation of that great religious principle whereby the nation, and we as its members, are bound up

---

[120] Levy, *supra* n. 22, at 86 and accompanying citations (1993).

[121] W. K. Jordan, *The Development of Religious Toleration in England*, vol. 1, at 86 (1932).

[122] Ibid. at 88.

[123] Professor Levy has written that the debate was opened with the publication by Sebastian Castellio of Basel, a professor of Greek and epic poet, of his *Concerning Heretics*, 'the sixteenth century's first book on religious liberty' (Levy, *supra* n. 22, at 67).

in a solemn relationship to *Christ Jesus* as our common head. . . . We look upon it as a great remaining bond, whereby. . . our nation, shall not be moved! . . . But if you seek to deprive us of that bond, you rend asunder the very life of the nation: and you will see, ere many years have passed by, the unnatural excitement of partial and divided life exhibited here and there amid the nation that has hitherto been one; preying inwardly upon its own vitals; continually fighting in a fearful strife, part against part; wasting its own forces by an inward fever; instead of developing the functions of the united body in wholesome action towards those who bear an external relationship to it.[124]

The good vicar seems almost to have foreseen, as a consequence of Jewish emancipation, the terrible urban traffic jams that Professor Etzioni (above, Ch. 5) now cites as evidence of modern social unravelling.

Over time, fortunately, the 'religious struggle which marked the history of this era etched deep into the fabric of Anglican thought a profound distrust of all coercive practices and a stalwart disavowal of the fanatical devotion to sectarian ends from which persecution springs'.[125] Queen Elizabeth I had already allowed recusants to avoid the established sacraments with a small fine.[126] The last two persons executed for heresy in England died in 1612, in the reign of James I, who eventually recognized the unwisdom of creating martyrs, preferring that 'heretics hereafter, though condemned, should silently, and privately, waste themselves away in the prison'.[127]

Enlightenment, however, did not come all at once or without reversals. The temporary reforms of Oliver Cromwell's Commonwealth recognized, despite the efforts of the more extreme Puritans, that the right to 'individual faith' is 'of such transcendental importance that the state dare not touch it'.[128] In 1650, Parliament passed its first Toleration Act repealing all legal enforcement of religious uniformity. Briefly, there was a secularization of England that proceeded from 'recognition that social order could rest on another basis than religious agreement'.[129] But the Protectorate failed to perpetuate itself, and even before its demise, toleration of dissent was being undermined by a tendency to limit it to mainstream Protestants. Only one month before enacting the 1650 Toleration Act, Parliament had criminalized the beliefs of a sect called the Ranters, and many of its followers (who, perhaps paradoxically, believed in neither heaven nor hell) were jailed, whipped, hanged, or had their tongues bored through with a hot iron.[130] Moreover, whatever tolerance there was at that time had been strongly opposed by many of the Presbyterians, even though they themselves, before the Commonwealth, had been cruelly persecuted by the Anglican establishment under Archbishop Laud.

---

[124] In an unpublished collection of pamphlets in Trinity College Library, Cambridge, no. 289-C 80 46, at 8. The author is Henry MacKenzie, MA, later Anglican Bishop of Nottingham.
[125] W. K. Jordan, *The Development of Religious Toleration in England*, vol. 4, at 422–3 (1940).
[126] Levy, *supra* n. 22, at 89. But see ibid. at 91.     [127] Ibid. at 99.
[128] C. John Sommerville, *The Secularization of Early Modern England* 108–9 (1992).
[129] Ibid.     [130] Levy, *supra* n. 22, at 158.

Typically, one John Bastwick, a Presbyterian, on being released from prison by the Protectorate, demanded, in the name of the Bible, death for 'atheism, blasphemy, profanation of the Sabbath, and all manners of impiety and toleration of all religions'.[131] This he thought to be the due not only of Catholics and Anglicans, but also Unitarians, congregationalist sects, and any who disagreed with Presbyterian orthodoxy. Adam Stewart, another of that faith, urged that, while persecution could not extirpate wrong beliefs, magistrates 'could cut away an ill tongue'.[132] The imprisonment and trial of Paul Best by the Long Parliament, beginning in 1645,[133] three years later led to enactment of 'An Ordinance for the Punishing of Blasphemies and Heresies' which once more imposed the death penalty on atheists and the anti-Trinitarian Socinians and imposed lesser punishment on Baptists.[134] Almost immediately, however, Pride's Purge cleared the Presbyterians out of parliament and suspended the enforcement of that law.

Following the Protectorate came the Stuart Restoration and a revival of Anglican supremacy. The Act of Uniformity of 1662 prescribed the Church of England's Book of Common Prayer for all churches. During the brief Restoration, thousands of nonconformists, ranging from Quaker to Presbyterian, died in jail.

The end of the Stuart dynasty was marked, however, by a new Toleration Act.[135] That law has been described by the historian Macaulay as 'among those great statutes which are epochs in our constitutional history'.[136] Yet, while it formally ended persecution of nonconformists, it required teachers and preachers to continue to subscribe to all but three of the Anglican Articles of Religion. It did not extend toleration to Roman Catholics, nor to those who denied the doctrine of the Trinity, and it did not repeal laws requiring attendance at some place of worship. For all this, as we have noted, the Act was scorned by Roger Williams in Rhode Island. The Test and Corporation Acts of 1673 also remained in force, formally restricting public office to communicants of the Church of England,[137] although society increasingly turned a blind eye to dissenters, dubbed 'occasional conformists', who were willing to take Anglican communion on a few formal occasions.[138]

Not only was this 'toleration' still severely circumscribed at the end of the seventeenth and beginning of the eighteenth centuries, it may even be discounted as little more than a tactical rallying of the tolerated, the better to

---

[131] Ibid. at 111.    [132] Ibid.    [133] Ibid. at 111–15.

[134] Ibid. at 120–1 and accompanying citations.

[135] 1 William and Mary, ch. XVIII (1688).

[136] J. Macaulay, 2 *History of England* 282 (Everyman edn., 1972).

[137] Ernest A. Payne, 'Toleration and Establishment: 1, A Historical Outline', in *From Uniformity to Unity* 1662–1962, at 259 (Nuttall & Chadwick eds., 1962).

[138] Daniel Defoe is quoted by Payne as calling it 'playing Bo-peep with God Almighty'. He cites Sir Thomas Abney, onetime Lord Mayor of London and Member of Parliament, as an example (ibid. at 261–2).

inflict greater intolerance on others. Daniel Neal's preface to his *History of the Puritans* (1731–2), for example, notes approvingly that, after passage of the Toleration Act, nonconformists delivered from the 'Yoke of Oppression', now in company with Anglicans, 'may with greater success bend their united Forces against the common Enemies of Christianity'.[139] In 1698, Parliament passed a law 'for the more effective suppressing of Blasphemy and Profaneness'.[140] Prosecutions under it and under common law continued for another two hundred years.[141]

The Schism Act of 1714 forbade teaching by anyone who could not demonstrate that he had taken Anglican communion during the previous year.[142] It was repealed five years later,[143] but the use of law and the state's power to entice and bully individuals into religious conformity continued to be seen as an essential antidote to civil war and the unravelling of the social contract. In *Rex v. Woolston*, in 1729, the English court declared that 'whatever strikes at the root of Christianity, tends manifestly to the dissolution of civil government'.[144] According to Blackstone, blasphemy was a common law criminal libel which consisted of a 'public affront to religion and morality, on which all government must depend for support'.[145] 'The English', one writer comments, 'seem peculiarly attached to the notion that the individual and his innermost thoughts are part of the bonds holding society together and that society may therefore act to prevent, as far as possible, external influences from leading those thoughts from the established path.'[146]

Not until the nineteenth century were there notable further steps in the direction of toleration, progress having been slowed by, among other factors, public reaction against the excesses of the French Revolution's campaigns against religion. In 1812 the Conventicle and Five Miles Acts were repealed,[147] and the following year the law of blasphemy was amended[148] to make it lawful to deny the doctrine of the Trinity, thereby exempting from criminalization the doctrines of Unitarians and Jews. In 1828 the Test and Corporation Acts were repealed[149] and the following year the Catholic Emancipation Act put Roman Catholics on a par with nonconformist Protestants.[150] The Marriage and Registration Acts of 1836 and 1856 at last legitimated marriages conducted by nonconformist ministers, although a registrar still has to be present. In 1858

---

[139] Ibid. at 263.      [140] 9 & 10 Will. 3, c.32 (1698).

[141] Note: *Blasphemy*, 70 Col. L. Rev. 694, 696 (1970).

[142] 13 Anne, Cap. 7, 1713.      [143] 5 Geo. I c.4.

[144] *Rex v. Woolston*, 93 ER 881 (KB 1729). This case was cited approvingly in New York in 1811 in *People v. Ruggles*, 8 Johns 290 (NY 1811).

[145] William Blackstone, Commentaries 58–9.

[146] Note: *Blasphemy* (*Law Note*), *supra* n. 141, at 698, citing Sir Patrick Devlin, *The Enforcement of Morals* 9–14 (1965).      [147] 52 Geo. IV c. 155, §1.

[148] 9 and 10 Wm. III ch. 32.

[149] The Repeal of the Test and Corporations Acts, 9 Geo. IV. cap. 17, 1828.

[150] 10 Geo. IV, ch. VII (1829).

parliament passed the law that had so exercised the Vicar of Yarmouth, an Act for the Relief of Her Majesty's Subjects professing the Jewish religion.[151] It dropped the uniform religious oathing requirements that had excluded Jews from public office.[152] In 1859, religious tests for appointments at Oxford and Cambridge were deleted.

These battles for and against toleration were fought with immense vigour only a century and a half ago. In 1830, Zachary Macaulay had written: 'why a man should be less fit to exercise [the civil powers of full citizenship] because he wears a beard, because he does not eat ham, because he goes to the Synagogue on Saturday instead of going to Church on Sunday, we cannot conceive.' These differences, he argued, had no more to do with his fitness to be a magistrate, legislator or Chancellor of the Exchequer than with his fitness to be a cobbler.[153] His reasoning did not carry for almost another thirty years.

Macaulay and other Christians, in demanding full tolerance for the Jews, and Sydney Smith in pursuing the cause of Catholic emancipation, adopted particularist arguments somewhat later developed more generally by John Stuart Mill. It was Mill's contention, building on Locke, that church and state must be altogether separate and that the accommodation of difference in philosophy and belief is a sign of a society's intellectual strength and resilience. By the latter part of the nineteenth century, as one historian remarked, 'Advanced opinion . . . had already shown signs of growing weary of divine decrees and infallible dogma, all of which helped to make the life of men in society disturbed and fratricidal.'[154] At last, a clear distinction between church and state—rather than an enforced code of religious conformity—was becoming the conventional wisdom upon which to erect a peaceable kingdom. As Locke had insisted, the prerogative of force now increasingly resided with the state only to compel conformity with laws enacted to promote true civil interests.

Leading churchmen of the established church had been arrayed on both sides during this battle for and against conscientious toleration. For example, in the House of Lords debates in 1707 on the Act of Union with Scotland,[155] which recognized the Presbyterians as the established church in Scotland, the liberal Archbishop of Canterbury, Tenison, said, 'he had no scruple against . . . confirming [the Act] within the bounds of Scotland [since] he thought that the narrow notions of all the Churches had been their ruin and he believed the Church of Scotland to be as true a Protestant Church as the Church of England

---

[151] Ch. 48, 21 & 22 Vict. 149 (1858).

[152] See the account of the struggle for Jewish emancipation in Ursula Henriques, *Religious Toleration in England, 1787–1833*, at 183–205 (1961).

[153] Zachary Macaulay, 'Civil Disabilities of the Jews', Edinburgh Review, Oct.-Jan., vol. 53, 365 (1830–1), quoted and paraphrased in Henriques, ibid. at 201.

[154] Edward Carpenter, 'Toleration and Establishment: 2, Studies in a Relationship', in *From Uniformity to Unity, supra* n. 137, at 291.        [155] 6 Anne C.40.

though he could not say it was so perfect'.[156] Yet as late as 1887, the Bishop of Winchester in Convocation warned against participation in public worship with the Dissenters, who believe 'that for very slight differences of opinion you may separate from a great national Church, and that any body of men that like may set up a new Church of their own . . .'.[157] In 1880, twenty-one years after the publication of J. S. Mill's classic essay *On Liberty*, and with the support of many Anglican clergy—but with 16,000 of them petitioning *against* it—the Burial Laws Amendment Act for the first time granted non-Anglicans the equal right to decay in churchyards.[158]

The Anglican religion is still England's state church, headed by the British monarch and only Anglican bishops hold *ex officio* appointments to the House of Lords. Both the archbishops, as well as all bishops of the Church of England continue to be appointed by the Crown on the advice of the Prime Minister who usually, but not invariably, accepts the counsel of the Church's Crown Appointment Commission.[159] Beyond those vestiges of establishment, however, little else remains, in Britain, to qualify or disqualify persons on account of conscientious belief.[160] In 1967, Parliament revoked the Blasphemy Act of 1698,[161] although as we have noted, blasphemy was still recognized by the High Court as a common law offence in the 1991 *Rushdie* case.[162]

While the effort to prosecute *Rushdie* failed, a 1979 prosecution did succeed. It had been brought by a private citizen against a newspaper and its publisher for printing a poem by James Kirkup, a British poet teaching at Amherst College (USA) that depicted Jesus as homosexual.[163] In the House of Lords, the conviction was sustained by Lord Scarman as necessary to protect 'religious beliefs . . . from scurrility, vilification, ridicule and contempt'.[164] Moreover, freedom of religious expression and critique of religion is still chilled in modern Britain by a raft of other speech-curbing laws on scandal, incitement to disorder, profanity, and obscenity.[165] In 1995, moreover, the European Court of Human

---

[156] From 'The Chronicle of Convocation,' 12 May 1887. Quoted in Carpenter, *supra* n. 154, at 301–2, citing *State Papers and Letters* addressed to William Carstares, at 760 (J. McCormick ed., 1774).

[157] 'The Chronicle of Convocation,' ibid. at 301.    [158] Payne, *supra* n. 137, at 279.

[159] Peter Crumper, 'Freedom of Thought, Conscience and Religion,' in David Harris & Sarah Joseph, *The International Covenant on Civil and Political Rights and United Kingdom Law* 355, 362 (1995). The Church of England is not established in Wales or Northern Ireland. The Presbyterian Church is established in Scotland. Ibid. at 363.

[160] David Feldman, *Civil Liberties and Human Rights in England and Wales* 687 (1993).

[161] The revocation came in 1967 as part of the Criminal Justice Act. Criminal Justice Act, 1967, ch. 80 (Eng.). This rescinded several 'obsolete' laws on the recommendation of a government appointed law commission. It was thought that that was the end of the matter, but such a conclusion ignores the resilience of the common law of blasphemy as propounded by Blackstone.

[162] In 1985, the UK Law Commission unanimously had recommended the abolition by statute of the common law offence of blasphemy. That recommendation still awaits action (Law Commission Report no. 145, *Offences against Religion and Public Worship* (London: HMSO, 1985)), and many in England still believe that the law, instead of being repealed, ought instead to be enforced and extended to protect also all other religions from intemperate dissent (see Feldman, *supra* n. 160, at 693).

[163] See *R. v. Lemon* [1978] 3 All ER 175; [1979] AC 617.    [164] Ibid. at 658.

[165] St John A. Robilliard, *Religion and the Law: Religious Liberty in modern English law* 35–40 (1984).

Rights upheld a ban imposed by British censors on 'Visions of Ecstasy', a film about St Teresa of Avila who had erotic visions of Jesus. The Court sided with the British Government on the ground that the film would 'give rise to outrage' and that 'a reasonable jury properly directed would find that it infringed the criminal law of blasphemy'.[166] The European judges noted that blasphemy laws are still in force in various European countries and that, because the film could 'outrage and insult the feelings of believing Christians' the censorship 'could not be said to be arbitrary or excessive'.[167]

What does all this tell us? At very least, it makes clear that modern 'Western' liberal values, with their emphasis on individuated personal autonomy and human rights, are no emanation of some deep cultural tradition of the societies of Europe and North America: certainly not of England. It demonstrates that these values and the legal skein that gives them effect are a radical and very recent repudiation of everything that characterized these societies throughout their recorded history. It also tells us that there are still many exceptions to the liberalizing trends of recent years.

At best, the account would arouse us to ask what brought about the recent, remarkable reversal of social values and laws in some states, including England. And that, in turn, should cause us to inquire whether those so-called 'non-Western' societies which currently espouse some of the values and laws that were from time immemorial the conventional wisdom of England may, in time, be subject to the same visions and revisions that eventually compelled the inhabitants of England gradually to embrace toleration and freedom of conscience.

### (b) The Special Case of the USA

Britain's American colonies, with the notable exception of Roger Williams' Rhode Island, emulated the early English legal precepts, establishing religion and criminalizing blasphemous dissent. The colonial settlers simply replicated in America the ecclesiastical conflicts of England and their attendant intolerances.

The Revolution did not entirely extirpate this tradition. Much of the legal framework of intolerance survived into the post-colonial era in both the statutes and practices of the former colonies.[168] The American Revolution, unlike its French counterpart, was neither anti-clerical nor counter-theological and the Constitution and First Amendment forbade only the *federal* establishment of religion. It did not abrogate then-extant establishment in Massachusetts, Connecticut, Vermont, and New Hampshire. Not until the passage of the

---

[166] *Wingrove v. United Kingdom*, Case 19/1995. Judgment of 25 Nov. 1995. Reported in The Times (London), 5 Dec. 1995, at 8.                                                                [167] Ibid.

[168] Note: *Blasphemy (Law Note)*, *supra* n. 141, at 694, notes 2 and 3 and cases and statutes therein cited.

Fourteenth Amendment, ratified in 1868, was the federal prohibition applied at the state level.

More important, the 'free exercise' clause, like its 'free speech' twin, has never been treated as absolute, leaving room for the punishment of obscenity, libel, and incitements to violence. Each of these exceptions has been used, at one time or another, as justification for prohibiting speech and practices pertaining to religion and, even, for punishing blasphemy.[169]

Through much of America's nineteenth century, attitudes of public officials and some judges regarding the corrosive effect of conscientious dissent strongly resemble those of their English counterparts. In 1811, the New York State Supreme Court of Judicature in a decision written by the 'American Blackstone'[170] Chief Justice Kent, held that the defendant's public denunciation of Jesus as a bastard and his mother, Mary, as a whore constituted blasphemy. Kent noted 'that we are a Christian people, and the morality of the country is deeply ingrafted upon Christianity, and not upon the doctrines of worship of those impostors Mahomet and the Grand Lama'.[171] He thought that the English common law crime of blasphemy still applied to the former colony despite New York's having neither a blasphemy statute nor an established church. 'Nothing could be more offensive to the virtuous part of the community, or more injurious to the tender morals of the young,' he said on behalf of a unanimous court, 'than to declare such profanity lawful. . . . No government among any of the polished nations of antiquity, and none of the institutions of modern Europe (a single and admonitory case excepted), ever hazarded such a bold experiment upon the solidity of the public morals, as to permit with impunity, and under the sanction of their tribunals, the general religion of the community to be openly insulted and defamed.' (The reference to a 'single exception' obviously was directed at revolutionary France.) In the court's opinion, the defendant's words were punishable 'because they strike at the root of moral obligation, and weaken the security of the social ties'.[172]

The Ayatollah Khomeini could not have said it better. Although Kent was not a religious fanatic, he approved the view common at the time to persons of his class and station that religion was 'a bulwark of good social order'[173] and that without religion the poor might not be held in check.[174] Thus, only a century and a half ago, the value of personal conscientious autonomy was nowhere near as widely shared, nor as deeply felt, as it is today. It was not unusual for persons, even some deeply steeped in law and public philosophy, to think it essential to repress freedom of personal conscience for the sake of a social stability, and to express that view through punishment.

There are other examples, although the communitarian cause gradually

---

[169] Ibid. and citations throughout. See e.g. *Reynolds v. US* 145 (1879) (plural marriage); *Roth v. US* 354 US 476 (1957) (obscenity).   [170] Levy, *supra* n. 22, at 401.
[171] *People v. Ruggles*, 8 Johns. (NY) 290 (1811), at 294–5.   [172] Ibid. at 294–5.
[173] Levy, *supra* n. 22, at 402.   [174] Ibid. at 404.

ceased to find much public resonance. In 1821 a Mr Jared W. Bell was indicted for blasphemy in New York City. He was charged with having allowed himself to be 'seduced by the instigation of the devil' to vilify the Christian religion 'to the great dishonour of Almighty God'.[175] He was acquitted by the jury, as was the defendant in a similar trial in 1823.[176] John Adams, in his old age, found these goings-on 'a great embarrassment'[177] but the prosecutions occasionally succeeded. As late as 1837, Chief Justice John M. Clayton, of Delaware, applying a state criminal blasphemy statute of 1826 that specifically incorporated canon law, imposed a fine, ten days in solitary confinement, and steep surety against repetition of the offence;[178] and in 1838, in the most notorious of the cases, Chief Justice Shaw of Massachusetts—a Unitarian—wrote the majority opinion upholding the conviction of Abner Kneeland, a cantankerous free-thinking editor, writer, and preacher, under that state's criminal blasphemy law.[179] He was jailed for sixty days for 'speaking evil of the Deity with an impious purpose to derogate from the divine majesty, and to alienate the minds of others from the love and reverence of God'.[180]

By the 1840s, however, even in England 'the focus of the law had shifted from protection of Christian belief to the protection of Christian sensibilities'.[181] A book written under the pseudonym 'John Search', but believed to be by the Anglican Archbishop of Dublin, Richard Whately, argued vehemently *against* legal restraints on free expression of religious (or irreligious) views.[182] The cause was taken up by others, many of them deists, who were also libertarians. It gradually ceased to be unlawful to challenge the truth of scripture or doctrine, provided it was done in moderate and thoughtful tones. Lord Coleridge, in a much-quoted opinion, formulated the new distinction thus: 'the mere denial of the truth of Christianity is not enough to constitute the offence of blasphemy.' From this it followed that 'if the decencies of controversy are observed, even the fundamentals of religion may be attacked without the writer being guilty of blasphemy'.[183]

In the US, the constitutional rulings of the Supreme Court made it increasingly clear, as early as the mid-nineteenth and certainly by mid-twentieth centuries, that free conscience and speech could not be curtailed—particularly not to secure conformity of religious belief, but also not to protect the tender

---

[175] Ibid. at 406 and accompanying citations.

[176] See also *People v. Porter*, 2 Park Crim. Rep. (NY) 14 (1823); *Updegraph v. the Commonwealth*, 11 Serg. & Rawl. (Pa.) 394 (1824); *State v. Chandler*, 2 Harr. (Del.) 553 (1837).

[177] Adams to Jefferson, 23 Jan. 1825, in *The Adams-Jefferson Letters* 607–8 (Lester J. Cappon ed., 1971). [178] Levy, *supra* n. 22, at 413.

[179] *Commonwealth v. Kneeland*, 37 Mass. 206 (1838) at 211–25.        [180] Ibid. at 213.

[181] The felicitous phrase is from Slaughter, *supra* n. 40, at 183. The distinction appears in the opinion of Lord Erskine in *Shore v. Wilson*, 8 ER 450, 517 (H. of L. 1842).

[182] Levy, *supra* n. 22, at 424. The book is: John Search, Considerations of the Law of Libel, as Relating to Publication on the subject of religion (1833).

[183] *Ramsey v. Foote*, 48 LTR 733, 736, 739 (*Regina v. Ramsey*, 15 Cox Crim. Cas. 231 (QB 1883)).

sensibilities of believers.[184] In 1971, the State of Pennsylvania dropped its effort to prosecute for blasphemy several shopkeepers who had displayed 'wanted' posters of Jesus with the legend: 'Wanted for sedition, criminal anarchy, vagrancy and conspiracy to overthrow the established government.'[185] Still, it is notable that, in 1971, the state was still trying.

In the last years of the twentieth century, a blasphemy trial anywhere in the US is probably unthinkable. The prevailing American legal justifications for free speech, as Professor Slaughter accurately summarizes them, 'are ultimately based on the liberal values of individual autonomy, self-determination, and self governance'.[186] These are now rather firmly established, but perhaps more interesting is the fact that this has occurred only so recently. Only recently has it become the essentially uncontested common wisdom of courts 'that a union of government and religion tends to destroy government and to degrade religion . . .' and 'that governmentally established religion and religious persecutions go hand in hand'.[187] Only thirty years ago did the Supreme Court make it entirely clear that the 'First Amendment mandates governmental neutrality between religion and religion, and between religion and non-religion'.[188]

The recently dominant liberal perspective accepts that each person's 'self-evident', 'inherent', or 'inalienable' freedom includes an unfettered conscience able to make self-defining teleological choices.[189] It takes seriously the words of Article 18 of the UN Declaration of Human Rights, that 'Everyone has the right to freedom of thought, conscience and religion' and that this 'includes freedom to change his religion or belief . . .'.[190] There thus appears to be a convergence around Locke's notion of society as a compact that preserves most of the essential prerogatives of autonomy enjoyed by individuals in 'a state of nature'.[191]

While it may not be possible for modern Americans to live autonomously outside *any* community, there is nothing especially arduous, today, about them exercising their individuality by leaving one political, religious, professional, or social community—perhaps in disagreement with its perceived *nomos*—and entering another. Moreover, they increasingly are allowed to define their specific personal identities by creating a 'portfolio' of variegated loyalties to family, state, culture, religion, and transnational interest groups. They are relatively at liberty to alter the mix and hierarchy of affinity groups and allegiances, always

---

[184] *Vidal v. Girard's Executors*, 43 US (2 How.) 126, 198–9 (1844). See also *Hustler Magazine Inc. v. Falwell*, 485 US 46 (1988).

[185] Levy, *supra* n. 22, at 530. See also NY Times, 25 Apr. 1971, at 60.

[186] Slaughter, *supra* n. 40, at 184. See also 'Blasphemy' (Note), 70 Col. L. Rev. 694 (1970).

[187] *Engle v. Vitale*, 370 US 421, 431–2 (1962). See also *Lee v. Weisman*, 112 S.Ct. 2649 (1992) and *Cantwell v. Connecticut*, 310 US 296 (1940).

[188] *Epperson v. Arkansas*, 393 US 97, 103–4 (1968).

[189] The terms 'inherent' and 'inalienable' are used, *inter alia*, in the preamble of the Universal Declaration of Human Rights of 1948. UN Doc. A/811 of 10 Dec. 1948.      [190] Ibid.

[191] John Locke, *The Second Treatise on Civil Government* 55 (Prometheus 1986 edn.) (1690).

consciously seeking an individualized identity that reflects their free conscience, values and concept of the good. 'The ideal life', Slaughter points out, thus 'is found, not in fulfilling predefined roles and patterns, but rather in exercising autonomy by choosing roles and in changing identity.'[192]

In America's liberal democratic society, to quote a 1992 decision of the US Supreme Court regarding attempts by Pennsylvania to restrict abortions, the law protects 'the most intimate and personal choices a person may make in a lifetime, choices central to personal dignity and autonomy'.[193] Thus, at 'the heart of liberty is the right to define one's own concept of existence, of meaning, of the universe and of the mystery of human life'.[194]

The way freedom of conscience is accepted in America, today, leads some observers to draw the starkest contrasts to less tolerant societies, most of which, nowadays, are in the non-Western world.[195] Such starkness seems confirmed by the contemporary rhetoric with which intolerant theocracies still sometimes defend their policies against what they perceive as rampantly immoral, socially destructive and even Satanic Western liberalism. Despite such super-ficial evidence, however, the theory of a Great Fault between civilizations cannot withstand historical scrutiny. The 'liberal' West, certainly as exemplified by England and the United States, did not become 'liberal' until very recently. Mostly, it remained on the other side of any 'fault-line' that can now be discerned between tolerant and intolerant societies. That contemporary Eng-land and the US have lately come to espouse tolerant accommodation of individual conscientious autonomy thus cannot credibly be attributed to genetic, ethnic, or cultural inherencies but must, instead, be explored in terms

[192] Slaughter, *supra* n. 40, at 187.

[193] *Planned Parenthood v. Casey*, 505 US 833, 851 (1992).

[194] Ibid. at 851. Such a commitment, of course, does not obviate the difficult task of deciding, case by case, when a socially intrusive claim to free exercise — e.g., the practice of polygamy — must yield to the social order as defined by a community as its 'state interest'. *Reynolds v. United States*, 98 US 145 (1879). There appears more recently, however, to be a tacit governmental agreement not to prosecute polygamy among small Mormon sects. NY Times, 12 Oct. 1969, sec. 1, at 5. This problem, briefly noted in the text of this chapter, was faced in a 1996 indictment by a Nebraska prosecutor of recent immigrants from Iraq who had participated in a wedding of two daughters, aged 13 and 14, to Iraqi immigrant grooms aged 28 and 34. The father was charged with child abuse, the mother with contributing to the delinquency of a minor, and the putative husbands with statutory rape under Nebraska law prohibiting marriage of persons under the age of 17 and making it illegal for anyone 18 or older to have sex with someone under 18, even with such person's consent. The girls were taken into protective custody and the four adults arrested. 'You live in our state,' the prosecutor was quoted as saying, 'you live by our laws.' According to the defence attorney, however, such child marriage is approved among conservative rural Islamics, since it alleviates concern that the girls might otherwise be 'dishonoured'. Don Terry, 'Child Brides in Middle America: Mideast Culture Clashes With the Law', Int'l Herald Tribune, 3 Dec. 1996, at 11. Another example is the use of hallucinogenic drugs. *People v. Woody*, 61 Cal.2d 719, 394 P.2d 813 (1964), held that the use of Peyote by Indians as a religious practice could not be prohibited. For discussion of this difficult subject, see, e.g., *Sherbert v. Verner*, 374 US 398 (1963).

[195] For a defence of that difference from an Asian perspective see Bilahari Kausikan, 'Asia's Different Standard', 92 For. Policy 24 (1993).

of socio-cultural, technological, scientific, economic, and political variables. *Prima facie*, such variables can operate anywhere. They are not society-specific.

What English and American history demonstrate is that under the influence of various factors these societies—quite recently as intolerant of freedom and individualism as any today—have evolved towards an acknowledgement of personal autonomy. The experiences of England and America certainly do not fully account for the evolution of a 'Western' position on freedom of conscience, but suffice to undermine any unsupported claims that tolerant liberalism is an inherent characteristic of Western society that cannot be replicated elsewhere. This insight is reenforced when one considers the history of Sweden's famously tolerant, liberal, and democratic society. This, too, turns out to be entirely a recent construct and is not in any sense 'inherent'. Until quite recently, freedom of conscience was no more a Swedish idea than it is currently a Saudi Arabian one. The remarkable change that has only now transformed the Swedish social and cultural attitude towards conscientious autonomy should move one to inquire further into the factors that determine (and change) the attitude of any society towards personal freedom and protection of the expression of individualism.

### (c) The Special Case of Sweden

The Reformation in England did not usher in freedom of conscience; nor did the American Revolution end the use of law to enforce conformity. Both events, however, did undermine societal support for enforcing old certitudes in matters of faith. In Northern Europe, Anglican, Lutheran, and Calvinist doctrines, although often as fiercely asserted and brutally enforced as any of the Old Order, lacked the power and conviction that only a long pedigreed and universal hierarchy could muster. Mere national churches did not have quite the cachet of the universal Catholic and Orthodox churches or, for that matter, of universal Islam. A certain unwonted modesty was imposed on the claims of the new churches because they were demonstrably 'only' national (or, as with Geneva, civic) institutions, operating, in most instances, plainly under the direction of secular authorities. Moreover, Protestantism's restricted view of hierarchy and emphasis on personal salvation made the emergence of conscientious individualism almost inevitable, even if it was, at first, a fiercely resisted concomitant.

The new Protestant secular authorities often had wider interests which did not coincide with those of their own ecclesiastics. For example, however intolerant the rulers were of religious dissent at home, they tended to recognize the legitimacy of—and sometimes form alliances with—foreign states regardless of the religions these espoused. This made it harder to compel conformity at home. Then, too, the subordinate role of new national Protestant churches to the political power of kings and parliaments also in time led to the curbing of conformist zeal, as rulers found it prudent to sacrifice dogmatic uniformity to achieve domestic tranquillity. The political leaders, when they came to realize that tolerance for diversity promoted, rather than eroded, the social fabric, were able to make the national churches bend to that new revelation.

This historic progression, from state-sponsored and legally enforced theological conformity to modern liberal democratic pluralism, began in Western and Central Europe with the decline of the Holy Roman Empire and the rise of sovereign states after the Peace of Westphalia. It drew strength from the dramatic triumph of populist politics over ecclesiastical power in the French and Russian Revolutions. In Scandinavia, the progression was rather more peaceful and, when it came, it was swifter than elsewhere in the West.

The inaccessibility of Sweden had caused it to be late in accepting the authority of Rome, and the country's notoriously inclement clime had made missionary Roman churchmen less passionate than elsewhere about putting down deep roots. The Swedish branch of Catholicism thus was by default unusually independent and self-sufficient, even before the Reformation. In the words of one historian: 'Nowhere else did the Pope exercise so little influence and, alone in medieval Christendom, the Swedes possessed what amounted to a national Church,'[196] one dominated by a Swedish perspective. This was apparent even before King Gustav Vasa formally introduced the Lutheran Reformation. Beginning with his coronation in 1523, the church was methodically subordinated to the state as the new king assumed very wide powers over church appointments. All bishops were compelled to take a lengthy oath of allegiance to the Swedish royal house and the clergy were made subject to discipline in Swedish crown courts.[197] The first break with Rome only came in 1544. As in neighbouring states (Prussia, Saxony, and Holland)[198] the clergy became 'servants of the congregation and the state'[199] rather than independent servants of God.

Unlike England, Sweden went from Catholicism to a national Protestant church swiftly, without backsliding or significant conflict, and entirely. And its national church came quickly and wholly under governmental control. Sweden differed from England in many respects, but most significantly in that feudalism was not well established in the sense that the aristocracy served primarily as royal functionaries of the court. It lacked what England had since *Magna Carta*: a class of landowners with the trappings of baronial autonomy. The Swedish barons, in effect, were a caste of high bureaucrats. This made it almost inevitable that, when the church was nationalized, its now-Protestant bishops and clergy would fit into the prevailing pattern of subservience to the central political authority of the state. Moreover, when Protestantism did come to

---

[196] Roland Huntford, *The New Totalitarians* 16 (1972).
[197] Nicholas Hope, *German and Scandinavian Protestantism, 1700–1918* 82 (1995).
[198] Ibid. at 83–98.        [199] Ibid. at 94.

Sweden, it came in the form of an established state church with no claim to continuity with Catholicism (in contrast to England) and, thus, with no claim to institutionally independent, historically legitimated authority or power. It was incorporated as a part of the system of political governance, with no economic autonomy. All property, including church real estate and its income, was transferred to the Crown. 'The clergy obediently turned into ordained bureaucrats. Ruled directly by lay officials and royal secretaries, the Church became a government department.'[200] The clergy carried out poor relief for the state, kept registers of births and marriages, proclaimed royal edicts to their congregants, reported on the condition of local farms and estates, and, in general, 'represented the government in exactly those areas where government impinged most directly on the individual, and in the riksdag [parliament] it was most often they who could best express the sentiments of the common man. The most active and democratic local governing bodies were the parish meetings and the elected six-man vestries and church wardens'.[201]

While the nationalization of religion sought to ensure a degree of stability after the collapse in Northern Europe of Catholic pre-eminence, this new civil role of the church through marriage to the state made religious doctrinal power subordinate to those militant political forces which had already begun to press the state for greater freedom and toleration of conscientious dissent. These forces did not, however, come to the fore at once; as in England, the early Reformation moved defensively in the opposite direction. Catholics were banned from holding public services in 1595 and Catholicism itself was prohibited in 1617. The Conventicles Act remained in force until 1858 and in 1884, August Strindberg could still be prosecuted for sacrilege on the basis of a collection of short stories.[202]

Compared to Britain, however, the Swedish transition was far gentler. The sole punishment for remaining (or becoming) a Papist was not execution or imprisonment, but exile. When Queen Christina, Gustav Vasa's great-granddaughter, reverted to Catholicism in 1654, during the twenty-third year of her reign, there was no revolution. She quietly abdicated, left Sweden and never returned. The quite mild—for the times—intolerance that marked Sweden's transition to Protestantism was at least in part in response to the fact that it was remarkably unopposed, especially compared to England. 'In few other countries', Roland Huntford concludes, 'did the Reformation triumph, or Catholicism disappear, so swiftly, completely and effortlessly. By the end of the

---

[200] Irene Scobic, *Sweden* 21 (1972).

[201] Franklin D. Scott, *Sweden, The Nation's History* 195 (1988).

[202] Nor was this unique in Sweden. A draconian Danish press law of 1799 provided (sec. 5) that anyone 'who published anything which aimed to subvert Christian teaching on God's existence, or the immortality of the soul, or in print censured and insulted Christian doctrine, was to be exiled for three to ten years . . . [and] blasphemy was punished with a diet of bread and water for four to fourteen days'. Hope, *supra* n. 197, at 304.

seventeenth century, not a single Catholic remained in Sweden.'[203] This facilitated a policy of silken suppression. There was little of the blood, fire, and
clangour of the same period in Britain.

Still, the facts scarcely fitted the model of Western liberalism. Calvinism and
Catholicism were prohibited by law. Enforced conformity continued until late
in the nineteenth century. In 1848, Sweden's Baptists were forced to emigrate to
America and expulsions of nonconformists continued until 1855. Until 1860,
apostasy remained a crime and Free Churches were legalized only in 1870. All
persons were legally deemed to be born into the state church until the law's
repeal in 1970.[204] While the law, after 1860, permitted Swedes to embrace a
religion other than the state church, anyone wishing to do so, until 1952, had to
submit to personal examination of their motives by the established Lutheran
clergy, which had the power to refuse the application.[205] In particular, persons
were only permitted to leave the state church upon proof of having joined
another Christian denomination.[206]

Lutheranism's virtual state monopoly prevailed at least until the arrival of a
wave of new immigrants from the Mediterranean and Asia, after 1960. They
made Islam formally the 'second party' of Swedish religious beliefs, although it
remains a small minority. The real opposition to Lutheranism's monopoly in
Sweden, Norway, or Denmark, however, has arisen not from outside but from
within the big tent of the state religion. Indeed, the struggle for personal self-
determination in Sweden has become little more than a gentle slide into
unbelief, most of it occurring more or less unremarked behind the façade of
nominal adherence to an established Lutheran Church in a Christian nation. It
has been said that 'Sweden is one of the rare countries in which men are often
anti-religious, but rarely anti-clerical.'[207]

The Swedish church is to be disestablished by the year 2000[208] and, with
recent immigration, mostly from outside Europe, the traditional homogeneity of
Sweden—until recently a nation of persons who have 'never emerged from
behind the veil of the group'[209]—is no longer so apparent. Individual autonomy and assertion of personal identity appears belatedly to have supplemented,
if not altogether supplanted, the Swedish preference for a nation 'not of
individual citizens, but of groups and guilds'.[210]

In matters of religious conscience, however, the transition has been made in
Sweden as fully as in England—perhaps even more so—from mandatory
conformity to personal autonomy. It is a transition, however, of very recent
origins and its pace has been somewhat slower and much gentler than in

---

[203] Huntford, *supra* n. 196, at 23.     [204] Ibid.     [205] Ibid.
[206] Scott, *supra* n. 201, at 573.     [207] Huntford, *supra* n. 196, at 24.
[208] *Staten och trossamfunden* (Summary), Statens offentliga utredningar, Civil departementet, at 15–
17, 1994. A résumé of previous efforts to disestablish the Swedish Lutheran Church is in Scott, *supra*
n. 201, at 575.     [209] Huntford, *supra* n. 196, at 34.
[210] Ibid.

England. Nevertheless, the steps, their direction and the outcome are all unmistakably similar.

## 7. THE ROAD TO TOLERATION: HISTORIC PARALLELS AND INDEPENDENT VARIABLES

A gradual and uneven progression towards toleration appears to have occurred in Britain and in Sweden over a period of 450 years and in three distinct stages.

First, churches were regarded as partners in the exercise of temporal power in the community. The power of kings, at this stage, was still dependent on a 'fusion of mythical and genealogical' explanations[211] which the ecclesiastical authorities were called upon to validate. At the next, second, stage, governments wrested away power from the spiritual authorities, restricting them to jurisdiction over purely theological matters, and, even then, in a position of subordination. Now churches, whether formally nationalized or only *de facto* under state control, became dependent on the state to enforce religious conformity or restrain dissent. The church/state partnership, at this stage, resembled that between a horse and its rider, with the state in the saddle. Finally, at the third stage, religion became an independent contractor, neither supported nor restrained by the state. Instead, either a constitutional or a *de facto* separation occurred. The state renounced control over church governance in return for church renunciation of all official status and accompanying rights to protection and privilege. At this point, all religions and beliefs, including secular humanism, agnosticism, and atheism, are equally tolerated and none are enhanced or disadvantaged. The choice among them becomes entirely a matter for each person's individual, autonomous self-determination.

Western nations, and some non-Western ones such as India, have traversed all three of these stages. A few societies remain in the first stage, their governments being essentially theocracies, where religious and political power act in partnership and the state is an instrument for the suppression of religious autonomy and individual self-identification. Iran and Afghanistan, after a brief period in the second phase appear to have reverted to the first. Most Islamic societies, however, even quite conservative ones, appear to have entered the second phase. In Saudi Arabia, we have noted that the clergy have been largely co-opted into the governmental bureaucracy[212] in a manner reminiscent of Sweden after the Reformation. In nineteenth- and early twentieth-century China, too, the emperors gradually achieved preponderant control of theological as well as secular affairs by integrating both into the bureaucracy. With the transformation of China, after its revolution, into a Marxist state, all

---

[211] Niklas Luhmann, *The Differentiation of Society* 333 (Holmes & Larmore trans., 1982).
[212] Ayman Al-Yassini, *Religion and State in the Kingdom of Saudi Arabia* 135 (1985).

religions—whether Confucian, Christian, Buddhist, or Islamic[213]—endured the same subordination to the will of the political state. It remains to be seen whether these societies will proceed, like most 'Western' and 'Westernized' ones, to the third stage.

Article 36 of the 1982 Chinese Constitution, for the first time since the revolution, expressly recognizes that no 'state organ, public organization or individual may compel citizens to believe in, or not believe in any religion, nor may they discriminate against citizens who believe in or do not believe in any religion'.[214] True, the Chinese Communist Party still refuses to admit persons publicly professing religious beliefs,[215] and the religious authority of the Tibetan Buddhist establishment remains restricted.[216] Still, it seems that the days of coerced conformity in China may be numbered and that this will result from the operation of the same independent variables—urbanization, industrialization, the rise of an urban middle class, the information and communications revolutions—as have operated in Western societies to unlock the demand for individual autonomy-based rights. In 1981, China did not oppose the final adoption by consensus of the UN Declaration on the Elimination of all Forms of Intolerance and of Discrimination Based on Religion or Belief,[217] although it continues to repress the Roman Catholic faith,[218] permitting only a national Catholic church to operate. According to Human Rights Watch, although 'freedom of religious belief is guaranteed in China, religious practice for all officially recognized religions—Buddhism, Taoism, Catholicism, Islam and Protestantism—is severely circumscribed. . . . However, the stories of persecution of Chinese Christians . . . are out of proportion to proven offences'.[219] In 1997, Beijing announced that it would sign the Covenant on Economic, Social, and Cultural Rights,[220] and, the next year, it also signed the Covenant on Civil and Political Rights.[221] Unfortunately, as of mid-1999, neither instrument had as yet been ratified.[222]

A progression is also apparent in Eastern Europe. After the collapse of communism, in all countries of the region with the partial exception of

---

[213] Cymoine Rowe, 'Religious Freedom in the People's Republic of China', 2 ILSA J. Int'l & Comp. L. 723 (1996).

[214] Eric Kolodner, 'Religious Rights in China: A Comparison of International Human Rights Law and Chinese Domestic Legislation', 12 UCLA Pac. Basin LJ 407, 421 (1996).

[215] Ibid. at 419–20.       [216] Rowe, *supra* n. 213, at 736–8.

[217] GA Res. 36/55, UN GAOR 36th Sess., Supp. no. 51, at 171, UN Doc. A/36/51 (1981). See GAOR, 36th Sess., 73rd Plenary Mtg., 25 Nov. 1981.

[218] H. Kamm, 'China's Priests, Sticklers for Latin, Disavow Vatican', NY Times, 23 Mar. 1981, at A2; D. Holley, 'Graham Finds Chinese Like His Frog Sermon', LA Times, 18 Apr. 1988, at 6 (pt. 1).       [219] Human Rights Watch, Memorandum, 18 June 1997, at 1 (fax copy).

[220] The Wash. Post, 9 Apr. 1997, at A22.

[221] 'On Eve of Geneva Rights Talks, China Agrees to Sign UN Pact', NY Times, 13 Mar. 1998, at A8. China signed the CCPR on 5 Oct. 1998. The announcement of the signing was carried in the NY Times, 30 Sept. 1998, at A3.

[222] For US pressure on China to ratify see Jane Perlez, 'China Syndrome: Disputes Persist, Civility Rules', NY Times, 3 Mar. 1999, at A3.

Romania and Albania,[223] there is ambiguity and struggle about the appropriate role of church and state and the accommodation of individual freedom of conscience. Once-predominant churches seek now to re-establish themselves as the arbiters of social and political values under the aegis of post-communist governments, for example, by insisting on control over religious education in state schools, recriminalizing of abortion, and restrictions on 'alien' missionaries.[224] Thus, the Bulgarian Orthodox Church has attempted to replace earlier communist-nationalist efforts forcibly to assimilate Turko-Islamic Bulgarians with its own brand of pusillanimous repression.[225] In some instances, the state which, under communism, had made the church its lapdog, still seeks to use religion to advance a political agenda. On the other hand, as various Catholic and Orthodox churches have sought to reclaim their socio-political power in Eastern European countries, they have also engendered a backlash from a citizenry which has little appetite for replacing one kind of communitarian supremacy with another. That has led to a sharp drop in church attendance in places like Slovakia[226] and to the return to power of anti-clerical parties of 'reformed' ex-communists, as in Poland. Overall, there appears to be a readiness to enter a new, third phase marked by the enactment of laws in most of these countries that separate church and state and guarantee freedom of conscience.[227]

For example, the 1990 Hungarian law on 'Freedom and Conscience' stipulates that the 'state is completely neutral to all religions and ideologies and may not be antagonistic toward religions'.[228] In Romania, efforts by the Orthodox Church to re-establish itself as the state religion have been opposed vociferously not only by free-thinkers but also by Latin-rite and Greek-rite Catholics.[229] Gradually, Eastern Europe seems to be navigating the same journey as the West to disestablishment and freedom of conscience. It no longer makes sense to characterize so widespread a phenomenon as 'Westernization', except as a subtle rhetorical device to subvert what is evidently a much wider-spread aspiration and trend.

What determines the pace at which different societies travel this common road? A number of indicators suggest that the pace of the historic shift to personal freedom of conscience, and to individual liberty in general, is determined not by ideology, but by the more exogenous and inexorable forces of economics, technology, and communications. To quote V. S. Naipaul, Western

---

[223] James E. Wood, Jr., 'Rising Expectations for Religious Rights in Eastern Europe', 33 J. of Church & State 1, 4 (1991).

[224] Paul Mojzes, *Religious Liberty in Eastern Europe* 308–9 (1992).     [225] Ibid. at 155.

[226] Ibid. at 186. See also Jonathan Luxmore, 'Eastern Europe 1994: A Review of Religious Life in Bulgaria, Romania, Hungary, Slovakia, the Czech Republic and Poland', 23 Religion, State and Society 213, 215–16 (1995).

[227] See e.g. the Hungarian law of 1990 entitled 'The Right to Freedom and Conscience' which guarantees the free exercise of religion and prohibits state intrusion into religious affairs. Mojzes, ibid. at 268 and Wood, *supra* n. 223, at 7.     [228] Mojzes, ibid. at 268.

[229] Luxmore, *supra* n. 226, at 213.

civilization is becoming the 'universal civilization' that 'fits all men'.[230] Naipaul's formulation, however, is unhelpful: the civilization that 'fits all' is *not* Western, as even the most cursory examination of history has amply demonstrated. It is a civilization of tolerance, freedom, and personal self-determination that is no more *inherently* Western than was the civilization of communitarian conformity and enforced subordination of the individual to state and church, which until so recently held sway in the West.

Rather, what is emerging is a civilization of *modernity*, in which the needs of urbanizing, industrializing, communicating, and information-networking have provoked a demand for civil society in which is clearly demarked a large area reserved for private choice and action in matters including, but by no means limited to, belief and affiliation. This demand governments increasingly find difficult to resist and to it churches increasingly have accommodated themselves.

That claim warrants careful consideration of supporting and countervailing evidence. If true, it suggests that liberal societies and autonomous persons have good reason for patience: for, the outcome of the cultural conflict with illiberal communitarians—so confidently predicted by Huntington and others—will be waged, if at all, not by political or military power but by economic, social, and cultural forces that have already transformed many societies and must eventually do so wherever the embers of social vigour still wait to be fanned.[231]

One indicator is the flow of immigration, which is overwhelmingly in the direction of the liberal-democratic societies, most of it from the communal-authoritarian ones. But for immigration restrictions, the flow from communitarian to individualistic societies would be a global version of the stampede out of Eastern Europe that marked the 1988–9 crumbling of communism's Great Wall. True, immigrants do not come solely for conscientious but also for economic freedom. Increasingly, however, it is becoming apparent that dynamic economic initiative and personal autonomy are indivisible.

There are other, suggestive, indicators. The extent to which communications, information, and higher education continue to be dominated by so-called 'Western' institutions has an inevitable impact on global intellectual trends; and these, in turn, filter into the consciousness of other segments of society. The idea of an Arabic-language service of CNN, for example, is rightly seen as potentially insidious by some Islamicists. One way or another, however, the universalization of information and communications is likely to continue and it will benefit most the cultures that welcome and lead, rather than resist it. Here, again, the advantage is with open societies that are able to accommodate a multiplicity of identities, values, and beliefs: that is, societies constituted by free individuals. And it is precisely in those societies that individuals, freed of the

---

[230] Quoted in Huntington, *supra* n. 88, at 40.
[231] I am indebted to Professor Philip Allott for the felicitous phrase.

deadening hand of conformism, lead the great advances in science, technology, and culture, which, in turn, propel the expansion of their influence.

This advantage, implicit in open societies competing with closed ones, is not so readily apparent from the internal perspective of either. From the internal vantage of the open society, its tolerance for diversity creates an impression of messy stasis: since all individuals theoretically are valued equally and autonomously, the society cannot have any one ideological or cultural 'programme', much less could it mount a concerted project of ideological or cultural expansion. The value it attaches to autonomy and nonconformity seem to vitiate the basic missionary premise imputed to 'the West' by outsiders. A similar delusion prevails in the opposite camp. From the internal vantage of closed communitarian societies, they seem impregnable and thus invulnerable to the chaotic forces of individuation. One is always being told by such governments that their streets are safe at night and that front doors need never be locked. Their intolerance of nonconformity creates the illusion of inexorable unity at home and a vibrant capacity for concerted external expansion. Both perspectives, however, are misleading.

The liberal society may lack epistemic certitude, but that has proven to be no handicap in achieving economic, cultural, and scientific progress and expansion. And the communitarian society may seem cohesive and united, but is still rendered vulnerable by internal stagnation symptomatic of the suppression of social vibrancy and private initiative as well as the society's lack of priming by exposure to external competition. It is difficult to think of a predominantly communitarian society in which the controlled flow of information has not caused social, cultural, and economic stagnation. One dramatic example is Japanese architecture, which, for a millennium, underwent little significant transformation even as architecture evolved, functionally and conceptually, in the West.[232] This made it difficult to introduce new ideas and created a gap now filled by much truly dreadful modern commercial architecture imported willy-nilly as Japan plunged into the 'modern' world. Once liberated, however, Japanese architects have begun to conceive new forms of expression equal to the best (and, of course, also the worst) to be found anywhere.

## 8. CONCLUSIONS

Toleration of diversity by a society and its institutions is that which enables each individual to exercise choice and manifest autonomous conscientious self-definition. While toleration is usually perceived in religious terms, it transcends religion to influence most facets of the individual, social, and political state of being. In England, for example, the party system, and with it parliamentary

---

[232] Kazuo Nishi & Kazuo Hozumi, *What is Japanese Architecture?* 53–92 (Eng. edn., 1985).

democracy, emerged as a concomitant of religious toleration, which, from the mid-seventeenth to nineteenth centuries was gradually extended first to the nonconformist chapels, then to the Roman Catholic Church and, finally, to Jews.[233] To the growth of religious toleration may be attributed the notion of peaceful political change, secular education, the emergence of a civil society, the 'idea of the limited State within which voluntary associations have their own sphere',[234] and, most especially, the theory of individual civil rights.

The milestones in this evolution are the monumental legal enactments, the judicial decisions and rescissions, and the shifts of power to parliaments and to broadened electorates. These slowly ended the long era of enforced conformity in matters of personal belief and expression, but also unleashed a great whirlwind of social, cultural, and economic creativity. From the internal perspective of traditional communitarian societies, it must be recognized, the prospect of such 'unleashing' represents what Professor Dianne Otto calls 'modernity's threat of universality'.[235] Otto's is a much more realistic appraisal of confrontation between communitarian and individualistic values than is offered by Samuel Huntington's 'clash of civilizations', for it understands—that is, it welcomes, or regrets, but, either way, perceives—the tactical advantages of the latter over the former, and its inherent potential for universality.

In any conflict between advocates of freedom of conscience and the guardians of communal authority, one modern tactical advantage that accrues inherently to the former seems particularly decisive. Only those who believe conditionally: that is, are willing to accept an unfettered right of each person to profess any system of belief (or unbelief), when in power are able comfortably to accommodate those who believe in absolute, or merely different, truths. In a liberal society, these latter need not fight, emigrate or die for their beliefs, but can conscientiously join in building a successful and peaceable civil society. Such accommodation is not reciprocal, however. Those who believe themselves possessed of invincible truths, if able to enforce their claim, must inevitably generate conditions of perpetual fight, flight, and stagnation.

In an era in which conflict is itself seen as antisocial and wasteful rather than ennobling, the tide would seem to be running towards belief systems that favour accommodation and conscientious *laissez-faire*. Precisely because religious certitude and enforced conformity have such a history of provoking men to war and mayhem, states have negotiated a global Convention on Civil and Political Rights that makes toleration the universal norm in matters of belief and professions of faith. The ICCPR purports to require all societies to guarantee everyone's right to freedom of thought, conscience, and religion and the right to manifest this in worship, observance, practice, and teaching.[236] While the text of

---

[233] Payne, *supra* n. 137.          [234] Ibid. at 257.

[235] Dianne Otto, 'Subalternity and International Law: the Problems of Global Community and the Incommensurability of Difference', 5 Social and Legal Studies 337, 354 (1996).

[236] ICCPR, art. 18. 999 UNTS 171, 6 ILM 368 (1967).

the Convention may not accurately reflect practice in some societies, it does evidence a general, if still grudging, acknowledgment by governments that intolerance and enforced conformity are irreconcilable with peaceful and prosperous development, as well as with the personal identity-aspirations of persons everywhere.

This does not mean that the human rights canon, although of universal application, should never be interpreted contextually. Obviously, a society in which there has been a recent history of devastating racial, religious, or cultural wars may have good reason to tailor its protection of conscientious freedom and conscientious expression in a mode different from that now prevailing in peaceable Sweden, Britain, or the United States. If it is correct that the prevalence of personal freedom in a society is determined essentially by exogenous factors, then the absence of individual freedom must rightly be seen as a factor requiring the international community to marshal not merely criticism and opprobrium but also international help to enable such societies to deal with the underlying causes.[237]

Finally, it is increasingly being realized that the tension between individualism and its enemies should not be seen, simplistically, as a zero-sum game. For one thing, the state and the individual are not the only contenders. As is more fully explicated in Chapter 9, there are trilateral tensions evident in virtually all societies between rights-based claims of the state seeking to preserve unity, the groups (cultural, ethnic, religious, etc.) seeking to preserve their particularity, and the individual seeking freedom of expression and identity. This tension obviously cannot always be resolved in favour of the individual, but requires careful equilibration. Thus, for example, the Human Rights Committee, applying the ICCPR, has ruled, applying article 18 of the ICCPR's religious freedom clause, that a Canadian conscientious objector is not entitled to withhold those taxes used to defray military expenditures.[238] Similarly, the Committee rejected the religion-based claim of a Canadian Sikh railway worker to be allowed to wear a turban at work, instead of the mandatory hard-hat.[239] These efforts at the balancing of social or communitarian with individual rights are neither 'Western' nor 'Eastern' but evidence of the search for accommodation and convergence.

The President of Sri Lanka, Mrs Chandrika Kumaratunga, has expressed the

---

[237] However, as the Human Rights Committee observed in a case in which it found that Cameroon had violated a prisoner's rights under ICCPR article 7 (prohibiting torture, and cruel, inhuman or degrading treatment), 'certain minimum standards of detention must be observed regardless of a State party's level of development . . .'. *Albert Womah Mukong v. Cameroon*, case no. 458/1991, Report of the Human Rights Committee, GAOR, 49th Sess., Supp. no. 40 (A/49/40) (1994), vol. 1, at 73–4, para. 420.

[238] Case no. 446/1991 (JP v. Canada), Report of the Human Rights Committee, 9 Oct. 1992; GAOR, 47th Sess., Supp. no. 40 (A/47/40), p. 158, para. 633 and annex X, sect. 25.

[239] Case no. 208/1986 (*Bhinder v. Canada*), Official Records of the Human Rights Committee, 1989/90, vol. II, CCPR/9/Add.1 (1995), at 362, para. 625.

view that 'the free market has become universal, and it implies democracy and human rights'. Asked whether this does not imply a preference for 'Western values' over Asian ones, she said that, 'of course, every country has its own national ethos, but in the modern world, it is largely cultural, not a political system. When people talk about a conflict of values, I think it is an excuse that can be used to cover a multitude of sins'.[240] Kofi Annan, the African Secretary-General of the United Nations, has expressed the same point of view even more emphatically. Speaking to the summit meeting of the Organization of African Unity in 1997, he rejected the idea that different societies and cultures view fundamental human rights differently. 'Some view this concern as a luxury of the rich countries for which Africa is not ready,' he told the heads of state. 'I know that others treat it as an imposition, if not a plot by the industrialized West. I find these thoughts truly demeaning, demeaning of the yearning for human dignity that resides in every African heart.'[241]

Something of the same point was made in a more strictly legal sense by Dame Rosalyn Higgins, currently a Judge of the International Court of Justice but, previously, a member of the ICCPR's Human Rights Committee. Summing up her experience on that body of elected experts, representing the world's major social and political systems, she observed: 'Third World members have taken the lead in insisting that human rights are not a set of imposed western ideas, but are of universal application, speaking to the human condition.'[242] Similar views have lately been expressed by Bertrand G. Ramcharan, the Guyanan Director for Africa in the UN Department of Political Affairs,[243] and Dato Param Cumaraswamy, the former chair of the Bar Council of Malaysia and UN Special Rapporteur on the Independence of Judges and Lawyers.[244]

To test that analysis we will next examine the direction in which various states and their legal systems are moving in respect of other matters pertaining to individual identity: the choice of occupations, of gender, and of personal names. Once again, the evidence will suggest that societies everywhere—in Western and non-Western societies—begin by enforcing communitarian uniformity, then move cautiously towards accommodating divergence and eventually assume a position of neutrality or benevolent protection towards the proliferating forms

---

[240] Interview conducted by Joseph Fitchett, Int'l Herald Tribune, 29 Nov. 1996, at 4.

[241] Anthony Lewis, 'It Tolls For Thee', NY Times, 23 June 1997, at A17.

[242] Rosalyn Higgins, DBE, 'Ten Years on the Human Rights Committee', Eur. H. Rts. L. Rev., no. 6, 570, 575 (1996).

[243] Bertrand G. Ramcharan, 'The Universality of Human Rights', The Review, International Commission of Jurists, nos. 58–9, 105 (1997).

[244] Dato Param Cumaraswamy, 'The Universal Declaration of Human Rights—Is It Universal?' The Review, ibid. at 118.

of individual self-expression.[245] What we will see is not a withering away either of the state or of community, but a gradual redirection of the state's enforcement power towards new areas of regulatory concern and a transfer to autonomous individuals of a right to private choice regarding matters as to which uniformity has ceased to demonstrate its social utility.

[245] In legal terms, this progression has also been hypothesized by Professor Robert C. Post, who proposes three kinds of laws: 'assimilationist, pluralist and individualist. Each postulates a different kind of relationship between . . . heterogeneity and the legal order. Assimilationist law strives towards social uniformity by imposing the values of a dominant cultural group; pluralist law safeguards diversity by enabling competing groups to maintain their distinct perspectives; individualist law rejects group values altogether in favour of the autonomous choices of individuals.' Robert C. Post, 'Cultural Heterogeneity and Law: Pornography, Blasphemy, and the First Amendment', 76 Cal. L. Rev. 297, 305 (1988).

# 7

## Constructing the Self: Name, Gender, Career, and Privacy

> Others say, Law is our Fate;
> Others say, Law is our State;
> Others say, others say
>    Law is no more
>    Law has gone away
> And always the loud angry crowd
> Very angry and very loud
>    Law is we
> And always the soft idiot softly Me.
>
> W. H. Auden, 'Law Like Love',
> *The Collected Poetry of*
> *W. H. Auden* 74 (1945)

Consider this: In 1996, M. Le Chevallier, the mayor of the French port of Toulon, quashed an award at the Toulon Book Fair to the Jewish writer Marek Halter. He gave it instead to the actress Brigitte Bardot, whose husband is a National Front member.

'Halter has an internationalist vision, whereas we are for family and nation,' the mayor explained.[1]

## 1. INTRODUCTION

In the preceding chapter, we examined one of the great claims individuals advance against compelled communitarian conformity: the claim to freedom of conscience. We turn now to what may seem to be lesser claims: the right of each person to determine autonomously such matters as choice of a name, sex, and career. To persons denied these rights, however, the struggle for them is not a trivial pursuit, but rather one of scarcely less importance than that for freedom of conscience. Whether one agrees or not, it does appear that progress towards individual self-definition in these additional areas may be seen as

---

[1] Barry James, 'French Intellectuals Take On the National Front', Int'l Herald Tribune, 15–16 Feb. 1997, at 2. Bardot ultimately declined the honour.

further redrawing the line between legally compelled communitarian conformity and legally protected individual autonomy.

Different societies, and the same societies at different times in their evolution, have extended varying degrees of tolerance to individual choice in such matters. The social indicator, usually, is a legal one: whether the law makes it relatively easy or difficult for persons in a particular state or system of law to exercise their autonomously derived preferences and whether law protects those individual choices from external interference. In recent times most Western and some non-Western societies have moved in the direction of greater systemic tolerance for individual choice, even when those choices confound the preferences and values of the majority. Or, perhaps more accurately, many people in liberal democracies have ceased to feel that society has a legitimate interest in controlling individual preference by enforcing conformity in such matters or in maintaining communitarian solidarity with common values and standards. Another way to put this is that much about the identity of each person has been reassigned from the province of legally enforced morality to that of freely exercised individual preference.

Seen in that light, a growing accommodation by previously restrictive communitarian societies of the right of persons to choose their own names (and that of their children) seems far from a marginal triumph for the individualist cause.

## 2. PERSONAL AUTONOMY IN CHOICE OF NAME

Guiliano Pisapia, a lawyer, member of the Italian Parliament and chairman of its Justice Committee, as well as a member of the orthodox Communist Reformation Party, introduced legislation in 1996 which would require children to assume the maiden name of their mother, rather than the father's surname. His purpose was to acknowledge in law each offspring's 'special relationship' with the mother, one 'different with respect to the father'.[2] This untraditional initiative had the partial support of Italy's left-centrist Government. The idea, it appears, was to bring patriarchal Italy into line with Northern European law, where—in Germany, for example—the law permits families to take the surname of the father, the mother, or both.[3]

Oddly, Pisapia's proposal, although coming from the far left, received strong support from Benito Mussolini's granddaughter, one of the parliamentary leaders of Italy's neo-Fascist National Alliance Party. Allesandra Mussolini volunteered that, because her family's name would otherwise face extinction, she had petitioned a court to allow her infant daughter Caterina to take the surname of the former Italian dictator, rather than her husband's. Refusal, she

---

[2] NY Times, 24 Aug. 1996, at 4.     [3] Ibid.

said, would make her feel 'penalized as a woman'. 'The obligation to assume the father's name is absurd,' she said: 'stuff from the Middle Ages.'[4]

Franco Ferrarotti, a leading Italian sociologist, commented that it was 'evident that in Italian society the autonomy of the personality of women is growing'.[5] However, he also recognized that Pisapia's measure, rather than promoting personal individualism, merely substituted one state-decreed value preference for another. The choice of names, he noted, 'should not be imposed as norms, but rather contemplated in a voluntary way, by joint agreement of the couple'.[6] His view was seconded by Italy's Minister for Equal Opportunity, Anna Finocchiaro, who stated a preference for a 'solution that guarantees freedom of decision, rather than imposing another obligation, even if in the opposite direction'.

This peculiar little cameo illustrates a number of relevant points. It makes self-evident that the matter of choosing a person's name is widely regarded, even by those who agree on little else, as within the realm of creating that person's identity. It also shows that, traditionally, the naming of persons is addressed not exclusively by the individual preference of parents but also by law, the latter being empowered to reflect and impose community values. Finally, the cameo illustrates an underlying socio-political fissure: not, as superficially appears, between proponents of matriarchy or patriarchy, but, more profoundly, between those who believe that such matters must be addressed by laws to ensure social conformity, order, and coherence and those who believe the choice should not be governed by law but by autonomous individuals in accordance with their personal taste.

Western thought has wavered, historically, between these positions: whether one's family, or given, names should be of public or only of private concern. Should our names reflect the state's, or community's, interest in a stable system of identification and in preserving family cohesion, or should the choice be left to personal preference? Under the laws of Imperial Rome, first names were followed by the genitive of the father's name and women usually had no first name but a female version of the second name used in her gens or clan (e.g., Claudia for Claudius), sometimes followed by a number or adjective to distinguish one from another.[7] A citizen could change his name at will, unless the proposed change was fraudulent in intent or effect.[8]

With the rise of Christianity and the fall of Rome, Christian names became the sole means of identification among the Gauls and Franks, until the notion of

---

[4] NY Times, 24 Aug. 1996, at 4.        [5] Ibid.        [6] Ibid.

[7] Walter Pintens & Michael R. Will, 'Names,' 4 *International Encyclopedia of Comparative Law*, ch. 2 (*Persons and Family*) (Mary Ann Glendon ed., 1995), at 45, 46.

[8] 'Très vite la loi romaine s'applique, en Gaule: . . . liberté absolue de changer de nom.' Armelle Cressard, Le Monde, 23 Sept. 1991, Lexis-Nexis p. 7 (Load 8 Nov. 1991). See also Pintens & Will, ibid. at 46: 'there was complete freedom in names, making it possible to change the name.' See also Constitutio de plutatione nomine of Diocletian and Maximinian, Codex 9.25.

a hereditary surname gradually spread from Constantinople beginning in the ninth century.[9] Nevertheless, the Roman tradition of allowing free change of name remained dominant until the eighteenth century, despite occasional efforts of the state to impose continuity.[10] In France, for example, uncontrolled nomenclature remained the rule until the sixteenth century. With the spread of unrest and the unravelling of social control, however, King Henri II, by the edict of Amboise of 1555, forbade all further changing of names except upon prior royal dispensation.[11] Under the new law, long usage of a family name would effectively preclude change except in the most extraordinary circumstances.[12] The legal innovation was not successful, but it began the tendency in many nations to make the state the arbiter of personal nomenclature, a tendency extending both to given and surnames, which has persisted to the present day.

After the French Revolution, the Decree of 26 brumaire an I, of 16 November 1793, reflecting the heady liberationist atmosphere, allowed everyone a change of name by simple declaration to public authorities. This resulted in a deluge of changes in the midst of post-revolution turmoil and, within a year, the fearful authorities had introduced new measures to protect the social fabric. The Convention passed a decree forbidding the use of any names other than those given or inherited at birth.[13] This law of '6 Fructidor an II, art. 1' made both given and family names essentially unchangeable.[14] A law of '11 Germinal an XI' further provides that parents' choice of first names be restricted (by the state registry) to names in use 'in the different calendars and those of persons known in ancient history'.[15] Especially commended by law are the names listed in the Republican calendar of Fabre d'Eglantine.[16] These requisites of social stability, as they appeared alike to successive French republican and imperial regimes, remained essentially unaltered until a law of 1985 at last gave persons the right to adopt last names consisting of the family names of both parents.[17]

In the 1980s French judicial decisions also began to modify other limitations.[18] Only in 1993, however, did the French Civil Code establish the presumption that 'the child's given names are chosen by the father and mother' and only if these are unknown may the civil registrar control or choose the child's names.[19] Even

---

[9] Pintens & Will, ibid. at 47.    [10] Ibid.    [11] Le Monde, 23 Sept. 1991, *supra* n. 8.

[12] Henri Capitant, *Les grands arrêts de la jurisprudence civile*, 9th edn. (François Terré and Yves Lequette, eds.) 84, 85 (1991). The authors cite a case in the Cour de Cassation, 'Saintecatherine v. Prosecutor General of Limoges) in which the appellate tribunal reversed a decision by the Limoges Tribunal 'de grande instance' that had refused to change the petitioner's surname back to its ancestral form of Sainte Catherine because several generations had accepted its misrendering by the registry as Saintecatherine. The lower court had cited sixteenth-century prohibitions refusing this rectification.    [13] Ibid.

[14] *Juris-Classeur Administratif*, Fasicule 1054, 'Compétence en Matière d'État et de Droits Fondamentaux des Personnes' (par Rosy Baclet-Hainque), at 8, para. 75 (1995).

[15] Dalloz, *Code Civil*, 93rd edn., p. 93 (1993–4).    [16] Ibid. at Art. 57, p. 91.

[17] Le Monde, 23 Sept. 1991, *supra* n. 8.

[18] Law no. 93–22 of 8 January 1993. Dalloz, *supra* n. 15, at Art. 57, p. 91.

[19] Ibid. at 90.

so, this emancipation retains the injunction to use 'usual names',[20] and preserves the registrar's option to refuse to register first names regarded as too unusual. In such cases, the registrar submits the matter to a Family Court judge, who may disallow names considered to be against the child's interest.[21]

The French state still has an active interest in controlling not only the giving of names, but also any subsequent changes in nomenclature. By the law of 1993, requests to change family names are still subject to strict standards of legal scrutiny administered on behalf of society by the judiciary.[22] To change one's surname, one must still overcome the force of Article 1 of the law of '6 Fructidor an II' which forbids the taking of a name other than that stipulated by birth or filiation. The Cour de Cassation 'on several occasions, and recently has cited [it] as still being in force'.[23] This rule is not absolute and may be modified in practice by change of status—for example, inheritance of a title, as also by legitimization, marriage, or adoption. Beyond that, the French judiciary 'has acquired a certain latitude in ordering or preventing a change of name'.[24]

Nevertheless, in each instance the onus is still on persons seeking a change of name to demonstrate a legitimate interest to the Court's satisfaction.[25] According to recent decisions, such an interest may be recognized if the name is 'grotesque or that of a criminal, or if one wishes to distinguish oneself from another family [of the same or similar name] or to revive an illustrious name which would otherwise be extinguished'.[26] There are also administrative procedures for the *francisation* of family names on acquisition of French citizenship,[27] or to perpetuate the name of citizens killed fighting for France.[28] However, the mere fact that a name is foreign-sounding is insufficient reason to allow a change, for, as courts have pointed out, French regions like Alsace, Corsica, and Nice are full of people bearing Germanic or Italian names.[29] 'Ridiculous or obscene' names, on the other hand, may readily be changed,[30] as also names that have been 'dishonored'.[31]

Under contemporary French legal standards, first names remain even harder to change than family names.[32] In this respect, the 'law of 6 Fructidor an II' remains quite rigorously in force.[33] The principle of 'immutability' applies.[34] In law, there are but three recognized exceptions: adoption,[35] acquisition of French nationality (to permit *francisation* of foreign given names)[36] or, in the

---

[20] Law no. 93–22 of 8 January 1993. Dalloz, *supra* n. 15, at Art. 57, p. 91.     [21] Ibid.

[22] Ibid. at 91–8. Encycl. Dalloz, *Repertoire de Droit Civil (2ᵉ) Mise a Jour 1996*, Tome VI, ch. 1, Indivisibilité à Nom-Prenom, Recueil 5 (1996).     [23] Ibid., para. 180.

[24] Ibid., para. 183.     [25] Ibid., para. 189.     [26] Ibid.

[27] The procedures for *francisation* are in ibid., paras. 260–75.

[28] Ibid. para. 184. See e.g. Cour de Cassation, First Civil Chamber, 6 April 1994, Arret no. 92-15.170. Lexis-Nexis. See also ibid., 9 Jan. 1996, Arret no. 94-20.800. Lexis-Nexis. There are at least a dozen other reported cases of this sort that were decided by the Cour de Cassation in the past decade.     [29] Ibid. para. 223.

[30] Ibid. para. 222.     [31] Ibid. paras. 272, 277.     [32] Ibid. para. 332.

[33] Ibid. para. 330.     [34] Ibid. para. 331.     [35] Ibid. para. 335.

[36] Ibid. para. 337.

case of children, where permission has previously been obtained for a change of the family name (to permit the first name to adjust to the new surname).[37] In no case, however, are diminutives allowed. Recently, a request to register 'Toni', instead of 'Antoine', was rejected.[38] It has, however, been decided that a person has a legitimate interest in changing a Jewish first name to escape possible racial persecution.[39]

In 1981, under the law of '11 Germinal an XI', the Cour de Cassation heard and denied an appeal from the Appellate Court in Orleans refusing parents' application to name their child Cerise ('Cherry').[40] In 1990, the Cour de Cassation of France denied parents permission to change their son's given name to one that had been commonly used for years by family and friends. 'The exclusive use of a first name', the Court said, 'does not suffice to establish a legitimate interest' in changing the name to accord with that in actual use.[41] What makes the case especially notable is that this name, Lesrague, was originally chosen at his birth by the Algerian mother, had been certified by the Algerian consul to be in common use, yet had been rejected at the time by the French registrar.

The French practice in making both given and family nomenclature the subject of legislative and administrative control is still widely followed to a greater or lesser degree in other countries. In 'some legal systems the name is partly treated as a police institution or at least as a matter of administrative law and the obligatory and—in principle—unchangeable character is emphasized'.[42] Policy on nomenclature is also deployed by states to promote assimilation of foreigners[43] or, conversely as in Nazi Germany, where Jews were forced to adopt Old Testament first names, to promote persecution.[44] Islamic religious rules usually prohibit change of name as a matter of communal conscience,[45] and Korean law, too, forbids change of surname.[46]

In many countries besides France, a person desiring a change of name must prove an exceptional legitimate interest as defined by law, demonstrating both a good motive for desiring a change and valid grounds for preferring a proposed new name. Obtaining such a change requires undergoing an administrative or judicial procedure. Examples, in addition to France, include: Belgium, Switzerland, Albania, Denmark, Poland, Germany, Netherlands, and Austria.[47] These legal systems stand in stark contrast to the practice in common law countries where 'there is complete liberty to change one's name. The simple

---

[37] Ibid. para. 338.      [38] Ibid. para. 326.

[39] Ibid. para. 342, citing Civ. 1re, 26 Jan. 1965, D.1965.216, Rev. trim. dr. civ. 1965. 335 obs. H. Desbois.

[40] Cour de Cassation, First Civil Chamber, 10 June 1981, Arret no. 626. Lexis-Nexis.

[41] Cour de Cassation, First Civil Chamber, 14 Feb. 1990, Arret no. 209. Lexis-Nexis.

[42] Pintens & Will, *supra* n. 7, at 48.

[43] For France see Law no. 72–964, art. 2, regarding relative ease in Frenchification of immigrants' names.      [44] Pintens & Will, *supra* n. 7, at 50.

[45] Ibid. at 73.      [46] Ibid.      [47] Ibid. at 74–6 and laws cited therein.

intention to change one's name is sufficient, whatever the motivation, except in cases of deceit. . . . The government does not exercise any supervision and there is not even a duty of registration'.[48] In England there is a system of registering a change which is used 'not to carry out an effective change of name, but merely to formalize an actual change of name'. Registration is purely optional.[49] 'In the United States, all states have a procedure for change of name with, mostly optional, registration.'[50] Nevertheless, one can freely change one's name by recourse to common usage in accordance with the common law tradition. The same applies in Australia. A few US states and Canadian provinces require registration of a change but otherwise refrain from any control.[51] There is also total freedom of choice in the US and the UK for adopted persons in deciding whether to assume the name of the adoptive family.[52] The same rule applies in Spain and in most of Latin America, but not elsewhere.[53] However, as will be further noted below, the liberal attitude of British law regarding change of name does not extend to applicants, such as transsexuals, seeking a change of sex classification on their birth certificate.

It cannot therefore be said that the British legal system is wholly indifferent to issues of communitarian social control that conflict with personal autonomy: only that that society has chosen to fight on another field of battle. Many governments, however, draw the line precisely at questions of nomenclature, as if to grant persons control over their own names would mark the beginning of the end of communitarian power over individual identity. Already in 1492, at a time when neighbouring Mediterranean countries like France and Italy still took a very relaxed view of persons' choice of names, Spain ordered its Jews to adopt Spanish names or leave the country. In a recent echo of this, Spanish dictator Francisco Franco insisted that parents eschew giving regional (Basque, Catalan, etc.) first names to their children. As one might expect, after Franco's death in 1975, there was a rush on the state registry to regularize names secretly bestowed at baptism.[54]

A more recent, and especially egregious example was the effort of the Bulgarian government to ban its citizens from using Turkish names to identify themselves.[55] In 1985, the communist dictatorship required all of its one million Turkish-speaking Muslims, about 10 per cent of the population, to suppress their Turkish identity by assuming Slavic names, while also closing Turkish-language newspapers and broadcast stations.[56] By 1990 this had led to the

---

[48] Pintens & Will, *supra* n. 7, at 50, 74.      [49] Ibid.      [50] Ibid.
[51] Ibid.
[52] But see Rose L. Hubbard, 'Gender Discrimination—It's Still With Us', Ore. St. Bar Bull. 70, Jan 1998.                              [53] Pintens & Will, *supra* n. 7, at 63.
[54] Letter of Nerea Prieto de Apraiz, New York, 11 Sept. 1996. NY Times, 12 Sept. 1996, at A22.
[55] Celestine Bohlen, 'A Junction of Ottoman Hate and Today's Mistrust,' NY Times, 28 Oct. 1991, at A4.
[56] Elliot Abrams, Assistant Secretary of State for Human Rights and Humanitarian Affairs, quoted by Don Oberdorfer, 'Bulgaria Oppressing Ethnic Turks, US Says', Los Angeles Times, 2 Apr. 1985, at 18.

massive flight of more than 300,000 persons across the Turkish border.[57] The International Human Rights Committee, charged with invigilating states' compliance with the International Covenant on Civil and Political Rights (the ICCPR), was stymied by Bulgaria's refusal, throughout this period, either to ratify the Optional Protocol allowing individual complaints to be lodged with the Committee, or even to file the periodic country reports required under article 40.[58] At last, in 1990, after the ouster of hard-line communist leader Todor Zhivkhov, the Bulgarian parliament unanimously voted to reverse this policy, allowing ethnic Turks to return and to resume use of their own names. Simultaneously, other aspects of forcible assimilation were also discarded.[59] In 1993, the new Bulgarian government reported that all discriminatory and forced-assimilation laws had been repealed and that compensation was being paid to those victimized by the prior regime.[60] Nevertheless, the Human Rights Committee used a case before it from the Netherlands to emphasize the view that 'if a State were to compel all foreigners to change their surnames this would constitute interference in contravention of article 17 [of the ICCPR]'.[61]

In many other countries, the state has maintained a long-standing interest in people's names in the hope of furthering social stability.[62] This may conflict with strongly held private desires insofar as a name may be an important expression of personal identity. Disputes tend to arise primarily in four cluster-areas: when a woman seeks to retain her maiden surname, when parents choose a first name for their children, when a change in family name is sought and when a person who has undergone a gender change seeks to adopt a name consonant with his or her new status.

International law has begun to make itself felt in each of these areas of confrontation, always siding with the right to personal autonomy. For example, the ICCPR takes its stand squarely on the side of personal autonomy as regards the right of women to retain their family name after marriage. By article 23(4), state parties undertake to 'ensure equality of rights and responsibilities of spouses as to marriage, during marriage and at its dissolution'—a formulation that would appear to cover the right of both spouses to retain their premarital surnames. This is made even more explicit by the Convention on the Elimination of All Forms of Discrimination Against Women,[63] article 15(1) of which

---

[57] Stephen Franklin, 'Ethnic Turks Hope Change is For the Better in Bulgaria', Chicago Tribune, 11 Feb. 1990, at 5C.

[58] Report of the Human Rights Committee, 1993, UN Doc. A/48/40, at 156, para. 745 and 156–57, para. 748.

[59] Reuters, 'Bulgarians Vote to Let Moslims Use Own Names', Chicago Tribune, 6 Mar. 1990, at 6C. Approximately 140,000 ethnic Turks had returned to their homes in Bulgaria by the end of 1994. Tim Judah, 'Bulgarian Hamlet of Hope for Balkans', Times of London, 29 Dec. 1994, at 3.

[60] Report of the Human Rights Committee, 1993, *supra* n. 58, at 155, para. 723.

[61] *Coeriel v. the Netherlands*, *infra* n. 90.

[62] See Pintens & Will, *supra* n. 7, at 45–91.

[63] Convention on the Elimination of All Forms of Discrimination Against Women, GA Res. 180 of 18 Dec. 1979. Entered into force on 3 Sept. 1981.

obliges the state parties 'to accord to women equality with men before the law' and specifies that this equality extends to the wife's right to choose the surname she will bear in marriage.[64]

While this precise matter has not been litigated before the Human Rights Committee, it has arisen with some frequency under the European regional human rights system, where it implicates articles 8 and 14 of the European Human Rights Convention. In *Burghartz v. Switzerland*[65] a husband had been denied the right to conjoin his surname with that of his wife's family. The Court found that this refusal by the Swiss authorities constituted a violation of both provisions (articles 8 and 14) of the Convention.[66] The tribunal said:

> As a means of personal identification and of linking to a family, a person's name none the less concerns his or her private and family life. The fact that society and the State have an interest in regulating the use of names does not exclude this, since these public-law aspects are compatible with private life conceived of as including, to a certain degree, the right to establish and develop relationships with other human beings . . .[67]

It thereby clearly recognized the link between autonomy in nomenclature and personal self-determination in matters of identity and affiliative choice. The majority of the European Human Rights Commission, which had earlier examined the complaint, was explicit about this, stating that 'the right to develop and fulfill one's personality necessarily comprises the right to identity and, therefore, to a name'.[68]

That the nomenclature aspect of autonomy is increasingly recognized may be seen by contrasting the 1994 *Burghartz* decision with earlier opinions of the European Commission. In these, the Commission had denied petitioners access to the Court on the ground that their article 8-based claims were ill-founded. In 1977, for example, the Commission saw no violation of article 8 in a Swiss refusal to allow a married woman to campaign for a parliamentary seat under her maiden name, upholding, instead, the state's interest in precise identification of families.[69] In 1983, the Commission, under very similar circumstances arising in the Netherlands, came to the same conclusion.[70]

After *Burghartz*, the Commission's earlier line of reasoning may now be said to have been revised to protect both wives and, occasionally, husbands seeking enhanced individual autonomy through the personal symbolism of nomenclature.[71] Whatever the merits of the communitarian arguments that became prevalent in Europe in the Middle Ages, they have been repudiated in inter-

---

[64] Ibid., art. 16(1)(g).
[65] *Burghartz v. Switzerland*, 280-B Eur. Ct. HR (ser. A) at 19 (1994).    [66] Ibid. at 30.
[67] Ibid. at 28.
[68] The Commission's report is cited in Court's opinion: ibid. at 37–8.
[69] *Hagmann-Husler v. Switzerland*, App. no. 8042/77, 12 Eur. Comm'n HR Dec. & Rep. 202 (1977).
[70] *X v. The Netherlands*, App. no. 9250/81, 32 Eur. Comm'n HR Dec. & Rep. 175 (1983).
[71] However, the European Court of Human Rights has not so far held that there is a general right of persons to change their names without convincing or specific reasons. *Stjerna v. Finland*, 299-B Eur. Ct. HR (ser. A) at 29–30, 39, 42–5 (1995).

national and (European) human rights law, and even the more traditionalist states are beginning to fall in line.

The same development is occurring with respect to the naming of children. Choosing a first name for children at birth still appears to provoke similar confrontations between community authorities and individual parents. Here, again, the international treaty system sides with those asserting autonomy against the state. Article 18(4) of the ICCPR[72] calls for states to 'respect . . . the liberty of parents and, when applicable, legal guardians to ensure the religious and moral education of their children in conformity with their own convictions'. The naming of a child may be part of parents' strategy for the religious and moral education of their offsprings. It is clear that a country's legal requirement that all children born there must be given Christian names would offend the religious and moral values of an immigrant Islamic family, even though (or because) intended to promote their cultural assimilation. It would also offend the Convention on the Rights of the Child[73] which specifically makes provision for 'the right of the child to preserve his or her identity, including . . . name . . .' (article 8(1)) and protects 'privacy' (article 16(1)) as well as the 'parents . . . responsibilities for the upbringing and development of the child' (article 18(1)). All of these are relevant to individual control over nomenclature.

The European Convention for the Protection of Human Rights and Fundamental Freedoms[74] reinforces this support for individual preference over statist policy by guaranteeing in article 8(1) the right of everyone 'to respect for his private and family life'. This has been interpreted by the European Court of Human Rights to include choice of children's names by the parents, rather than by the state. A case that recently capped a surprisingly heated and protracted battle had its origins in a 1984 decision by French authorities to reject the application of Mr and Mrs Guillot to name their daughter 'Fleur de Marie' (Flower of Mary). The Government, of course, prevailed in its own courts and, at first, in the European forum. The European Human Rights Commission, in considering the complaint, reported that the French action did not violate the girl's right under article 8 of the European Convention.[75] It affirmed, instead, the interest of the state in protecting children from harmful, frivolous, or socially divisive names chosen by the parents. However, on 24 October 1996, the European Court of Human Rights at last concluded that 'the choice of a

---

[72] International Covenant on Civil and Political Rights [hereafter ICCPR], 999 UNTS 171. Adopted by GA Res. 220 of 16 Dec. 1966.

[73] Convention on the Rights of the Child, adopted by GA Res. 44/25 of 20 Nov. 1989. Entered into force 2 Sept. 1990.

[74] European Convention for the Protection of Human Rights and Fundamental Freedoms, 213 UNTS 221, ETS 5. Signed 4 Nov. 1950. Entered into force on 3 Sept. 1953. The large majority of European states are now parties.

[75] *Lassauzet and Guillot v. France*, App. no. 22500/93, Report adopted by the Commission on 12 April 1995.

first name of their child by the parents is of an intimate and effective nature' and was thus, after all, in the 'private sphere' envisaged by article 8 of the European Human Rights Convention. Even so, the Court was saved from a head-on collision with the French Government when the latter agreed to allow the parents to register a compromise—'Fleur-Marie.' The European tribunal thus was able to conclude that the actual infringement on article 8 parental and privacy rights had become so minimal as not to warrant a further remedy.[76]

To some, it may seem exceedingly strange that society, through its legal machinery, should be involved at all in such matters of personal identity and preference.[77] The protracted litigation and governmental insinuation into the intimate choices made by parents does appear, however, to reflect the continuing importance which French society attributes to names as instruments of social cohesion. Michel Foucault, more generally, has referred to France as the 'society of normalization' and describes the 'homogenizing techniques' by which it seeks its goal.[78] This, evidently, is one of these.

France, however, does not stand alone in this respect. For example, a similar complaint under the European Convention was brought against Austria in 1989,[79] after authorities there had refused to register the name of a child as 'Keren Katharina Ingeborg' by virtue of Austria's law banning uncommon names. The parents claimed that the 'common name' requirement was a violation of article 8 of the Convention. When the Austrian authorities agreed to enter the name 'Keren' in the registry, the application was dropped before it could be considered by the Commission.[80]

The European Human Rights Convention was also recently invoked in a complaint filed by ex-King Constantine of Greece against a law denying him a passport and access to Greek courts unless he and his family agreed to adopt a surname—'Glucksborg' appears to have been proposed—and drop the usage 'King' or even 'ex-King'. Constantine alleged that such legal compulsion regarding his name violates provisions of articles 3 and 14 of the European Convention. He also alleged that the law constitutes degrading treatment or punishment imposed for political purposes in violation of articles 6(1) and 14 and which, in violation of article 8, violates his and his family's right to respect for their private and family life. The complaints were ruled inadmissible by the Commission on the ground that 'it is legitimate in a Republic to require anyone,

---

[76] *Guillot v. France*, European Ct. of HR, Decision of 24 Oct. 1996, no. 52/1995/558/644.

[77] Cf. Aeyal M. Gross, 'Rights and Normalization: A Critical Study of European Human Rights Cases on the Choice and Change of Names', 9 Harv. Hum. Rts. J. 269, 280 (1996).

[78] Michel Foucault, *Discipline and Punish* 184 (A. Sheridan trans., 1979) (1975). See also Gross, *supra* n. 77, at 279.

[79] *K.K.I. v. Austria*, App. no. 14562/89 (1992) [unpub.].

[80] Ibid. at 3. See also Gross, *supra* n. 77, at 279–80. Decision of 20 May 1995.

including the former King and members of his family, who wishes to apply for citizenship or a passport to have a surname of their choice . . .'.[81]

Similar conflict between public and private interests occurs when a person, or a family, propose a change of surname. We have noted the resistance of French law to any such changes, but, again, it is far from unique in this respect. Both the European Human Rights Commission and the Court have had occasion to consider complaints by persons who were denied the right to change their family names. These complaints have arisen from Sweden,[82] Finland,[83] the Netherlands,[84] and even from Britain.[85]

The complained-of British refusal to permit a change of name was unusual in that it ran counter to the general tradition of British common law. As noted, this ordinarily makes changing one's given and family names extremely easy. The exceptional denial of the right occurred in respect of an incarcerated person,[86] where the authorities believed the change would make it harder to keep track of him. The liberal common law tradition, however, is largely followed not only in Britain but also in the United States, although a few states have sought, mostly unsuccessfully, to legislate to require legitimate children to bear the father's surname and illegitimate ones to bear that of the mother.[87] These provisions tend to be struck down by US courts under the constitutional 'equal protection' requirement,[88] and under the constitutionally protected right to privacy.[89] Autonomy in matters of nomenclature ordinarily being protected by common law and constitutional principles, there is no need of recourse to prevailing international norms.

Although most of the effort to impose international protection of personal autonomy in nomenclature has come from the European Court of Human Rights, interpreting the European Convention, at the global level the Human Rights Committee, too, has broadened the ambit of individual discretion, interpreting article 17 of the ICCPR. This states that 'no one shall be subject to arbitrary or unlawful interference with his privacy . . .'. In *Coeriel v. the Netherlands*,[90] the Committee considered whether article 17 protects a person's right to change his name in connection with a decision to pursue Hindu religious studies. It decided that 'a person's surname constitutes an important

---

[81] Press communiqué issued by the Secretary to the European Commission of Human Rights, Applic. no. 25701/94, hearing of 21 April 1998, *The former King Constantine of Greece and 8 members of his family v. Greece*, available at http://www.dhcommhr.coe.fr/eng/25701CP.Ehtml.

[82] *Borj v. Sweden*, App. no. 16878/90.     [83] *Stjerna v. Finland, supra* n. 71.

[84] *X v. the Netherlands*, App. no. 18806/91 [unpub.]. See also Gross, *supra* n. 77, at 277.

[85] *Lant v. United Kingdom*, App. no. 11046/84, 45 Eur. Comm'n HR Dec. & Rep. 236 (1985).

[86] Ibid.

[87] For a full discussion of the common law and American state statutory laws see L. A. Foggan, 'Parents' Selection of Children's Surnames', 51 Geo. Wash. L. Rev. 583 (1983).

[88] See e.g., *Jech v. Burch*, 466 F.Supp. 714 (D. Hawaii 1979).

[89] *Sydney v. Pingree*, 564 F.Supp. 412 (SD Fla. 1982).

[90] *Coeriel v. the Netherlands*, Case no. 453/1991, Report of the Human Rights Committee, GAOR, 50th Sess., Supp. no. 40 (A/50/40), 3 Oct. 1995, at 91, para. 531.

component of one's identity and that the protection against arbitrary or unlawful interference with one's privacy includes the protection against arbitrary or unlawful interference with the right to choose and change one's own name'.[91]

Finally, there is the cluster of disputes arising out of sex reassignment. Typically, a person changing from male to female, or female to male, will seek to signify the new identity by altering his or her given name. Even where states permit, and financially sometimes assist, operative sex change, there may be reluctance to change the transsexual's Christian name as registered at birth. Obviously, the communitarian policy behind this reluctance is not generated by opposition to autonomy in sex selection but by concern for the social stability thought to depend upon the objectivity and immutability of the state registry.

The policy of states that refuse change of name for post-operative transsexuals has been the subject of considerable litigation in the European Court of Human Rights.[92] Indeed, 'in most parts of the world, . . . operated transsexuals had to undergo years of litigation, and the higher the court, the less the chance to see their physical change accompanied by the desired change of their name'.[93] In more and more countries, however, judges, legislators, and administrators, sometimes prodded by the international rights regimes, have taken steps to remedy this situation: Switzerland, Canada, South Africa, some US states, Panama, all Scandinavian states, Austria, Israel, Germany, Italy, Spain, Netherlands, and Turkey being among these.[94] The subject is of sufficient significance as an indicator of growing sensitivity to individuals' desire for self-expression to warrant consideration under a separate heading.

## 3. PERSONAL CHOICE AND ADAPTION OF SEXUAL IDENTITY[95]

As science develops new options for individual identity-construction, that process becomes both more complex and, potentially, more fulfilling. In recent decades, medical science and genetics have created prenatal and postnatal options regarding sex which have both seemed to raise profound moral issues and enhanced the range of personal choices pertaining to individual identity.

Before actual birth, choice of a child's sex by the parents is possible by a

---

[91] *Coeriel v. the Netherlands*, Case no. 453/1991, Report of the Human Rights Committee, GAOR, 50th Sess., Supp. no. 40 (A/50/40), 3 Oct. 1995, at 91, para. 531.

[92] *B. v. France*, Eur. Ct. H. Rts. 1992 A no. 232 considering earlier judgements including *Oosterwijck v. Belgium*, *Rees v. United Kingdom* and *Cossey v. United Kingdom* which are discussed below.

[93] Pintens & Will, *supra* n. 7, at 81.          [94] Ibid. notes 832, 833, 835, 836, 837.

[95] The terms gender and sex have different meanings in different contexts. Gender is sometimes the term used to describe the self-definition of a person in psychological terms and identity, while sex is sometimes used to refer to a person's physical features, or biological encryption. It will be readily apparent that, by some definitions, this distinction creates the possibility that a person's gender can be the opposite of his or her sex. In this essay, to avoid a definitional controversy irrelevant to the intended exposition, the terms are used interchangeably, but an effort is made to indicate clearly the intended meaning from the context of usage.

calculated combination of prenatal testing and abortion. Some societies permit this, others do not. In the US, the state of Illinois has enacted a law criminalizing the performing of abortions 'with knowledge that the pregnant woman is seeking an abortion solely on account of the sex of the fetus'.[96] Pennsylvania has a similar law,[97] but the other states and federal government have enacted no such restrictions on parental choice. No jurisdiction in the US has legislated to control access to the various methods for determining the sex or other genetic characteristics of children prior to conception.[98]

In several non-Western societies, however, the practice of fetal sex selection is both much more common and, in some, is prohibited or constrained by law. Since 1994, prenatal disclosure of the sex of a child and the aborting of female fetuses have been criminalized by South Korean law, even as it continues to be a common practice.[99] In China, where parents are in theory limited to one or two children, it is widely reported that one million females are 'missing' due to prenatal or postnatal intervention in the process.[100] In India, from 1978 to 1982 it is reported that 78,000 female fetuses were aborted,[101] despite the banning in 1975 of amniocentesis to determine sex.[102] The concern of these societies can be understood in purely consequentialist—as opposed to moral—terms. In both China and India the twinned desire for boys and for population control has led to severe constraints on the reproduction of females, so that in China the population ratio of males per 100 females recently shifted from the normal 105 to 153 during the period of strict enforcement of a one-child policy.[103]

The issue of individual autonomy, here, is often shaped by one's personal opinion of the sentient 'personhood' of the parties to the selection process. Parents, obviously, are persons with liberty-based rights pertaining to reproductive freedom, child-bearing,[104] and child-rearing.[105] It is also relatively clear that sperm and ovules, until combined in vitro and inserted in a woman's body, are incapable of asserting claims of liberty or autonomy that depend upon sentient personhood. As regards sex selection by the abortion of foetuses, opinions will vary more or less along the same lines as those drawn more generally in respect of abortion, with one exception. Among some feminist writers in the US there is a further factor at work: the belief that all sex

---

[96] 720 ILCS 510/6(8).     [97] Title 18, Pa.CS §3204 (1996).

[98] These include, for example, Preimplantation Genetic Diagnosis combined with in vitro fertilization (IVF). See J. Tarin & A. Handyside, 'Embryo Biopsy Strategies for Reimplantation Diagnosis', 59 Fertility and Sterility 943 (1993).

[99] Sheryl Wu Dunn, 'It's a Boy! Koreans Exult', Int'l Herald Tribune, 15 Jan. 1997, at 2.

[100] Amartya Sen, 'More than 100 Million Women Are Missing', NY Rev. Books, 20 Dec. 1990, at 61–6.

[101] Rada Krishna Rao, 'Move to Ban Sex Determination', 33 Nature 467 (1988).

[102] John A. Robertson, 'Genetic Selection of Offspring Characteristics', 76 B.U. L. Rev. 421, 458 (1996).     [103] Ibid. at 457.

[104] See *Griswold v. Connecticut*, 381 US 479, 503 (1965); *Planned Parenthood v. Casey*, 505 US 833, 871 (1992); *Meyer v. Nebraska*, 262 US 390, 399 (1923).

[105] See *Wisconsin v. Yoder*, 406 US 205, 210 (1972).

selection, whether in the form of 'engineering' the union of spermata and ovules, or in abortion, is wrong and ought to be prohibited by law because (1) it has undesirable demographic consequences in increasing the numerical ratio of men to women; (2) that this male numerical advantage has political consequences in perpetuating male dominance; and (3) it also has psychological consequences in demeaning the value of women as such.[106] Those who believe this, may seek on purely political, rather than moral, grounds to have the government prohibit or regulate the autonomy of parents in selecting the sex of their children. Some of the same reasoning also causes a few advocates for the handicapped to favour banning all selection of genetic characteristics pertaining to a potential child's physical or mental condition. So far, however, at least in Western nations, these efforts have had limited success in restricting parental choice,[107] and, in the US, such intervention by the public sector into what has so far been reserved to private choice would encounter significant constitutional obstacles.[108]

Sex selection opportunities offered by new scientific techniques do not end at birth, but merely shift from choices available to parents to options available to the persons affected. Those with the genetic and biological characteristics of one sex but a powerful desire to manifest the lifestyle and physiological characteristics of the opposite one, now usually can avail themselves of surgical and hormonal procedures by which some of the preferred characteristics can be acquired. This capacity poses an important issue: will society permit that identity-choice to be made autonomously in the private realm of conscience and taste? Or is the matter assigned to the public realm of morality, good order, and decorum?

In many nations, this matter, too, is increasingly relegated to the private sphere. Thus, sex-change operations performed on adults as a result of personal choice with due professional counselling are now no longer regarded as bizarre in Western states, as they were forty years ago, when, under the glare of maximum publicity, such an operation was first performed in Denmark on Christine Jorgensen.[109] Families, peer groups, and professional associations are becoming more tolerant of this still-exotic exercise of private preference. For example, the Presbytery of Greater Atlanta, in the US, recently decided that one of its ordained ministers, Rev. Erin Swenson, upon completion of transsexual medical procedures, could retain the ordained vocation she had previously exercised for twenty-three years as a married man with grown children.[110]

---

[106] These arguments are ably summarized in Jodi Danis, 'Sexism and "The Superfluous Female"': Arguments for Regulating Pre-Implantation Sex Selection', 18 Harv. Women's LJ 219 (1995)
[107] See, however, efforts in France and Britain to impose governmental restrictions. R. Saltus, 'France Weighs Restrictive Biomedical Science Law', Boston Globe, 23 Oct. 1993, at 6. See also the 1990 British legislation creating the Human Fertilization and Embryo Authority and its licensing regulation, discussed in Danis, ibid. at 260.          [108] Robertson, *supra* n. 102, at 478–82.
[109] See 'Bronx "Boy" is Now a Girl', NY Times, 2 Dec. 1952, at A18.
[110] 'Presbyterians Vote to Keep Transsexual Minister in Fold', The Atlanta J. & Const., 23 Oct. 1996.

When, in 1995, China's 28-year-old leading choreographer and dancer, Jin Xing, decided to have a sex change operation, the Government at first ordered her off the stage, then relented. She reappeared in 1996 in great triumph as a ballerina in her own ballet, staged at the Beijing Theatre owned by the People's Liberation Army.[111]

That such a choice exists at all is due to recent strides in the practice of psychological and physiological intervention. More persons seem to avail themselves of the resultant opportunities. There are now an estimated 65,000 post-operative transsexuals in Britain, with a 50 per cent rise in demand for the operation since the mid-1980s.[112]

Has the law taken similar strides to facilitate such individual self-determination?[113] Is the medical profession permitted to practise sex reassignment? Will the state recognize its legal concomitants? Will the public (or private) health services cover the cost of reassignment procedures in the same way as other medical treatments? The answers vary from one legal system to another, and to a degree they depend on how sex reassignment is itself classified. To some persons it is a religious or moral issue, to others a communitarian issue to be determined by law in the name of civic values, order, and cohesion, to still others a professional issue to be determined by physicians on application by a patient, and to many it is a private issue to be determined by reference to personal taste and individual preference.

Which? This question is currently still being fought out in the various courts and parliaments, especially in Western Europe and anglophonic North America, where issues pertaining to transsexual rights have begun to attract public notice, resulting in litigation and legislative action.

On 30 April 1996, the European Court of Justice in Luxembourg, the court of the European Union, ruled that a person discharged by an employer for being a transsexual is protected by the Community's laws regarding equal treatment of men and women and prohibiting sex-based discrimination. In a case brought against the Cornwall County Council, the tribunal ruled that there had been a violation of the European Union's Council of Ministers' directive 76/207 EEC of 9 February 1976, article 5(1), which pertains to the implementation of the principle of equal treatment of men and women as regards access to jobs, vocational training, and working conditions.[114]

The issue had arisen from the discharge, on 31 December 1992, of the plaintiff, P, employed as a manager in the education office of England's

[111] U. Schmetzer, 'Leading Dancer Wins Battle', Chicago Trib., 20 Jan. 1996, at N4.

[112] Jojo Moyes, 'When a Man Loves Being a Woman', The Independent, 22 Feb. 1997, at 19.

[113] The tolerance for autonomous choice shown by the Atlanta Presbytery is not echoed by some courts, for example, in denying parental rights to a parent who undergoes sex change. Cf. *Daly v. Daly*, 102 Nev. 66, 715 P.2d 56 (1986). Other courts have taken the opposite position: *In re the Custody of T.J., child*, no. C2–87–1786 (unpub.), 1988 Minn. App. LEXIS 144 (1988).

[114] *P v. S. and Cornwall County Council*, Reuter Eur. Community Rep., 30 Apr. 1996. Also (1996) All ER (EC 397); (1996) 2 CMLR 247.

Cornwall County Council.[115] Upon starting to dress as a woman and undergoing a series of operations to provide 'women's characteristics',[116] the manager was given notice of dismissal, which led to the bringing of proceedings against the school's director and the Cornwall County Council. Plaintiff alleged sexual discrimination. While defendants claimed that the reason was overstaffing, the Truro Industrial Tribunal, based in Cornwall, rejected this defence, finding instead that 'plaintiff was wrongly terminated . . .'.[117] However, those judges, interpreting Britain's 1975 Sex Discrimination Act,[118] were unable to find a basis for awarding damages.[119] They instead requested that the European Court of Justice issue a preliminary ruling on whether or not 'the dismissal of a transsexual for a reason related to a gender reassignment constitutes a breach of the [Community] directive'[120] and, more generally, whether sex discrimination prevention laws apply to such persons. To both questions the European Tribunal answered affirmatively.

That conclusion is all the more remarkable because the United Kingdom Government and the European Commission had both maintained in the pleadings that the dismissal of a person because of transsexuality or on the grounds of having had a sex change operation 'did not constitute sexual discrimination under the terms of the directive'.[121] The EU Court, however, concluded that the non-discrimination directive is 'simply the expression in the relevant field, of the principle of equality, which is one of the fundamental principles of Community law'.[122] It does, therefore, 'apply to discrimination arising, as in this case, from the gender reassignment of the person concerned'. Where a person is dismissed on the ground that he or she intends to undergo, or has undergone 'gender reassignment', he or she is indeed being 'treated unfavourably by comparison with a person of the sex to which he or she was deemed to belong before undergoing gender reassignment'.[123]

The implications both for the Court and for the British Government and public were considerable. Guiseppe Tesauro, the European tribunal's advocate general, put it in terms of the law's obligation to reflect contemporary reality: 'To my mind, the law cannot cut itself off from society as it actually is and must not fail to adjust to it as quickly as possible.'[124] Tesauro was reportedly influenced by the 'Richards' case, named after Dr Renée Richards, a male-to-female transsexual who in 1977 had won an action in the Supreme Court of New York to compel the US Open Tennis Federation to allow her to play in the Women's competition despite the Federation's claim that 'masculine muscle structure'

---

[115] European Information Service, Eur. Rep., 1 May 1996, at 3 (Load: 7 May 1996), Lexis-Nexis.
[116] Ibid.
[117] Reuter Eur. Community Rep., 20 Mar. 1995, at 7 (Load: 21 Mar. 1996), Lexis-Nexis.
[118] Sex Discrimination Act, 1975, 6 Halsbury 753 (4th edn., 1992).
[119] Reuter Eur. Community Rep., 20 Mar. 1995, at 7 (Load: 21 Mar. 1996), Lexis-Nexis.
[120] Ibid.
[121] European Information Service, Eur. Rep., 1 May 1996, at 4 (Load: 7 May).
[122] Ibid.          [123] Ibid.
[124] Daily Mail, 15 Dec. 1995, at 61 (Load: 18 Dec. 1995), Lexis-Nexis.

gave Richards an unfair advantage. The wisdom of rejecting that claim seemed to be confirmed when Dr Richards was beaten by his opponent in only two sets: 6-1 and 6-4.[125]

Elsewhere than in Britain, the 'P' decision caused little stir. In Sweden, Germany, the Czech Republic, Finland, Greece, Italy, the Netherlands, and Switzerland, national legislation already allows post-operative transsexuals to marry, adopt children, and receive social benefits under their new identity.[126] In Denmark, transsexuals have long been entitled to change their status under a 1935 law on voluntary castration. In France, Belgium, Spain, Portugal, and Luxembourg the matter has so far been addressed not by legislation but only by the courts.[127]

Nevertheless, some European nations' legal systems are having problems with ancillary matters. In France and in Austria, while the civil legal status of the individual undergoing sex-change may be revised by *ad hoc* administrative or judicial fiat, the courts by-and-large have refused to order the state registry to amend the sex classification, or even the given names of persons who have undergone medical procedures.[128] British law has been particularly obdurate in

[125] Reuter Textline, Agence Europe, 5 Mar. 1996, at 5 (Load: 5 Mar. 1996), Lexis-Nexis. While the matter of 'P,' the case of the Cornwall teacher, was moving towards judicial determination, a 3-judge panel of the British Court of Appeal, in Nov. 1995, had upheld the dismissal of four armed services personnel—three male soldiers and a female nurse—for homosexuality. These cases were being prepared for appeal to Britain's highest tribunal, the House of Lords, even as the European Court made its pronouncement (Ibid.). The larger implications were not lost on the then British Defence Minister Nicholas Soames, who heatedly proclaimed that British armed forces 'do not go along with politically correct claptrap.' Daily Mail, 15 Dec. 1995, at 15 (Load: 18 Dec. 1995), Lexis-Nexis. There was much talk in Parliament of resisting more such interference by Europe. Nevertheless, in March 1997, a British High Court judge sent to the EU Court of Justice for decision the case of Terry Perkins, a naval medical assistant with nearly five years of exemplary service, who had been discharged after the Royal Navy's investigative branch had concluded that he was homosexual. P. W. Davies, 'Judge Sounds Last Post for Forces Gay Ban', The Independent (London), 14 Mar. 1997, at 8. The European Community Court will now have to decide whether that discharge—there are reportedly more than a hundred such, each year—violates the Community's Equal Treatment Directive. The Labour Government elected in Britain in 1997 has announced that it will abide by the European Court's decision and will reverse the previous policy.

There is considerable further jurisprudence emanating from the European Court, although not directly on the point of discharge from the armed forces. For example, in a 1993 decision (8 to 1), *Monidos v. Cyprus* (1993), 16 EHRR 485, 22 April 1993, the European judges ruled that the criminal code of Cyprus, insofar as it prohibits and criminalizes homosexual activity between consenting male adults, 'violates his right to respect for his private life' which is guaranteed by article 8 of the European Rights Convention. This violation was held not mitigated by the fact that, since 1981, the Cypriot Attorney General, using his discretionary powers, had brought no prosecutions. Rather, it was found that the mere failure of Cyprus to repeal the offending sections 171, 172, and 173 of its criminal code constituted a continuing violation. The Cyprus Government thereupon decided to amend the law, despite countervailing pressure from militant clerics of the Orthodox church.

[126] Jerold Taitz, 'Judicial Determination of the Sexual Identity of Post-Operative Transsexuals', 13 Am. JL & Med. 53, 57, n. 22.

[127] Conclusions of Advocate General Tesauro, Reuter Textline, 5 Mar. 1996, at 6 (Load 5 Mar. 1996) Lexis-Nexis.

[128] See e.g. the case of Mlle. Santa, Maria Vasta. Cour de Cassation, First Civil Chamber, 21 May 1990, Arret no. 598; case of Mme Dominique Nadaud, ibid., 21 May 1990, Arret no. 599; case of Mme Suzanne, Josephine Jacquin, ibid., 21 May 1990, Arret no. 600. All: Lexis-Nexis.

refusing to change the sex designation on a person's birth certificate or give any other official recognition to sex redesignation, making it legally impossible for a person, after sex change, to marry, obtain remedies on divorce, or to adopt children. It leaves the transsexual in constant fear of exposure that could result in discharge from employment. Male to female transsexuals also risk imprisonment in men's prisons and are denied protection of the rape laws.[129] All this jibes oddly with the provision of free operative procedures by Britain's National Health Scheme.

Lord Justice Ormrod, an eminent British judge and former medical practitioner, has explained his country's long-standing reluctance to alter such persons' birth certificate:

The law, which is essentially an artefact, is a system of regulations which depends upon precise definitions [in] . . . a binary system. . . . Biological phenomena however, cannot be reduced to exclusive categories so that medicine often cannot give Yes or No answers . . . [p]eople are not either tall or short, they are taller or shorter or about average. This fundamental conflict lies at the root of all relations between medicine and law.[130]

The binary view became law in Britain as a result of the 1970 judicial decision in the case of a former merchant seaman, a post-operative transsexual who, as April Ashley, had been denied a change in her birth certificate. Her registration at birth was regarded by the court as an 'historic fact' rather than as evidence of Ashley's present sexual self-definition.[131] As a result, the court declared Ashley's marriage to Arthur Cameron Corbett (a female-to-male transsexual) dissolved as void at the latter's instigation without any provision for alimony.[132] The court adopted what became known as the 'Ormrod test', which held that a person's sex depends on the congruence of three biological factors: (1) the chromosomal, (2) the gonadal (i.e. presence or absence of testes or ovaries), and (3) the genital, which includes internal organs at the time of birth.[133] This decision, by the aforementioned Judge Ormrod, found the post-operative female transsexual to be male,[134] although the decision was carefully restricted to the right to marry.

---

[129] See Liz Hodgkinson, 'The Minority Without Real Rights', The Times, 10 Sept. 1991, Features, (Load 11 Sept. 1991), Lexis-Nexis; Steve Doughty, 'Euro Ruling Paves the Way for Transsexuals' Rights', Daily Mail (UK), 10 June 1996, at 7. One of the many strange consequences of the application of the Ormrod test in England is that a person who forces sex on a transsexual female could not be charged with rape, since it is defined as an offence that can be committed only against a woman, even though a post-operative male-to-female transsexual may have suffered precisely the trauma against which the law is directed. *S.Y. v. S.Y.*, (1963) at 37, 60 (CA). But see *R. v. Cogley*, Supreme Court of Victoria, [1989] VR 799, where the Supreme Court of the Australian State of Victoria held that the question of whether the victim was a woman as defined in *Corbett, infra* n. 131, or a transsexual 'was not relevant to the matters in issue'. Ibid. at 803.

[130] Ormond, 'The Medico-Legal Aspects of Sex Determination', 40 Medico-Legal J. 78 (1972).

[131] *Corbett v. Corbett (otherwise Ashley)* [1970] 2 All ER 33. The decision, in the Probate, Divorce and Admiralty Division of the Court of King's Bench, was by the aforecited Lord Ormond. Ibid. and accompanying text.

[132] *Corbett v. Corbett (otherwise Ashley) (no. 2)* [1970] 2 All ER 654, 656–7.

[133] See Taitz, *supra* n. 126, at 106.          [134] Ibid. at 100, 106.

This reluctance of Britain to accord ordinary sex-based rights to transsexuals became, in time, the subject of litigation before the European Court of Human Rights. The case was brought in 1996 by a person who had undergone female to male gender selection. The applicant's 'wife' had borne a child by insemination of a donor's sperm and the litigation sought to overturn the British authorities' refusal to register the applicant as the father on the child's birth certificate. The couple had been in a stable relationship since 1979 and the European Human Rights Commission, making a preliminary determination, found that Britain could be said to have violated article 8 of the European Convention's guarantee of 'respect for . . . private and family life' (article 8(1)).[135] The case, *X, Y and Z v. United Kingdom*, then went to the European Court of Human Rights, which held that the British authorities' refusal was not violative of article 8, because each state is entitled to a 'margin of appreciation' in balancing parental rights against the child's interests.[136] The Court also noted that nothing in British law prevents the 'father' from holding himself out as the ordinary parent of the child and from making provision for appropriate testamentary succession in his will.

Britain is not alone in these odd mixtures of new permissiveness and old restraints. Some recent French cases denying a change of given names make reference to article 57(3) of the *Civil Code* and find that these provisions do not recognize change of sex as a legitimate reason for permitting a name change. French courts have also considered, in this context, the aforementioned article 8 of the European Convention on Human Rights, guaranteeing to all persons respect for their private and family lives, but found that this does not require the official attribution to transsexuals of a sex category that 'is not in reality theirs'.[137]

This view, too, has been challenged in the regional human rights system. A 1992 case before the European Court, *B. v. France*,[138] called into question a French law prohibiting the applicant, a male-to-female transsexual, from adopting any name other than that recorded on the person's birth certificate. Applicant had been refused a change of name from 'Norbert Antoine' to 'Lyne Antoinette' by several levels of French tribunals. These had insisted that the applicant select from among approved 'gender neutral' first names such as Claude, Dominique, or Camille, none of which suited her. The European Court of Human Rights found that the French government's refusal had denied her

---

[135] Comm. Applic. no. 21830/93 of 13 Sept. 1995. See Stephen Bates, 'Transsexual's Plea to European Court', The Guardian (UK), 28 Aug. 1996, Home Page, at 5.

[136] *X, Y and Z v. United Kingdom*, no. 75/1995/581/667 of 22 April 1997. Note the dissent by Judge Gotchev.

[137] See cases nos. 599 and 600, *supra* n. 128.

[138] *B. v. France*, 232-C Eur. Ct. HR (ser A) (1992).

the respect for private life guaranteed by article 8 of the Convention, by not allowing her to indicate her new sex through a new name.[139]

The European Convention thus has been interpreted to vouchsafe to transsexuals at least the intimate decisions about name, although not yet those

---

[139] Ibid. This case indicates some movement in the European Court's conservative view of the right to freely choose at least some aspects of one's gender identity that do not pertain specifically to children. For several decades, transsexuals in Europe trying to have their gender reassignment recognized through a concomitant change in official records had mostly failed to establish any rights under the terms of the European Human Rights Convention. In the 1981 *Van Oosterwijck* case, the European Commission of Human Rights did hold that, in failing to correct Van Oosterwijck's birth register, Belgium had violated his 'right to private and family life'. The Commission criticized the refusal 'to recognize an essential element of his personality: his sexual identity resulting from his changed physical form, his physical make-up and his social role' (*Van Oosterwijck v. Belgium*, App. no. 7654/76; Commission Report adopted 1 Mar. 1979. The Court refused relief on technical grounds. (1981) 3 EHRR 557, emphasizing the personal, psychological nature of a person's private decisions regarding gender affiliation. That view, however, failed to prevail when the matter came before the European Court of Human Rights. The European Court of Human Rights applies to European Human Rights Convention and should not be confused with the European Court of Justice, which applies the treaties and orders of the European Union.

Likewise, in two cases from Britain, decided in 1987 and 1990 (*Rees v. United Kingdom*, 17 Oct. 1986, (1988) 9 EHRR 56, 68, paras. 48–51; *Cossey v. United Kingdom*, 27 Sept. 1990, (1990) 13 EHRR 622, 642, paras. 43–45) the judges in Strasbourg ruled that a government's refusal to provide a transsexual with an amended birth certificate stating the new gender did not constitute a violation of the Convention's article 8. The Court noted that the applicant had encountered no difficulty in legally changing his name in all other official documents and decided that the birth certificate testifies to the facts as of the time of birth. Nevertheless, the Court passed over the key fact that what was at stake for the applicant was 'the right to marry' which article 12 of the Convention vouchsafes to 'men and women of marriageable age'. The Court, instead, took it for granted that the article intended only to protect the matrimonial rights of persons of opposite biological sexes, since the article spoke of a right to marry 'and to found a family' and further made the right subject 'to the national laws governing the exercise of this right'. The Court thereby avoided the real, if elusive issue: what is the sex (gender) of the applicant, and: who is to answer that question, and by reference to what standards? For a critique see Taitz, *supra* n. 126, at 66–7. 'The European Court avoided the real issue, i.e. the determination of the sexual identity of the post-operative transsexual. Its failure to decide this essential question at the outset forced the Court to regard Rees throughout as a biological female instead of as a post-operative transsexual male, and thereby prejudiced his case.' Ibid. at 67.

The European Human Rights Court's second case from the UK, *Cossey v. United Kingdom*, decided in 1990, again concluded that the right to marry is always 'subject to the national laws of the contracting States . . . [although] limitations . . . introduced must not restrict or reduce the right in such a way or to such an extent that the very essence of the right is impaired. However, the legal impediment in the United Kingdom on the marriage of persons who are not of the opposite biological sex cannot be said to have an effect of this kind.' Ibid. at 634. However, this drew a stinging dissent from Judge Martens. 'Why', he asked, 'should an individual who—although having since birth the chromosomes of a male—at the moment he wants to marry no longer has testes or a penis but, on the contrary, shows all the (outward) genital and psychological factors of a female (and who is socially accepted as such), nevertheless, for the purpose of determining whether that individual should be allowed to marry a man, be deemed to be still a man himself? To attach so much weight to the chromosomal factor requires further explanation. That explanation, moreover, should be based on at least one relevant characteristic of marriage, for only then could it serve as a legal justification for the differentiation between the individual just described and an individual who is similar in all respects, save for having since birth the chromosomes of a female.' *Cossey v. UK* (1990) 13 EHRR 622, 657 (diss. op. Martens). See also Gross, *supra* n. 77, at 282. This article also cites two additional opinions regarding transsexuals and nomenclature: *D.N. v. France*, App. no. 17557/90 (1993) (unpub.) and *X v. Fed. Rep. Ger.*, App. no. 6699/74, Rep. of 11 Oct. 1978 (unpub.).

concerning marriage and children. As to these latter, the community's member states retain a 'margin of appreciation', including the right to apply the 'Ormrod Test', which purposefully ignores the individual's choice.[140]

The international and regional systems may yet take a more liberty-enhancing posture. Since 1992, with its decision in *B v. France*,[141] the European Court appeared to have rethought at least some of the legal issues surrounding restrictions on transsexuality. According to Judge Luzius Wildhaber, now President of that Court, the tribunal in rendering its opinion 'went to great lengths to explain that it did not mean to overrule' its prior refusal to enter this area 'but in fact it may well have done just that'.[142]

Indeed, the Ormrod test, where applied by states, increasingly leads to such odd results that change seems inevitable, whether pressed by national or international engines of reform. The *status quo* invented by Ormrod is simply too ludicrous to endure for much longer. For example, in the 1983 English case of *Regina v. Tan*,[143] the respondent, Gloria Greaves, a post-operative male-to-female transsexual, was charged under the 1956 Sexual Offences Act's provision criminalizing a man's conduct in living off the earnings of prostitution. Gloria argued that as she had undergone both a sex-change operation and hormonal treatment and thus was no longer a man, the law did not apply to her. She also pointed out that the British National Health Service, for twenty years, had recognized her as female. Nevertheless, she was convicted as a male.

Some evidence of a willingness to reform such an incongruous state of the law already is appearing in common law jurisdictions where the binary categories postulated by Lord Ormrod are being challenged by more flexible approaches. Some have begun to evolve a third alternative, a middle path between, on the one hand, adopting the 'objective' Ormrod test and, on the other, embracing entirely subjective individual self-definition.

This third approach recognizes individual and personal preferences, according transsexuals rights pertaining to sex reclassification, marriage, children, choice of first names, as well as health, tax, matrimonial, retirement, and succession benefits. On the other hand, it preserves some communitarian values

---

[140] In a later letter referring to the *Corbett* case, Sir Roger Ormond comments: 'There is nothing to stop our legislature from enacting that the homosexual can "marry" but they have not yet done so. . . . Would anyone regard intercourse per pouch as better than intercourse per anum?' Henry Finlay, 'International Commentaries: Legal Recognition of Transsexuals in Australia', 12 J. Contemp. HL & Pol'y 503, 508. On the other hand, Ormond does suggest that the law simply take a different tack: 'recognize and define the legal incidents and consequences of cohabitation and forget about the genitals.' Ibid. at 509.      [141] *B v. France, supra* n. 138.

[142] Luzius Wildhaber, 'The Right to Respect for Private and Family Life: New Case-Law on Art. 8 of the European Convention on Human Rights', in *The Modern World of Human Rights* 106 (Antonio A. C. Trinidade ed., 1996). But see *Sheffield v. UK*, no. 31–2/19097/815–16/1018–19, 30 July 1998, in which the European Court of Human Rights once again refused to compel the British authorities to extend legal recognition to the altered status of a post-operative transsexual. (The Court voted by a majority of 11–9.)

[143] *Regina v. Tan*, (1983) QB 1053 (CA). For Australia see *R. v. Cogley* [1989] VR 799.

by superimposing a different—i.e. non-chromosomal but still objectively physical—standard as a check on arbitrary or capricious exercises of personal
preference. The new rule extends legal validation to personal choices, but
only when they are ratified by undergoing the onerous medical steps necessary
for sex reassignment.

The state of South Australia, in 1988, enacted legislation giving effect to this
third alternative. Section 8 of the Sexual Reassignment Act establishes a registry
for transsexuals and provides that '(1) a recognition certificate is conclusive
evidence that the person to whom it refers—(a) has undergone a reassignment
procedure; and (b) is of the sex stated in the certificate'.[144]

Some recent Australian court decisions have also switched to the third
alternative, focusing on whether the transsexual has undergone the requisite
medical procedures for change of sex. For example, in the 1988 case *R. v. Harris
and McGuiness* in the New South Wales court of Criminal Appeal, two persons,
both claiming to be transsexual women, were charged with criminal indecency
towards third persons. The criminal offence is defined as an act by a 'male
person'. The court interpreted the law to apply to the pre-operative, but not to
the post-operative defendant.[145] *Corbett*, to that extent, was specifically
rejected.[146] Thus, as one Australian authority has observed, the 'hare of science
and technology lurches ahead. The tortoise of the law ambles slowly behind'.[147]

Australia's effort to wrestle with the status of transsexuals in a criminal
context is replicated in the area of civil entitlements. Here, again, the recent
cases turn neither on chromosomal nor on psychological factors, but on medico-
operative and physiological distinctions. In the 1991 Administrative Appeals
Tribunal case brought by 'H.H.' against the Commonwealth Department of
Social Security, the three-judge bench unanimously decided that a post-
operative male-to-female gender reassignee was entitled to a pension at age
60, as a woman, rather than having to await the male entitlement age of 65.
The court said that a 'requirement that reassignment surgery be completed
before the law recognizes the reassigned sex of an individual protects the public
against possible fraud and acknowledges that an irreversible medical decision
has been made affirming the patient's psychological sex choice'.[148] A similar
rationale was employed (in reverse) to deny women's benefits to a pre-operative
transsexual who had not yet undergone the surgical/medical transformation
from male to female, despite medical evidence of a wholly feminine psychological
status.[149]

New Zealand now follows similar reasoning. Thus, the Wellington High
Court has held that, under s.23 of the Marriage Act of 1955, 'from a purely
legal point of view there is no impediment to this Court holding that a post-

---

[144] Sexual Reassignment Act, 1988, no. 49 (S. Austl.).
[145] *R. v. Harris and McGuiness*, (1988) 17 NSWLR 158, 191–3.      [146] Ibid. at 191–4.
[147] Finlay, *supra* n. 140, at 520.      [148] (1991) 23 ALD 58 at 64.
[149] *Re Secretary, Dept. of Social Security v. SRA* (1992) 28 ALD 361.

operative transsexual can enter into a valid marriage . . .'.[150] Moreover, transsexuals 'exist in our society . . . allowing those few who qualify [by operative
procedure] to marry will not impact greatly on society, but it will provide relief
and recognition for the few individuals affected'.[151] (None of these decisions
explain, however, why the 'chosen' sexual identity should have had to have been
selected by irreversible operative procedures, thereby precluding any subsequent choice. If freedom of religious identity were similarly limited to one
irreversible change of belief in a lifetime, such an arbitrary limitation presumably, at least, would need some explaining in principled terms.)

One recently reported case from Singapore follows the Ormrod test, voiding
*ab initio* a marriage between a woman and a female-to-male post-operative
transsexual.[152] The case is unusual because the petitioner's 'wife' had pleaded
that she did not know of her 'husband's' true condition, thereby introducing the
element of fraud. Had the court held the marriage fraudulent and thus voidable
at the instance of the petitioner (rather than void), it could have ordered
annulment, thereby preserving the wife's right to ancillary relief. The court,
instead, chose to proceed by a declaration of nullity *ab initio* on the ground that
a transsexual, even after operative procedures, cannot contract a valid marriage
in Singapore: a much broader ground than necessary to the resolution of the
case and an outcome arguably less fair to the petitioner.[153] Although the case
strictly follows the precedent established by *Corbett*, the result nevertheless was
incongruous, given Singapore's historically indulgent attitude to transsexuality
and to sex-change operative procedures. Indeed, the Singaporean authorities
had actually issued the respondent with a new identity card in which he was
classified as male. Eventually, the peculiarity of the Court's opinion was recognized by the government, whose Minister of Community Development, Abdul-
lah Tarmugi, proposed legislation that would permit sex-reassigned persons to
register their new sex, to marry, and to adopt children.[154]

In the United States, the matter is governed primarily by state law, with
consequent wide variations. At least sixteen states and the District of Columbia
allow change in a person's sex designation to be recorded on the birth certificate
after sex reassignment surgery.[155] These jurisdictions, obviously, have adopted
the third or physiological test, rather than the *Corbett*, or chromosomal, test.

---

[150] *Attorney-General v. Otahuhu Family Court*, (1995) 1 NZLR 603, 622–3.          [151] Ibid. at 630.
[152] *Lim Ying V. Hiok Kian Ming Eric* [1992], 1 SLR 184.
[153] Coincidentally, in 1996, the ethics committee of Saitama Medical College became the first to
approve sex change operations. The Daily Yomiuri, 3 July 1996, at 1.
[154] Rohania Saini, 'Transsexuals Keeping Their Fingers Crossed', The Straits Times, 26 Jan.
1996, at 1.
[155] *M.T. v. J.T.*, 140 NJ Super. 77 (1976) specifically rejects the Corbett test to uphold the marriage
of a male-to-female transsexual. D. Douglas Cotton, 'Note: Ulane v. Eastern Airlines: Title VII and
Transsexualism', 80 NWUL Rev. 1038, 1038, n. 1 (1986). The jurisdictions are Arizona, Arkansas,
California, District of Columbia, Georgia, Hawaii, Illinois, Iowa, Louisiana, Massachusetts,
Michigan, Mississippi, New Mexico, North Carolina, Oregon, Utah, and Virginia.

Other states—New York is an example—permit only the issuance of a new birth certificate which does not disclose sex.[156] In the states that recognize sex reassignment, marriage of the reassignee appears to be legally sanctioned.[157] In a New Jersey case, it was held that, if 'such sex reassignment surgery is successful and the post-operative transsexual is, by virtue of medical treatment, thereby possessed of full capacity to function sexually as a male or female, as the case may be, we perceive no legal barrier, cognizable social taboo, or reason grounded in public policy to prevent that person's identification at least for purposes of marriage to the sex finally indicated'.[158] In such instance, the court added, 'the transsexual's gender and genitalia are no longer discordant; they have been harmonized through medical treatment'.[159]

Despite the New Jersey court's rather quaint language, the line drawn is quite as bright as the chromosomal test of *Corbett* and at least somewhat closer to the social reality of what marriage means today, when neither procreation nor even continual sexual relations can any longer be said to be the matrimonial *sine qua non*. Moreover, since pre-operative cross-dressing may be 'a necessary therapy in preparation for such surgery' a Chicago city ordinance prohibiting that conduct 'was an unconstitutional infringement of liberty' where state law permits 'sex-reassignment surgery'.[160]

Nevertheless, some US state courts have refused to take this direction,[161] and some state courts still hold, with *Corbett*, that it 'is generally accepted that a person's sex is determined at birth by an anatomical examination by the birth attendant'.[162]

Not only are post-operative transsexuals legally capable of marriage in some states, a male-to-female post-operative wife may also be entitled to the support for which law makes provision in the event of divorce.[163] In rejecting *Corbett's* test, the New Jersey court held that 'a person's sex or sexuality embraces an individual's gender, that is, one's self-image, the deep psychological or emotional sense of sexual identity and character. Indeed . . . the "psychological sex of an individual," while not serviceable for all purposes, is "practical, realistic and humane".'[164] On the other hand, US federal courts, unlike the European Court of Justice, have refused to interpret Title VII of the Civil Rights Act of 1964[165] to include 'transsexuals' among those whose rights are protected

---

[156] *In the Matter of Deborah Hartin*, 347 NYS.2d 515 (1973). But see also 'Note: Transsexuals in Limbo: The Search for a Legal Definition of Sex,' 31 Maryland L. Rev. 236 (1971).

[157] *M.T. v. J.T.*, 140 NJ Super. 77, 355 A.2d 204 (1976).       [158] Ibid. at 210.

[159] Ibid.

[160] *City of Chicago v. Wilson*, 75 Ill.2d 525, 389 NE. 2d 522 (1978).

[161] *In re Declaratory Relief for Ladrach*, 32 Ohio Misc.2d 6; 513 NE. 2d 828, 832.

[162] Ibid.        [163] *M.T. v. J.T., supra* n. 157, at 83.

[164] Ibid. at 86–7, quoting *Comment*, 56 Cornell L. Rev. 969–70 and citing *In re Anonymous*, 57 Misc.2d 813, 293 NYS.2d 834, 837 (Civ. Ct. 1968).

[165] 42 USC §2000c et. seq.

against sex discrimination.[166] Even in New Jersey, the courts are still influenced by England's jurisprudence. A teacher dismissed after a sex change operation was held not protected by a contractual tenure provision providing job security 'during good behaviour and efficiency' except 'for inefficiency, incapacity, unbecoming conduct, or other just cause'.[167] Although the court found the teacher's 'proficiency as a teacher . . . not in question'[168] it was 'convinced that where, as has been found in this case, a teacher's presence in the classroom would create a potential for psychological harm to the students, the teacher is unable properly to fulfill his or her role and his or her incapacity has been established within the purview of the statute . . . We express no opinion with respect to her fitness to teach elsewhere . . .'.[169] The court also found no violation of plaintiff's constitutional right to 'equal protection of the laws'.[170]

In at least some US states, the courts have refused to overrule administrative denials of public assistance (Medicaid) to persons seeking sex reassignment,[171] sometimes on the ground that this procedure is still 'experimental'.[172] On the other hand, some state courts have come to the opposite conclusion. A federal appellate bench, in 1980, awarded an applicant the costs of a sex change operation, plus damages, finding that the refusal by the state's Department of Social Services to apply the Medicaid statute to such procedures 'reflects inadequate solicitude for the applicant's diagnosed condition, the treatment prescribed by the applicant's physicians, and the accumulated knowledge of the medical community'.[173]

That the procedures are still 'experimental' is hardly credible. While Western societies' public interest in the transsexual phenomenon burgeoned in the early 1960s after the gender reassignment operation of Christine Jorgensen, there has been public notice of the phenomenon at all periods of history and, apparently, also in many non-Western civilizations.[174] There are exact accounts from ancient Greece and Rome. For example, Philo, the Jewish philosopher of Alexandria, reported frankly on the matter.[175] There are accounts of the Roman Emperor Heliogabalus' marriage to a slave, 'whereupon he assumed wifely duties and offered half the Empire to the physician who could equip him

---

[166] *Voyles v. Davies*, 403 F. Supp. 456, 457 (1975); *Powell v. Read's Inc.*, 436 F. Supp. 369 (1977); *Holloway v. Arthur Anderson and Co.*, 566 F.2d 659 (1977); *Cornish v. Budget Marketing, Inc.*, 667 F.2d 748 (1982); *Ulane v. Eastern Airlines, Inc.*, 742 F.2d 1081 (1984).
[167] *Grossman v. Township of Bernards*, 127 NJ Super. 13, 316 A.2d 39 (1974).
[168] Ibid. at 29.      [169] Ibid. at 32.      [170] Ibid. at 33–4.
[171] *Rush v. Parham*, 625 F.2d 1150, 1157 (5th Cir. 1980). See *Rush v. Johnson*, 565 F. Supp. 856 (1983).      [172] *Rush v. Johnson*, ibid. at 867.
[173] *Pinneke v. Preisser*, 6 F.2d 546, 549 (1980).
[174] See L. Lothstein, *Female-to-Male Transsexualism* 7 (1983); R. Green, *Sexual Identity Conflict in Children and Adults* 3–5 (1974); *Note: Ulane v. Eastern Airlines, Inc., supra* n. 166, at 1037, 1041.
[175] Green, ibid. at 5. 'Expending every possible care on their outward adornment, they are not ashamed even to employ every device to change artificially their nature as men into women—some of them craving a complete transformation into women, they have amputated their generative members.'

with female genitalia'.[176] Reports abound of transsexualism among North and South American Indians.[177] In sum, '[n]umerous descriptions from classical mythology, classical history, Renaissance and nineteenth century history, plus many sources of cultural anthropology, point to the long-standing and wide-spread pervasiveness of the transsexual phenomenon.'[178]

The origins of transsexual behaviour are not known to science, although experiments conducted on animals just before or after birth suggest to some that it can be induced by the introduction of sex hormones and their effect on the brain. On the whole, however, the matter remains as much a mystery as other aspects of how the human bio-system organizes and facilitates the establishment of gender role behaviour.[179] Since we do not know precisely what determines sex or gender, we have difficulty characterizing it. If we choose, with Mr Justice Ormrod, a binary chromosomal characterization, we are faced with a sizeable array of deviations — homosexuality, transsexuality, bisexuality, hermaphroditism — which, in turn, have deviations of their own. In the absence of scientific knowledge of causality, or even of reliable medical characterizations and typologies, communities are left with only two choices: to do something or to do nothing.

Doing something generally takes the form of enforcing a pretence of communitarian conformity against deviating individuals. This social choice may be motivated by concerns for morality, often based on divinely inspired but (thus) unverifiable information, or simply on the utilitarian or historically rooted penchant for social order and cohesion. In this area, as in so many others, there are always persons ready to predict the demise of the community if individual deviation from the norm were permitted to dissolve the glue that holds society together.[180]

Doing nothing usually takes the form of removing legal constraints on the exercise of autonomous personal choice — 'leaving it to individual taste'. Choice may or may not need to be manifested, and thus controlled, by legal requirements to undergo surgical or medical transformative procedures. Whether in this area the individual is capable of truly autonomous choice is an interesting question, but one which could as well be addressed to many other issue-areas now reserved by law to private decisions.[181] Even if an answer were at hand, it

---

[176] Ibid. at 6.     [177] Ibid. at 8–12.

[178] R. Green, 'Mythological, Historical, and Cross-Cultural Aspects of Transsexualism', in *Transsexualism and Sex Reassignment* 18, 22 (R. Green & J. Money eds., 1969).

[179] See Lothstein, *supra* n. 174, at 180. I am indebted to Cotton, *supra* n. 155, for pointing out most of the sources here cited and for others equally helpful if inconclusive.

[180] Columnist and sometime US Presidential candidate Pat Buchanan exemplifies this oratory, proclaiming that 'gays' are the 'aggressors in our cultural wars' in which they seek 'to use schools and media to validate and propagate their moral beliefs, to convert all of America . . .'. John M. Broder & James Risen, 'Buchanan Measured by Life of Sharply Honed Rhetoric', LA Times, 25 Feb. 1996, at 1.

[181] Carey Goldberg, 'Shunning "He" and "She" They Fight for Respect', NY Times, National Report, 8 Sept. 1996, at 24.

might not prove decisive in allocating this particular issue either to private preference or public morality.

As with other aspects of individual human rights, there is also in this area a continuous and reciprocal interaction between domestic and international legal norms, as also between the interpretative modalities applied to these norms by domestic and international courts. Uncertain as this discourse and its outcome may appear at this time, there is reason to expect the law to follow the gradual evolution of public opinion in recognizing sex preference to be a matter of private taste or proclivity and not suitable for the enforcing of conformity to arbitrary communitarian standards.

4. PERSONAL AUTONOMY IN CHOICE OF CAREER

### (a) New Norms Defined by the Treaty System

It is often asserted, especially in Western nations, that a person can become anything he or she wants, given adequate spirit and aptitude. But are individuals, today, really free to choose what they want to be? Or is this freedom still restricted: by law, social class, race, economics or other distortions? While these questions can generate vibrant disagreement, it is generally acknowledged that persons have more career opportunities now than was the case until quite recently.

The recentness of this change may surprise us. Well into the nineteenth century there was widespread, legally sanctioned slavery. Until the twentieth century, the law could still compel persons to fulfil personal service contracts. Only in recent years have many craft guilds and unions begun to admit persons who are not sons or close relatives of members. It is only within living memory that women, the largest excluded group, have had equal access to professional schools. Moreover, if real choice of occupations has only very recently, and quite imperfectly, been realized in democratic, industrialized Western societies, it has scarcely been broached in some other regions. In many societies, persons' occupations are still largely determined by birth, gender, class, or tribe and are enforced by law and social custom.

Obviously, how choices about career are made has a profound effect on personal identity: whether, in the case of African-Americans, an individual can opt to be an opera singer or is assigned to cooking, cleaning, and child-bearing; whether, as a woman, one may choose to be a lawyer or only, at best, to be a teacher or nurse; whether, as a Jew, one may decide to become a doctor or is forced by religious quotas at medical schools to become a merchant. Here, as in other aspects of personal identity, there have been important recent strides towards personal autonomy and away from communal values imposed by elites on the powerless. In this gathering momentum, international norms have played a role, both in clearly demarcating the goals and in slowly nudging and cajoling societies in the direction of change.

The International Covenant on Economic, Social, and Cultural Rights,[182] for example, obliges states to extend equal rights to persons, regardless of 'race, colour, sex, language, religion, political or other opinion, national or social origin, property, birth or other status'[183] and to ensure 'the right of everyone to the opportunity to gain his living by work which he freely chooses or accepts'. States are required to 'take appropriate steps to safeguard this right'.[184] Specifically, '[h]igher education shall be made equally accessible to all, on the basis of capacity, by every appropriate means, and in particular by the introduction of free education . . .'.[185] The Convention on the Elimination of Racism requires states to provide 'free choice of employment' as well as 'the right to education and training' to 'everyone, without distinction as to race, colour, or national or ethnic origin'.[186] The obligation's implementation is subject to review by an elected Committee of Experts.[187] The Convention on the Elimination of All Forms of Discrimination Against Women requires states to take measures to 'eliminate discrimination against women in the field of employment'.[188] They are to ensure the same rights 'on a basis of equality of men and women'[189] including 'the free right of profession and employment, the right to promotion, job security, and all benefits and conditions of service . . .' as well as by 'equal remuneration and . . . equal treatment in respect of work of equal value . . . .'[190] To oversee implementation, the Convention establishes a Committee of twenty-three experts which receives periodic reports and makes recommendations to governments found not to be in compliance.[191]

At a regional level, the European Convention prohibits 'forced or compulsory labour'.[192] The European Court of Human Rights is empowered to hear allegations of non-compliance.[193] Working conditions, particularly for women, are regulated by the European Social Charter.[194] In the Western Hemisphere,

---

[182] International Covenant on Economic, Social and Cultural Rights, 993 UNTS 3, 6 ILM 360 (1967). Adopted by the UN General Assembly on 16 Dec. 1966, Annex to GA Res. 2200, 21 GAOR Supp. 16, UN Doc. A/6316 at 490. Entered into force 3 January 1976.

[183] Ibid. at 2(2). See also art. 3, on equal rights of men and women.

[184] Ibid. art. 6(1).     [185] Ibid. art. 13(2)(c).

[186] International Convention on the Elimination of All Forms of Racial Discrimination, 660 UNTS 195, 5 ILM 352 (1969), adopted by GA Res. 2106 of 21 Dec. 1965, 21 GAOR, Supp. 14, UN Doc. A/6014, at 47. Entered into force on 4 January 1969, arts. 5 and 5(e)(V).

[187] Ibid. Part II.

[188] Convention on the Elimination of All Forms of Discrimination Against Women, GA Res. 180(XXXIV 1979) adopted 18 Dec. 1979, 19 ILM 33 (1980). Entered into force 3 Sept. 1981, art. 11(1).     [189] Ibid.

[190] Ibid. art. 11(2)(c) and (e).     [191] Ibid. Part V.

[192] European Convention for the Protection of Human Rights and Fundamental Freedoms, 213 UNTS 221, ETS 5. Signed at Rome on 4 Nov. 1950; entered into force on 3 Sept. 1953.

[193] Ibid. Secs. III and IV.

[194] European Social Charter, 529 UNTS 89, ETS Nos. 35. Done at Turin, 18 Oct. 1961. Entered into force 26 Feb. 1965, art. 8.

the American Convention on Human Rights[195] stipulates that no one 'shall be required to perform forced or compulsory labour . . .'.[196] and promotes implementation through the Inter-American Commission and Court of Human Rights.[197] By an Additional Protocol to this Convention (the 'Protocol of San Salvador'), the state parties 'guarantee in their internal legislation' to provide that everyone shall enjoy 'the right . . . to follow his vocation and to devote himself to the activity that best fulfills his expectations and to change employment in accordance with the pertinent national regulations . . .'.[198] In Africa, equality of treatment on the basis of 'race, ethnic group, colour, sex, language, religion, political or any other opinion, national and social origin, fortune, birth or other status' is established as a right under the Charter on Human and Peoples' Rights (The 'Banjul Charter'),[199] which also guarantees 'equal pay for equal work'[200] and commits states to 'ensure the elimination of every discrimination against women . . .'.[201] Compliance is monitored by a Commission of eleven elected independent experts.[202]

There can be little doubt as to the direction in which these legal regimes are pulling: towards a global convergence on the principle that individuals are entitled to pursue career-choices determined only by personal preference and competence, uninhibited by such traditional but extraneous factors as race, caste or gender.

### (b) Women and the Professions

One of the most potent examples of the old order is the limitation on choice of careers long imposed on women in the name of communal values and decorum. Nowadays, in the West, this is often dismissed as the exotic problem of some Islamic, Asian, and African societies whose disregard for women's autonomy and personal self-determination is thought to contrast so vividly with the emancipated sexual equality characteristic of the West. As with freedom of conscience, however, the illusion of a Great Chasm between Western and non-Western societies is sustainable only by disregarding latitudinal social and historic evidence to the contrary. How can it be reconciled with four great Asian nations—Pakistan, India, Sri Lanka, and Bangladesh, together accounting for

---

[195] American Convention on Human Rights, OAS Off. Rec. OEA/Ser.K/XVI/1.1, Doc. 65, Rev. 1, Corr. 1, 7 Jan. 1970. 9 ILM 101, 673 (1970). Signed San Jose, 22 Nov. 1969. Entered into force 18 July 1978.                                                      [196] Ibid. art. 6(2).

[197] Ibid. Chs. VII and VIII.

[198] Done 17 Nov. 1988. Reprinted in 28 ILM 156 (1989), art. 7(b). Not yet in force.

[199] African Charter on Human and Peoples' Rights (The 'Banjul Charter'), OAU Doc. CAB/LEG/67/3/Rev. 5, reprinted in 21 ILM 5 (1982). Adopted by the OAU on 27 June 1981. Entered into force 21 Oct. 1986.                                                      [200] Ibid. art. 15.

[201] Ibid. art. 18(3).

[202] Ibid. Part II. For a recent survey of the African Commission's decisions and reports see 18 H.Rts. LJ 28–36 (1997).

one-third of the world's population—having been led by women in recent years? One has but to study the role of women in Singapore to see how absurd is the stereotype of subservient Asian women.

The illusion of a Great Chasm is nurtured by ignorance of contemporary social conditions in non-Western states and sustained by a short, selective memory of Western resistance to women's rights. Longitudinally, women's progress in Europe and America has been achieved only recently, against formidable obstacles. As with freedom of conscience, there is no reason to believe that this progress is a manifestation of 'Western' culture. Much more likely, the same independent variables that advanced freedom of conscience have also promoted the rights of women.

Women's rights advanced in the wake of changes in class structure, which followed political changes that were prompted by radical economic transformation. The industrial revolution in England and America created a large merchant class, which demanded new goods and services, the universal male franchise, and quality education for its young. By the beginning of the nineteenth century, a middle-class electorate, swollen by lowering of property qualifications, had won universal free schooling for its sons. This demand, paradoxically, could only be met by opening the teaching profession to women.[203] The emancipation of women thus began as a by-product of the invention of general public education for boys.[204]

The tremendous demand for teachers to work in the new elementary schools made it inevitable that women would have to gain access to higher education, 'so that they could become minimally adequate instructors of young children'.[205] Oberlin College, in 1833, and Mt. Holyoke, in 1837, were the first to respond, although the former did not initially allow women to pursue any of the 'professional' subjects.[206] In our cultural myopia, we lose sight of how recently this has happened. The transformation began less than a century-and-a-half ago. Previously, it was generally acknowledged in Western society that, except for a few hereditary aristocrats and privileged eccentrics, the place of women was in the kitchen and the nursery, whether as wives or domestic servants.

In law, Blackstone's view predominated: 'By marriage, the husband and wife are but one person in law, that is the legal existence of the woman is suspended during marriage, or at least is incorporated into that of the husband, under whose protection and cover she performs everything.'[207] In French law the married woman was a 'femme couvert' who existed 'under the protection of her husband, her baron or lord, and her condition during marriage is one of coverture'.[208] She could not own or inherit property, enter into contracts, sue or

---

[203] David L. Madsen, *Early National Education, 1776–1830* 65–6 (1974).

[204] Joellen Lind, 'Symbols, Leaders, Practitioners: the First Women Professionals', 28 Valparaiso UL Rev. 1327, 1330 (1994). [205] Ibid.

[206] Ibid. at 10.        [207] 1 William Blackstone, *Commentaries* 442.

[208] Lind, *supra* n. 204, at 13.

be sued. The first legal reform allowing women to own certain forms of property in New York State was only enacted in 1848.[209]

Not until the 1840s did women in America begin to seek admission to professional schools. Most were rejected outright. Antoinette Brown, one of a tiny number of women ministers ordained before the civil war, was rejected by the seminaries, 'often with church officials citing Scripture to justify their treatment'.[210] As for women in law, it was unheard of at this time, the practice being regarded as 'especially imbued with "male" characteristics. . . . It seemed particularly unnatural and unfeminine for women to engage in legal combat in public. . . . Worries of these sorts were effective impediments to women's visible legal practice [they sometimes helped their lawyer husbands] and they continued to function as barriers to women's formal licensure until well into the 1890s'.[211] Exceptionally, Belle A. Mansfield was admitted to the Iowa bar in 1869, after studying in a home office. Thereafter, a handful of other women gained admission to their state bars in the middle west, and to the law schools of the University of Iowa in 1869, the University of Michigan in 1870, and Boston University in 1872.[212] The Harvard Law School, however, did not begin to admit women until the 1950s.[213] The US census reported ten women attorneys in 1870, seventy-five in 1890, and slightly over 1,000 in 1900.[214] By 1920, no state any longer excluded women from practice and, currently, most law schools report an approximately 1:1 male-to-female ratio in their enrolment.

Progress for women in medicine was only slightly faster. The first female candidate for a medical degree was Elizabeth Blackwell, who graduated from a rural medical college in Geneva, New York, in 1849, but left America to continue her training at La Maternité hospital in Paris.[215] She continually 'faced formidable obstacles, intense prejudice and severe hostility from male physicians'.[216] By 1880 there were almost 2,500 female physicians in the US, partly in response to the need for medical personnel during the civil war. In 1910, women made up 6 per cent of enrolment in medical schools,[217] and by 1920 there were 8,800 women doctors in US practice.[218] Similar, if uneven, rises in the 1920s occurred in such professions as the clergy, architecture, dentistry, and even engineering.[219] The passage of the Nineteenth Amendment in 1920, at last enfranchising women, undoubtedly helped, as did the need for professional 'manpower' during the first and second world wars.

This sketch of female career-emancipation, however encouraging, should also

---

[209] Ibid. at 14.    [210] Ibid. at 23.

[211] Ibid. at 24. Cf. *Bradwell v. Illinois*, 83 US (16 Wall.) 442, 446 (1873).

[212] Lind, ibid. at 35.

[213] Robert Stevens, *Law School: Legal Education in America From the 1850s to the 1980s* 24 (1983). A few public institutions such as the University of Michigan and the University of Iowa began to admit a few women to legal studies before the end of the nineteenth century. Lind, ibid. at 31.

[214] Lind, ibid. at 36.    [215] Ibid. at 22.

[216] Ibid. See also Mary Roth Walsh, *Doctors Wanted: No Women Need Apply* 213 (1977).

[217] Lind, ibid. at 37.    [218] Ibid. at 47.    [219] Ibid.

remind us how very recently the career choices of half the population of America was still curtailed by imposed 'communitarian' values enforced by law and custom. Whatever emancipation Western women were able to achieve in the recent past cannot obscure the preceding millennia of subordination.

Such subordination, insofar as it still prevails in some societies, is now vigorously challenged not only by women activists but also by the new global ethos of individualism that demands equal treatment for all persons. Women's rights are expanding in tandem with the new global emphasis on individual human rights. Although there is, now, an international convention specifically on the rights of women, those rights are also part of the older, general canon of protected civil and political rights. For example, in 1989, the ICCPR's Human Rights Committee found article 168 of the Peruvian Civil Code in violation of article 26 of the International Covenant.[220] Article 168 prohibits married Peruvian women from suing on matrimonial property claims. The ICCPR Committee concluded 'that the facts before it reveal that the application of article 168 . . . resulted in denying [the applicant] equality before the courts and constituted discrimination on the ground of sex'.[221] Still, the 1995 United Nations Development Programme's *Human Development Report* states that 'Husbands can restrict a wife's employment outside the home in Bolivia, Guatemala and Syria.'[222] Evidently, the fight to establish equal rights for women is far from won, but it has now been joined by influential international institutions and laws.

In particular, however, progress in women's rights proceeds everywhere in response to the same, or similar exogenous factors. Labour needs, urbanization, education, democracy, changing gender norms are among the omnific factors that determine the direction and rate of this progress. Despite aberrational variances (the Taliban of Afghanistan, for one), that direction is not in doubt, and is reinforced by pressure to conform to increasingly universal standards and a growing body of international and national law.

### (c) Slavery and Indentured Labour

As with the subjugation of women, so, too, involuntary servitude was long thought necessary to uphold social stability and important communal values. Nowadays, slavery is outlawed by almost all national legal systems, and is clearly prohibited by international customary and treaty law.[223] Yet, in 1996, UN

---

[220] *Ato del Avellanal v. Peru*, case no. 202/1986. Report of the Human Rights Committee, GAOR, Supp. no. 40 (A/44/40), at 149, para. 656 and annex X, sect. C, para. 10.2.                    [221] Ibid.

[222] UNDP, Human Development Report, 42–4 (1995). See also Berta Esperanza Hernández-Truyol, 'Sex, Culture and Rights: A Re-Conceptualization of Violence for the Twenty-First Century', 60 Alb. L. Rev. 607, 615 n. 31, 619 n. 51 (1997). The Hernández-Truyol article also notes that, under Kenyan law, a married woman may obtain a passport only with the permission of her husband. Ibid. at 615 n. 31.

[223] See *Restatement (Third) of the Foreign Relations Law of the United States* § 702(b) and comment (e) (1987); Theodor Meron, *Human Rights and Humanitarian Norms as Customary Law* 20 (1989).

Secretary-General Boutros Boutros-Ghali, marking the International Day for the Abolition of Slavery, reported that, far from being resolved, the problem of 'traffic in human beings has become a serious challenge to the entire international community', adding that it has become 'a highly organized and international trade with links to organized crime' in whose hands it 'can and often does lead to prostitution, forced domestic service and pornography'.[224] Evidently, even the clearest legal prohibition has not entirely succeeded in transforming oppressive traditional behaviour or entrenched social and legal structures.

The institution of slavery is as old as human history and as universal as humanity itself.[225] It is sanctioned by the Old Testament.[226] What is striking is the temporal length of its dominion and the extent to which slavery was regarded by communities as 'normal' and 'right'. Although not all nations have practised slavery, there was little objection by governments until late in the eighteenth century.[227] In a landmark 1772 decision in *Somerset v. Stewart*, Lord Mansfield at the King's Bench Division refused to give effect to the status of slavery in English law, not even in an instance where the slave's foreign domicile did recognize the legality of bondage. He ordered the freeing of a man brought along on a visit to London by his West Indian master.[228] It had been argued that if British courts failed to recognize the status of slavery that was legal in the place of the master's usual domicile, it would undermine the comity between legal systems that made for orderly relations among jurisdictions and would undermine respect for property rights. In rejecting these arguments and thus banishing the last vestiges of slavery from English soil, Mansfield proclaimed '*fiat justicia, ruat coelum*': let justice be done, though the sky may fall. Slavery was prohibited in metropolitan France in 1794 and in French Saint Domingue in 1804.[229] It was not outlawed in the United States until the entry into force of the Thirteenth Amendment, in 1865, although it had been abolished earlier in some northern states and had been roundly condemned

---

[224] 'Secretary-General Urges Action to Address Contemporary Forms of Slavery', in Statement to General Assembly. Press Release SG/SM/6121, 6 Dec. 1996.

[225] Renee C. Redman, 'The League of Nations and the Right to be Free of Enslavement', 70 Chic.-K. L. Rev. 759, 765–77 (1994).

[226] See e.g. Exodus 21: 2, 26, 27, 32; Leviticus 25: 39; Deuteronomy 15: 12; and Ecclesiastes 2: 7.

[227] Contrary to public myth, slave-carrying vessels captured on the high seas by British vessels on the high seas were usually not treated as prize by British courts in the 18th, 19th, and early 20th centuries but were either returned to their owners or surrendered to the state whose flag the vessel had flown. See 1 L. Oppenheim, *International Law* 616–17 (H. Lauterpacht ed., 8th edn. 1955); see also *The Diana*, 1 Dods. 95, 165 ER 1245 (Adm. 1813) at 97–8, 101; *The Antelope*, 23 US (10 Wheat.) 66, 90 (1825). These cases seem to contradict J. Story, in *La Jeune Eugenie, infra* n. 230.

[228] [1772] 98 ER, 27 KB 499, 509, Lofft 1, 17.

[229] Guyora Binder, 'The Slavery of Emancipation', 17 Cardozo L. Rev. 2063, 2079 (1996).

by Supreme Court Justice Story, for 'the vast extent of misery and cruelty occasioned by its ravages'.[230]

International action was still slower in coming. Not until 1841 did the Great Powers of Europe (Austria, Britain, Prussia, Russia, and France) sign a treaty to consider the seaborne trade in slaves as an act of piracy, thereby authorizing all state parties to inspect each other's vessels in prescribed zones.[231] France failed to ratify the accord,[232] and the United States did not join the interdiction until 1862.[233] Efforts altogether to abolish slavery awaited the Berlin Act of 1885,[234] the Brussels Act of 1889,[235] and the Convention of St. Germain-en-Laye of 1919.[236]

While these measures indicated enlightened intentions, they did little to curb slavery and slave trading in the Middle East, Ethiopia, Liberia, and parts of Asia. They also did not cover various surrogate practices such as the indenturing or bonding of labour.

Noncompliance in non-Western states was first systematically addressed in 1927 by the International Labour Organization, which negotiated and still oversees the implementation of a global prohibition of forced labour.[237] A further 1930 Convention[238] covers not only slavery but also analogous forms of forced labour. It has been ratified by 132 states and obliges them to respect their citizens 'right to free choice of employment'.[239] Forced labour is also

---

[230] The quotation comes from *Miscellaneous Writings of Joseph Story* 122 (William W. Story ed., 1852). See also Story's opinion in *US v. La Jeune Eugenie*, 26 F. Cas. 832, 834 (CCD Mass. 1822) (no. 15,551). See further his charges to juries as a Circuit Judge: In *Fales v. Mayberry*, Story railed against slavery as 'a most odious and horrible traffic', which was 'contrary to the plainest principles of natural justice and humanity' and so 'cannot have a legal existence'. *Fales v. Mayberry*, 8 F. Cas. 970 (CCD RI 1815) (no. 4,622), at 971. In *La Jeune Eugenie*, he asserted that the practice 'begins in corruption, and plunder, and kidnapping' destroying 'all the ties of parents, and of children, and forcing the brave to untimely death in defence of their humble homes . . .'. Ibid. at 845.

[231] Treaty of London of 1841, Treaty between Austria, Great Britain, Prussia and Russia for the Suppression of the African Slave Trade, signed at London, 20 December 1841, 92 Consol. TS 437, arts. 1 and 2.　　　　　　　　　　　　　　　　　　[232] Redman, *supra* n. 225, at 773.

[233] Treaty for the Suppression of African Slave Trade [Treaty of Washington], 7 Apr. 1862, Stat. 1225, § I(12).

[234] General Act of the Conference at Berlin Respecting the Congo, 26 Feb. 1885, 7 Hertslet's Com. TS 62.

[235] Suzanne Miers, 'The Brussels Conference of 1889–90', in *Britain and Germany in Africa* (P. Gifford & W. R. Louis eds., 1967), at 81, 85. 27 Stat. at 887, 1 Bevans 134–5.

[236] Convention Revising the General Act of Berlin of 1885 and the General Act and Declaration of Brussels of 1890, 49 Stat. 3027, 2 Bevans 261 (10 Sept. 1919).

[237] See e.g. Slavery Convention of 1926, entered into force 1927. 60 LNTS 253. Convention Concerning Forced or Compulsory Labour (no. 29), 28 June 1930, reprinted in 1 International Labour Conventions and Recommendations (ILCR) 155 (1982). See also the Convention Concerning the Abolition of Forced Labour (no. 105), 25 June 1957, in 1 ILCR 618 (1982), with 110 ratifications.

[238] Convention Concerning Forced or Compulsory Labour (ILO no. 29), adopted 28 June 1930, 39 UNTS 55 (entered into force 1 May 1932). See also the Convention Concerning the Abolition of Forced Labour (ILO no. 105), adopted 25 June 1957, 320 UNTS 291 (entered into force 17 Jan. 1959).

[239] Hurst Hannum, 'The Status of the Universal Declaration of Human Rights in National and International Law', 25 Ga. J. Int'l & Comp. L. 287 (1995/6).

prohibited by the more recent International Covenants on Economic, Social, and Cultural Rights[240] and on Civil and Political Rights.[241] Article 6(1) of the former[242] also recognizes the 'right . . . of everyone to gain his living by work which he freely chooses or accepts' and requires state parties to 'take appropriate steps to safeguard this right'. More recently, the General Agreement on Tariffs and Trade and the World Trade Organization[243] authorized remedial and retaliatory measures[244] when a state's exports are produced in ways that offend 'public morals' or by prison labour.[245]

Beginning in the inter-war period, some global efforts have been made to compel recalcitrants to comply with these prohibitions. The League of Nations' Advisory Committee on Slavery focused attention on states that blatantly continued to tolerate the practice, including Hedjaz and Nejd (Saudi Arabia), Yemen, Hadramuth, Oman, Kowait (Kuwait), and Abyssinia (Ethiopia). Liberia found itself threatened with expulsion from the League if it did not take measures to abolish slavery and the slave trade.[246] In 1937, the League of Nations congratulated Saudi Arabia for having made the import of slaves illegal and prohibiting the purchase or enslaving of free persons. Even so, these measures did not actually prohibit slavery itself, which persisted. In the British Aden Protectorate, due to League pressure, slavery was outlawed in 1938.[247] The 1996 report of the UN Secretary-General indicates, however, that international efforts at eradication are still far from achieving their goal. Like a weed treated with chemical eradicators, slavery, outlawed, tends to re-emerge from the hospitable soil of traditional communities, sometimes slightly mutated but usually still virulent.

Advances also generated reaction. In the same year as Mansfield's decision in *Somerset*, a Scottish court confirmed the legality of contracts of lifetime bondage.[248] This was reversed on appeal by the Court of Session which held that such contracts are unenforceable: 'a service for life, without wages, is, in fact, slavery. The law of Scotland would not support a voluntary contract in these terms; and, even where wages are stipulated, such a contract has been voided by the court . . .'.[249] Still, a century after *Somerset*, the US Supreme Court decided

---

[240] International Covenant on Economic, Social and Cultural Rights, 993 UNTS 3 (entered into force 3 Jan. 1976), arts. 6–8.
[241] ICCPR, 999 UNTS 171 (entered into force 23 March 1976), art. 8.
[242] International Covenant on Economic, Social and Cultural Rights, 993 UNTS 3, 6 ILM 360 (1967). Adopted by GA Res. 2200 of 16 Dec. 1996. Entered into force on 3 Jan. 1976.
[243] The latter incorporates the former. Final Act Embodying the Results of the Uruguay Round of Multilateral Trade Negotiations, Agreement Establishing the Multilateral [World] Trade Organization, GATT Doc. MTN/FA (5 Dec. 1993) reprinted in 33 ILM 13, art. XX(a) and (e) and XXIII(2).
[244] General Agreement on Tariffs and Trade, 61 Stat., p. 5 at A3, 55 UNTS 194 (entered into force 1 Jan. 1948). Ibid. at VI(3).     [245] Ibid. at art. XX(a) and (e).
[246] For a history of these efforts and others by the League see Redman, *supra* n. 225, at 777–90.
[247] Ibid. at 787–8 and cites therein.
[248] *Knight v. Wedderburn*, 20 How. St. Tr. 1–12 (1772).
[249] *Knight v. Wedderburn*, 8 Fac. Coll. 5, 8 (1778).

that a seaman who had contracted to serve on an American merchant ship, the *Arago*, could be compelled against his will to complete the term of his service on pain of arrest by US marshals, imprisonment, and forcible return to his ship.[250] This was held not to be in violation of the thirteenth constitutional amendment's prohibition of 'involuntary servitude'. The judges thought that 'the business of navigation could scarcely be carried on without some guaranty, beyond the ordinary civil remedies upon contract, that the sailor will not desert the ship at a critical moment . . .'.[251] They seemed convinced that seamen, as a class, were 'deficient in that full and intelligent responsibility for their acts which is accredited to ordinary adults' and thus, like children, could be recommitted to their, as it were, 'parents and guardians'.[252]

Although such compulsory service of civilians is probably no longer regarded as constitutional in the United States, except perhaps in extreme emergencies, several countries make specific constitutional provision for it.[253] In the case of Vietnam, for example, civilians may be required by law to work 'on public projects'.[254]

For some time after the abolition of slavery, in almost every society, there ensued efforts to replace it with mandatory service based on debt or long-term contracts. In Britain, these efforts were repelled by the judges. In the mid-nineteenth century, the Lord Chancellor's Court in England, in the case of *Lumley v. Wagner*,[255] held that the law would not enforce a contract between an impresario and an artist by compelling the latter to perform. For the three months stipulated in the contract she could be enjoined from performing elsewhere, but the English court refused 'to enforce the specific performance of the whole of this contract'.[256] The diva could not be made to sing.

In 1905,[257] and again in 1910,[258] the US Supreme Court, too, rejected calls to enforce involuntary servitude. In the latter instance, it declared unconstitutional an Alabama statute which had made the refusal or failure to perform labour contracted for, without refunding the money or paying for property received, *prima facie* evidence of the commission of a crime. The law's effect, the Court ruled, was 'to enforce involuntary servitude by compelling personal service in liquidation of a debt' in violation of the Thirteenth Amendment.[259]

Peonage, or involuntary servitude of various kinds, has now largely been eliminated in most other Western nations. In France, a judgement for specific

---

[250] *Robertson v. Baldwin*, 165 US 275 (1897).    [251] Ibid. at 283.    [252] Ibid. at 287.

[253] Pakistan (art. 11(4)(b)); Nepal (art. 13); Malaysia (art. 6(2)); Singapore (art. 10(2)).

[254] Vietnam (art. 80).

[255] *Lumley v. Wagner*, [1843–60] All ER Rep. 368.    [256] Ibid. at 373.

[257] *Clyatt v. US*, 197 US 207 (1905). 'Peonage is sometimes classified as voluntary or involuntary, but this implies simply a difference in the mode of origins, but none in the character of the servitude. . . . But peonage, however created, is compulsory service, involuntary servitude. . . . A clear distinction exists between peonage and the voluntary performance of labour or rendering of service in payment of a debt.' Mr Justice Brewer, ibid. at 215.

[258] *Bailey v. Alabama*, 219 US 219 (1911).    [259] Ibid. at 227.

performance is no longer given in respect of those 'positive obligations which require personal performance and those negative obligations the enforcement of which would result in such an interference with personal liberty as would be offensive to current morality'.[260] In a famous case, the Cour de Cassation refused to compel the painter James McNeill Whistler to hand over to Sir William Eden the portrait of Eden's wife, for which payment had already been made. The decision was 'regarded as a vindication of an artist's right to decide when his work was complete'[261] and of all persons' right freely to dispose of their labour.

This is not yet universally conceded, however. Bonded labour is common in Nepal among the Tharu tribe of the Terai region, usually based on compounded debt which descendants are held to have inherited from their ancestors.[262] Such debt servitudes, enforced by law or custom, are also said to be common in China,[263] the Dominican Republic,[264] and in parts of India.[265]

It thus appears that the right of individuals freely to determine whether, and how, to work, and to choose their occupations, is both recent and as yet far from universally implemented. It is also clear, however, that the momentum of recent history and current sentiment is in the direction of the emancipation of persons everywhere from old communitarian traditions that bound individuals to compelled servitude.

### (d) Monopolization and Manipulation of Access to Professions and Trades

Sex discrimination, slavery, and servitude are among the traditional means by which a society prevents persons within it from aspiring to free choice in disposing of their skills and labours. There are many other, more subtle means which also have proven resistant to change.

A prime example is professional self-regulation. Intended to maintain high standards of training and performance, the systems by which various trades and professions control intake can readily serve to limit access. Although ostensibly protecting consumers from charlatans and incompetents, professional self-regulation may operate primarily to exclude persons not of a privileged kinship group. The history of guilds is replete with examples.

---

[260] Barry Nicholas, *The French Law of Contract* 218–19 (1992), citing the French Civil Code, art. 1142–5. 'Any obligation to do or not to do is resolved into damages in case of inexecution' (art. 1142).

[261] Ibid. at 219, citing Civ. 14.3.1900, D.1900.1.49, S.1900.1.489, Source-book, 502.

[262] Sherab Posel, '*Kamaiya*: Bonded Labor in Western Nepal', 27 Col. H. Rts. L. Rev. 123 (1995).

[263] Daniel S. Ehrenberg, 'The Labor Link: Applying the International Trading System to Enforce Violations of Forced and Child Labor', 20 Yale J. Int'l L. 361, 366, 369, 371 (1995).

[264] Ibid. at 369–70.

[265] Ibid. at 371–4; Posel, *supra* n. 262, at 161–4. Posel also includes information on Pakistan at pp. 164–6 and on Bangla Desh at pp. 166–7.

Although there were social guilds in the Roman Empire, the Western origins of the modern self-regulatory occupations may be traced to the eleventh-century medieval guilds of Holland, Italy, France, England, Scotland, and Germany,[266] beginning with Guilds Merchand and culminating in the fourteenth- to sixteenth-century craft guilds. From Italy, the Rhineland, and the Low Countries, guilds spread quickly over all of Western Europe.[267] Similar developments have been traced in medieval and modern China, Japan, India, and Islam.[268]

The guilds' overall purpose was to establish a high standard of production and income for groups of skilled artisans. They sought 'to maintain the fixed number of small independent producing masters in each craft. To this end, competition had to be limited', which ensured that the guild 'was pitted against . . . would-be newcomers to the trade . . .'.[269] Although theoretically based on merit, guilds became 'increasingly restrictive in membership', often confining 'intake to the masters' sons . . . .'.[270] The excluded became day-labourers, an urban proletariat that performed services for a middle class of licensed artisans without hope of entry into the profession.[271]

In the French town of Limoges, for example, only six barbers were allowed to practise at any one time. Only after one of them had died could another be chosen for admittance to the guild.[272] A contemporary Paris Statute of the napery weavers stated that 'no one may be a master weaver except the son of a master'.[273] Artisans learned to combine to monopolize their trade and soon 'strengthened this monopoly by conferring special privileges on the sons of members of their fraternity . . . .'.[274] The system of apprenticeship gradually became the sole means by which the applicant could join a trade or profession. By restricting the number apprenticed to any craftsman it was possible to control competition.[275]

With the growth of national governments, the power of the guilds declined, not least their rights of self-regulation. Nevertheless, even in the modern industrialized West there are still traces of the tendency arbitrarily to exclude certain persons from various crafts and professions. In large east coast US cities, at least until the mid-1950s, it was exceedingly difficult for anyone not closely related to a licensed plumber—least of all an African-American—to become apprenticed. In Britain, in 1997, the Ford Motor Company reluctantly paid $170,000 in damages to settle a case brought by Asian and black workers who had been denied highly paid jobs as lorry drivers at the company's Dagenham

---

[266] Georges Renard, *Guilds in the Middle Ages* (D. Terry trans., 1968).
[267] Antony Black, *Guilds and Civil Society in European Political Thought from the Twelfth Century to the Present* 6 (1984).          [268] Ibid. at 7.
[269] Ibid. at 9.          [270] Ibid. at 9–10.          [271] Ibid. at 9–11.
[272] Renard, *supra* n. 266, at 39.          [273] Ibid. at 39–40.
[274] Jonathan F. Scott, *Historical Essays on Apprenticeship and Vocational Education* 14 (1914).
[275] Harry E. Barnes, *An Economic History of the Western World* 185 (1937).

plant. These jobs, by tradition, were reserved for children of drivers.[276] Because of that tradition, less than 2 per cent of the drivers were blacks or Asians, although fully 45 per cent of the Dagenham work force were non-white.

While the West largely may have overcome its communitarian tradition of male white dominance in the professions and occupations, the dismantling of that legacy and its replacement by open access based on individual preference and ability is very recent and remains incomplete. For example, while polemics in America are focused on affirmative action programmes in colleges and professional schools, very little attention has been directed at 'the fact that applicants who are children of alumni receive an advantage greater than that enjoyed by any minority student' in gaining scarce places at top institutions.[277] Quietly, this vested policy of preference for 'legacies' has been allowed to continue with the tacit approval of universities and the US Department of Education,[278] despite evidence that it increasingly penalizes other applicants with higher qualifications. Thus, 'white children of alumni' are 'more than twice as likely to be accepted at Harvard than more-qualified high school students lacking an alumni connection'.[279] This state of affairs recalls the much more blatant quotas that were imposed on Jewish and Catholic applicants by Columbia, Harvard, Princeton, and Yale in the 1920s and 1930s.[280]

In some non-Western societies the same exclusionary practices flourish through the operation of communitarian caste systems. In India, communitarian group exclusions are very deeply rooted. Caste is believed to have evolved around 1000 BC.[281] The system eventually produced (between AD 400–600) the 'untouchables' at one end of the social scale and Brahmins at the other. The power of the latter over the former was ascribed directly to God. Untouchables were 'treated as subhumans and forced to be scavengers and indentured labourers in agricultural lands owned by the upper castes'. They remain, 'penalized even today throughout India'.[282] This communal system, with its many castes and subcastes, 'has refused to accept the individual as a basic unit. Instead, the individual's rights are limited in such a way to serve the interests of society'.[283] Those 'interests of society', however, are always defined by those at

---

[276] Barrie Clement, 'Ford Pays Truckers 100,000 Pounds as Race Battle Comes to End', The Independent (UK), 28 Jan. 1997, at 4. The truckers' power derives from the fact that 'they deliver Ford parts from plant to plant throughout Europe' so 'they can bring the whole operation to a halt within days' (ibid.).

[277] John D. Lamb, 'The Real Affirmative Action Babies: Legacy Preferences at Harvard and Yale', 491 (1993) and citations therein. [278] Ibid. at 492.

[279] Ibid. at 496 and fn. 39, citing Statement of Findings of Office for Civil Rights, Compliance Review 01-88-60099 sent to Harvard President Derek Bok on 4 October 1990. See also Lamb, ibid. at 499. [280] Ibid. at 492–5, 496–8.

[281] Roshani M. Gunewardene, 'The Caste System: A Violation of Fundamental Human Rights?', 11 H. Rts. LJ 35, 37 (1990), citing D. N. Sandanshiv, *Reservations for Social Justice* 16–17 (1986).

[282] Gunewardene, ibid.

[283] Ibid. at 38, citing Sandanshiv, *supra* n. 281, at 127–8.

the top, usually by reference to natural or divine law that favours them and their interests.

Hindu authorities long sanctioned this oppressive normative system of stratification and allocation, 'even perpetuating it when certain groups converted to other religions'.[284] Despite these religious underpinnings, however, it has become increasingly clear to Indians, especially since the teachings of Mahatma Gandhi, that 'caste is a gross form of social and economic discrimination by so-called higher caste groups against the so-called lower castes'.[285] In recent years, there have been concerted efforts to eradicate, or at least mitigate, the pernicious role-assigning function of caste and to liberate the individual from its bondage. Lord Buddha, Mohandas K. Gandhi, the British raj, and, after independence the Constitution of India, especially as interpreted by the Indian Parliament and Supreme Court, have all resorted to various remedial measures including outright prohibitions.[286] Various forms of affirmative action have been introduced that favour the scheduled (lowest) castes and tribes,[287] many of them going far beyond anything attempted in the United States. For example, a percentage of seats have been set aside in the Lok Sabha (federal House of Representatives) equal to the scheduled castes' and tribes' proportion of the national electorate.[288]

India's national effort to eradicate caste are being re-enforced by international norms. The International Covenants on Economic, Social, and Cultural Rights, and on Civil and Political Rights, to which India is a party,[289] prohibit many aspects of the caste system.[290] Nevertheless, it is an uphill battle to liberate the individual from a deeply ingrained communal value-system. As a recent study notes, '[e]mployment discrimination against Harijans [untouchables] is a fact of life in most parts of India' even now,[291] and, in practice, land ownership is still largely restricted by caste.[292]

Such exclusion of categories of persons, and arbitrary communitarian role-assignment, at last may be diminishing worldwide. In Japan, the constitution

---

[284] Ibid., citing Louis Dumont, *Homo Hierachius: the Caste System and Its Implications* 24–5 (1980).

[285] Ibid. at 39.

[286] Articles 14, 15, 16 and 17 of the Indian Constitution of 26 November 1949, as amended. See V. D. Mahajan, *Constitutional Law of India* 104 (7th ed., 1991).

[287] See e.g. *Indra Sawhrey v. Union of India*, 80 AIR (SC) (1993), which upholds quotas of up to 50 per cent for scheduled castes, tribes, and other lower-caste individuals from low-income families applying for places at the universities or for jobs in the civil service. See Marc Gallanter, *Competing Equalities: Law and Backward Classes of India* (1984) and E. J. Prior, 'Constitutional Fairness or Fraud on the Constitution? Compensatory Discrimination in India', 28 Case W. Res. J. Int'l L. 63 (1996).

[288] Lance Liebman, 'Equalities Real and Ideal: Affirmative Action in Indian Law' (Rev. of Galanter), 98 Harv. L. Rev. 1679, 1682 (1985).

[289] GA Res. 2200(xxi), 21 UN GAOR Supp. no. 16 at 52, UN Doc. A/6316 (1966). Gunewardene, *supra* n. 281, at 42.

[290] See e.g. Covenant on Economic, Social and Cultural Rights, *supra* n. 240, arts. 2(2), 6, 7, 10(1) and 10(3).

[291] Gunewardene, *supra* n. 281, at 45.          [292] Ibid. at 48.

explicitly protects individuals' right to choose their occupations,[293] and the Japanese Supreme Court struck down a Pharmaceutical Business Act on the ground that, in severely restricting the number of pharmacies that could operate in any one zoning district, it arbitrarily denied access to the profession.[294] In America, the Supreme Court during the charged McCarthy period, reversed as unconstitutional a decision of the New Mexico Board of Bar Examiners denying a law graduate the right to take the bar examination on the ground that he had once been a member of the communist party.[295] Although once-endemic categorizations and exclusions of persons die only slowly, they do now seem to be almost everywhere in retreat.

## 5. A RIGHT TO PRIVACY?

The individual's right to define a personal identity by freely choosing among conscientious beliefs, personal nomenclature, gender, and occupation can only be realized when the political community relaxes its demand for absolute universal adherence to community standards. Such relaxation requires the community not only to recognize each individual's right to be different, but to practise those differences sheltered from public pressures to conform: whether political, social, cultural, or legal. The rights of nonconforming individuals thus require the protection afforded by an overarching right to privacy. Without it, individual identity-formation is inhibited by the pressure to conform to the communitarian norm, a pressure many persons find irresistible.

Among the 'freedom from' rights claimed by individuals, the right to privacy is particularly contentious, both in national and international law. To libertarians, the right entails a prohibition of government interference with the personal autonomy of their bodies and homes, a right sometimes traced to King John's Magna Carta of 1215 and its restatement in the Great Charter issued as 9 Henry III in 1225. Nevertheless, except among extreme libertarians, a concomitant need for balance between the community's interests and those of the individual is also accepted, but only on condition that it be applied by independent courts on the basis of general principles of law: the essential

---

[293] Japan: 1947 Const. art. 22 ('Every person shall have freedom to . . . choose his occupation to the extent that it does not interfere with the public welfare.'). See P. R. Luney, Jr. & Kazuyuki Takahashi, *Japanese Constitutional Law* 321 (1993). Similar free choice provisions are found in the constitutions of Austria (art. 18), the Federal Republic of Germany (art. 12(1)), Italy (art. 4), Netherlands (art. 19(3)), Portugal (art. 47(1)), Spain (art. 35(1)) and Turkey (art. 48), among others, but is sometimes explicitly made subject to governmental regulatory powers.

[294] (The Pharmacy Case), 29 Minshu 572 (Sup. Ct., GB, Ap. 30, 1975. See Luney, ibid. at 265. The Court appeared not to accept the Government's argument that competition among pharmacists would lead to substandard medicines.

[295] *Schware v. Board of Bar Examiners of New Mexico*, 353 US 232 (1957). See also David Caute, *The Great Fear: the Anti-Communist Purge Under Truman and Eisenhower* 140–58 (1978) and citations therein.

propositions of Section III of Magna Carta[296] which are still the foundation of the 'rule of law'.

One of the major developments in the constitutional jurisprudence of the United States was the acknowledgement by the Supreme Court in recent years of a protected individual right to personal privacy. It has accepted the principle of an 'area of protected freedoms' including 'the zone of privacy created by several fundamental constitutional guarantees'.[297] This entitlement to 'privacy' has been extended to include the sale of contraceptives to adults[298] and to minors[299] as well as the right of women to an abortion.[300] According to the Supreme Court, 'it is clear that among the decisions that an individual may make without unjustified government interference are personal decisions relating to marriage, procreation, contraception, family relationships and child rearing and education'.[301]

While a wide mantle of protection has been thrown by the US judiciary around privileged personal choices in these matters, its coverage is not absolute. The cases still do recognize the community's 'interests in safeguarding health, in maintaining medical standards and in protecting potential life'.[302] Government interest in interfering with personal privacy, in pursuit of these or other narrow community objectives, must, however, be 'sufficiently compelling'[303] and the means used must be the least intrusive available.[304] There is thus a recent but strong American 'constitutional protection of individual autonomy'[305] through limits on intrusion into the individual's private realm.

Despite these favourable auguries it should be noted that the US Supreme Court, in 1985, upheld the constitutionality of a Georgia statute criminalizing private homosexual conduct between consenting adults.[306] A slim majority of five judges characterized the case as a demand by the citizen, who had been investigated but not charged by Georgia's district attorney, for a declaration of the law's unconstitutionality and thus a judicial affirmation of 'a fundamental right to engage in homosexual sodomy'.[307] The four-judge minority opinion, on the other hand, characterized the case as being 'about "the most comprehensive of rights and the right most valued by civilized man," namely, "the right to be let alone"'.[308]

Since then, on 18 October 1990, one of the Supreme Court's majority, Judge Lewis Powell, publicly recanted his stand[309] and the law upheld by the US

---

[296] Section III of Magna Carta proclaims: 'No freeman shall be taken or imprisoned, or disseised, or outlawed, or exiled, or in any way destroyed, nor will we go upon him, nor will we send upon him, except by the lawful judgement of his peers, or by the law of the land.'
[297] *Griswold v. Connecticut*, 381 US 479, 485 (1965).     [298] Ibid.
[299] *Carey v. Population Services International et al.*, 431 US 678 (1977).
[300] *Roe v. Wade*, 410 US 113, 152 (1973).
[301] *Carey, supra* n. 299, at 684–5. Citations omitted.     [302] *Roe v. Wade, supra* n. 300, at 153.
[303] Ibid. at 154.     [304] Ibid. at 155–6.     [305] *Carey, supra* n. 299, at 687.
[306] 478 US 186 (1986).     [307] Ibid. at 191.
[308] Ibid. at 199, quoting *Olmstead v. United States*, 277 US 438, 478 (1928) (Brandeis, J. dissenting).
[309] Nat Hentoff, 'Infamous Sodomy Law Struck Down', *The Village Voice*, 22 Dec. 1998, at 30.

Supreme Court was itself struck down by Georgia's State Supreme Court as 'violative of the privacy rights protected by that state's own constitution'.[310] Moreover, by 1999, thirty-one US states had decriminalized consensual private sodomy.[311]

This has resonance in many jurisdictions. A recent decision by the Constitutional Court of South Africa voided legal prohibitions against sodomy, likening them to the *apartheid* regime. Judge Sachs, in his concurrence, stated that the nation's 'future . . . depends in large measure on how we manage difference. In the past difference has been experienced as a curse, today it can be seen as a source of interactive vitality. The Constitution acknowledges the variability of human beings (genetic and socio-cultural), affirms the right to be different, and celebrates the diversity of the nation'.[312]

In recent years, a 'right to privacy' has been widely recognized in international and regional law. Article 12 of the Universal Declaration of Human Rights of 1948 states that 'No one shall be subject to arbitrary interference with his privacy, family, home or correspondence' and the ICCPR of 1966 enacts that declaration, almost verbatim, into binding international law. All persons, by article 17 of the ICCPR must have 'the right to the protection of the law against such interference . . .'.

The enunciation of this right in international legal instruments has strengthened the claim to privacy under national law. Interpreting article 17 of the ICCPR, the Human Rights Committee recently decided that the Australian state of Tasmania had violated individuals' privacy by criminalizing consensual adult homosexual conduct.[313] The Committee held that 'adult consensual sexual activity in private is covered by the concept of "privacy" in article 17' and that the Tasmanian law interferes with that privacy right.[314] Following this decision, the Commonwealth of Australia enacted a Human Rights (Sexual Conduct) Act of 1994, which provides that 'sexual conduct involving only consenting adults in private shall not be an offence under any law of the

---

[310] Kevin Sack, 'Georgia's High Court Voids Sodomy Law', NY Times, 24 Nov. 1998, at A16.

[311] Sodomy laws have been repealed in: Alaska (1980), California (1976), Colorado (1972), Connecticut (1971), Delaware (1973), Hawaii (1973), Illinois (1962), Indiana (1977), Iowa (1978), Maine (1976), Nebraska (1978), Nevada (1993), New Hampshire (1975), New Jersey (1979), New Mexico (1975), North Dakota (1975), Ohio (1974), Oregon (1972), South Dakota (1977), Vermont (1977), Washington (1976), West Virginia (1976), Wisconsin (1983), Wyoming (1977). Sodomy laws have been held unconstitutional in Kentucky, Louisiana, Massachusetts, Michigan, New York, Pennsylvania and Texas. The right privately to keep and view pornography had earlier been upheld by the US Supreme Court in *Stanley v. Georgia*, 394 US 557 (1969).

[312] Constitutional Court of South Africa: *National Coalition for Gay and Lesbian Equality v. Minister of Justice*, CCT 11/98 (9 Oct. 1998), 1 *International Law in Brief*, no. 3, at 7 (Nov. 1998).

[313] *Nicholas Toonen v. Australia*, case no. 488/1992, Report of the Human Rights Committee, vol. I, GAOR, 49th Sess., Supp. no. 40 (A/49/40) (1994), at 80, para. 445. See also Communication no. 488/1992, *Nicholas Toonen v. Australia*, views adopted on 31 March 1994, fiftieth session, Report of the Human Rights Committee, vol. II, GAOR, A/49/40, Supp. no. 40, at 226.

[314] Ibid. See Report of the Human Rights Committee, vol. I, GAOR A/49/40, Supp. no. 40, at 80–1, para. 445.

Commonwealth, a State or a Territory',[315] thereby rescinding the Tasmanian law. The Committee has called for similar repeal of US states' remaining anti-sodomy laws.[316] The Committee has expressed its concern at some governments' use of personal data obtained for privileged telecommunications, banking, and health purposes.[317] In its 'general comment' on the right to privacy, the Committee called for prohibitions against interception of correspondence, wire-tapping, and recording of conversations in all but exceptional cases.[318]

At the regional level, Article 8 of the European Convention on Human Rights applies a reasonable balancing test as between the right to personal privacy and community interests:

1.  Everyone has the right to respect for his private and family life, his home and his correspondence.
2.  There shall be no interference by the public authority with the exercise of this right except such as is in accordance with the law and is necessary in a democratic society, in the interests of national security, public safety or the economic well-being of the country, for the prevention of disorder or crime, for the protection of health or morals, or for the protection of the rights and freedoms of others.

The European Convention's privacy requirements have been interpreted by its judicial organs.[319] Adult sexual acts in private are 'an essentially private manifestation of the human personality'[320] and national laws governing such conduct, even when not enforced, are unlawful because they 'continuously and directly affect[ed] the applicant's private life'.[321] Protected, too, by the European right to privacy are most changes of name and of sex.[322]

Also under the heading of privacy the European Court has insisted that the mere existence of legislation which permits secret telephonic or other intrusive surveillance measures 'constitutes an interference with the right to respect for private and family life . . . under art. 8 . . .'.[323] Such interference can only be

---

[315] Report of the Human Rights Committee, 16 September 1996, A/51/40; GAOR, 50th Sess., Supp. no. 40, at 88, para. 456.

[316] Report of the Human Rights Committee, vol. I, GAOR, A/50/40, Supp. no. 40, 1996, at 46, para. 287.

[317] Report on Sweden. Report of the Human Rights Committee, GAOR, A/46/40, Supp. no. 40, 1991, at 83, paras. 336–9. See also report on the United Kingdom, ibid. at 99, para. 399–400. See, further, report on Poland, Report of the Human Rights Committee, GAOR, A/47/40, Supp. no. 40, 1992, at 37, paras. 162–3, and, as to Russia, Report of the Human Rights Committee, vol. I, GAOR, A/50/40, Supp. no. 40, 1996, at 62, 65, paras. 380, 399.

[318] CCPR/C/21/Add.6, 31 March 1988. General Comment Under Article 40, para. 4 of the Covenant, 23 March 1988, at 3, paras. 7, 8.     [319] See e.g. Wildhaber, *supra* n. 142.

[320] *Dudgeon* case, 45 Eur. Ct. HR (ser. A) (1981). See also *Norris* case, 142 Eur. Ct. HR (ser. A) (1988); *Modinos v. Cyprus*, 259 Eur. Ct. HR (ser. A) (1993).

[321] *Modinos v. Cyprus*, ibid. at §§ 17–26.

[322] See *Burghartz v. Switzerland*, *supra* n. 65; and compare *Stjerna v. Finland*, *supra* n. 71.

[323] Wildhaber, *supra* n. 142, at 109 and cases cited therein.

justified by article 8(2)'s exception in favour of acts essential to protect the public health or security when taken in accordance with established legal proce- dures.[324] The European Court has also prohibited unwarranted police searches and seizures.[325]

The 'right to privacy', or 'to be let alone', is among the most controversial of the claims persons have recently been authorized to make in exercise of their right freely to create and enjoy their individuality. Like almost all other claims to personal autonomy, the rights being asserted are not claimed as absolutes, but they are an important new shield against the hitherto absolute, usually irrefu- table, demands of communitarian conformity. The rules and values of govern- ing elites, or even of an electoral majority, are no longer regarded as sacrosanct and unchallengeable. In the past, such rules and values restricted the opportu- nity for individual self-expression and self-realization. Now, increasingly, the utility and morality of legally enforced conformity to communitarian standards is open to re-examination, coming under close scrutiny both in the political and judicial arenas of national, regional, and global governance.

In Chapters 8 and 10, personal autonomy will be discussed as 'freedom from' communitarian interference with individual choice in the designing of personal identity. In that discussion, the 'right to be let alone' will be weighed alongside (1) the right of the community to protect its cohesion, health and security, and (2) the right of underprivileged individuals to public assistance in overcoming their disadvantages. 'Weighing' notably implies balancing. That the right to privacy must be balanced against these legitimate communitarian concerns cannot obscure the fact that claims advanced in the name of social cohesion and respon- sibility no longer automatically trump those advanced by individuals in the name of personal freedom. This development—so recent and so incomplete—is truly an historic watershed.

---

[324] *A v. France*, 277-B Eur. Ct. HR (ser. A) § 36 (1993).
[325] *Niemitz v. Germany*, 251-B Eur. Ct. HR (ser. A) (1992).

# 8

## *The Individual as Emerging International Rights-Holder*

> The makers of our Constitution undertook to secure conditions favourable to the pursuit of happiness. . . . They conferred, as against the Government, the right to be let alone—the most comprehensive of rights and the right most valued by civilized men.
>
> Justice Louis D. Brandeis Dissenting in *Olmstead v. United States*, 277 US 438 at 478

### 1. FROM WARD OF THE STATE TO SHAREHOLDER IN A GLOBAL SYSTEM

The Second World War featured several states' massive betrayal of the lives and liberties of persons, including even their own civilians. Since then, a tectonic shift has occurred in the law of nations. In the words of Professor Louis B. Sohn:

Just as the French Revolution ended the divine right of kings, the human rights revolution that began at the 1945 San Francisco Conference of the United Nations has deprived the sovereign states of the lordly privilege of being the sole possessors of rights under international law. States have had to concede to ordinary human beings the status of subjects of international law, to concede that individuals are no longer mere objects, mere pawns in the hands of states.[1]

The traditional law of nations had been built on the prevalent feudal assumption that each person 'belonged' to a sovereign liege-lord, rather the way slaves had belonged to masters and women to their husbands. From this subordination followed several consequences, each limiting the 'subject's' personal autonomy. In particular, each person injured by his or her sovereign was entitled by national law only to whatever remedy the sovereign grudgingly chose to allow. In most jurisdictions, at least until quite recently, this meant, in practice, that there could be no realistic expectation of redress. For example, the maxim—'The King can do no wrong'[2]—largely immunized British governments from litigation initiated by a citizen seeking a remedy for alleged wrongs.

---

[1] Louis B. Sohn, 'The New International Law: Protection of the Rights of Individuals Rather Than States', 32 Am. UL Rev. 1 (1982).

[2] Edwin M. Borchard, 'Government Liability in Tort', 34 Yale LJ 1, 2 (1924). See also Note, 'Rethinking Sovereign Immunity After *Bivens*,' 57 NYUL Rev. 597, 606 (1982) (noting that the maxim was intended to suggest not 'that the king was above the law and thus immune from legal process; rather, because the king could personally do no wrong, wrongs done in the king's name by his officers were not attributable to the king'). In Britain, however, the maxim also for long virtually immunized the king's ministers and ministries.

In international law, the consequences were equally dire. Each subject injured while in a foreign state and denied redress by its laws could do no more than petition his or her ruler to confront the offending foreign authorities through diplomatic channels, or—most unlikely—by state-to-state litigation or armed reprisal. The offended person could also petition the authorities to issue 'letters of marque and reprisal' authorizing a victim personally to seize vessels or cargoes belonging to the victimizer.[3] For most persons, these were no more than very limited or even illusory remedies. The state rarely had an interest in its subject's private cause, especially if it thereby risked antagonizing a fellow-sovereign with whom it had mutually beneficial relations. Even if a letter of marque and reprisal could be obtained, the cost of initiating such a private act usually exceeded the victim's purse.[4]

These remedies, although in occasional use until quite recently,[5] seem entirely obsolete when viewed in retrospect from the end of the twentieth century. In most instances, they provided the individual with too little recourse. In a few others, they provided excessive recourse, making an individual's private claim a *cause célèbre* that was disproportionate to the wrong inflicted or alleged.

There were exceptions, of course. A few bilateral treaties dated before 1914 established claims, or capitulatory, regimes purporting to grant recourse or protection to the citizens of one party in the territory of the other. Normally, however, individuals who lived as aliens, abroad, had few, if any, rights enforceable through international law. Thus, 'a person's protection depended on the conduct of his state, and stateless persons were entitled to no protection whatsoever'.[6] Moreover, 'a state's own citizens were almost completely at its mercy, and international law had little to say about mistreatment of persons by their own government'.[7] Just as in domestic law a woman had been a 'femme couvert', incapable of acquiring rights in her own name, so all persons in international law remained, essentially, 'persons couverts' under the prevailing Vattelian system that recognized only the rights of sovereign states.

The first significant exception was the setting up of the International Labour Organization in Geneva in 1919.[8] Intended as a forum for negotiating universal

---

[3] E. Colbert, *Retaliation in International Law* 9–50 (1948). For an example of litigation between states based on a private claim of wrong see *Interhandel* case (Switz. v. US), 1959 ICJ Rep. 6, 27 (Prelim. Obj. Judgment, 21 Mar. 1959).     [4] Sohn, *supra* n. 1, at 2.

[5] As late as 1858, however, the US government still threatened to issue letters of reprisal to Boston merchants ejected by Venezuela from the disputed Aves Islands. Ibid. at 3. The dispute was settled by Venezuela's agreeing to pay $130,000 in compensation. Ibid., and citations therein. In 1902, Germany, Great Britain and Italy still effectively blockaded the Venezuelan coast to compel its government to accept arbitration of disputes involving their citizens. See *Venezuelan Preferential Claims Case* (Germany, Great Britain, Italy v. Venezuela), Hague Ct. Rep. (Scott) 55 (Perm. Ct. Arb. 1904).

[6] Sohn, *supra* n. 1, at 9.     [7] Ibid.

[8] Constitution of the International Labour Organization, 28 June 1919. 225 Consol. TS 373 (part XIII of the Treaty of Versailles, 225 Consol. TS 189). See also Victor-Yves Ghebaldi, *The International Labour Organization: A Case Study as the Evolution of UN Specialized Agencies* 1–17 (1989); Walter Galenson, *The International Labor Organization: An American View* 4–5 (1981).

labour standards, the ILO created many of the building blocks of the modern human rights system. For the first time, non-governmental parties—labour and management—were introduced as equals to the international treaty-making process.[9] Once standards were agreed, it monitored compliance through a Committee of Experts and examined complaints before a Commission of Inquiry. It developed a fledgling institutional capacity for fact-finding, concilia-tion, and even for collective decisions against defaulters taken by its Governing Body and Conference.[10] Nevertheless, the ILO addressed the rights of persons principally in terms of group rights—as workers or employers—rather than as individuals: a new category of collective rights claims discussed below in Chapter 9.

The Second World War created better understanding of the inextricable connection between international protection of human rights and the maintaining of world peace. Strong personalities like Eleanor Roosevelt, first to chair the newly established UN Human Rights Commission, determined to reconfigure the entire relationship in law between the power of governments and the freedoms of the individual. By 1945, widespread revulsion at the massive wrongs perpetrated by Germany and Japan against individuals, conquered nations, and ethnic and other groups, generated the momentum needed to empower persons to pursue effective legal remedies against such oppressors, whether foreign governments or their own.

The ensuing canon of human rights laws has only partially fulfilled the aspirations of those heady postwar years.[11] Nevertheless, its coverage is extensive both in terms of the rights defined and the number of states that have voluntarily agreed to be bound by the new rules.[12] It includes the International Convention on Civil and Political Rights (ICCPR),[13] and some fifty other instruments cover-ing such subjects as the rights of women and children, racial discrimination,

---

[9] See 'Handbook of procedures relating to international labour Conventions and Recommenda-tions', International Labour Standards Department, International Labour Office, Parts VI and XI, 1995.

[10] These procedures are not here discussed in detail. They are outlined in 'Handbook of procedures relating to international labour Conventions and Recommendations', International Labour Standards Department, 1995. This also contains the titles of the many standard-setting Conventions adopted by the ILO from 1919 to 1995. For a summary of action taken on Repre-sentations and Complaints see, e.g., Report of the Committee of Experts on the Application of Conventions and Recommendations, General report and observations concerning particular coun-tries, Report III (Part 4A), International Labour Conference, 83rd Sess. 1996, and International Labour Conventions and Recommendations, 1919–1991, vol. I, ILO.

[11] For a critique of its shortcomings see *Enforcing International Human Rights Law: the Treaty System in the 21st Century*, Papers for a Conference, York University, 1997 (Anne Bayefsky, director).

[12] For texts of these documents, see *United Nations, Human Rights: A Compilation of International Instruments*, UN Doc. ST/HR/1 Rev.1 (1978).

[13] International Convention on Civil and Political Rights, entered into force 23 March 1976. GA Res. 2200A, 21 GAOR Supp. (no. 16) at 52, UN Doc. A/6316 (1966). 999 UNTS 171, 6 ILM 368 (1967). [Hereafter, ICCPR].

torture, and religious intolerance.[14] It consists primarily of binding treaties supplemented by a nimbus of non-binding declarations.[15] The latter, usually adopted by a consensus of states at the UN General Assembly, depend for credibility on their principles being incorporated into state law and applied in state conduct. When that happens, the principles, over time, evolve into binding international customary law.[16]

While less than triumphant, the new international system of human rights norms, in its first fifty years, has embarked on making all states accountable for many wrongs against most persons. Especially significant is the extent to which these new rules open the way for the previously excluded individuals and non-governmental groups to participate in monitoring compliance. Persons are not only the holders of legal entitlements but also, in some instances, can be the authorized initiators of legal and political actions against violating states and governments.

The treaty instruments vary as to how, and how much, they may be invoked by individuals. Many envisage a system of complaints to an expert body: the process pioneered by the ILO and adapted in 1966 by the new Human Rights Committee established under the ICCPR. In other instances, human rights violations are taken up by an interstatal political body, notably the UN Human Rights Commission, established by the UN Economic and Social Council in 1946, and its subsidiaries.[17]

In addition to the universal declarations, conventions, and covenants that make up the global human rights canon, there are the regional instruments. Notable among these is the 1950 European Convention on Human Rights[18] which, while originally a modest compact among the traditional democracies of Western Europe, more recently has been embraced by most of the former communist nations of Eastern Europe, including Russia and some other

[14] Convention against torture and other cruel, inhuman or degrading treatment or punishment, GA Res. 39/46, UN GAOR, 39th Sess., Supp. no. 51, UN Doc. E/CN.4/1984/72 (1984). 1465 UNTS 85, 23 ILM 1027 (1984), as modified 24 ILM 535 (1985). The relevant dates are: adopted by GA 10 Dec. 1984, entered into force 26 June 1987, for US 20 Nov. 1994, Sen. Treaty Doc. no. 100–20.

[15] For example, Mrs Eleanor Roosevelt, although a principal author of the Universal Declaration of Human Rights, was instructed, in her capacity as US delegate to the UN, to say on the occasion of its adoption by the General Assembly that it 'was not a treaty or international agreement and did not impose legal obligations'. 3 UN GAOR (pt. 1, 3d Cttee) at 32 (1948).

[16] All international legal rules depend for their credibility upon sure and swift enforcement against transgressors. To the extent violators are not identified, sought out, subject to a hearing and the guilty punished, the law is brought into disrepute. In this, international law is not very different from domestic legal systems, which also oft-times suffer valid criticism for being slow and uncertain in enforcement against the powerful, while acting with speed and a certain callousness against the poor. The recent record of revived death-sentencing in some US states is one example of inconsistent and unequal implementation of laws.

[17] ECOSOC Res. 5(I), 16 Feb. 1949 and 9(II), 21 June 1946. UN Yearbook, 1946–7, at 524. See Howard Tolley, Jr., *The UN Commission on Human Rights* 101–86, 205–20 (1987).

[18] Convention for the Protection of Human Rights and Fundamental Freedoms, 4 Nov. 1950, 213 UNTS 222.

European parts of the former Soviet Union.[19] This Convention has pioneered in creating instruments—including a court with full-time judges—through which claims can be adjudicated and remedies decreed; and, also, in establishing a route by which such claims can be pursued against states by individuals.[20] As of late 1997, the Court had jurisdiction over 40 states.[21] So well-established is this remarkable new process for protecting personal rights that the European Court has become the world's broadest jurisdiction, covering a larger number of persons in more states than any national tribunal. It is, as one might expect, one of the world's busiest tribunals, its chambers often engaged in several cases concurrently.[22] Its caseload rose from seven judgements in 1980 to 126 in 1996. As of the end of 1996, it had given 711 judgements and decisions.[23]

The European example has echoes elsewhere. In the Americas, the American Convention on Human Rights[24] entered into force in 1978 and in Africa the Charter on Human and Peoples' Rights was approved in 1981.[25]

The norms of the American Convention on Human Rights are applied, under article 33, by a Commission and by an Inter-American Court of Human Rights. The Commission's mandate extends not only to the Convention but also to the obligations and rights of members under the OAS Charter.[26] It 'is an international quasi-judicial body that can hear cases, make findings of fact and conclusions of law, and issue reports publicizing the results. It can also issue recommendations to governments' although it has no enforcement powers.[27] Complaint petitions may be brought by states, victims, or by NGOs and other groups.[28] The Court, consisting of judges elected in their individual capacities, may hear cases arising out of alleged violations of the Convention brought

---

[19] The European Convention on Human Rights has been ratified by Albania, Bulgaria, Croatia, Czech Republic, Estonia, Hungary, Latvia, Lithuania, Moldova, Poland, Romania, Slovakia, Slovenia, Ukraine, and FYROM. Russia had signed but not ratified the Convention as of 13 Nov. 1997. See Council of Europe, *Chart showing signatures and ratifications of Conventions and Agreements concluded within the Council of Europe*, Europ. TS, no. 5 (1997).

[20] Ibid. art. 25(1). The 'right of individual petition is applicable to any person who files a complaint against a state party to the Convention which has declared that it recognizes the competence of the European Court of Human Rights (formerly the Commission) to receive such individual petitions'.

[21] Chart of Signatures and Ratifications, Council of Europe, European Treaties, 13/1/97 (Pub. by C. of Eur. Treaty Section).

[22] The caseload of the ECHR has grown from 2 references and 1 decision in 1960, and 8 references and 7 decisions in 1980, to 165 references and 126 decisions in 1996. See 39 *Y'book Euro. Conv. Hum. Rts.* 180 (1996).

[23] Council of Europe, ibid.

[24] American Convention on Human Rights, OEA/Ser.K/XVI/1.1, Doc. 65, Rev. 1, Corr. 1, OAS Treaty Ser., no. 36 (1970), 9 ILM 101, 673 (1970). [Hereafter American Convention.]

[25] Charter on Human and Peoples' Rights, 21 ILM 58 (1982); OAU Doc. CAB/LEG./67/3/Rev. 51.

[26] Charter of the Organization of American States (OAS), 2 UST 2394, TIAS 2361, 119 UNTS 3. Signed 30 April 1948, entered into force 13 Dec. 1951.

[27] Robert O. Weiner, 'Trying to Make Ends Meet', 26 St. Mary's L.J. 857, 865 (1995).

[28] American Convention, *supra* n. 24, art. 44; Scott Davidson, *The Inter-American Court of Human Rights* 16, 22 (1992).

either by a state party or by the Commission[29] and may make findings of law, order remedies and award damages.[30] Both the Commission and the Court have become increasingly active in recent years, although not nearly as much as their European counterparts. Professor Andrew Moravcsik attributes this disparity to evident differences in internal social and political conditions of the respective state-systems,[31] and several authorities have pointed to evidence that, although 'the advisory jurisdiction of the Court may be said to have functioned well, it is clear that its contentious jurisdiction is not working as it should'.[32] Delays occasioned by the requirement that individual applications for relief be first submitted to the Commission and the latter's slow procedures have also been cited by critics.[33]

The African Charter was adopted in 1981 and entered into force in 1986. By 1998, it had been ratified by fifty-one states. It establishes a Commission of Experts, elected by the parties, which began to operate in 1987. It is authorized to receive complaints by one state against another and, also, by operation of article 55, such 'communications other than those of states parties to the [Banjul] Charter' as a simple majority of its members decide to examine. If the Commission determines 'after deliberations—that one or more communications apparently relate to special cases which reveal the existence of a series of serious or massive violations of human and peoples' rights, the Commission shall draw the attention of the Assembly of Heads of State and Government to these special cases'.[34] On being notified, the Assembly may then decide to request the Commission to make a factual report and submit findings and recommendations to it.[35]

The Commission has begun to operate and in its first decade, received some 200 non-statal communications. It has found violations of the African Charter by Nigeria for imposing the death penalty without benefit of trial by an impartial tribunal[36] and for enacting a decree that suspends not only the national constitution but also purports to nullify any domestic effect of the Charter.[37] It has held Malawi in violation of article 6 of the Charter which

---

[29] American Convention, ibid. art. 61(1). In its 1995 Report the Commission reported that five cases had been brought before the Court by the Commission. OEA/ser.L/V/II.91, Doc. 7, 1995 IACHR, p. 2.                                                                                                       [30] Ibid. art. 63(1).

[31] Andrew Moravcsik, 'Explaining International Human Rights Regimes: Liberal Theory and Western Europe,' 1 Eur. J. Int'l Rel. 157, 159, 178–82 (1995). See also Davidson, *supra* n. 28, at 195–204.                                                                                                      [32] Davidson, ibid. at 3.

[33] Ibid. at 4.

[34] Charter on Human and Peoples' Rights, 21 ILM 58 (1982); OAU Doc. CAB/LEG./67/3/ Rev. 51, art. 58(1).                                                                                  [35] Ibid. art. 58(2).

[36] *Constitutional Rights Project v. Nigeria*, Opinion of 3 Nov. 1994 (16th Ordinary Session), 28 June 1995 [AHG/Res. 240(XXXI)], Communication 60/91. *Also Constitutional Rights Project v. Nigeria*, Opinion of 3 Nov. 1994 (16th Ordinary Session), 28 June 1995 [AHG/Res. 240(XXXI)], Communication 89/93. Reported in 18 H.Rts. LJ, nos. 1–4, at 28, 30 (1997).

[37] *Civil Liberties Organization v. Nigeria*, Opinion of 22 March 1995 (17th Ordinary Session), 10 July 1996 [AHG/Res. 250(XXXI)], Communication 129/94. Reported in 18 H.Rts. LJ, ibid. at 35–6.

provides: 'Every individual shall have the right to liberty and to the security of his person . . .'. The violations consisted of the 'massive and arbitrary arrest of office workers, trade unionists, Roman Catholic bishops and students' as well as of the political leaders Orton Chirwa and Aleke Banda.[38] In respect of the Government of Zaire, the Commission found 'serious and massive violations' of seven articles of the Charter pertaining to protections against torture and inhuman or degrading treatment, the right to liberty, life, freedom of conscience, fair trial and other provisions.[39] These opinions of the Commission were reported to the African Heads of Government at their annual conference, which adopted them and made them public.[40]

This modest but significant experience of the African Commission of Experts in 1998 led 30 states to sign a new protocol to the Charter establishing an African Court of Human and Peoples' Rights.[41] It is to enter into force when ratified by fifteen signatories.[42] The new Court is additionally authorized to receive complaints and requests for advisory opinions from Non-Governmental Organizations, providing the state involved has made an (optional) declaration accepting such jurisdiction, an innovation also found in the Inter-American system.[43] According to a study of Nico Krisch, these unusually broad rights allotted to NGOs 'follow at least partially from the success of their cooperation with the Commission'. For example, more than half the communications addressed to it during the first decade of its operation were initiated by such human rights advocacy groups.[44]

## 2. THE ICCPR SYSTEM AND ITS PROGENY

Of these various regimes, the European one has established the most effective machinery for monitoring compliance and promoting individuals' entitlements. The ICCPR's global system, however, may be even more significant

---

[38] *Amnesty International on behalf of Orton and Vera Chirwa v. Malawi*, Opinion of 3 Nov. 1994 (16th Ordinary Session), 28 June 1995 [AHG Res. 240(XXXI)], Communication 69/92. Reported in 18 H.Rts. LJ, ibid. at 29.

[39] *Free Legal Assistance Group, Austrian Committee Against Torture, Centre Haitian des Droits de l'Homme et des Libertés (all affiliated to World Organization Against Torture), and Les Témoins de Jéhovah v. Zaire v. Zaire*, Opinion of 4 April 1996 (19th Ordinary Session), 10 July 1996 [AHG/Res. 250(XXXII)], Communication 25/89. Reported in 18 H.Rts. LJ, ibid. at 32–3.

[40] See Banjul Charter, Arts. 52 and 59. See The Commission's 8th Annual Activity Report, adopted by the Assembly of Heads of State and Government of the OAU, 31st Ordinary Session, Addis Ababa, Ethiopia, 26–8 June 1995, AHG/Res. 240(XXXI); also Commission's 9th Annual Activity Report, adopted by the Assembly of Heads of State and Government of the OAU, 32nd Ordinary Session, Yaoundé, Cameroon, 8–10 July 1996, AHG/Res. 250(XXXII).

[41] See N. Krisch, 'The Establishment of an African Court on Human and Peoples' Rights', 58/3 Zeitschrift für Ausl. u. Öff. R. u. V. 713 (1998). The text of the new Protocol is reproduced, ibid. at 727.          [42] Protocol, art. 34(3), ibid. at 731.

[43] Ibid. at 724.          [44] Ibid.

precisely because it has near-universal reach, with 140 state parties as of mid-1998.[45]

The Covenant, opened for state ratification or accession in 1966, relies first on national measures for its enforcement: that is, executive, legislative, judicial, and administrative action by each state party to give effect to its normative obligations.[46] Each party, by article 2(3), must ensure that persons complaining of a violation of their rights have an effective remedy in domestic (national) law and access to appropriate national procedures of redress.

The rights enumerated by the ICCPR, for the most part, protect individual freedoms: to life (article 6), liberty and personal security (article 9); to humane treatment (articles 7, 8, 10), liberty of movement within the state and the freedom to leave it (article 12); to judicial proceedings without delay upon detention (articles 9, 14); to privacy and the sanctity of family and home (article 17), freedom of thought, conscience, and religion (articles 18, 19) and to peaceful association, assembly, participation in democratic public affairs and politics (articles 21, 22, 25); to equality before the law (article 26). Three groups (as opposed to individuals) are also proffered protection: children (article 24), families (article 23), and 'persons belonging to [ethnic, religious or linguistic minorities]' who 'shall not be denied the right, in community with other members of the group, to enjoy their own culture, to profess and practice their own religion, or to use their own language' (article 27).

The implementation of the ICCPR is not relegated exclusively to the parties. By article 40, states are required to prepare periodic reports evaluating their own implementation of, and compliance with, these legal obligations. The reports are studied by the 18-member Committee of Experts elected by the state parties for renewable four-year terms.[47] At oral hearings, representatives of the reporting state, usually high officials, appear to respond to questions arising out of the reports. Such hearings may continue for several days and representatives may be asked to follow up with new information.[48] In its annual report to the General Assembly, the Committee may make observations concerning a state's compliance.[49] The Committee also, from time to time, issues more general observations on the meaning and implementation of various articles of the ICCPR.[50] While these procedures help

---

[45] Multilateral Treaties Deposited with the Secretary-General, Status as at 5 August 1998, ST/LEG./SER.E. See also Report of the Secretary-General on Human Rights Questions, A/52/446, p. 2, 3 Oct. 1997.

[46] ICCPR, GA Res. 2200(XXI), 21 GAOR Supp. (no. 16) 52, Dec. 19, 1996. Entered into force Mar. 23, 1976. Arts. 2(1) and 2(3).    [47] ICCPR, ibid., arts. 28–32.

[48] Dominic McGoldrick, *The Human Rights Committee: Its Role in the Development of International Covenant on Civil and Political Rights* 86–8 (1991).

[49] See e.g. Report of the Human Rights Committee, 16 Sept. 1996, GAOR, 51st Sess., Supp. no. 40 (A/51/40), at 13–65, paras. 26–367.

[50] e.g., 'General Comments under art. 40, para. 4', Report of the Human Rights Committee, 16 Sept. 1996, GAOR, 51st Sess., Supp. no. 40 (A/51/40), Annex V, at 111.

turn an embarrassing spotlight on non-compliant parties, they also help to develop the applicable law.

Such general review of a state's compliance is augmented by optional means for addressing actual disputes. The Committee may hear a complaint by one state against another when both states have declared their general acceptance of this procedure.[51] Currently forty-four states[52] have done so, but no actual interstate disputes have arisen. More utilized is the procedure for individual complaints. By the end of 1996, ninety-two states[53] had accepted the Optional Protocol[54] that permits the Committee to consider petitions from persons who, having exhausted local remedies,[55] claim 'to be victims of a violation by [a] State Party of any of the rights set forth in the Covenant'.[56] It is a measure of the momentum for protection of individual rights that, a decade earlier, a mere thirty-seven states had endorsed this Protocol.[57] Particularly noteworthy are the recent accessions of such formerly totalitarian states as Belarus, Bulgaria, Hungary, Mongolia, Poland, Russia, and the Ukraine. The Optional Protocol has also been adopted by a large number of states in Africa[58] and Latin America[59] in addition to the Western European nations and Canada.

This individual complaints process is now widely utilized. Victims are often aided by lawyers provided by non-governmental organizations and professional networks. NGOs also play an important role in providing the Committee with information withheld by states, or information on states that fail to file the required periodic reports.

What does all this presage? As Professor Sohn has written: 'No longer is an individual's international protection limited to the state of his nationality and subject to its whims.'[60] States can now complain to impartial global and regional forums against treatment of their citizens by another state; and citizens, increasingly, can lodge complaints against their own governments. These complaints allege violations of personal rights that are now formally protected by international law and are judged in accordance with principles of law and legal reasoning, much as if the same issues had been raised before the Supreme Courts of India or the United States.

A brief review of the work of the Human Rights Committee of Experts under Optional Protocol I is indicative of the new direction in which global society has

---

[51]  ICCPR, art. 41(1).

[52]  Report of the Secretary-General on Human Rights Questions, *supra* n. 45, at 2.

[53]  Ibid.

[54]  Optional Protocol I, 999 UNTS 171, 6 ILM 383 (1967).          [55]  ICCPR, art. 5(2)(b).

[56]  ICCPR, art. 1.

[57]  *Yearbook of the Human Rights Committee*, 1985–6, vol. II, CCPR/5/Add. 1; GAOR Doc. A/41/40.

[58]  Algeria, Angola, Benin, Cameroon, Central African Republic, Chad, Congo, Equatorial Guinea, Gambia, Libya, Madagascar, Malawi, Mauritius, Namibia, Niger, Senegal, Seychelles, Somalia, Togo, Uganda, Zaire, and Zambia. Ibid. at 95.

[59]  Argentina, Barbados, Bolivia, Chile, Colombia, Costa Rica, Dominican Republic, Ecuador, El Salvador, Guyana, Jamaica, Nicaragua, Panama, Paraguay, Peru, Saint Vincent, Suriname, Trinidad and Tobago, Uruguay, Venezuela.          [60]  Sohn, *supra* n. 1, at 23.

embarked. Since beginning its work in 1977 and up to late 1996, the Committee received 716 communications from individuals asserting violations pertaining to fifty-one states. It decided 239 of these cases. Another 224 were dismissed as inadmissible. One hundred and fifteen complaints were withdrawn before being decided, forty-two were found admissible but not yet concluded and ninety-six were still pending.[61]

A cross-section of the Committee's decisions under Optional Protocol I may impart some flavour of this new jurisprudence of personal rights. For example, the Committee has held that, although a French law prohibiting challenges to the conclusions and verdict of the International Military Tribunal at Nuremberg might in some circumstances constitute a violation of the Covenant's right to freedom of expression, it did not do so in an instance where the law was applied to a published denial of the holocaust. Such expression was held to fall under the exception to the expressive right set out in article 19, being of such a nature as to violate the Jewish community's right 'to live free from fear of an atmosphere of anti-semitism'.[62] The Committee has also held that article 22's provision regarding trade unions is not violated by a Canadian municipality's restriction on the right of its employees to strike.[63] Article 26's provision for equal protection before the law was held to permit differentiations that are 'based on reasonable and objective criteria'.[64] Nevertheless, in establishing criteria for receiving unemployment benefits, 'a differentiation [the "breadwinner"] which appears on one level to be one of status [but] is in fact one of sex, placing married women at a disadvantage compared with married men is not reasonable.'[65]

The Committee has found Madagascar in violation of article 13 of the Covenant for failing to grant an alien 'full facilities for pursuing his remedy against expulsion so that this right in all the circumstances of his case be an effective one'.[66] Peru was found in violation of article 12(2) for keeping an arrest warrant against complainant pending for seven years without either apprehending him or bringing him to trial while denying him the right to leave the country.[67] Ecuador has been advised that it must bring a prisoner to trial within a reasonable time or free him[68] and Jamaica has been told that egregious conditions of imprisonment, especially in capital cases, constitute 'cruel and inhuman treatment'.[69] Long detention of prisoners on 'death row', however,

---

[61] Report of the Human Rights Committee, 1996, *supra* n. 49, at 66–7, paras. 370–2.

[62] *Faurisson v. France*, Decision of 8 Nov. 1996, Communication no. 550/1993, para. 9.6 of the decision, reprinted in 18 H.Rts. LJ, *supra* n. 36, at 40, 46. The exception is based on the Covenant's art. 19(3)(a).  [63] *J.B. et al. v. Canada*, case no. 118/1982.

[64] *F.H. Zwaan-de Vries v. Netherlands*, case no. 182/1984. Report of the Committee to the General Assembly, GAOR, 42nd Sess., Supp. no. 40 (A/42/40) (1987), at 279, para. 407.

[65] Ibid. See also *Blom v. Sweden*, case no. 191/1985.

[66] *Eric Hammel v. Madagascar*, case no. 155/1983, ibid. at 280, para. 410.

[67] *Miguel Gonzales del Rio v. Peru*, case no. 263/1987.

[68] *Floresmilo Bolaños v. Ecuador*, case no. 265/1987. See also *Muñoz v. Peru*, case no. 203/1986.

[69] *Pratt and Morgan v. Jamaica*, nos. 210/1986 and 225/1987.

has been held not to constitute, *per se*, a violation of the Covenant's article 7,[70] although defendants in capital cases must be provided with 'effective representation'.[71] When a prisoner awaiting execution has lodged a complaint, the Committee, invoking interim measures authority under Rule 86, has requested states not to carry out the death sentences until 'the Committee has had the opportunity to render a final decision in this case'.[72] This procedure has produced its own backlash, however, with several of the Anglophonic Caribbean states recasting their acceptance of the optional protocol in ways intended to prevent the Committee from delaying executions. Some of these delays had pushed executions beyond a mandatory five-year period after which, by operation of a decision of the Judicial Committee of the Privy Council— some of these nations' highest court of appeal—the 'death row phenomenon' bars execution on constitutional grounds.[73]

Even such a cursory sampling of the Committee's extensive, carefully reasoned jurisprudence demonstrates that a radical new idea has gained currency: that individuals can hold their governments accountable before an international tribunal applying globally adopted principles of personal rights. The Committee, on several occasions, has taken pains to 'point out that it is not an instance of final recourse intended to review or reverse decisions of domestic courts and that it cannot be used as a forum for pursuing a complaint on the basis of domestic law'.[74] Nevertheless, it has become a court of last resort for many of the world's least privileged and most oppressed.

The Committee has also had occasion to venture beyond individual rights into the field of group rights. In cases involving the Samis of northern Sweden and Finland, it has had to weigh the state's duty to protect 'cultural activity' against plans for economic development. In reviewing a Sami's application of Sweden's Reindeer Husbandry Act, the Committee held that, although the 'regulation of economic activity is normally a matter for the State alone, where that activity is an essential element in the culture of an ethnic community, its application to an individual may fall under article 27 of the Covenant'.[75] In *Länsman et al. v. Finland*, other Saami complainants charged that Finland was permitting quarrying which interfered with their tradition of reindeer husbandry. Finland replied that it was merely balancing and regulating various competing

---

[70] *Howard Martin v. Jamaica*, no. 317/1988, Report of the Human Rights Committee, GAOR, 48th Sess., Supp. no. 40 (A/48/40), at 169, para. 802.

[71] *Robinson v. Jamaica*, case no. 223/1987.

[72] Report of the Human Rights Committee, GAOR, 42nd Sess., Supp. no. 40(A/42/40), 1987, at 279, para. 404.

[73] Larry Rohter, 'In the Caribbean, Support Growing for the Death Penalty', NY Times, 4 Oct. 1998, at 14.

[74] Report of the Human Rights Committee, GAOR, 51st Sess., Supp. no. 40 (A/51/40), 1996, at 70, paras. 390–1.

[75] *Kintock v. Sweden*, Report of the Human Rights Committee, GAOR, 43rd Sess., Supp. no. 40 (A/43/40), 1988, at 157, para. 668.

economic activities and that reindeer husbandry, now not carried out in the ancient manner, was no longer a protected cultural activity. The Committee disagreed, reasoning that article 27 'does not only protect *traditional* means of livelihood of national minorities. . . . Therefore, the fact that the [complainants] may have adapted their methods of reindeer-herding over the years and may practice it with the help of modern technology does not prevent them from invoking article 27 . . . '.[76] It held that '*if* mining activities were to be approved on a large scale in the future, this might constitute a violation of the [complainants'] rights . . .'.[77]

On the other hand the Committee has firmly rejected efforts by ethnic groups to use the Optional Protocol complaint procedures to pull the Committee towards defining the right of self-determination, which the Covenant's article 1 vouchsafes to 'all peoples'. In *Bernard Ominayak and the Lubicon Band v. Canada*, the Committee observed that 'the question whether the Lubicon Lake Band constitutes a ."people" is not a question for the Committee to address under the Optional Protocol. . . . [which] provides a procedure under which individuals can claim that their individual rights have been violated'.[78] Self-determination is not such an individual right.[79] In reply to a similar request from several persons seeking self-determination for Italy's German-speaking minority in the South Tyrol, the Committee came to the same conclusion: 'the Committee . . . can receive and consider communications only if they emanate from individuals who claim that their individual rights have been violated by a State party. . . . [Therefore] no claim concerning the question of self-determination may be brought under the Option Protocol.'[80] Thus, while the ICCPR does protect certain group rights, the Committee has refused to be party to the enforcement of a right to self-determination through the procedures of the optional protocol.

Nevertheless, this bright line has not precluded the Committee's consideration of group rights when their violation affects an individual in his or her personal capacity. For example, the Committee has decided that a Sikh's cultural and religious right to wear a turban must yield in situations where use of hard-hats is mandated for valid reasons of health and safety.[81] The 'legislation requiring that workers in federal employment be protected from injury and electric shock by the wearing of hats', it wrote, 'is to be regarded as reasonable and directed towards objective purposes that are compatible with the Covenant'.[82] However, when the right of the predominantly French

---

[76] *Länsman et al. v. Finland*, Report of the Human Rights Committee, GAOR, 50th Sess., Supp. no. 40 (A/50/40), 1995, at 94, para. 541.  [77] Ibid.

[78] Case no. 167/1984, Official Records of the Human Rights Committee, 1989/90, vol. II, CCPR/9/Add.1, 1990, at 360, para. 615.

[79] But see applicability of article 27 to the Lubicon Lake Band, ibid. at 363, para. 628.

[80] *A.B. et al. v. Italy*, case no. 413/1990. Annual Report of the Human Rights Committee, GAOR, 46th Sess., Supp. no. 40 (A/46/40), 1991, at 432, para. 684.

[81] *Bhinder v. Canada*, case no. 208/1986.

[82] Ibid., Report of the Human Rights Committee, GAOR, 45th Sess., Supp. no. 40 (A/45/40), 1990, at 362, para. 625.

Canadian province of Quebec to prohibit external advertising in any language other than French was challenged by English-speakers, the Committee ruled in favour of the expressive rights of those individuals, rejecting the argument that the law permissibly protected the rights of the province's French-speaking majority. The Committee found that 'the commercial element in an expression taking the form of outdoor advertising cannot have the effect of removing this expression from the scope of protected freedom'.[83] It also ruled that Quebec's French Canadians' 'right to use their own language . . . is not jeopardized by the freedom of others to advertise in other than the French language'.[84]

In a subsequent decision on the same issue, the Committee said, 'a State party may choose one or more official languages, but . . . it may not exclude, outside the sphere of public life, the freedom to express oneself in a language of one's choice'.[85] This line of disputes illustrates both the problem of reconciling group rights with the countervailing rights of other groups or individuals—a matter further considered in Chapter 9—and also the problem federal states like Canada may encounter in having to take international responsibility for violations of the Covenant by sub-statal units such as Quebec, over whose actions they do not have the constitutional jurisdiction necessary to bring them into compliance.

Securing compliance has become a major concern of the Committee, whose efforts in that direction have placed it at the forefront of international systemic innovations. Since 1979, up to late 1996, it has found that states were in violation of the Convention in 168 cases.[86] Because, in the early years of its operation, states frequently failed to inform the Committee of any remedial measures taken, it established, in 1990, a new post of 'special rapporteur for the follow up on views'.[87] This member's task is to systematically request follow-up information whenever the Committee has found a violation. The annual Committee Reports list the states' replies and judges their compliance record 'satisfactory' or not.[88] By 1996, such information had been received in respect of 90 cases, of which only one third were characterized as 'satisfactory'.[89] The 1996 Report concluded that 'the overall results of the experience with the follow-up procedures are encouraging, yet they cannot be termed fully satisfactory'.[90]

The Committee's annual Reports provide a glimpse of the Committee's efforts to obtain remedial action by governments to bring themselves into

---

[83] *John Ballantyne, Elizabeth Davidson, and Gordon McIntyre v. Canada*, case nos. 359/1989 and 385/1989. Report of the Human Rights Committee, GAOR, 51st Sess., Supp. no. 40 (A/51/40), 1993, at 173, para. 820.

[84] *Allan Singer v. Canada*, case no. 455/1991. Ibid. at 174, para. 821.

[85] Report of the Human Rights Committee, GAOR, 49th Sess., Supp. no. 40 (A/49/40), 1994, at 81, para. 448.

[86] Ibid. at 78, para. 424.

[87] Ibid. at 78, para. 425.     [88] Ibid. at 79–83, para. 429.

[89] Ibid. at 78, paras. 426–7.     [90] Ibid. at 83, para. 430.

compliance after a complaint has been found to be justified. Such measures include the release of prisoners, lifting of bans on free movement, amending of legislation, changes in administrative practices, and the payment of compensation.[91] Whereas these follow-up reports were initially confidential, in 1993 the Committee decided to make them public in order to bring additional pressure to bear on recalcitrants.[92] It was also decided that the Committee would welcome 'information which non-governmental organizations might wish to submit as to what measures States parties have taken, or failed to take, in respect of the implementation of the Committee's Views'.[93] To expedite its operations, the Committee now selects from its ranks Special Rapporteurs with responsibility for preparing complaint dockets for Committee consideration and, as noted above, for establishing 'contacts with particular Governments and Permanent Missions to the United Nations to inquire further about the implementation of the Committee's Views'.[94] Its Reports now summarize these 'follow-up consultations' and the results of occasional on-site visits made by a Member at the Committee's behest.[95]

The ICCPR's canon of rights has been significantly augmented in various other instruments. Under the Convention on the Elimination of All Forms of Racial Discrimination,[96] state parties are obliged to prevent governmental and, by article 2(1), non-governmental, discrimination 'by any person, group or organization'. This Convention, too, establishes a Committee of Experts elected in the same way as the Committee of the ICCPR, with very similar compliance monitoring procedures, utilizing periodic state reporting. Its findings are reported to the General Assembly, together with 'suggestions and general recommendations based on the examination of reports and information received from the State Parties'.[97] States may declare their acceptance of the Committee's optional individual complaint jurisdiction.[98] When a state lodges a complaint against another, however, this Committee—unlike its ICCPR counterpart—has mandatory jurisdiction to consider the matter.[99]

These examples are intended to demonstrate a little noted but notable trend. A pattern is emerging of individual human rights recognition and protection. It is further evident in the Convention on the Elimination of All Forms of Discrimination Against Women (CEDAW).[100] A 23-member Committee of Experts, elected by the parties,[101] is empowered to receive and review periodic

---

[91] Ibid. at 83–4, paras. 431–5 and 85–90, paras. 438–62.    [92] Ibid. at 84, para. 437.
[93] Ibid. at 84–5, para. 437.    [94] Ibid. at 85, para. 437.
[95] Ibid. at 85–90, paras. 438–62.
[96] International Convention on the Elimination of All Forms of Racial Discrimination, GA Res. 2106, 21 GAOR Supp. 14, UN Doc. A/6014, at 47. 660 UNTS 195, 5 ILM 352 (1966). Entered into force 4 Jan. 1969.    [97] Ibid., art 9(2).
[98] Ibid. art. 12.    [99] Ibid., Part II, art. 11.
[100] Convention on the Elimination of All Forms of Discrimination Against Women, GA Res. 180 of 18 Dec. 1979. 19 ILM 33 (1980). 1249 UNTS 13. Entered into force 3 Sept. 1981.
[101] Ibid., art. 17.

) ·

:e reports[102] and to make public its findings together with recommendations
... reports to the General Assembly via the Economic and Social Council.[103] By
its article 29, CEDAW authorizes states to refer disputes regarding the
Convention's interpretation to the International Court of Justice. (A similar
provision in article 9 of the 1948 Genocide Convention[104] has recently been
held by the Court to give it jurisdiction over complaints alleging non-
compliance even when the alleged violation is by a state against its own
citizens.[105]) Unfortunately, many state parties to CEDAW have entered reservations to its article 29.[106] Also, CEDAW, as yet, makes no provision for individual
petitions. However, in 1999 an optional protocol was drafted which, on
adoption by ten states, will create jurisdiction to receive complaints from, or
on behalf of, individual victims and victimized groups.[107]

Regarding protection of women's rights, the Organization of American States
has ventured further. In 1994, it opened for signature a Convention on the
Prevention, Punishment, and Eradication of Violence Against Women[108]
which, in Chapter II, contains more extensive obligations than does CEDAW.
It also establishes novel 'mechanisms of protection' including a provision for
receiving complaints brought by non-governmental organizations.[109]

Another progeny of the ICCPR is the 1984 Convention Against Torture and
Other Cruel, Inhuman or Degrading Treatment or Punishment (CAT).[110] It,
too, establishes an independent expert committee (the Committee Against
Torture) consisting of ten members elected by the parties.[111] As of May 1996,

---

[102] Ibid. art. 18.    [103] Ibid. art. 21.

[104] Convention on the Prevention and Punishment of the Crime of Genocide, GA Res. 2670, 3
GAOR, Pt. 1, UN Doc. A/810, p. 174. Entered into force 12 Jan. 1951. 78 UNTS 277.

[105] *Republic of Bosnia-Herzegovina v. Federal Republic of Yugoslavia (Serbia-Montenegro)*, *(Jurisdiction and
Admissibility)*, Judgement of 11 July 1996, ICJ.

[106] Declarations, reservations, objections and notifications of withdrawal of reservations relating
to the Convention on the Elimination of All Forms of Discrimination against Women, Annex II, at
65, UN Doc. CEDAW/SP/1996/2.

[107] Draft Optional Protocol to CEDAW, art. 2 (1999). See further A. Byrnes & J. Connors,
'Enforcing the Human Rights of Women: A Complaint Procedure for the Women's Convention?',
21 Brooklyn J. Int'l L. 679 (1996). See also Report of the World Conference on Human Rights,
UN GAOR, 48th Sess., Pt. II, UN Doc. A/CONF.157/24 (1993) (the 'Vienna Declaration'),
para. 40.

[108] Convention on the Prevention, Punishment and Eradication of Violence Against Women, 33
ILM 1534 (1994).

[109] Any person or group of persons, or any non-governmental entity legally recognized in one or
more member states of the Organization, may lodge petitions with the Inter-American Commission
on Human Rights containing denunciations or complaints of violations of Article 7 of this Convention
[Duties of the States] by a State Party, and the Commission shall consider such claims in accordance
with the norms and procedures established by the American Convention on Human Rights and the
Statutes and Regulations of the Inter-American Commission on Human Rights for lodging and
considering petitions. Ibid. Article 12, ch. IV.

[110] Convention Against Torture and Other Cruel, Inhuman or Degrading Treatment or Punishment (hereafter CAT), GA Res. 46 of 10 Dec. 1984. UNTS no. 24841, 24 ILM 535 (1985). Entered
into force 26 June 1987.    [111] Ibid. art. 17(1).

there were ninety-six states party to the Convention.[112] Under article 19 of the CAT, State Parties are required to submit quadrennial reports on compliance. The Committee examines and reports on these and makes recommendations to the General Assembly. By article 21, the treaty makes provision for state-to-state complaints if both parties have previously declared their acceptance of the Committee's jurisdiction for such purposes.[113] Its optional article 22 allows individual victims to petition for remedies. As of September 1996, 36 states had accepted this option.[114]

While generally following the ICCPR precedent, the CAT departs from it in one noteworthy respect. It allows its Committee of Experts to receive anonymous complaints of violations even when brought by individuals and groups that are not themselves victims. Under article 20:

If the Committee receives reliable information which appears to it to contain well-founded indications that torture is being systematically practiced in the territory of a State Party, the Committee shall invite that State Party to co-operate in the examination of the information and to this end to submit observations with regard to the information concerned.

Taking such information and the state's reply into account, the Committee is empowered to designate one or more members 'to make a confidential inquiry and to report to the Committee urgently'.[115] Such an inquiry does not require the prior agreement of the affected state. Consent is required, however, for the Committee to proceed with an on-site visit.[116]

Inquiries by the Committee under article 20 of CAT are confidential and its meetings are closed.[117] However, the Committee 'may, after consultations with the State Party concerned, decide to include a summary account of the results of the proceedings in its annual report' to the UN General Assembly.[118] For example, an investigation of Egypt under article 20, begun by the Committee in November 1991 and concluded three years later,[119] eventually led to publication in May 1996 of a summary account of the investigation and subsequent negotiations with the Egyptian government.[120]

The Committee summary reveals that this investigation was initiated by Amnesty International,[121] later joined by other non-governmental organizations and by a Special Rapporteur of the Human Rights Commission on questions related to torture.[122] The Committee invited and received observations by Egypt on the allegations.[123] An informal working group of three members of

---

[112] Report of the Committee against Torture, GAOR, 51st Sess., Supp. no. 44 (A/51/44), 1996, at 1, para. 1.　　　　　　　　　　　　　　　　　　[113] CAT *supra* n. 110, art. 21.

[114] Report of the Committee against Torture, *supra* n. 112, at 37, para. 223.

[115] CAT, *supra* n. 110, art. 20(2).　　　[116] Ibid. art. 20(3).

[117] Ibid., art. 20(4) and Rules of Procedure 72, 73, 84. See Report of the Committee against Torture, 1996, *supra* n. 112, Annex VI, at 88.　　　　[118] CAT, *supra* n. 110, art. 20(5).

[119] Report of the Committee against Torture, *supra* n. 112, at 30, para. 181.

[120] Ibid.　　　[121] Ibid. at 30, paras. 182–3.　　　[122] Ibid. at 30, para. 183.

[123] Ibid.

the Committee was established to analyse information and propose action. After receiving more comments from Egypt in April 1993, the Committee decided to open a 'confidential inquiry'[124] and named two members for that purpose.[125] They addressed specific questions to Egyptian authorities, and met with a human rights expert designated by that Government.

In November 1993, the Committee asked Egypt to permit on-site inspection of certain prisons by its two designated members. Until November 1994, modalities were discussed by high ranking officials of Egypt's Ministries of Justice and the Interior.[126] When these proved fruitless, the Committee in mid-November 1994, adopted the conclusions proposed by its designated team. These were transmitted to Egypt which was 'invited to inform the Committee by 31 January 1995 of the measures it intended to take concerning the Committee's conclusions'.[127]

While Egypt met this deadline, evidently its response was not satisfactory. In May 1995, the Committee asked Egypt for its views on the proposed publication of a summary account of the results of the inquiry.[128] In its reply, Cairo urged the Committee not to encourage terrorists who, the previous month, had staged a 'sad and barbaric' incident in Cairo.[129]

Nevertheless, the Committee decided, under article 20(5), to proceed with publication. It also recognized the severe problems caused in Egypt by terrorism, but refused to accept this in mitigation. 'Torture seems to be used not only to obtain information and extort confessions,' it reported, 'but also as a form of retaliation to destroy the personality of the person arrested in order to intimidate and to frighten the family or the group to which the person arrested belongs.'[130] The obligations states voluntarily assume under CAT's article 2(2) permit no exceptions—'whether a state of war or a threat of war, internal political instability or any other public emergency'—that justify recourse to torture.[131]

While agreeing with Egypt that its legal system already has means 'to combat torture in an effective way' it concluded that judicial remedies 'are often a slow process leading to the impunity of the perpetrators of torture' and seemed inoperative against 'the role of State Security Intelligence . . .'.[132] It observed that torture can be found to be 'practiced systematically when it is apparent that the torture cases reported have not occurred fortuitously, in a particular place or at a particular time, but are seen to be habitual, widespread and deliberate in at least a considerable part of the territory of the country in question'.[133]

In an important ruling on evidence, the Committee concluded that Egypt, by interminable delays in its negotiations with the Committee, had made an on-site visit impossible. Thus, the Committee had no choice but to accept as valid those

[124] Ibid. at 31, para. 186.    [125] Ibid.    [126] Ibid. at 32, para. 195.
[127] Ibid. at 32, para. 196.    [128] Ibid. at 32, para. 198.    [129] Ibid. at 32, para. 199.
[130] Ibid. at 33, para. 204.    [131] Ibid. at 34–5, para. 211.
[132] Ibid. at 34, paras. 206–9.    [133] Ibid. at 35, para. 214.

numerous unrebutted allegations, coming from many different sources that had proven reliable in the past. It had been forced to draw its conclusions 'on the basis of the information available to it'.[134] It acknowledged indebtedness to evidence obtained from the UN Human Rights Commission, Amnesty, the Egyptian Organization for Human Rights and the World Organization Against Torture.[135] 'On the basis of this information,' the Committee concluded, 'torture is systematically practiced by the security forces in Egypt . . .'.[136] To ameliorate this, a set of recommendations are made to aid the government in coming into compliance with CAT's legal requirements.[137]

From the foregoing discussion it will be seen that the human rights protection system constructed after World War II has made the individual central not only to the definition of internationally protected rights but also to the process by which those rights are applied in instances of non-compliance. By making the individual an active, and not merely a passive, rights-holder, the law improves on the previous, exclusively state-centred, system. However, it has also become evident that, by focusing on individual complaints, the new system of protection has some shortcomings. Individual complaint procedures may not be the most efficient way to deal with large-scale violations. And complaint procedures, being dependent on proof of violations that have already occurred, are incapable of addressing anticipated wrongdoing preventively.

There have been several recent efforts to mitigate these shortcomings. During the drafting of CAT, Costa Rica suggested a new procedure which, while not incorporated into that instrument, was adopted in 1987 as part of a regional counterpart, the European Convention on the Prevention of Torture and Inhuman or Degrading Treatment or Punishment.[138] This instrument, while establishing the usual procedures for state complaints and, optionally, individual petitions, incorporates a non-adversarial supervisory system which, while triggered by states' or individuals' complaints, is essentially non-judicial and preventive. It envisages periodic or occasional Committee on-site visits to places of detention to ensure that prisoners are not subject to treatment violating the treaty. The Committee's role is primarily to suggest improvements in conditions of detention. This procedure is mandatory. Under article 2, State Parties must 'permit visits . . . to any place within its jurisdiction where persons are deprived of their liberty by a public authority'. Turkey has already been the object of such on-site visits.

The 1989 Convention on the Rights of the Child,[139] which has 187 parties as

---

[134] Ibid. at 36, para. 218.     [135] Ibid. at 33, para. 201.
[136] Ibid. at 36, para. 220.     [137] Ibid. at 36, para. 221.
[138] European Convention on the Prevention of Torture and Inhuman or Degrading Treatment or Punishment, 27 ILM 1154 (1988).
[139] Convention on the Rights of the Child, GA Res. 44/25, 20 Nov. 1989. Entered into force 2 Sept. 1990.

of June 1996,[140] establishes less intrusive procedures: it requires governments to submit periodic compliance reports to a committee of ten experts elected by the parties.[141] Reporting states may be requested to provide further information.[142] Reports by the Committee, setting out its findings regarding compliance, go to the General Assembly via the Economic and Social Council.[143] These may 'recommend to the General Assembly to request the Secretary-General to undertake on its behalf studies on specific issues relating to the rights of the child . . .'[144] and may make 'suggestions and general recommendations based on information received' to 'any State Party concerned . . .'.[145] There is no provision, however, for state-to-state complaint procedures nor for receiving individual petitions, which may account for the fact that this Convention quickly became the most widely ratified of the human rights instruments.

The pending Migrant Workers' Convention of 1991,[146] which is not yet in force, while envisaging similar supervision by a Committee of Experts, does permit (in article 77) petitions from persons 'subject to [a Party's] jurisdiction who claim that their individual rights as established by the present Convention have been violated by that State Party'.[147] They must, as usual, first exhaust their local remedies in the state being charged.[148] However, the Committee may waive even that prerequisite where 'in the view of the Committee, the application of the remedies is unreasonably prolonged or is unlikely to bring effective relief to that individual'.[149]

## 3. TACKLING UNDERLYING SOCIAL AND ECONOMIC CAUSES OF VICTIMIZATION

Most victims are poor; many are underprivileged and have little education, let alone legal or diplomatic training. To make these new regimes work, such persons need both *pro bono* legal services and, alternatively, some less cumbersome process through which to bring their problems to the attention of the rights regimes. As noted, innovative non-judicial procedures are included in the European Torture Convention. These are of a preventive nature, indirectly triggered by individual complaints but formally initiated by the supervising committee of experts themselves. Inquiries are conducted in a non-adversary, advisory manner, although they can include on-site investigations of circum-

---

[140] For list of ratifications see Convention on the Rights of the Child; Reservations, Declarations and Objections, Note by the Secretary-General, CRC/C/2/Rev.5, 30 July 1996, at 1 ff. But the Convention had not been ratified by the US as of mid-1996.

[141] Convention on the Rights of the Child, *supra* n. 139, at arts. 43, 44.

[142] Ibid. art. 44(4).          [143] Ibid. art. 44(5).          [144] Ibid. art. 45(c).

[145] Ibid. art. 45(d).

[146] International Convention on the Protection of All Migrant Workers and Members of Their Families, GA Res. 45/158, UN GAOR 45th Sess., Supp. no. 49 at 261, UN Doc. A/45/49 (1990), 30 ILM 1517 (1991). Opened for signature 2 May 1991. (Hereafter MWC.)

[147] Ibid. art. 77, in 30 ILM 1517, 1549.          [148] Ibid. art. 77(3)(b).          [149] Ibid. art. 77.

stances and conditions that may have occasioned a pattern of complaints. Investigators are authorized to conduct interviews with persons in detention.[150]

A further advantage of such alternate dispute-resolving procedures is that they place alleged victims in less danger of retribution than does a formal complaint. The less formal and non-adversary procedure also helps obviate the costs and complexities of initiating quasi-legal proceedings. It also potentially expedites remedial action by transforming the process from one based on time-consuming hearings and the evaluation of oral and written evidence to one of direct investigation of actual conditions by the supervising body itself. This new procedure needs more time to prove its utility, but it has the potential for addressing underlying conditions directly and preventively, rather than reacting solely to complaints by individuals who may already have been injured and whose allegations about past events may be hard to verify.

Planning to anticipate victimization by timely preventive action inevitably leads to consideration of the underlying social, cultural, and economic causes of abuse and of ways to address these preventively and remedially. The 1966 International Covenant on Economic, Social, and Cultural Rights makes an effort to do this.[151] Although parts of it are worded in vague and non-binding language,[152] it gives early credence to the evident but long-ignored proposition that genuine personal autonomy cannot be realized in the absence of personal security in employment, condition of work, family, education, and health. The right to property, a fundamental precondition of personal autonomy and individual rights, is also addressed by Protocol I of the European Human Rights Convention which guarantees to '[e]very natural or legal person . . . the peaceful enjoyment of his possessions' and provides that no one 'shall be deprived of his possessions except in the public interest and subject to the conditions provided for by law and by the general principles of international law'.[153]

This European Convention also addresses several other human rights not yet so clearly protected by international treaty. Protocol Seven, for example, restricts states' power arbitrarily to expel aliens.[154] As with other rights protected by the Convention, state-to-state complaints, and, optionally, individual petitions, provide recourse to the Council of Europe's judicial procedures.[155]

---

[150] European Convention on the Prevention of Torture and Inhuman or Degrading Treatment or Punishment of 1987, *supra* n. 138, especially arts. 7–14. Visits may only exceptionally be postponed on restrictive grounds asserted by the state to be visited. Ibid. art. 9(1).

[151] International Covenant on Economic, Social and Cultural Rights, Annex to GA Res. 2200 of 16 Dec. 1966, 21 GAOR Supp. no. 16, UN Doc. A/63/6 at 490. 993 UNTS 3; 6 ILM 360 (1967).

[152] Ibid. Article 2 only obliges parties to 'take steps . . . to the maximum of its available resources with a view to achieving progressively the full realization of the rights recognized' in the Covenant.

[153] Protocol to the Convention for the Protection of Human Rights and Fundamental Freedoms, 20 March 1952, ETS 9, art. 1.

[154] European Human Rights Convention, Protocol Seven (22 Nov. 1984), entered into force 1 Nov. 1988. 24 ILM 535 (1985).

[155] European Human Rights Convention, done on 20 Mar. 1952. Entered into force on 18 May 1954. ETS 9; 213 UNTS 262.

The European Social Charter,[156] however, goes further. This treaty has been in force since 1965 and, as of 1996, had twenty parties.[157] It seeks to give persons within its jurisdiction an ambitious ambit of those personal rights and securities that make individuality practically feasible. It is not limited to freedom of conscience, personal expression, and democratic participation, but also seeks to protect those social and cultural rights that are not always protected by political freedom alone. The Charter contains a number of non-binding aims, but also several legally binding provisions,[158] in particular those pertaining to persons' right freely to choose their occupation,[159] their right to organize 'for the protection of their economic and social interests . . .',[160] to bargain collectively,[161] to enjoy a system of social security at least equal to that established by the relevant International Labour Convention,[162] to social and medical assistance as needed when unemployed or ill,[163] and several other enumerated and defined entitlements for families[164] and migrant workers.[165]

As usual, there is provision for monitoring compliance through periodic state reports[166] which are reviewed by a 9-member committee of independent experts elected by the European Parliamentary Assembly.[167] The reports and the experts' conclusions regarding compliance are submitted to a Subcommittee of the Governmental Social Committee of the Council of Europe which consists of representatives of the States Parties to the Charter. The Subcommittee draws its own conclusions and submits these, together with the Committee of Experts' report, to the Council's Committee of Ministers. In parallel, a copy of the report of the experts is also submitted to the Council's Parliamentary Assembly, which also communicates its views to the Ministers. These, acting by two-thirds majority, may take decisions or make recommendations to the State Party whose policies have been reviewed.[168]

A shortcoming implicit in remedies based solely on individual complaints is addressed by a 1995 Protocol to the European Social Charter. A new European System of Collective Complaints,[169] patterned on procedures pioneered by the ILO that facilitate complaints by national organizations of employers and trade unions, also borrows from the experience of class actions in various national jurisdictions. It authorizes unions, employer organizations, and, for the first time, international and national non-governmental organizations to lodge

---

[156] European Social Charter, done on 18 Oct. 1961. Entered into force on 26 Feb. 1965. ETS 35; 529 UNTS 89. The following states were parties as of the end of 1995: Austria, Belgium, Cyprus, Denmark, Finland, France, Germany, Greece, Iceland, Ireland, Italy, Luxembourg, Malta, Netherlands, Norway, Portugal, Spain, Sweden, Turkey, United Kingdom.

[157] 34 ILM 1453 (1995). Introductory note by Andreas Zimmermann. See also European Social Charter, *supra* n. 156. See D. J. Harris, *The European Social Charter* (1984).

[158] Ibid. art. 20(1)(b).      [159] Ibid. art. 1.      [160] Ibid. art. 5.

[161] Ibid. art. 6.      [162] Ibid. art. 12.      [163] Ibid. art. 13.

[164] Ibid. art. 16.      [165] Ibid. art. 19.      [166] Ibid. art. 21.

[167] Ibid. art. 25, as amended by Protocol of 21 Oct. 1991, art. 3.

[168] Ibid. arts. 27–9, as amended by Protocol of 21 Oct. 1991, art. 5.

[169] Council of Europe, 9 Nov. 1995. 34 ILM 1453 (1995).

complaints with the Charter's Committee of Independent Experts.[170] As with complaints lodged by individuals, when a complaint is held admissible, the Committee examines its merits and makes a report to the Council's Committee of Ministers. If a violation is found, the Ministers, by two-thirds majority, may recommend measures to be taken by the violator to bring it into compliance with the Charter.[171] When this Protocol comes into force it will become an important new tool in building an effective new system of remedies.[172]

## 4. THE RESOLUTION 1503 SYSTEM

In addition to these convention-based methods of supervising compliance with legal obligations in the respective areas of human rights, there are institutional UN 'Charter-based' procedures, especially one centred on the Human Rights Commission: the 'Resolution 1503 procedure'.[173] Under it, the Commission, a subsidiary organ of the UN Economic and Social Council, may receive complaints from individuals and NGOs. If the Commission's Subcommission on Discrimination and Protection of Minorities perceives 'a consistent pattern of gross and reliably attested violations of human rights' it reports to the full Commission, which may take up the complaint with the state accused of violations and, if necessary, can take certain further steps. These include appointing a country rapporteur with authority to investigate and report on efforts to obtain compliance. In addition, the Human Rights Commission has developed the approach of setting up 'thematic mechanisms'—rapporteurs and working groups to address discrete subjects such as torture, violence against women, interference with judicial independence, and religious intolerance. There is no requirement that a state agree to this form of scrutiny, but there may well be a duty not to interfere with it.[174]

These intergovernmental procedures are augmented by the determined investigation and reporting of violations by NGOs. Amnesty International, for example, 'makes full use of all the relevant UN human rights mechanisms and procedures and sends huge volumes of information and case material to the UN for action . . . principally the Commission on Human Rights and its . . .

---

[170] Additional Protocol to the European Social Charter Providing for a System of Collective Complaints, 9 Nov. 1995. 34 ILM 1456, arts. 1(b), 2 and 3.

[171] Ibid. arts. 1(b), 2, 3, 6, 7, 8.

[172] The Protocol, opened for signature on 9 Nov. 1995, enters into force after ratification by 5 states. As of Jan. 1998, 10 states had signed and 2 had ratified it. Newsletter on the European Social Charter of the Council of Europe, no. 6, Jan. 1998. Entry into force is expected by the end of 1998.

[173] ECOSOC Res. 1235(XLII) (1967) and ECOSOC Res. 1503(XLVIII) (1970).

[174] See e.g. International Court of Justice, Request for Advisory Opinion transmitted to the Court pursuant to Economic and Social Council decision 1998/297 of 5 Aug. 1998, *Difference relating to Immunity from Legal Process of a Special Rapporteur of the Commission of Human Rights*, 1998 Gen. List no. 100, 8/19/98.

Sub-Commission on Prevention of Discrimination and Protection of Minorities, as well as ECOSOC and the General Assembly'.[175] So, to varying extent, do many other transnational and national groups.

## 5. HUMAN RIGHTS RESPONSIBILITY OF THE WORLD BANK

The proliferation of international treaty-based human rights protective regimes has been a feature of the era following the Second World War. These regimes have been influential in securing the compliance of governments with newly formulated minimum standards protecting the rights of persons. At the same time, in bringing compliance pressure on states, they are being augmented by other influential international institutions that increasingly are displaying sensitivity to human rights considerations even when these are not within their traditional mandate.

The 'World Bank', or International Bank for Reconstruction and Development and its International Development Association are prime examples. For many years, non-governmental organizations have been consulted in formulating development strategies.[176] These influential international lending institutions now regularly include some human rights considerations among the factors relevant to assessing a state's eligibility for loans.[177] For example, in 1994, the World Bank won a pledge from the government of Burkina Faso to take steps to stop female genital mutilation.[178] Environmental rights and the rights of indigenous peoples are given specific consideration in making decisions on proposed projects.[179]

---

[175]  Helena Cook, 'Amnesty International at the United Nations', in *The Conscience of the World* 181, 187 (Peter Willetts ed., 1996).

[176]  See Seamus Cleary, 'The World Bank and NGOs', in *The Conscience of the World* 63, 70–4 (Peter Willetts ed., 1996). Cleary concludes that, while the 'Bank has taken on board many NGO criticisms' nevertheless there 'is now a general consensus among development and environmental NGOs that the Bank and the IMF structural adjustment programmes are highly damaging to the people and the environment in developing countries'. This is made worse because 'the NGOs are clearly divided on what should be the political response'. Ibid. at 86–7.

[177]  See *The Inspection Panel*, Operating Procedures, IBRD and IDA, Aug. 1994; World Bank Operational Directive 4.20: Indigenous Peoples, Sept. 1991; *The Inspection Panel*, IBRD and IDA, Annual Reports, 1 Aug. 1994 to 31 July 1996, and 1 Aug. 1996 to 31 July 1997. See also Cleary, ibid. at 63, 68–73; Laurence Boisson de Chazournes, 'Applicable Standards for Review of Complaints, with Emphasis on Operational Policies and Procedures of the Bank', statement prepared for the Expert Meeting on the Inspection Panel of the World Bank, held at the Raoul Wallenberg Institute of Human Rights and Humanitarian Law, Lund, Sweden, 23–5 Oct. 21997 (MS). For a criticism of the Bank's selectivity in pressing human rights concerns see Daniel Bradlow & Claudio Grossman, 'Limited Mandates and Intertwined Problems: A New Challenge for the World Bank and the IMF', 17 Human Rts. Q. 411 (1995).

[178]  George Graham, 'Pledge Over Female Mutilation,' Financial Times, 22 Apr. 1994, at 6.

[179]  The World Bank Operational Manual, Manual Transmittal Memorandum, Operational Directive 4.20: Indigenous Peoples, 17 Sept. 1991. Alaka Wali & Shelton Davis, 'Protecting Amerindian Lands: A Review of World Bank Experience with Indigenous Land Regularization Programs in Low and South America', Report no. 19 (1992).

The Bank has also begun to play a role in implementation of these rights. In 1994, it established a procedure by which persons claiming that their rights have been violated by Bank-financed projects can complain to a 3-member Independent Inspection Panel. Requests for such a project review may be made by 'any two or more persons who share common interests and concerns'[180] and are 'affected parties':[181] that is, persons who are in the territory of the borrowing government and claim that their 'rights or interests have been, or are likely to be, adversely affected directly by an action or omission of the Bank . . .'.[182] After a preliminary consultation and investigation, the Panel is authorized to advise the Bank's Executive Directors whether the complaint warrants a full-scale investigation. On completing their investigation, the Panel, reporting to the Bank's Executive Directors, may recommend continuation, alteration, or termination of a project. If the project has not yet commenced, the Panel may advise whether, and how, the project might be made more consistent with the rights and interests of the petitioners.[183]

By May 1997, the Bank's Inspection Panel had received ten requests to investigate projects ranging from a power generating facility in India to a Brazilian Amazon development. The various complaints allege, for example, a failure to 'implement a sustainable health plan for indigenous people' (in the Brazilian project), a failure to consider the effect of a power generating plant on the health of local residents (India), and effects on the livelihood of local providers of services that may be displaced by a project (Paraguay and Bangla Desh). While some petitions were held inadequately founded, others have been sustained. For example, complaints that a planned hydroelectric development would impose involuntary resettlement on persons in the area and would violate IDA policies regarding the rights of indigenous populations led the Bank to reassess and withdraw its proposed financing of one project.[184]

While the world's financial institutions are not in the business of protecting individual rights of persons, the inclusion of such considerations in assessing the impact of a bank-financed development is a justified broadening of the definitional indicators by which eligibility for funding is measured by prudent lenders. At the same time, investors' heightened awareness of the connection between individual freedom and the sustainability of economic growth is giving the cause of liberty a potent new set of allies in the struggle for human rights.[185]

---

[180] IBRD and IDA, 'Review of the Resolution Establishing the Inspection Panel; Clarification of Certain Aspects of the Resolution,' IBRD Memo, p. 1, 17 Oct. 1996. [181] Ibid.

[182] IBRD and IDA, 'The Inspection Panel for the IBRD and IDA', Apr. 1997, at 1 (updated).

[183] Ibid. at 1–2. See also 'The Inspection Panel, IBRD and IDA', *Report*, 1 Aug. 1994 to 31 July 1996; 'The Inspection Panel, IBRD and IDA', *Operating Procedures*, Aug. 1994.

[184] The complaint concerned the Arun III Hydroelectric Project. 'The Inspection Panel', Apr. 1997, *supra* n. 182, at 2.

[185] Some advocates for human rights and environmental concerns have concluded, however, that the Bretton Woods institutions are hopelessly mired in traditional secrecy and outmoded definitions of fiscal priority. See e.g. Bruce Rich (international director, Environmental Defence Fund), in BankCheck Quarterly, Sept. 1993, cited in Cleary, *supra* n. 176, at 87–8 and n. 34.

Similarly, international trade regimes are beginning to be summoned to use their leverage with participant governments to enforce international human rights and similar public-interest standards, even if these are not directly related to trade. One example is the North American Agreement on Environmental Cooperation,[186] negotiated as companion to the North American Free Trade Agreement (NAFTA).[187] Without agreement on these procedures for enforcing environmental standards, the US government would probably not have been able to muster the public support necessary to obtain congressional acquiescence in NAFTA.[188] Such considerations increasingly influence national commercial policies. It is inevitable that they will also begin to influence the international trade regime.

### 6. SOME PROTECTIVE COMMONALITIES

Several points emerge from the texts and practices of the new transnational institutions for the protection of human rights. *First*, each represents significant progress towards the recognition, by international and regional law and institutions, that individuals are legitimate and globally recognized claimants and rights-holders. *Second*, each manifests a growing global and regional recognition that the protection of personal rights cannot be left solely to states but must also be the responsibility of global and regional institutions. *Third*, most of these new rights regimes recognize that not only governments but also victims, victim-support groups, and human rights experts each have important parts to play in invoking and implementing the new rights. *Fourth*, the circumference of the international human rights regime is expanding with the inclusion of international institutions created for other functional purposes, but which increasingly include human rights factors in their political, economic, and fiscal calculations.

While these developments affect the formerly exclusive role of the state in the international system, they generally redound also to the states' advantage. Historically, human rights violations have ended in misery and war. Disputes over human rights can now be resolved on a low-profile, case-by-case basis. In some instances, problems can even be addressed in a non-adversarial, preventive mode. Increasingly, there is a realization that some states may need international help to improve their capacity to comply with the new rights. It is helpful that disputes are now often handled by standing bodies. This

---

[186] North American Agreement on Environmental Cooperation, 14 Sept. 1993, Canada–Mexico–US, 32 ILM 1482 (entered into force 1 Jan. 1994).

[187] North American Free Trade Agreement, 17 Dec. 1992, Canada–Mexico–US, 32 ILM 296 (Parts One through Three); 32 ILM 612 (Parts Four through Eight) (entered into force 1 Jan. 1994).

[188] Kal Raustisala, 'International "Enforcement of Enforcement" Under the North American Agreement on Environmental Cooperation', 36 Va. J. Int'l L. 721 (1996).

encourages consistency of practice and the evolution of a body of principled expectations.

Nevertheless, current practice also validates some complaints. For example, it is true that the proliferation of human rights treaties imposes a burden of multiple periodic reporting that is especially onerous for poor nations. It is not surprising that many states' reports are becoming both cursory and tardy, making them altogether unsatisfactory vehicles for overseeing compliance. Various solutions to this problem have been proposed. Consolidation of the many treaty regimes would make reporting easier, but would also impose a heavy burden on those charged with overseeing such a large and varied body of specialized law. Even more radical is the suggestion that supervision of compliance with all the rights treaties should be judicialized: that periodic reporting should be replaced with adjudication before a global Human Rights Tribunal exercising case-by-case jurisdiction over compliance with all human rights treaties. A variation on this theme envisages regional tribunals, with limited right of appeal to a global forum. Such judicialization, as will be discussed in the next section, has advantages but also entails new costs that victims are often unable to bear alone.

7. ORGANIZING THE SHAREHOLDERS: NETWORKS FOR THE PROTECTION OF PERSONAL AUTONOMY

It is hardly credible that most victims—a jungle farmer in Brazil, a filmmaker in Austria, a journalist in China, a housewife in Pakistan—should spontaneously avail themselves of the new international norms and institutions designed to protect their personal freedoms. Those protections, being new, are not well known. More to the point, they are both procedurally complex and couched in normative language that, being nuanced and intended to balance personal rights with the requisites of public order, health, and safety, are difficult for ordinary persons to penetrate.

This complexity is illustrated by article 19(2) of the ICCPR, which extends to all persons 'the right to freedom of expression' but makes the exercise of that entitlement 'subject to certain restrictions . . . provided by law' that 'are necessary . . . [f]or the protection of national security or of public order . . . or of public health or morals'. Similarly, the 1991 Convention on Migratory Workers provides that their protected freedom to manifest or adopt a religion of choice, is 'subject . . . to such limitations as are prescribed by law and are necessary to protect public safety, order, health or morals or the fundamental rights and freedoms of others'.[189] What all that means, in practice, can only be fathomed by persons, usually lawyers, who are versed in the law's drafting and

---

[189] MWC, *supra.* n. 146, art. 12(3).

institutional history and have kept up with its subsequent case-by-case application. Clearly, an individual or group bringing a complaint against a powerful state usually will need the help of professional specialists.

Not surprisingly, a transnational network of just such professionals is springing up and beginning to provide services, often at little or no cost to impecunious clients. Others assist the expert committees and the various instrumentalities charged with overseeing implementation. 'Friends' of these implementing bodies volunteer advice pertaining to specific, often complex, complaints and help produce relevant evidence.

Advice is regularly given to some members of the Human Rights Committee on questions of fact and law by non-governmental human rights organizations. This is especially useful to elected experts from smaller or poor countries who cannot count on their governments' research support. Increasingly, that gap is being filled by law students and practitioners who provide *pro bono* support services and help 'prep' the elected experts, for example, when they are to cross-examine a reporting country's representatives. Other non-governmental networks of investigators and reporters within a reporting country provide evidence of abuses that can be used to challenge the official version of events and conditions. When complaints are lodged with some human rights treaty bodies, such as the Banjul (African) Commission, an NGO representative may act for the complainant, helping in the preparation of the complaint and presenting relevant evidence. The World Bank's system for receiving 'requests' for review of a planned or existing project (see above) provides that those who believe their 'rights or interests' to have been 'adversely affected' by a Bank project may be represented by 'a duly appointed local representative acting on explicit instructions as the agent of adversely affected people; or . . . in the exceptional case . . .' by 'a foreign representative acting as agent of adversely affected people . . .'.[190]

According to a leading NGO advocate, since the end of the Cold War the human rights treaties' supervisory expert committees have 'begun to acknowledge their dependency on NGO information'.[191] A 1994 meeting of the committees' chairs concluded that the time was ripe for NGOs to play a more formal role: they 'could be allowed, in particular, to make oral interventions and to transmit information relevant to the monitoring of human rights provisions through formally established and well-structured procedures'.[192]

Another example of the volunteer-expert's growing role in implementing the new human rights canon is an emerging practice of expert interventions in international litigation. In a procedural move common to courts of the United States but not hitherto well known in international tribunals, the International

---

[190] IBRD, IDA, Inspection Panel, Operating Procedures, Aug. 1994, at 8.

[191] Felice Gaer, 'Reality Check: Human Rights NGOs Confront Governments at the UN', in *NGOs, the UN, and Global Governance* 51, 56 (Thomas G. Weiss & Leon Gordenker eds., 1996).

[192] Ibid., citing UN Doc. A/49/537, 19 Oct. 1994, para. 41.

Tribunal for the Prosecution of Persons Responsible for Serious Violations of International Humanitarian Law Committed on the Territory of the Former Yugoslavia since 1991, decided in June 1995 to grant leave to various experts in human rights and humanitarian law to file *amicus curiae* ('friends of the Court') briefs in the *Dusko Tadic* case.[193] NGO lawyers and others also played an important role assisting smaller states to file written briefs and enter oral pleadings in the 1995–6 World Court proceedings regarding the legality of the threat to use, or actual use, of nuclear weapons.[194] No doubt, in future, the role of lawyers as volunteers will increase as the legal protection of individual rights continues to expand.

---

[193] Briefs were filed by Professor Christine Chinkin of the Law Faculty of the London School of Economics and by a group of professors and attorneys on behalf of the Jacob Blaustein Institute for the Advancement of Human Rights, as well as by human rights clinics at the City University of New York and at the Harvard Law School. Prosecutor v. Dusko Tadic a/k/a 'Dule', Opinion and Judgement, 7 May 1997, Case IT-94-1-T, at 5.

[194] See *The Case Against the Bomb* (R. Clark & M. Sann eds., 1996), esp. p. 5, where members of the supporting NGO consortium are listed in the text and in n. 5.

# 9

## *The Individual against the Group*

1. TRIAD: THE STATE, THE GROUP, AND THE INDIVIDUAL

In preceding chapters we have reviewed the emergence of a new kind of individual: rights claiming, consciously assertive, aggressively self-determining persons exercising a high degree of creative autonomy. We have observed such persons' struggle for personal space within which, newly freed from the vestiges of communitarian control, they seek to shape their unique identity through the exercise of unfettered choice in such matters as citizenship, conscience, expression, education, occupation, sexuality, and other aspects of self-definition.

In recent decades the individual has made progress in asserting personal autonomy, while the sovereign state has lost some ground: both to individualism and to internationalism. There has been symbiosis here. The state's retreat before the demands of individuals has been accelerated by a burgeoning global human rights regime.

The symbiosis is dramatic in its invigoration of the hitherto dormant international legal order. While much of the struggle for individuality traditionally has occurred in older venues—the town, the church, the state—we now begin to observe the growth, in recent decades, of an international legal system which, abandoning its earlier Vattelian deference to state sovereignty, participates actively in curbing states' previously unchecked power to compel individuals to conform. Thus assisted, significant victories are being won almost everywhere by persons seeking the right to construct their personal identity through autonomous choice among ever-expanding options.

The emerging victory of personhood, if still contingent, is already being celebrated as the emancipation of individuals from communitarian conformity. Large domains previously ruled by governments have been ceded to personal preference or individual taste.

Just as this has been happening, however, another set of rights-claimants has emerged, militantly asserting a different agenda. This third contender for power is the group—ethnic, tribal, or other—organized around linguistic, genetic, religious, historic, and territorial commonalities. It seeks group autonomy, and sees that claim in confrontation both with the state and the individual. We are thus witnessing the birth of a rights triad: individual, state, and group.

Group rights are not new. Indeed, the concept has a longer, perhaps stronger, provenance than does either modern state sovereignty or even more contemporary individual autonomy. Early empires, including the Roman and the Chinese, granted considerable self-rule to ethnic, tribal, and linguistic groups, especially at the outer marches of their domains. Nowadays, such 'groups' are returning to the fore, more numerous and widespread than ever.

There are many contemporary manifestations of this militant group-rights resurgence. One of the best organized is the global movement of 'indigenous people'. It is estimated to have more than 300 million adherents in some seventy countries, organized not only locally but also in a transnational network that provides mutual support for each group's national struggle.[1]

These and many other newly assertive groups in some respects do not much differ from the great and small nationalisms that emerged in Europe in the wake of the French Revolution.[2] However, the modern groups have tended to splinter existing multi-ethnic political entities, emphasizing their differentness, whereas the eighteenth-century nationalisms of Europe, as we noted in Chapters 1 and 3, tended to unify different ethnie and religions in the spirit of America's motto—*e pluribus unum.*

Such particularism seems in the ascendant at the close of the twentieth century, and not only in the former communist fiefs of Europe. In Africa, several thousand tribal and other kinship groups, submerged in the 1960–80 struggle for national liberation, now seem poised for revival. With the end of the Cold War, moreover, the big powers seem less concerned than hitherto about these groups' potential for destabilizing world order. Gone is the vigour with which the United Nations in the 1960s resisted Katanga's attempt to secede from Zaire and the benign insouciance with which the world watched Nigeria suppress the Biafran secession. Were those wars for tribal independence being fought today, rather than decades ago, there might well be a worldwide demand for intervention on the side of the secessionists.

## 2. EQUALITY VS. AUTONOMY IN GROUP RIGHTS STRATEGY

While the contemporary group-rights claimants see themselves as different from, and often adversary to, both the state and the individual, they tend still to be ambiguous about other aspects of their self-definition. In particular, there is within many groups a bipolarity between integrationists and separatists. The former engage the state's and international community's political and juristic processes to militate for equality of opportunity within the multicultural communities in which they live, relying primarily on antidiscriminatory measures and programmes of affirmative action. The latter, in sharp contrast, advocate either the creation of independent states in which the group predominates, or, if that is impossible, then political, social, and cultural autonomy, with rights and

---

[1] S. James Anaya, *Indigenous Peoples in International Law* (1996). Shelton Davis & William Partridge, 'Promoting the Development of Indigenous People in Latin America', 31 Finance and Development 38 (1994). [2] For discussion see Chs. 1 and 3, above.

laws different from those of an encompassing state with which they wish to remain only loosely associated. Both integrationist and secessionist advocates of group rights have had their periods of ascendancy in the twentieth century.

The integrationist ascendance had some ambiguous support between the world wars, as we shall see. Its influence was at its greatest, however, with the rise of African nationalism in the mid-1950s, and with the emergence of the US civil rights movement led by Martin Luther King. As the new, multi-tribal nations of Africa and Asia struggled for cohesion, separatism—the demand for tribal autonomy—fell out of favour. Integrationist group-advocacy, on the other hand, survived as a viable adjunct to the new emphasis on individual human and civil rights and the fight against apartheid. In mid-century, both in South Africa and the United States, the demand was not for black rights but for equal rights. To the extent special claims were advanced—affirmative action is the most important example—they were presented as transitional measures meant to compensate groups of persons for past injustices and to facilitate categories of previously deprived persons' assimilation into a society of equal *individuals*. That, in the event, is how minority rights were accepted in the period after World War II, both in national and international forums and law. As Justice Blackmun observed at the time, 'In order to get beyond racism, we must first take account of race. There is no other way.'[3] The integrationists' long-run efforts, however, were aimed primarily at making race irrelevant in order to better equalize the prospects of the essential individual. Followers of King and Mandela, in good Lockean tradition, thought the individual, regardless of race, ethnie, or other group-affiliation, to be the authentic holder of rights. These rights were to be redeemed through legally mandated broadening of opportunity.

In that spirit, several rights campaigns of that post-World War II era involved individuals seeking to integrate fully while yet preserving elements of their group identity: Sikhs wishing to work as ordinary London bus conductors while wearing turbans; Jews serving in the US army claiming the right to wear yarmulkes under their service caps. What these persons sought was a right to integrate as individuals, to join as equals the larger community's common enterprises, while still retaining some symbols of their particular group affiliation.

The secessionist group-rights claimants have a quite different agenda. Their claim is not advanced on behalf of individuals who happen to be members of a group, but on behalf of the group itself. They assert a rights-based claim against *both* the once-omnipotent state and the increasingly assertive individual. They distrust both. Somewhat like the individualists, the group-separatists have demanded that the state cede control in matters of language, education, culture, religion, and those aspects of the legal system that pertain to careers, marriage,

---

[3] *Regents of the University of California v. Bakke*, 438 US 265, 407 (1978) (sep. op.).

land-ownership, inheritance, and children. But whereas individualists seek to have all persons control these choices for themselves, the advocates of group autonomy want that control exercised by the group collectively. Their demand is for transfer of power over these matters not to individual persons but to the designated group as such, which is to be empowered to set and enforce values, rules, and policies for all its members. Their autonomy claim, in effect, asks that groups be allowed to opt out of the larger polis in respect of matters that intimately define them. Naturally, they do not wish to be integrated into the sort of liberal democracy in which, as put by John Rawls, the *individual* is the sole 'self-originating source of valid claims'.[4] Will Kymlicka, restating this opposition, argues that Rawls' desideratum of granting all persons in a multicultural society the benefits of common and equal rights, far from conducing to universal happiness, is likely to galvanize groups that want to live by their own laws and traditions into an aggrieved minority in open revolt against a system that reflects and imposes the values and aims of the preponderant culture.[5]

The campaign for both kinds of group rights, waged concurrently in national and international law, has a long provenance. It gained international recognition in the period following World War I, when the Wilsonian concept of ethnic self-determination was applied to rearrange boundaries as part of the dismantling of the German, Austro-Hungarian, and Ottoman empires in Europe. Even in that period, however, it soon became apparent that the Powers were unwilling to embrace all the destabilizing consequences of fulfilling the impossible Hegelian dream that each European 'nation' emerge as a self-contained state. To compensate for denying to some what had been given to others, several minorities were guaranteed degrees of autonomy as a means by which the international system could recognize their special status without prompting the further splintering of states.

The inter-war period was thus one in which the anti-integrationist wing of the group-rights movement received significant recognition by the state system. Professor Adeno Addis has pointed out that under the aegis of the League of Nations and the watchful eye of the Permanent Court of International Justice, there emerged

a system of treaties and other arrangements to protect minorities as minority groups rather than as individuals, as current human rights law tends to do. . . . Under the League system, minority rights included the positive right of cultural identity. And unlike the United Nations system, which conspicuously downgraded the question of protection of minorities . . . the League system provided formal guarantee of minority rights by the international community's most powerful agency, the League Council itself.[6]

[4] John Rawls, 'Kantian Constructivism in Moral Theory', 77 J. of Phil. 515, 543 (1980).
[5] Will Kymlicka, *Multicultural Citizenship* 181–91 (1995).
[6] Adeno Addis, 'Individualism, Communitarianism, and the Rights of Ethnic Minorities', 67 Notre Dame L. Rev. 615, 636 (1992), and cites therein.

Although this period was by no means the first flourishing of demands for group autonomy, it was a time when those particularist rights were embraced as legitimate by the international legal systems, which set about their implementation through new norms and processes.

### 3. THE LEAGUE REGIME OF GROUP RIGHTS

Professor Nathaniel Berman has observed that the regime of new nation-states created after World War I may be seen as

> the replacement of the Central European empires with 'national' states, such as Poland and Czechoslovakia. This implementation of the principle of nationalities or 'objective' self-determination was foreshadowed in [the Allies'] . . . promise to create a Polish state out of those regions with 'indisputably Polish' populations. In certain frontier regions, such as Schleswig, the 'objective' principle of nationalities gave way to the 'subjective' plebescite principle.[7]

In this way, group rights were further accommodated by allowing a group to secede from one state to join a more compatible one next door.

This partial redrawing of the political map of Europe along unprecedented national-ethnic lines may have given self-determination to some populations, but only at the price of denying it to others. It featured wholesale, rather than retail, definition of persons' identity. While that solved some problems, it did so only by creating others for which new solutions were then needed. The new nations celebrated their emancipation by adopting constitutions stressing their 'national' character in terms of the dominant ethnic group or culture.[8] In so doing, they immediately became the objects of new, antagonistic group-rights claims of the minorities stranded in their midst. These claims could not be ignored in any principled way, but neither could they be fully satisfied by an infinite regression to a system of group-exclusive nations that satisfied every possible group-claimant. 'Accordingly,' Berman notes, 'as an accompaniment to the implementation of self-determination in its various guises, the new or greatly enlarged states of Central Europe were compelled either to sign minority protection treaties or to make declarations guaranteeing various rights to their minority groups.'[9] While, in some instances, outright secession had been allowed, where it was denied, the consolation prize was a regime of internationally mandated and monitored minority group rights imposed by the international community on states forced to accept such diminution of traditional

---

[7] Nathaniel Berman, '"But the Alternative is Despair": European Nationalism and the Modernist Renewal of International Law', 106 Harv. L. Rev. 1792, 1822 (1993).

[8] See Berman, ibid., and C. A. Macartney, *Nation States and National Minorities* 208–10 (1934) citing the constitutions of Austria, Czechoslovakia, Estonia, Poland and Romania.

[9] Berman, ibid.

sovereignty. This was new: sovereignty had traditionally meant being free to persecute nonconformists and alien others.

Thus, reluctantly, Austria, Hungary, Bulgaria, and Turkey undertook to protect minorities in their respective peace treaties. Poland, Czechoslovakia, Yugoslavia, Romania, and Greece signed minorities protection treaties with the principal allied and associated powers. Albania, Lithuania, Latvia, Estonia, and Iraq made minority protection declarations as conditions for entry into the League of Nations.[10] These treaties and declarations contained formal guarantees of personal equality between members of the majority and minority, thereby seeking to satisfy the integrationist group claimants: the ones who only wanted the right to wear their yarmulkes to work at the state school. But they also contained provisions guaranteeing some collective group rights that were not integrationist at all. Indeed, they provided a degree of collective group autonomy. For example, the Polish Minorities Protection Treaty, in article 8, granted minorities the right to 'establish, manage and control at their own expense charitable, religious and social institutions . . . and . . . educational establishments' while article 9 guaranteed primary instruction in a minority's own language in parts of Poland 'in which a considerable proportion of Polish nationals of other than Polish speech are residents', with an 'equitable share' of public funds being allocated to such educational, religious or charitable purposes.[11]

To summarize: in an apparent effort to mitigate the inherent contradiction between a universal 'right' of peoples (i.e. groups, tribes, or nations) to self-determination—that is, to statehood through secession—and the denial of that right to others dictated by harsh logistic, geographic, economic, and strategic realities, the international system after 1919 established a regime of group rights. It was the compensation prize for failing to achieve statehood, and it had two notable characteristics. First, it stopped short of granting outright independence. Instead, it offered a model of limited autonomy. Second, it accorded rights not only to individual members of minorities (to equality of treatment by the state in economic, cultural, and political matters) but also to groups as such (to maintain separate cultural, educational, religious, charitable, and sometimes legal institutions and practices).

This must have seemed a Solomonic compromise. As Berman says, while '[i]nternational minority protection infringes on sovereign authority' it still falls short of granting full 'national' rights to the affected group.[12] And it applied another compromise in granting rights to minority persons both as individual citizens and also as members of a recognized group. It granted special rights to individuals to live out their group identity, but it also granted strong rights to

---

[10] Inis L. Claude, Jr., *National Minorities* 16 (1955). See e.g. the Minorities Treaty Between the Principal Allied and Associated Powers and Poland, 28 June 1919, 225 Consol. TS 412.
[11] Polish Minorities Treaty, ibid. art. 9, at 418.    [12] Berman, *supra* n. 7, at 1825.

the group itself, as distinct from its members. These group rights were extended by state law, but, for good measure, were also guaranteed by a regional or international treaty regime. Underlying the new rights was the assumption 'not only that a Polish citizen of German speech and ancestry can be a loyal Pole but also that the only way to make him so is to leave him unmolested in the possession of his German cultural heritage'.[13]

This latter insight was not new, but, rather, a clever reinvention of older applications of cultural autonomy as a tactic for securing the group's adhesion to a larger *polis*. After the defeat of France at Quebec City, for example, Britain enacted laws guaranteeing the residents of Lower Canada continuing protection of French civil law, the primacy of the Catholic religious establishment, and the right to continue to use the French language. The Quebec Act of 1774[14] waived application to Quebec of Britain's Test Act, which had disenfranchised Britain's Roman Catholics. The idea was to make Quebec British by allowing it to remain (almost) French. After World War I, the same strategy was applied to make German Poles more Polish by ensuring their right to remain culturally German. Whatever the actual effects of these strategies, they reintroduced into modern law the ancient idea of autonomous 'peoples' with rights (and, perhaps, duties) in important respects different from those of the general citizenry. In a sense, it reinvented in modern Eastern Europe the sort of niche King Herod's Judaea had occupied in Roman times.

Within the affected states, the emergence of group regimes transformed what had for several centuries been essentially a dyad into a modern rights triad. At least, since the English revolution of 1688 and the American and French revolutions of the late eighteenth century, individuals had been emerging as contenders for serious rights, entitled to make claims on, or even against, their rulers.[15] With the establishing of minority protection regimes after World War I, the state and the citizen were joined by the group as the third recognized rights

---

[13] Macartney, *supra* n. 8, at 278, quoted in Berman, ibid.

[14] The British North America Act of 1774, 14 Geo. 3, ch. 83, reprinted in 6 Halsbury's Statutes of England 296 (Burrows, 2nd edn., 1948).

[15] After the American and French revolutions, the state had begun to recede as the sole holder of rights. The maxim: 'the king can do no wrong' was repealed in the new republics. For origins and application of the maxim see Edwin M. Borchard, 'Government Liability in Tort', 34 Yale LJ 1, 2 (1924); Note, 'Rethinking Sovereign Immunity After *Bivens*', 57 NYU L. Rev. 597, 604–7 (1982). Instead, individuals were newly empowered and the state strictly limited in its share of unopposable entitlements. This shift to limited state sovereignty, while amply evident domestically, was less apparent from the perspective of the international legal system. The prevalent Vatellian international legal system adhered strictly to notions of state sovereignty (and to the invisibility of persons as rights claimants) for another 150 years. Instead of moving with the times, international law shunned individual rights even as it reinvented and recognized a concept of group rights that were protected and implemented in derogation of state sovereignty. This fitted uncomfortably with the old Vattelian order, without actually repealing it; and it suited not at all the revolutionary doctrines of individuality, equality and inherent personal autonomy that had already come to the fore a century earlier and found recognition in the domestic law of many nations. Thus began a struggle for place among a triad of rights claimants: the state, the individual and the group.

claimant, empowered to make claims against the state and, occasionally, also against individuals: claims the members of a group and sometimes the group itself could advance for the protection of their special group identity.

It should be noted that after the First World War, this triad was distinctly asymmetrical. Group rights were being recognized in international law and foisted on states' governments. National protection for groups, spelled out in state constitutions, were given their footing in international law by incorporation into treaties and other agreements. The rights of individuals, in sharp contrast, although well-established for more than a century in the legal systems of liberal Western states, still remained but dimly recognized by international law, which, between the wars, continued to operate essentially under the unchanged Vattelian assumption that its rules protect the prerogatives of states, but never those of individuals. Only after the end of the Second World War did the rights of individuals come to be recognized as a proper subject for international legal protection.

This inter-war imbalance, by seeming in part to validate the modern romantic claims of ethnie as unique bearers of cultural identity and historic memory worthy of special protections, may have helped create the climate in which a Nazi racist *Übermenschen* ideology could blossom. To the extent the peace settlements following the Treaty of Versailles husbanded the bio-cultural identity once celebrated by Rousseau and Hegel, these might, indeed, have contributed, however unintentionally, to the ethnic and cultural wars that debauched Europe for most of the rest of the century, and do so still.

That was not, of course, their intent. What the inter-war protection regimes did try to promote was a delicate equilibrium between the traditional sovereign rights of the state and ethnic minorities newly protected by international law, as well as between the integrationist and autonomist tendencies within these groups. Equilibrium requires a fulcrum. When these new regimes were established by treaty, the Permanent Court of International Justice (PCIJ; 'World Court') was given jurisdiction to interpret rights and resolve disputes, an entirely new role for that young institution.[16]

Its judges used several cases to elaborate the Court's new balancing mandate. In 1928, in a suit filed by Germany, they[17] interpreted provisions of the German–Polish Convention relating to Upper Silesia.[18] At issue, in general, was access to minority education. In its formerly German territories, Poland had instituted an enquiry into the 'authenticity of applications for admission to the minority schools and to ascertain whether such applications emanated from

---

[16] See e.g. Advisory Opinion no. 7, *Acquisition of Polish Nationality*, 1923 PCIJ (ser. B) no. 7, at 13–16. See also Advisory Opinion no. 6, *German Settlers*, 1923 PCIJ (ser. B) no. 6, at 37; Advisory Opinion no. 7, ibid. at 23–5 (observations by Lord Finlay).

[17] Judgment no. 12, *Rights of Minorities in Upper Silesia*, 1928 PCIJ (ser. A) no. 15.

[18] German–Polish Convention relating to Upper Silesia of 15 May 1922, 16 Martens Nouveau Recueil (IIIe Série) Tome XVI 645 (1926).

persons authorized to submit them' on behalf of their children.[19] The Polish authorities, anxious to promote integration, claimed the right to refuse German education to anyone deemed insufficiently German. Germany challenged this practice[20] and the Court essentially upheld the claim, deciding that every person had the right to 'freely declare according to his conscience and on his personal responsibility that he does or does not belong to a racial, linguistic or religious minority . . .' although 'these declarations must set out what their author regards as the true position'. Such declarations, however, 'are subject to no verification, dispute, pressure or hindrance whatever on the part of the authorities . . .'.[21]

This decision, at one level, supported the group autonomy of persons of German origin in Poland. On another level, it ratified the right of individuals to decide for themselves, on reasonable grounds, whether or not to be identified as part of a group. Over time this solution was perceived as more threatening to group-interests than to the sovereign rights of the state. Advocates of group autonomy have become dissatisfied with the implications of this compromise. They came to see it as subversive of communal law and governance, leaving too much to individual preference, which they regard as manipulable by the powerful state. In ensuing years, the issue of who controls entry to and exit from a group—the state? the individual? the group?—has been the focus of severe tension within the rights triad. No other front in the identity wars has seen more intense conflict.

Group rights also featured in the 1930 advisory opinion of the PCIJ regarding *The Greco-Bulgarian 'Communities'*[22] which interpreted a 1919 Convention Between Greece and Bulgaria Respecting Reciprocal Emigration.[23] The agreement had obligated the parties to 'facilitate' the 'right of those of their subjects who belong to racial, religious or linguistic minorities to emigrate freely to their respective territories' and to take with them personal and community property and to receive compensation for immovables.[24] Among the immovables for which 'communities' might seek compensation were churches, schools, convents, hospitals, and cultural foundations.[25]

The treaty thus accorded rights to 'communities' as well as to individuals.[26] As Berman points out, 'the "communities" could not comfortably be assimilated [in law] either to states or to individuals; by forcing a debate on the meaning of such ambiguous intermediate groups, the case implicated the question of the attitude of the new system to non-state "national" identities generally'.[27]

In the Bulgarian view 'communities' were legal fictions. Only individuals could be deemed rights-holders under the treaty. Bulgaria's interpretation thus

---

[19] Judgment no. 12, *supra* n. 17, at 10.    [20] Ibid. at 5.    [21] Ibid. at 46–7.

[22] Advisory Opinion no. 17, *Interpretation of the Convention Between Greece and Bulgaria Respecting Reciprocal Emigration*, 1930 PCIJ (ser. B) no. 17.    [23] 1 LNTS 67 (1919).

[24] Ibid. arts. 6, 7, 10, at 69–71.    [25] Ibid. art. 6, at 69–70.

[26] Berman, *supra* n. 7, at 1844.    [27] Ibid.

excluded property claims by Greek churches and monasteries that were not owned by persons: 'community' property.[28]

The Court rejected this interpretation, recognizing the 'community' as a distinct legal entity, separate from its individual members,[29] and entitled to compensation for concomitant loss of its property.[30] In so holding, the judges carefully balanced recognition of rights accruing to individuals as members of a protected group and the rights of the collective, autonomous entity.

In 1935, the Court revisited these issues in the dispute over *Minority Schools in Albania*.[31] Here, the PCIJ was asked to review a 1933 Albanian law which made primary education in state schools free and compulsory for all nationals and ordered the closing of all private schools.[32] This law was challenged by religious minorities as a breach of their rights granted in a Declaration Albania had made on 2 October 1921, as a condition of membership in the League of Nations. In it, Albania had pledged legal equality for all Albanian nationals and their enjoyment of full civil and political rights, without distinction as to race, language, or religion.[33] It had also promised that 'Albanian nationals who belong to racial, linguistic, or religious minorities, will enjoy the same treatment and security in law and in fact as other Albanian nationals. In particular they shall have an equal right to maintain and control . . . schools and other educational establishments, with the right to use their own language and to exercise their religion freely therein.'[34]

The Albanian Government argued that, since *all* schools had been nationalized, the equality principle had not been violated. The Court rejected this, pointing out that Albania had promised equality of treatment in law and *fact*.[35] 'Equality in law', the opinion states, 'precludes discrimination of any kind; whereas equality in fact may involve the necessity of different treatment in order to attain a result which establishes an equilibrium between different situations.'[36] Institutions such as separate schools 'are indispensable to enable the minority to enjoy the same treatment as the majority, not only in law but also in fact. The abolition of these institutions, which alone can satisfy the special requirements of the minority groups, and their replacement by government institutions, would destroy this equality of treatment, for its effect would be to deprive the minority of the institutions appropriate to its needs, whereas the majority would continue to have them supplied in the institutions created by the State.'[37] In effect, the Court's opinion further confirmed that groups have rights transcending the right to equality of treatment. It proceeds from an assimilationist legal notion of an equal right on the part of minorities to a

---

[28] Advisory Opinion no. 17, *supra* n. 22, at 16.     [29] Ibid. at 21.     [30] Ibid. at 21–3.
[31] Advisory Opinion no. 64, *Minority Schools in Albania*, 1935, PCIJ (ser. A./B.), Fascicule no. 64.
[32] Quoted in Advisory Opinion no. 64, at 13.     [33] Ibid. at 17–18.
[34] Ibid. at 18–19.     [35] Ibid. at 19.     [36] Ibid.
[37] Ibid. at 19–20.

secessionist one of particularist rights that accrue collectively and differentially to a protected group.

It is apparent that these inter-war regimes for the protection of minorities established a system of group rights with the purpose of enabling minorities to elect integrations on the basis of equality but, alternatively, to sustain their collective separateness by permitting individuals to merge their personal identities into autonomous group regimes, with a special rights regime of their own, operating loosely within a larger state *polis*. This compromise sought to empower and balance the integrationist and the secessionist tendencies within the nascent group-rights movement. On the one hand, the new regime emphasized group entitlements. At the same time, the notion of group rights remained generally framed in terms of *individual* rights, albeit rights to which persons became entitled by reason of their membership in a linguistic, ethnic, or religious minority. In this uneasy legal balancing, the protection of a group's integrity was characterized as broadening the associational rights of the *individual* members of a sub-statal community, while the group's collective rights were seen as a voluntary bundling of the members' individual entitlements. It is easy to surmise that this compromise satisfied none of the parties to the new rights triad and certainly not the different tendencies uneasily marching under the banner of group rights.[38]

The precariousness of the balance sought should not detract from the importance of the innovations. Their significance must be understood in the context of the previously predominant Vattelian rules, which had recognized neither group rights nor personal rights. For the preceding three centuries, Vattelian jurisprudence had anointed the state exclusive repository of rights recognized by international law. In the years between 1918 and 1939, groups within states became subjects of various international protective regimes: this at a time when individual rights, although extensively developed within the national legal orders of some liberal democracies, were still little recognized by the international system.

---

[38] It will at once be evident that efforts to balance individualism and communitarianism in the context of group autonomy claims are more likely to succeed when the group is essentially liberal — that is, open-ended, amenable to unimpeded individual entry and exit at will, and nontotalitarian in its internal governance. Professor Kymlicka clarifies this important distinction between liberal groups and those that 'suppress rather than support the liberty of their members' and deny them the most basic of freedoms, including the right to change their identity by renouncing the group affiliation. Kymlicka, *supra* n. 5, at 75. He would readily accord communitarian autonomy to the former, but, as to the latter, his views become precariously balanced, leaving him to argue that in some respects liberal societies should not accommodate illiberal practices of groups under the rubric of self-governance. Ibid. at 94–5. That conclusion, however, places Kymlicka outside the pale of at least the more absolutist communitarians, for he believes that there 'is a genuine conflict here, which we need to face honestly. If we wish to defend individual freedom of conscience, and not just group tolerance, we must reject the communitarian idea that people's ends are fixed and beyond rational revision. We must endorse the traditional liberal belief in personal autonomy'. Ibid. at 163. See also Will Kymlicka & Ian Shapiro, 'Introduction', in *Ethnicity and Group Rights*, 39 *Nomos*, 7 (I. Shapiro & W. Kymlicka eds., 1997).

Despite its audacity, the version of group rights endorsed by various internationally supervised regimes during this period was far from satisfactory either to advocates of group rights or to individualists already beginning to organize under the banner of universal human rights. To individualists, minority status is always a singular attribute, never a collective one. To communitarians, individual rights derive meaning solely from association with the group. By the end of World War II, these tensions became more palpable. What emerged was an intricate rights triad, as tensile and delicate in its ever changing balance as a Calder mobile.

4. THE UNITED NATIONS REGIME OF AUTONOMOUS INDIVIDUAL RIGHTS:
A CHALLENGE TO BOTH GROUPS AND STATES

The post-war changes wrought by the advent of a United Nations human rights system have been detailed in Chapter 8. Primarily, the emphasis was on *individual* rights meant to shield persons against conformist pressures and repressions by both states and groups.

This summary of the United Nations' human rights explosion needs careful calibration. Not all developments in this period have re-enforced individual rights. Some of the gains in group rights made during the inter-war era have been retained and even expanded. For example, the International Covenant on Civil and Political Rights universalizes key provisions of the earlier country-specific minority treaties.[39] Its article 27 says:

In those states in which ethnic, religious or linguistic minorities exist, persons belonging to such minorities shall not be denied the right, in community with other members of their group, to enjoy their own culture, to profess and practice their own religion, or to use their own language.

The regime emerging after 1945 also for the first time extended special conservancy rights to some 'endangered' ethnie. A 1989 ILO Convention on Indigenous and Tribal Peoples[40] provides that 'special measures shall be adopted as appropriate for safeguarding the persons, institutions, property, cultures and environment of [indigenous and tribal peoples]'.[41] A further

---

[39] International Covenant on Civil and Political Rights, 999 UNTS 171, 6 ILM 368 (1967). Adopted by the UN General Assembly on 16 December 1966 (GA Res. 2200, 21 GAOR, Supp. 16, UN Doc. A/6316 at 52). Entered into force on 23 March 1976. [Hereafter ICCPR.]

[40] Convention (no. 169) Concerning Indigenous and Tribal Peoples in Independent Countries. LXXII ILO Off. Bull., Ser. A, no. 2 at 63 (1989). Entered into force 5 Sept. 1991. See also ILO Convention 107 on Indigenous and Tribal Populations (1957).

[41] ILO Convention no. 169, ibid. art. 4.

universal Declaration on the Rights of Indigenous Peoples is currently being drafted by a Working Group of the Human Rights Commission.[42]

Unlike the inter-war regimes that applied to a specified country, these new instruments intend to protect groups everywhere. So, too, did a 1991 Operational Directive of the World Bank, to which reference was made in Chapter 8. It establishes special project review procedures 'where Bank investments affect indigenous peoples, tribes, ethnic minorities, or other groups whose social and economic status restricts their capacity to assert their interests and rights in land and other productive resources'.[43] The object 'is to ensure that the development process fosters full respect for their dignity, human rights, and cultural uniqueness' as well as to 'ensure that indigenous peoples do not suffer adverse effects during the development process, particularly from Bank-financed projects, and that they receive culturally compatible social and economic benefits'.[44] Thus, each proposed lending project's feasibility study must include a 'plan for the development component for indigenous peoples' and its actual implementation by a loan recipient is subject to Bank supervision.[45]

Indigenous peoples are not the only subjects of remedial group rights recently recognized by the international legal system. Article 2(2) of the 1966 Convention on Racial Discrimination provides:[46]

States Parties shall, when the circumstances so warrant, take in the social, cultural and other fields, special and concrete measures to ensure the adequate development and protection of certain racial groups or individuals belonging to them, for the purpose of guaranteeing the full and equal enjoyment of human rights and fundamental freedoms.

This provision purports to make affirmative action applicable when necessary to protect racial minorities and rectify past injustice. It is thus not true that the post-1945 system of international human (individual) rights has been purchased at the expense of group rights.

At the regional level, too, group rights have been adumbrated. The Organization for Security and Co-operation in Europe (OSCE) recently established a High Commissioner on national minorities[47] who, in situations where the rights of minorities may have been violated, acting with the consent of any nine members

---

[42] See E/CN.4/Sub.2/1989/33 (1989); E/CN.4/Sub.2/1994/2/Add 1. See also draft annexed to Res. 1994/45 of 26 Aug. 1994 of the Subcommission on Prevention of Discrimination and Protection of Minorities of the Human Rights Commission; GA Res. 214, UN GAOR, 49th Sess., 94th plen. mtg. at 337, UN Doc. A/RES/49/214 (1994); GA Res. 78, UN GAOR, 51st Sess., 82nd plen. mtg. at 218, UN Doc. A/RES/51/78 (1996).

[43] The World Bank Operational Manual, Operational Directive, Indigenous Peoples, OD 4.20, at 1, Sept. 1991.                                                                [44] Ibid. at 2.

[45] Ibid. at 6. See also Davis & Partridge, *supra* n. 1, which discusses the implementation of these procedures by the Bank to 1994.

[46] Convention on Racial Discrimination, 660 UNTS 195 (1966). Entered into force 4 Jan. 1969.

[47] Document of the Helsinki Meeting of the Conference on Security and Co-operation in Europe, 10 July 1992, reprinted in 13 Hum. Rts. LJ 284, 289 (1992).

of the Organization, is authorized to dispatch a crisis-management mission.[48] This, at least potentially, is a powerful new tool for the defence of groups' interests.[49]

All this demonstrates a continuing interest, after World War II, in regimes and institutions for the protection of groups. Despite these, the principal innovations of the past half-century have been in the legal protection of individual rights. At last, this has brought about international recognition of 'rights of man' that, two centuries earlier, had already been expressed in the constitutions of liberal states.

It was almost inevitable, after 1945, that the global system should embrace the rights of individuals. World War II had occasioned a rethinking about the causes of war. It had become apparent that states which begin with domestic persecution of nonconformists often advance to aggression beyond their borders. This realization, together with a new awareness of nations' interdependence in matters of trade, security, and well-being, has eroded the traditional notions of state sovereignty. Earlier minorities' protection regimes, although selective, went some way to legitimizing intrusive norms and compliance supervision. After 1945, previously sacrosanct state sovereignty became far more permeable, partly as a result of lessons learned in the war and also as a consequence of the many factors that are gathered under the head of 'interdependence'. Part of this new permeability has been used to gain new protections for individuals asserting autonomy against totalizing communitarian pressures.

Inevitably, these myriad innovations, surveyed in Chapter 8, have stirred reaction. As personal rights have taken the spotlight, practitioners of older communitarian values—both the statist and the group-based varieties—have felt challenged by this systemic encouragement of individualism.[50] Some

---

[48] Document of the Moscow Meeting of the Conference on the Human Dimension of the CSCE, 3 Oct. 1991, reprinted in 12 Hum. Rts. LJ 471, 472 (1991).

[49] The High Commissioner's mandate 'is to identify—and seek early resolution of—ethnic tensions that might endanger peace, stability or friendly relations between the participating States of the OSCE . . .: an instrument of conflict prevention at the earliest possible stage'. *OSCE: High Commissioner on National Minorities, Factsheet*, p. 1, 30 June 1998. In mid-1998, his office was engaged in situations involving 11 states (Albania, Croatia, Estonia, Hungary, Kazakhstan, Kyrgyzstan, Latvia, Romania, Slovakia, Macedonia and the Ukraine). He has examined the relations of various governments towards Greek, Russian, Slovak, and Albanian minorities and has conducted OSCE-wide studies regarding the Roma and Sinti people. Ibid. at 1–2. In large part, the High Commissioner's early-warning, advisory and mediating roles are self-starting, although, if action by the OSCE is desired, the support of member states is necessary. The office is precluded from considering individual complaints, which would otherwise put it in competition with the Human Rights Committee of the ICCPR and the European Human Rights Court. While it is briefed to promote minority rights, it is to do so 'within the framework of the state' rather than by 'territorial expression' of 'identity' (ibid. at 4. See also *OSCE Newsletter*, vol. 5, no. 4, April 1998, and earlier numbers reporting on HCNM activities): a discreet way of saying that the Commissioner should not aid secessionist groups.

[50] See Amitai Etzioni, *The New Golden Rule: Community and Morality in a Free Society* (1997). Professor Etzioni is founder and director of the Communitarian Network.

governments, and many communitarians, have expressed their concern that the new international emphasis on personal rights would weaken the social fabric. In Chapter 10 we will explore one recent manifestation of this concern: a spate of recent proposals that the international system codify the *duties* of persons and their *social obligations* in order better to balance and contain recent advances in individual human rights.

It is not only the communitarian society of the traditional state which has feared for the cohesion of its social fabric in an era of burgeoning individualism. Similar concerns have alarmed the smaller, less established cultural, ethnic, and religious groups that see the coddling of individuals and self-expressive freedoms as incompatible with the preservation of their group's particularist norms.

Groups, like the state itself, cite recent normative texts to support their unease. Article 1(3) of the UN Charter, for example, while requiring 'respect for human rights and for fundamental freedoms for all without distinction as to race, sex, language or religion' makes no mention whatever of minority or group rights. Similarly, the Universal Declaration of Human Rights does not deal with community and status-based entitlements. This leads Professor Adeno Addis to conclude that the new rights canon is an example 'of methodological individualism given legal and textual expression'.[51] Moreover, a close reading of article 27 of the ICCPR, which seems to protect 'ethnic, religious or linguistic minorities' only confirms to Addis 'that what is protected is the right of the individual to choose with whom to associate and under what conditions, rather than the rights of the groups . . .'.[52]

In such expressions of concern, one readily identifies a reprise of the issues raised in the inter-war period concerning control over entry into, and exit from, groups. The critics have claimed that, to whatever extent group rights are still the focus of entitlement regimes, it is only open-ended groups, rather than the traditional exclusivist ones that are the beneficiaries. Moreover, it is charged that primarily individuals in groups rather than the groups themselves, are the preferred rights-holders. 'Article 27 of the Covenant', Addis says, 'does not create, as it appears with a first reading, a space for group rights . . . but it reaffirms an important dimension of the individualist project: the individual right to freedom of association. . . . The explicit concern with ethnic minorities as a group here is in fact regarded as a first step towards making group affiliation irrelevant in the treatment of individuals.'[53] His observation reflects group advocates' fear of what they perceive as the assimilationist spirit in which group-protective regimes were instituted in the inter-war period and the outright preference for individual rights manifested by new international regimes

---

[51] Addis, *supra* n. 6, at 637.

[52] Ibid. at 638. This was confirmed by the refusal of the Human Rights Committee to consider a complaint against Canada purporting to be made as an assertion of a collective group right, as opposed to an individual assertion of a right under article 27. See *Lubikon Lake Band v. Canada*, Comm. no. 167/1984, UN Doc. A/45/40, vol. II, at 1 (1990).          [53] Ibid.

after World War II.[54] As if to confirm this suspicion, a recent study of minority protection in post-communist Poland notes that the law now combines 'the principle of non-discrimination (equality before the law) with principles of positive support and protection of individual rights of persons belonging to minorities (positive individual approach) . . .'.[55] Not all groups appreciate such a 'positive individual approach' to their claims.

Some advocates go so far as to charge that the focus on the rights of individuals not only leads to homogenization and the marginalization of their group cultures but actually robs all rights of content. Prevalent notions of human rights, these critics claim, may appear to entitle each person to undifferentiated equality; but the 'ideal of impartiality . . . masks the ways in which the particular perspective of dominant groups claim universality, and helps justify hierarchical decisionmaking structures'.[56] In Professor Will Kymlicka's terms, 'freedom . . . to be pursued for its own sake [is] empty. . . there has to be some project that is worth pursuing, some task that is worth fulfilling. . . . [A] valuable life, for most of us, will be a life filled with commitments and relationships'.[57] To this Adeno Addis adds: 'One cannot have a right as an abstract individual. Rather, one has a right as a member of a particular group and tradition, and within a given context.'[58] Moreover, in the view of radical communitarians, a regime that emphasizes individual rights encourages a 'concept of self that is normatively undesirable'[59] because, in Professor Michael Walzer's words, it 'generates a radical individualism and then a radical competition among self-seeking individuals'.[60] Addis adds that such a regime 'breeds social dislocation and social pathology among members of groups'.[61]

As we have observed, group-rights advocacy does not speak with one voice. Between Kymlicka, Addis, Walzer, and others there are as important disagreements as commonalities. Kymlicka's reservations regarding illiberal, authoritarian groups sets him somewhat apart from Addis and Walzer. So does his opposition, in most cases, to groups' pursuit of sovereignty as opposed to autonomy. Still others prefer that groups pursue their interests through more effective parliamentary representation rather than autonomy.[62]

---

[54] An example is the narrow interpretation of the educational rights provision (art. 2 of the First Protocol to the European Convention on Human Rights) given by the European Court of Human Rights in its opinion in the *Belgian Linguistics Case* of 1968. 6 Eur. Ct. H. Rts. Ser. A, no. 6 (1968). For a discussion see Ian Brownlie, 'The Rights of Peoples in Modern International Law', in James Crawford, ed., *The Rights of Peoples* 1, 3–4 (1988).

[55] Jerzy Kranz, *Law and Practice of Central European Countries in the Field of National Minorities Protection After 1989* 178 (1998).

[56] Iris M. Young, *Justice and the Politics of Difference* 97 (1990).

[57] Will Kymlicka, *Liberalism, Community and Culture* 48–9 (1989).

[58] Addis, *supra* n. 6, at 642.      [59] Ibid.

[60] Michael Walzer, *Radical Principles: Reflections of an Unreconstructed Democrat* 98 (1980).

[61] Addis, *supra* n. 6, at 645.

[62] Iris Marion Young, 'Deferring Group Representation', in *Ethnicity and Group Rights*, 39 *Nomos*, 349, 370–1 (I. Shapiro & W. Kymlicka eds., 1997).

What does appear to bring the different strands of thinking about group rights together, however, is a shared belief in the ineluctable force and authenticity of group identification. Kymlicka argues that group identity is indelible and points to 'the tenacity with which ethno-national groups have fought to maintain their distinct identity, institutions and desire for self-government'. He calls this 'a striking fact of twentieth century history: there are few examples this century of national minorities—that is, national groups who share a state with a larger national group—voluntarily assimilating into the larger society.'[63]

In making this argument for the ineluctable logic of the group, Kymlicka carefully distinguishes conquered minority groups—Indians, French Canadians, Puerto Ricans—from immigrant groups that left their homelands to settle in other states. For the latter, he concedes, assimilation and individuation is the natural route to emancipation.[64] Except for such special cases, however, he believes 'there are virtually no cases of national minorities accepting assimilation. If we focus on territorial nations, rather than immigrants, [group] nationalism has been a constant factor of twentieth century history.'[65] He claims that the 'cosmopolitanism' espoused by 'eighteenth-century Enlightenment theorists, nineteenth-century socialists and twentieth-century modernization theorists . . . has been decisively disproved in our age of [group] nationalism'.[66]

Against this it could be argued that a huge preponderance of the conquered indigenous population of America (and, probably, elsewhere) has already been assimilated and has joined the general gene pool through intermarriage: that what remains of a distinct native population is not so very different from immigrant groups which, for economic and cultural reasons, remain outside the integrating mainstream in inner cities and certain rural areas. Of course, this conquest occurred before the twentieth century, to which the application of the theory is confined. Kymlicka's argument, in any case, seems less descriptive than prescriptive. He argues that all cosmopolitan notions of individuation, personal self-determination, and autonomous construction of one's identity are illusory because for 'meaningful individual choice to be possible, individuals need not only access to information, the capacity to reflectively evaluate it, and freedom of expression and association. They also need access to a societal culture'.[67] He does not explain, however, why this need for 'societal culture' should tie any group to its historic identity when new choices become available.

Evidently, however, what some welcome as individual freedom of choice and emancipation from imposed loyalties is considered by others as an unrealistic, ahistorical chimera. Some abhor it because they believe such freedom presages the destruction of 'the framework within which choices can be made' and as imposed assimilation, which 'is nothing but one form of totalizing, in that it is

---

[63] Will Kymlicka, *Reading* from 'Human Rights and Ethnocultural Justice,' in *Review of Constitutional Studies* 3, draft, September 1997 (forthcoming).                    [64] Ibid. at 3–4.
[65] Ibid. at 4.        [66] Ibid. at 6.        [67] Ibid. at 9.

out to destroy the possibility of counter-narratives and, hence, the possibility of challenge and change'.[68] Thus, individualism, which, from one perspective, is an invitation to every person to constitute a selected self-definition in multi-layered affinities with persons chosen from among an infinite variety of 'others', can also be castigated as a siren call inviting persons to abandon their historically, ethnically and culturally validated identity: a poisoned invitation to join the omnivorous mass culture of an undifferentiated, homogenized majority.

What some deplore, however, is clearer than what they want. Addis deplores the 'insularity and parochialism implied by local communitarianism' just as much as 'the totalizing tendency of national communitarianism . . .'. In his view, 'ethnic minorities do not clearly see themselves as part of the 'we' the national communitarians embrace. Nor are they any more secure with the possibility of numerous insular and exclusionary communities proliferating at the local level. In sum, communitarianism [of both kinds] does not offer very much hope for minorities.'[69] But, then, what does? And how are the norms of group autonomy and cohesion to be reconciled with the requisites of a modern liberal democracy and of the recent human rights canon?[70] There is much conceptual work left to do, before the group-rights movement becomes a coherent and effective emanation of the new *Zeitgeist*.

## 5. THE ZEITGEIST AND THE NEW TRIAD

Whatever one makes of these radically different perspectives, it is important to locate their origins in the several recent *Zeitgeisten*. As we have seen, after 1919, the world's conscience was pricked by 'nationalities' that, for practical geopolitical or demographic reasons had been denied the promised land of self-determination. To compensate, various minorities, on receiving nation-statehood at Versailles and becoming masters in their own houses, were required to grant group rights to the new minorities in their midst. Germans benefited from these regimes in Poland, Hungarians in Czecho-Slovakia and Romania, Albanians and Slovenes in Yugoslavia. For these and other minorities, failure to achieve statehood was compensated by an internationally imposed and monitored group-rights regime. That *Zeitgeist* was overtaken by the new reality behind the Munich settlement, the repudiation of mere guarantees of minority rights in favour of the idea that Germans in another state had a *right* to become German by territorial cession. In Hitler's brief but terrible world, genetic solidarity trumped all else. The individual was meaningless except in solidarity with a people, and peoples' rights were the only real form of human rights.

---

[68] Addis, *supra* n. 6, at 645.     [69] Ibid. at 646–7.

[70] See e.g. Leslie Green, 'Internal Minorities and Their Rights', in Judith Baker, ed., *Group Rights* 101 (1994).

After Hitler's fall came the new wave of internationally guaranteed and monitored rules and institutions intended to protect the rights of individual expression and choice that nationalist demagogues had repressed. Inevitably, there was a strong reaction against the racist nationalisms of Germany, Italy, and Japan, and an emphasis on protecting the individual against any recurrence of pseudo-genetic politics. Only the communist version of social solidarity still lingered as an organizing ideology—of course there were still plenty of opportunistic tin-pot dictators around—to contest the progress of individualism and the new international regime of human rights.

This wave of post-war revulsion against politicization of race, nation, and tribe seems now to have ebbed. Fifty years on, just as effective international protection of individual rights is beginning to be realized, a new wave of claims has begun to break, introducing a different rights-discourse to a new *Zeitgeist*.[71] The post-1986 collapse of illiberal, totalitarian, and corrupt states, whether in Eastern Europe, Asia, or Africa, has led to a revival of interest in group-identity. In part this is another backlash, reflecting widespread popular disenchantment with the state in those places—there are many—where it has failed to meet basic human needs and expectations. This is compounded by feelings that many decisions of great importance to individuals are made at great distance from those whose lives they affect. Some of the disenchanted have turned to rabid capitalism, to be ruled by its invisible hand. Others reverted to the more proximate structures offered by long-repressed, more local tribal, religious, ethnic and cultural mores, beliefs and structures. In the search for new forms of order and stability, many rediscovered the older, nearer frameworks of half-forgotten group identity.

This most recent turn of the *Zeitgeist* has opened the way for new claims by advocates of group autonomy. What its advocates claim, today, is not the assimilationist, essentially egalitarian kind of minority rights invented for the inter-war period, but self-rule, with a promise of a permanent defence against loss of separateness.[72] They want, more or less, what, in 1938, the Sudeten Germans wanted (or were *said* by Hitler to want).[73]

Predominantly, group-rights advocacy today no longer seeks to protect and empower individuals who share a minority identity, but to promote the autonomy of groups that become the unique and exclusive expression of its members' collective identity.[74] This version of group rights challenges not only the

[71] See e.g. Larry Catá Backer, 'Harmonization, Subsidiarity and Cultural Difference: An Essay on the Dynamics of Opposition Within Federative and International Legal Systems', 4 U. Tulsa J. Comp. and Int'l L. 185 (1997).

[72] The subject is extensively canvassed in *Ethnicity and Group Rights*, 39 *Nomos* (Ian Shapiro & Will Kymlicka eds., 1997).

[73] See Nathaniel Berman, 'Beyond Colonialism and Nationalism? Ethiopia, Czechoslovakia and "Peaceful Change",' 65 Nordic LJ 421, 437–45 (1996).

[74] Graham Walker, 'The Idea of Nonliberal Constitutionalism', in *Ethnicity and Group Rights*, *supra* n. 72, at 154, esp. 162–5.

Vattelian supremacy of the state but also the post-1945 emphasis on individuality. In place of personal liberty, it imagines a non-liberal constitutionalism[75] that may bar exit and that sanctions intra-group inequalities. These inequalities are rooted in group values—for example, between men and women, between members and strangers—that are hard to reconcile with liberal democracy. Instead of personal freedom, these groups emphasize mandatory social cohesion, a political vision that is not necessarily democratic, and a particularist socio-political agenda.[76] Some North American Indian tribes seem to be moving towards a kind of communitarian self-definition that demands realization through illiberal political autonomy or independence.[77]

Kymlicka and others argue that most group-based versions of communitarianism are not infected with the xenophobia, paranoia, and superiority of the sort that characterized Nazi, Fascist, and Japanese Shinto romantic mythology.[78] They are undoubtedly correct in pointing out that many contemporary group-rights claimants intend to coexist peacefully with liberal and democratic concepts of human identity.[79]

But most demand to do so separately, on their own terms. Thus, the end of the twentieth century finds all three parts of the rights triad tautly balanced in vigorously adversary rival self-assertions. For the first time in history, it has become necessary to examine simultaneously three kinds of powerful and competing rights claimants. Moreover, we need to keep revising our notions of each claimant's identity. For example, claims of state sovereignty may now be advanced by interstatal authorities such as the Commission of the European Union, while group claims may now be advanced not only by revived tribes or religious groups but also by what Professor Iris Young characterizes as 'the claims of new group-based social movements associated with left-politics—such movements as feminism, Black liberation . . . and gay and lesbian liberation'.[80] Transnational corporations are also manoeuvring for recognition as autonomous rights-holders: resembling, in part, the state, the group, and even the fictive person.

International law is only now beginning to think about the appropriate balance between the claims of the state, the individual, and the revived traditional and new groups. What sort of future world do we want, what sort of governance should it have, and who or what will exercise power in it? In

---

[75] Walker, ibid. at 169.

[76] Ibid. at 176. '[T]he unequal protection of the laws is an established part of Indian tribal policy.'

[77] See e.g. the treaty for extensive self-government in an area of 750 square miles of British Columbia, Canada, approved in 1998 by the Nisga'a tribe in the remote Nass Valley near Alaska. NY Times, 11 Nov. 1998, at A8.

[78] See e.g. the circumspect version of group rights espoused in Thomas Pogge, 'Group Rights and Ethnicity', in *Ethnicity and Group Rights, supra* n. 72, at 187.

[79] Chandran Kukathas, 'Cultural Toleration', in *Ethnicity and Group Rights*, ibid. at 69.

[80] Young, *supra* n. 62, at 3.

accordance with what kind of political process are claims to rights and goods to be reconciled and configured? We have barely begun to examine such problems and opportunities, standing as we now do at the cusp of a global triage that will fix our identities in the third millennium.

### 6. GROUP-RIGHTS CLAIMANTS AND INDIVIDUALISTS: THE CONTRAST

There are efforts underway to fill that conceptual hiatus. The 'group-rights' perspective of Indian tribes and 'many nonwesterners' is described by Professor Robert Clinton, thus:

Deriving their legal vision from their tribal associations, tribal traditions, and the natural ecology. . . . native peoples see humans as inherently social beings . . . born into a closely linked and integrated network of family, kinship, social and political relations. One's clan, kinship and family identities are part of one's personal identity and one's rights and responsibilities exist only *within* the framework of such familial, social, and tribal networks. [They], therefore, naturally think of their rights as part of a group. Certain rights exist within each social group and other rights and responsibilities are attendant to their relations with members of other groups within the web of associations that forms the tribe or the state. For them, the tribe or state is merely composed of interlinked group associations and affiliations. . . . Thus, an individual's right to autonomy is not a right *against* organized society, as it is in western thought, but a right one has *because* of one's membership in the family, kinship and associational webs of the society.

While Clinton reports that 'individual rights are unthinkable except in contemplation of how those rights relate to the larger political group . . .' he nevertheless asserts that this 'conception of rights tends to provide [persons with] a richer, more realistic perspective . . .'.[81]

There is much similarity between this claim on behalf of group-communitarianism and that advanced by Professor Sandel (see Chapter 5, above) on behalf of the state's civic republican virtues. Although espousing different demographic units within which communitarian values should be paramount, their respective claims resemble each other in implacable opposition to the recent trend towards individualism.

Individualists perceive both these communitarianisms, despite their differences, as posing similar threats to the cause of personal autonomy. While the one seeks to confine the rights of individuals in the name of the state or 'society', the other would do so to preserve the integrity of a minority, group, or tribe. In the end, however, individualists have the same problem with both, because each seems determined to preserve by law the supremacy of traditional kinds of human affiliation. The community of the future foreseen by the individualist is

[81] Robert N. Clinton, 'The Rights of Indigenous Peoples as Collective Group Rights', 32 Ariz. L. Rev. 739, 742 (1990).

composed of persons voluntarily associated in mutual responsibility and common endeavours by a sense of shared or overlapping self-interest and values. That sense of community, with its absence of control over individual entry or exit and its ready acceptance of the idea of multiple layers of individually chosen affiliation, has little in common with the communitarian values of either the state or the group.

As noted in Chapter 5, most champions of individual rights do not oppose the ideal of community, of shared affiliative ventures and responsibilities. On the contrary, they are usually loyal citizens, albeit sometimes of more than one state; they often regard themselves as practising members of religious and ethnic groups, even if they reserve the right to change churches or reject some teachings and practices; they make personal commitments to local and transnational commercial, cultural, or social enterprises; and they participate actively in civic institutions and civil society. They differ from committed communitarians, however, in being affiliated contingently, by personal choice, and, often, with multiple demoi. They define themselves by associations they have personally chosen and feel free to change. While they may, at times, support causes of the state and the group, they see all loyalties primarily as something to be bestowed or rescinded freely and for cause. It was as a manifestation of this that the right to emigrate became so crucial an international human rights claim in the 1980s, pressed in spontaneous unison by persons all over the world on behalf of individual dissidents denied exit from the Soviet Union or China.[82] It is this same ethos that leads the individualist to oppose, on principle, group, national, or international censorship of literature, art, or the internet.

The individualist's concept of human rights is not anti-associational: rarely is it anarchic. It is described, but also circumscribed, by the international rights regime developed after 1945. Although this regime accords extensive rights to individuals, it does not seek to recreate 'man in the state of nature' as some communitarians fear.[83] Rather, for the four decades following the Second World War, it seemed to represent a balanced global consensus that also reserves extensive rights to states, including the right to suspend some personal rights in emergencies or for urgent cause.[84] It has also allotted special rights to groups, to enable those who so choose to satisfy their need for a more intense and local form of community. However, that consensus is now being challenged and the balance could be upset by newly militant communitarianisms.

---

[82] This 'right of exit' is discussed by Prof. L. Green, *supra* n. 70, at 108–12.
[83] See e.g. Clinton, *supra* n. 81, at 740.
[84] For example, see articles 15(2), 18(3), 19(30), 20, 21, 22(2) of the ICCPR, *supra* n. 39.

7. PRINCIPLES AND FULCRUMS: REACHING TRIADIAL BALANCE

Except among the most extreme advocates, it is widely accepted that the claims of individuals, groups, and states must coexist in a kind of balance. Thus, for example, reasonable persons would tend to agree that, at a minimum, each of the three categories of rights claimants should be able to enjoy rights that are essential to its survival. Let us call this point of agreement the *survival principle.*

Of course, the devil is in the details. For example, what constitutes 'survival'? A *person* may feel his or her survival threatened when denied some important liberty, even though he or she is in no actual, physical danger. Can survival of a person only be threatened by an actual deprivation of life, or also by severe constraints on liberty and pursuit of happiness? A *group* may feel the survival principle violated by the public education of its children, by mandatory vaccination, or by the corrosive social influence of television. Can a group's survival be said to be threatened by the unimpeded encroachment of popular culture or only by a forthright policy of extermination? To a *state*, survival may seem threatened by large rallies in opposition to the government's foreign policy, by press exposure of secret official memoranda, or by individuals' giving aid and comfort to a hostile foreign government. Does it matter whether this giving of aid and comfort takes the form of mere words, the dispatch of medical supplies, or the conveyance of classified defence information? Or can a state's survival be said to be threatened only by more drastic threats to its existence, such as terrorist attacks or popular insurrections?

Inevitably, left to their own devices, individuals, groups, and states are likely to define the requisites of their survival so broadly as to ensure conflict with the broadly defined survival requisites of the other parts of the triad. Yet, none of the triad's three components are likely to accept an interpretation of the survival principle that protects only their mere physical existence. Thus, conflicts arise less from abstract efforts to define a universal principle than from the way non-negotiable rights are asserted in a particular dispute.

Take the example of Afghan women, since 1997 denied all access to education in accordance with the strict theology of Afghanistan's Taliban rulers. Some of these women argue that, in the twenty-first century, a person denied education is robbed of her defining humanity. The Taliban rulers, on the other hand, reply that women, separated from all public obligation, have been freed to focus on the home and family. This freedom, they claim, is the cornerstone of the Islamic Afghan nation and they point scornfully to the degradation of women in other societies through pornography, prostitution, and other forms of exploitation.

Such profoundly irreconcilable survival claims have at various times and places been addressed by local option, assisted exodus or by the subordination of particularism.

## (a) Local Option

A big helping of local autonomy has sometimes mitigated the effects of culture-clash. Thus, within the Ottoman Empire, Christian Orthodox, Jewish, and Armenian millets were pacified by exemption from many Ottoman laws and practices.[85] In the United States, the Supreme Court has sustained a right of Indian tribes to a form of sovereign immunity against civil suit, subject only to limitations specified by federal legislation.[86]

Such pragmatic compromises, with elements of quasi-secession spliced onto a policy of continued integration, are more evidently applicable to groups living within a fixed area. Where they are not, group autonomy is harder to reconcile with the dominant liberal precepts of the state. Nevertheless, it may still be possible to separate control over some substantive areas of law along group lines, departing in agreed circumstances from the liberal principle of strict equality before the law. In practice, a state's general law pertaining to citizens' education, culture, welfare, land-law, matrimonial law, and religion could exempt persons in accordance with their group affiliations, regardless of their place of domicile.[87]

There are important precedents. Austro-Hungarian Social Democrats, before the First World War, proposed a reorganization of the empire on the basis of a non-territorial autonomy for its various nationalities. Members of each ethnie, whether living in Vienna, Budapest, Prague, or elsewhere, were to elect their own governing bodies empowered to regulate group social and cultural life. Matters affecting more than one group were to be governed by common institutions.[88] The idea continues to have currency in thinking about sovereignty and autonomy. For example, Professor Ruth Lapidoth, in a recent study, distinguishes this 'personal (or cultural) autonomy' from the better-known concept of 'territorial autonomy'.[89] She cites, as a recent example, the 1991 minorities law that grants a degree of personal autonomy to members of Latvia's Russian minority.[90] In Kenya, a person's religion may determine the applicable law of marriage, divorce, and testamentary succession.[91] Elsewhere,

---

[85] Ruth Lapidoth, *Autonomy: Flexible Solutions to Ethnic Conflicts* 37 (1997); Kemal Karpat, 'The Ottoman Ethnic and Confessional Legacy in the Middle East,' in *Ethnicity, Pluralism and the State in the Middle East* 35–53 (Milton J. Esman & Itamar Rabinovich eds., 1988); Hurst Hannum, *Autonomy, Sovereignty, and Self-Determination: The Accommodation of Conflicting Rights* 308–27 (rev. edn., 1996).

[86] *Kiowa Tribe of Oklahoma v. Manufacturing Technologies, Inc.*, 118 S.Ct. 1700 (1998).

[87] See R. Bartlett, *Subjugation, Self-Management, and Self-Government of Aboriginal Lands and Resources in Canada* (1986).

[88] Otto Bauer, 'Die Nationalitätenfrage und die Sozialdemokratie', in 1 *Werksausgabe* 325–6 (Manfred Ackermann et al. eds., 1975).           [89] Lapidoth, *supra* n. 85, at 37–40.

[90] 'Law on the Unrestricted Development and Right to Cultural Autonomy of Latvia's Nationalities and Ethnic Groups', cited in Lapidoth, ibid. at 38 n. 8.

[91] See e.g. *Mohd. Ahmed Khan v. Shah Bano Begum and Ors.*, S.Ct. India, (1985) 3 SCR 844 in which the secular Indian Supreme Court interprets Muslim divorce law. See also *Ephraim v. Pastory and Kaizilege*, High Court of Tanzania, (1990) 87 ILR 106 in which the court seeks to reconcile Haya tribal customary law with the Bill of Rights and Universal Declaration of Human Rights incorporated in the national constitution.

that which is forbidden may be selectively permitted to a specified group. Many countries permit native populations, but no one else, to engage in hunting and fishing for endangered or spawning species.[92] In the United States, the Supreme Court has upheld the right of Chippewa Indians to continue enjoying special usufructuary hunting, fishing, and gathering rights within the terms of an 1837 treaty made by the federal government with the tribe.[93]

In theory, the Sudan is governed by a similar system granting exemption from Islamicist laws and practices to the Christian and animist Southern regions.[94] In India, various religious communities enjoy large measures of autonomy over matters of most direct interest to them. For example, the crime of bigamy under India's penal code is not committed if the accused husband belongs to a religion or caste 'in which a second marriage is allowed'.[95] Muslim bigamy has been held to be protected, whereas Hindu bigamy is a punishable offence.[96] Marriage law is not the only example. Sikhs are constitutionally entitled to carry Kirpans (short daggers), a right not granted others.[97]

The Hungarian–Romanian basic treaty of September 1996 pledges to promote cultural and local autonomy for ethnic Hungarians of Transylvania in accordance with European standards.[98] In other recent developments, native Indian tribes in Canada[99] and aboriginal peoples of Australia[100] have moved towards accommodations on land title and other matters which grant them a high degree of group-autonomy. The survival principle's local option is further echoed in Canada's new Charter of Rights and Freedoms, which protects minority-language rights (section 23), Aboriginal rights (sections 25 and 35) and affirms multiculturalism.[101] Particularly precedent-setting is the agreement

---

[92] In Canada, Indians are normally not charged with game or fish law violations as long as they are hunting for subsistence or ceremonial reasons. T. Claridge, 'Ruling on Game Rights Upheld,' Tor. Globe & Mail, 10 Aug. 1996, at A5. Sec. 13 of the International Whaling Commission's Schedule, as amended at its annual meeting in July 1983, allows member governments to contract with any of its nationals for special permit to kill, take and treat whales for 'aboriginal subsistence whaling,' a provision used by the US to establish a limited quota for Alaskan Eskimo bowhead whale hunting. See Patricia W. Birnie, 'International Legal Issues in the Management and Protection of the Whale: A Review of Four Decades of Experience', 29 Nat. Resources J. 903, 929–30 (1989); International Convention for the Regulation of Whaling, 2 Dec. 1946, 62 Stat. 1716, TIAS no. 1849, 161 UNTS 72.

[93] *Minnesota et al. v. Mille Lac Band of Chippewa Indians et al.*, decided by the US Supreme Court 24 March 1999, 1999 WL 155689 (US Minn.).          [94] Hannum, *supra* n. 85, at 317–23.

[95] N.D. Basu's *Indian Penal Code*, S.494, p. 1221 (7th edn., Bose & Bose eds., 1986).

[96] *The State of Bombay v. Narasu Appa*, AIR (Bombay) 84 (1952).

[97] Constitution of India, Art. 25(1), Explanation I. See also Marc Gallanter, *Law and Society in Modern India* 103–40 (1989).          [98] 4 Human Rights Brief, no. 3, 4–5 (1997).

[99] Treaty between British Columbia and the Nisga's Nation, Final Treaty Agreement, 4 Aug. 1998. International Law: In Brief, 24–8 Aug. 1998. The Canadian Supreme Court's 1998 decision in *Delgamuukw v. British Columbia*, 37 ILM 261, is only the most recent of the land disputes being addressed by courts and parliaments in Canada.

[100] *Mabou v. State of Queensland*, (1988), 83 ALR 14.

[101] The change in law was supported by the Canadian Indian Congress, although not by several more traditional bands. See 'Move to Deny Women Status Dismissed by Supreme Court', Tor. Globe & Mail, 2 Dec. 1997, at D8.

between Canada and its Inuit population to create an autonomous Nunavut region.[102] In addition, the government has enacted measures to assist minorities to sustain their heritage through a Cultural Development Programme that subsidizes and helps groups preserve their native skills and traditions.[103]

## (b) Assisted Exodus

In the World Court's 1930 advisory opinion on the *Convention Between Greece and Bulgaria Respecting Reciprocal Emigration*, arranged exodus was regarded as admirably humane.[104] Large-scale population exchanges between Greece and Bulgaria avoided a potentially lethal clash between irreconcilable survival claims. Today, however, that sort of solution is tarred with the brush of 'ethnic cleansing' and has been characterized by the UN as a 'threat to the peace'.[105] In a particularly vulgar recent reprise, Slovakia's then-Prime Minister Vladimir Meciar, during a dinner honouring his visit to Budapest, offered Hungarian Prime Minister Gyula Horn 600,000 Slovaks of Hungarian origin in exchange for the ethnic Slovak population of Hungary.[106] Such an approach to the survival principle tends to shade into genocide, an extreme violation of basic international treaty and customary law.[107]

## (c) The Priority of Universal Norms

Mass emigration and local autonomy may not be feasible options in some instances. Neither, for example, could ameliorate the plight of Afghan women who decry their subordination. In some circumstances, the survival principle requires choice between irreconcilable claims. The international system of human rights described in Chapter 8, reserves to itself residual authority to referee such disputes in accordance with its common norms and procedures. Thus, for example, the ICCPR obliges of all states 'to ensure the equal rights of men and women . . .'.[108] It trumps, in its universality, the more general survival

---

[102] B. Laghi, 'Nunavut Vote to be Moved Up', Tor. Globe & Mail, 23 Mar. 1998, at A3.

[103] Torres, *infra* n. 118, at 135. For Australian application of its *Heritage Protection Act*, 1984, see *Kartinyeri v. The Commonwealth* [1998] HCA 22 (1 April 1998).          [104] See n. 22, above.

[105] SC Res. 688 (1991). See Douglas L. Donoho, 'Evolution or Expediency: The United Nations Response to the Disruption of Democracy', 29 Cornell Int'l LJ 329, 361–4 (1996).

[106] NY Times, 12 Oct. 1997, at 3.

[107] International Criminal Tribunal for Rwanda, Chamber I, *The Prosecutor v. Jean-Paul Akayesu*, Case no. ICTR-96-4-T, Judgment, 2 Sept. 1998, p. 95.

[108] ICCPR, *supra* n. 39, art. 3. As to racism, see also International Convention on the Elimination of All Forms of Racial Discrimination, 660 UNTS 195; adopted by the UN General Assembly on 21 Dec. 1965. Reprinted in 5 ILM 352, 1966. Entered into force 4 Jan. 1969 (Racial Convention). It has been ratified by more states than any other human rights treaty with the exception of one Geneva Convention on the laws of war. Theodor Meron, 'The Meaning and Reach of the International Convention on the Elimination of All Forms of Racial Discrimination', 79 Am. J. Int'l L. 283, 284 (1985).

claims advanced by any part of the rights triad. In the instance of Afghanistan, such trumping favours the rights of women over the particularism of Taliban theology and justifies the global community's pressure to compel the Taliban's compliance with globally ratified standards.

The Taliban is not the first power-elite to enforce a religiously imbued vision of domination. The same tactic was used by whites in South Africa, where the Afrikaans population used an extreme formulation of Dutch Reformed Calvinist predestinarianism to justify forcing non-whites into the biblically prescribed role of 'hewers of wood and drawers of water'.[109] This oppression of Africans through apartheid eventually encountered, and was forced to yield to, the global insistence that racism constitutes a violation of common human rights norms and a threat to world peace. In 1974, the UN General Assembly refused to seat South Africa's white delegates on the ground that they did not represent the population.[110] Five years later, the Security Council, acting under chapter 7 of the Charter, imposed a mandatory embargo on arms transfers[111] and, in 1985, successfully urged states to suspend all further investments in the country.[112] Similar action was taken after Rhodesia's racists made their Unilateral Declaration of Independence.[113] The UN's strong measures against these racist and apartheid regimes are important precedents for similar concerted trumping by the international system of claims by any part of the rights triad, whenever such claims lead to violation of universal norms of human rights protection.

It often turns out that oppressive practices defended by a state or group as essential to its survival are no more than the self-interested preferences of its current power-elite. Sandra Lovelace, a Canadian Indian, complained to the ICCPR's Human Rights Committee[114] that, having 'married out' of her tribe, the Maliseet of New Brunswick, tribal law, enforced as Canadian law,[115] had deprived her of the right to live on tribal land. Although this practice was defended as essential to the tribe's survival, the Committee found it trumped by the Covenant's universal rules.[116] It also noted that no similar exclusionary practices operated against men who chose to marry outside the tribe.

Thus prodded by the quasi-judicial body charged with interpreting the applicable international norms, the Canadian Government repealed most of

---

[109] Joshua 9: 21.
[110] UN GAOR, 29th Sess., 2281st mtg., 12 Nov. 1974, agenda item 3, Report of the Credentials Committee.                                                                                    [111] S. Res. 418 (1977).
[112] S. Res. 566 (1985) and S. Res. 569 (1985).           [113] S. Res. 232 (1966).
[114] Communication R.6/24. *Lovelace v. Canada*, 36 UN GAOR Supp. no. 40, Annex XVIII, Doc. A/36/40 (1981).
[115] Canadian Indian Act, Rev. Stats. Can., 1985 ch. I-5, § 5–6. See, also, D. Hawley, *The Annotated 1990 Indian Act.*
[116] Views of the Human Rights Committee under Article 5(4) of the Optional Protocol to the ICCPR, Case Submitted by Sandra Lovelace, UN GAOR, 36th Sess., Supp. no. 40, at 166, UN Doc.A/36/40 (1981) (annex 18).

the sexually discriminatory provisions of its Indian Act.[117] It turned out to be possible to do this with the consent of representative Indian institutions. Thereupon, 133,000 persons applied for reinstatement in their tribes. While the imposed changes caused great bitterness among some Indian traditionalists,[118] their insistence on discrimination against women as necessary to the tribe's cultural survival did not, in the event, represent evolving Indian views of the group's own traditions, nor was it justified by the facts pertaining to demographic survival.[119] Rather, the overruling of discriminatory practices regarding women succeeded in releasing the group's pent-up capacity for creative change and authenticity.

Similarly, once international pressure had forced the South African regime to abandon apartheid as a cornerstone of white survivalism, the emergence of a multiracial society has been embraced with astonishing vigour by all but diehards. A corresponding shift in public opinion was evident in the southern segregated states of the US once legally mandated segregation was repealed. Who, then, is to say that the men and women of Afghanistan truly believe that their society's survival depends upon the sort of aberrational confinement of women that almost all other societies, with varying vehemence, find unacceptable. At a minimum, any claim that survival depends on gross violations of universally accepted norms warrants closest scrutiny.

But scrutiny by whom?

A dynamic tension exists today between the interests of the group, the state, and the individual. For the most part, this tension leads to discourse and mutual accommodation. Where it does not—as in the case of the Taliban of Afghanistan or the Apartheid regime of South Africa—the international system may have recourse to measures of persuasion that range from ostracism to the use of force.[120]

---

[117] Bill C-3 (1985) (amending the Indian Act). John Borrows, 'Contemporary Traditional Equality: The Effect of the Charter on First Nation Politics', 43 UNBLJ 31–4 (1994). The ICCPR has continued to criticize Canada, however, for the failure of the 1985 legislation to extend status rights to subsequent generations of women, still denied membership in the community by an ancestor's marrying out. ICCPR, Consideration of reports submitted by State parties under article 40 of the Covenant. Concluding observations of the Human Rights Committee. Canada. CCPR/C/79/Add.105, 7 Apr. 1999.

[118] Borrows, ibid. at 35–6; Raidza Torres, 'The Rights of Indigenous Populations: the Emerging International Norm', 16 Yale J. Int'l L. 127, 135 (1991).

[119] Some Indian law authorities insist that gender discrimination in Indian law and custom is not native but imposed by the laws of the colonial 'oppressors.' Borrows, ibid. at 19.

[120] For example, on 4 Nov. 1991, the Peace Conference on Yugoslavia, chaired by Lord Carrington, constituted 27 Aug. 1991, EPC Joint Statement of 27 Aug. 1991, EC Bull, 1991/7–8, at 115–16, precisely detailed the human rights guarantees the new states emerging from the former Yugoslav Socialist Federal Republic would have to accept and the ways in which their compliance would be monitored. See Report of the Secretary-General Pursuant to Paragraph 3 of Security Council Resolution 713 (1991), UN Doc. S/23169, 1991, at 20 (Annex II). They were required to accede to relevant international and regional human rights treaties and to enact guarantees both for individuals and for the new minorities within their borders. EPC Joint Statement of 16 Dec. 1991; EC Bull. 1991/12, at 119–20. With varying degrees of enthusiasm, Slovenia, Croatia, Macedonia and Bosnia-Herzegovina all accepted these internationally mandated terms. Arbitration (Badinter) Commission, Avis nos. 6 and 7, 31 ILM 1992, at 1512 and 1507.

Many times, fortunately, adjudication helps prevent outright confrontation, although such increasing recourse to international legal institutions offends the *amour propre* of some watchdogs of state sovereignty and may also arouse the ire of group rights purists, who regard such forums as 'culturally biased'[121] and likely to superimpose 'outside' standards on the practices by which the group defines and governs itself.[122]

## 8. MORAL PRIORITY OF INDIVIDUAL RIGHTS

To acknowledge the need for balance and accommodation among the triad of rights holders—the state, the individual, and the group—is not quite the same as recognizing the equivalence of the three claimants. Morally, the claims of individuals are entitled to priority. In the words of Neil MacCormick, 'individual human beings are the primary bearers of moral value and of moral and legal rights'.[123]

Of the three components of the rights triad, only the person has a natural right to be.[124] In Professor Mulholland's terms, the 'status of a person is a right that cannot be derived from any higher moral principle, and is at least presupposed in any enumeration of rights'.[125] In this sense, personal autonomy claims are different in kind from the rights-based claims of groups and of states. Both the latter are non-inherent historico-social constructs. They are validated only derivatively by persons' identification with, and recognition of, their existence. In contrast, a person's rights are implicit and inherent in the objective fact of being.[126]

To put it another way: there are acquired rights and unacquired rights. States, groups, and individuals each may be holders of acquired rights, but only persons can also have unacquired rights.[127] 'An acquired right', Mulholland explains, 'is a right that is transferrable because the object of the right is transferrable. An unacquired right is not transferrable and pertains to the bearer unconditionally, i.e. without some external condition (such as transference) having to be met.'[128] The right to a retirement pension is an example of the former, but the right to life is an example of the latter. In simpler terms, the distinction between a community—whether it be a state or an historic group—and an individual person is that the former is a thing or construct, while the latter is not. The person, in Kantian terms, is an 'end in itself'.[129] A community can be disas-

---

[121] Will Kymlicka, 'Individual and Community Rights', in *Group Rights* 17, 19–20 (J. Baker ed., 1994).                                                        [122] Addis *supra* n. 6, at 664.
[123] Neil MacCormick, *Legal Right and Social Democracy* 247 (1982).
[124] Leslie A. Mulholland, 'The Innate Right to be a Person,' in *Ethics and Basic Rights* 131 (Guy LaFrance ed., 1989).                                      [125] Ibid. at 131.
[126] For a discussion of personhood as the basis for moral entitlements see Bernard Williams, *Problems of the Self*, esp. 230–49 (1973).                       [127] Mulholland, *supra* n. 124, at 131.
[128] Ibid.
[129] Immanual Kant, *Foundations of the Metaphysics of Morals* 46 (L. W. Beck trans., 1969).

sembled, scattered, and its component members will survive, as did the biblical Jews and contemporary Armenians. A person, disassembled, cannot remain a person and a person's scattered members will die.

Still another way to put this is that a person's moral claim to rights derives from original, autonomous personage and not from the sorts of contingent external events that shape the rights claims of such entities as the state, society, or tribe.[130] The rights of individuals in this sense may be said to have a natural or moral priority over the rights of a group or a nation, which is also to say that personal rights, in structural terms, have an irreducible (that is, irrefutable) functional utility and, in moral terms, claim an absolute value. The international system, while usually promoting equilibrium and accommodation, may also take account of this moral intuition.

Of course, persons tend to develop and to realize their desires in association and community; and in that secondary, or derivative, sense the various forms of human society—the nation, the tribe or ethnie, etc.—are also 'natural' manifestations of individuals' irrepressible associational drive. But, lexically, it is the individual who constitutes society. The group, nation, and state do not constitute the individual, except in the literature of romantic nationalism. This distinction makes slavery a violation of a basic natural or moral right, whereas anarchy is merely a failure of associational virtue. Or, to take another example, the state's taking of a person's life may be legal but is a primary moral wrong against the natural order, while a person's rebellion against government—as Thomas Jefferson understood[131]—may be legally wrong but is not a violation of the moral or natural order of things.

The distinction between the *moral* priority of rights-based claims and their *legal* priority is important. At many levels of governance—local, national, and international—the law itself usually establishes priorities that determine the outcome of any particular dispute between rival rights-claimants. In some instances, however, a conflict cannot be resolved by normative text. The canon may have internal contradictions, or more than one rights regime may be thought to be applicable to the same dispute. Or the legal texts may not have envisaged, and so do not cover, the particulars of a dispute. In the words of Judge Cardozo, there are times when 'the case at hand is not so governed by authority but that it may be dealt with upon principle'.[132] The 'principle' is ascertainable by recourse to moral reasoning.

If there is room for moral reason in adjudication, the more so is this true of

---

[130] On the historic and circumstantial forces that shape a community or nation see Bauer, *supra* n. 88, at 71, 73, 89, 172, 174.

[131] 'I hold it that a little rebellion now and then is a good thing, and as necessary in the political world as storms in the physical.' Letter from Jefferson to Madison (30 Jan. and 5 Feb. 1787), in 1 *The Republic of Letters: The Correspondence Between Thomas Jefferson and James Madison, 1776–1826* at 460, 461 (James Morton Smith ed., 1995). See also Carl T. Bogus, 'The Hidden History of the Second Amendment,' 31 UC Davis L. Rev. 309, 393 (1998).

[132] *Sokoloff v. National City Bank*, 239 NY 158, 165; 145 NE 917, 918 (1924).

other means of dispute settlement. The UN Security Council's decisions to use coercion against Rhodesia and South Africa are examples of a political, rather than a judicial, organ making weighty deliberative decisions that accord priority to one set of considerations (prohibiting racism) over another (protecting state sovereignty). The power of such a decision, its ability to pull states and populations continually towards compliance, depends in part on its value in the marketplace of principled reason and moral intuition.

# 10

## *Personal Freedom, Personal Responsibility, and their Democratic Reconciliation*

### 1. FREEDOM FROM/FREEDOM TO

This study has focused on the emerging right of individuals autonomously to design their personal identities by deliberately and freely selecting from among a range of options. It has sought to demonstrate that in recent years, just as individuals were being emancipated to create freely chosen identities, the range of available options was also broadening exponentially. This broadening has occurred as an incidental social consequence of progress in areas such as science, technology, and the economy.

Today, in many societies, decisions once dictated by enforced communitarian values have been relegated to personal preference and conscience. 'The right to be let alone', extolled by Justice Brandeis in *Olmstead v. US*,[1] is at last being realized with the help of national and international law as well as of changing social attitudes. In areas once tightly conformed by rules and rulers, persons are now on their own. And, in their own way, individuals are making the important choices and taking the personal initiatives that, in most instances, conduce not only to greater personal fulfilment and the general advancement of science, industry, and the arts, but also, as a secondary consequence, to the emancipation of less fortunate persons in their own and other societies. In many ways, the rising tide actually has succeeded in lifting most boats.

It must be acknowledged, however, that these salutary consequences of individualism's progress have not invariably followed. Personal freedom in some instances may actually have exacerbated inequalities and disadvantages. The right to be let alone, standing alone as a personal entitlement, almost inevitably magnifies the 'natural' advantage of those already most favoured: by social rank, family cohesion, education, and economic well-being. 'Leaving alone' the poor and those unable to cope often accords them no social benefit and their neglect promotes no social virtue. In an enlightened liberal democracy, the dark underside of the individual's cherished 'right to be left alone' must be redeemed by social commitment, first, to equalizing the conditions under which persons compete freely and, second, to ameliorating the lot of those who cannot compete well, or at all.

This is not a radical visionary prescription. Social responsibility, in a liberal

---

[1] 277 US 438, 478 (1928).

racy, is widely accepted as the due that each owes all: a sensible toll paid
se lucky to be driving fast cars on the open road to self-realization. Yet, in
.iternational community, this moral and political link between personal
autonomy and social responsibility has not always been recognized. Even quite
recently, the struggles for freedom of expression and religion, the fight against
racism and for the emancipation of women, as well as the conflict over persons'
right to emigrate or choose and change their careers, has so occupied the
agenda of rights activists that the definition and implementation of commensurate individual social responsibilities tended to be relegated to global
afterthoughts.

In matters of social responsibility, as in those of individual freedom,
twentieth-century international law and practice has developed far more slowly
than did commensurate domestic law and state practice. Only now that basic
human rights have been recognized universally has the international legal
system begun to acknowledge personal and societal *responsibilities*. It is beginning
to be understood that global recognition of a 'right of persons to be left alone'
must go hand in hand with a universal right of persons not to be left behind.

Internationally, disparities between advantaged and disadvantaged tend to be
greater and more resistant than within states. Stubbornly surviving racial and
gender biases still handicap personal achievement. The inordinate effort still
required of some to fulfil their basic needs for food, shelter, health services, and
quality education makes their personal autonomy illusory. Politics, moral
discourse, and the law must address these deprivations.

At both national and global levels, 'freedom from' is being challenged to
accept a linkage with 'freedom to'. It is not enough, the argument goes, to
neutralize the traditional oppressors of personal autonomy—the state, group,
church, and social class—or to achieve their passive acquiescence in the private
exercise of judgement in matters of conscience, education, occupation, sexuality,
nationality, or association. Rather, these former enemies of individualism must
be redirected to play an active role in empowering everyone to realize their full
potential in the pursuit of personal self-definition.[2]

What is asked of society and the law is to make individual autonomy
pandemic and effective. How this can be achieved depends on each person's
contextual particulars. The well-educated, socially and professionally secure,
may ask only that government and society leave them free to achieve. Others,
however, see such benevolent non-intervention as a nostrum. Freedom to choose
one's education guarantees neither access nor quality. Freedom to choose one's
occupation does not provide the remedial career guidance necessary to
compensate for a broken home or drug dependency. For many persons, genuine
autonomy is more closely linked with 'freedom to' than with 'freedom from'.

---

[2] For a parallel examination of this topic in US constitutional theory, which I found very helpful,
see James E. Fleming, 'Securing Deliberative Autonomy', 48 Stanford L. Rev. 1 (1995).

For some, self-realization requires more than getting the government off their backs. For these, only a boost onto the benign back of government—local, national, and transnational—can create opportunities to reach freedom's tantalizingly proffered goals.

In recent years, there have been a number of efforts to establish a symbiotic functional and ethical link between individual freedom and individual responsibility. While the 1948 Universal Declaration of Human Rights is concerned primarily with protecting individual rights, article 29 states that 'Everyone has duties to the community in which alone the free and full development of his personality is possible.' The Declaration has been criticized, however, for not elaborating on this theme.

Remedial efforts are underway. One is led by the prominent reformist Catholic theologian Hans Küng, whose 'Declaration Towards a Global Ethic' has received the imprimatur of an organization calling itself the Parliament of World's Religions. A 'Declaration of Human Responsibilities' was recently drafted under the auspices of the InterAction Council, a group comprised of activist former heads of state and government, including Jimmy Carter. Still more reforms are proposed by leaders of some South-East Asian countries. It remains to be seen what effect these will have.

The 1993 Declaration Towards a Global Ethic[3] restates the existing 'commitment to respect life and dignity, individuality and diversity, so that every person is treated humanely . . .' but links it to 'individual responsibility' for 'a just social economic order, in which everyone has an equal chance to reach full potential as a human being'.[4] It seeks 'to confirm and deepen' the 1948 Human Rights Declaration by adding the right to 'full realization of the intrinsic dignity of the human person, the inalienable freedom and equality in principle of all humans, and the necessary solidarity and interdependence of all humans with each other'.[5] These proposals seem to point in the right direction, while still lacking specificity.

More controversially, Küng has taken to criticizing the existing rights regime because 'individuals and groups constantly appeal to *rights against others* without recognizing any responsibilities of their own'. He complains about social stasis due to this proliferation of rights: 'Hardly anyone can build a house or a street, hardly an authority can enact a law or a regulation, without an appeal being made to rights in connection with it. Today countless claims can be advanced as rights, in particular against the state. . . . Don't we perhaps need a new concentration on responsibilities . . .?'[6]

Although Küng's Declaration appears reasonable in linking individual rights to personal social commitment, his emphasis on 'duties',[7] when put alongside

---

[3] *A Global Ethic* 43–53 (Hans Küng & Karl-Joseph Kuschel eds., 1993).     [4] Ibid. at 14–15.
[5] Ibid. at 20.
[6] Hans Küng, *A Global Ethic for Global Politics and Economics* 99–100 (1997).     [7] Ibid. at 100.

disparagement of 'our over-developed legalistic states . . .'[8] uncomfortably recalls the plaints of traditional authoritarians against personal freedoms.

This unfortunate linking of calls for greater personal responsibility with attacks on the legal culture of individualism has lately gathered some momentum. The InterAction Council, established in 1983 and counting among its members former heads of government of Australia, Austria, Britain, Brazil, Canada, France, Israel, Japan, Norway, Singapore, Spain, Thailand, the Soviet Union, the US, and Zambia, as well as Fr. Küng, Cardinal Franz Koenig of Vienna, and other eminent philosophers and theologians, in 1997 published a Universal Declaration of Human Responsibilities endorsed by 24 of its 29 members.[9] In part, it is merely vacuous. Article 3, for example, proclaims: 'Everyone has a responsibility to promote good and avoid evil in all things.' Article 4 sensibly but imprecisely urges all 'people, endowed with reason and conscience, [to] accept a responsibility to each and all, to families and communities, to races, nations, and religions in a spirit of solidarity'. Notably, however, the Declaration maintains utter silence regarding personal rights.

This silence becomes more ominous in the light of explanatory remarks by the Declaration's sponsors. Australia's former prime minister, Malcolm Fraser, in introducing the Council's Declaration dismissed the UN's 1948 Human Rights Declaration as reflecting only the views of the then-dominant Northern Hemispheric democracies. He urged that 'now that the [UN] membership had changed and been enlarged, there was need for a "balancing" declaration . . . that asserted the universal values of duties and obligations'.[10] Former German Chancellor Helmut Schmidt, more pointedly, observed that the 50-year-old Declaration reflects 'the philosophical and cultural background of its Western drafters' and called for a new 'balance' between 'the notions of freedom and of responsibility',[11] because 'the concept of rights can itself be abused and lead to anarchy'.[12]

The benevolent impulse to link new social responsibilities to human rights thus has evolved into attacks on the 'anarchy' of the 'over-developed legalistic' human rights regime. This has been expressed most bluntly by Malaysian Prime Minister Mahathir Mohamad. In September 1997, he marked the approaching fiftieth anniversary of the Universal Declaration of Human Rights by calling for it to be rewritten. According to local reports, 'the perception prevails within the top ranks of Malaysia's officialdom that existing human rights standards focus too much on individual rights. Malaysian officials say the rights of the majority

---

[8] Ibid. Küng's associate, Jürgen Moltmann, in an earlier work, only criticized the failure of states in the West to develop economic and social rights in tandem with individual rights. Jürgen Moltmann, 'Human Rights, Humanity and the Rights of Nature', in *The Ethics of World Religions and Human Rights* 121, 125–6 (Hans Küng & Jürgen Moltmann eds., 1990). See also *Yes to a Global Ethic* (Hans Küng ed., 1996).

[9] Pang Gek Choo, 'New Charter on Human Obligations Drawn Up,' The Straits Times (Singapore), 2 Sept. 1997, at 1.                                            [10] Ibid.

[11] Ibid. at 8.        [12] *The Age*, 31 March 1998, at 1.

or the common good, and even economic development, should take precedence over the rights of the minority or individual rights'.[13] His views roughly correspond with those of the Government of Singapore, which has long contended that the international rights regime fails to take into account 'Asian values'.[14]

While the call for a new emphasis on social responsibility of individuals, in itself, is both unexceptionable and commendable, it becomes less so when coupled with efforts to cut back on what some perceive as a pernicious emphasis on the rights of the individual. These moves to emphasize social responsibility by pruning personal rights have been confronted by Mary Robinson, former President of Ireland and, more recently, the UN Human Rights Commissioner.[15] She has rightly pointed out that the Human Rights Declaration, after 50 years, has come to reflect not just the best Western aspirations but also 'the differing cultural traditions in the world. The result is a distillation of many of the values inherent in the world's major legal systems and religious beliefs including the Buddhist, Christian, Hindu, Islamic, and Jewish traditions'.[16] Robinson has explained that the Declaration is now customary law and the basis for a significant canon of global and regional human rights treaties.[17] Responding to the InterAction Council, she said: 'It is right that we should focus more on duties and obligations, but, I believe, it would be wiser to avoid the distraction of seeking a new declaration. . . . Its universal vocation to protect the dignity of every human being has captured the imagination of humanity. . . . We tamper with it at our peril.'[18]

A strong refutation of Malaysia's Prime Minister has come from a countryman, Dato' Param Cumaraswamy, the UN Special Rapporteur on the Independence of Judges and Lawyers and former chairman of the Bar Council of Malaysia, who has criticized the cultural 'relativist' position, asserting, instead, that the universal nature of these rights and freedoms is beyond question and that the number of non-Western ratifications of the basic human rights instruments 'is further testimony of universal acceptance . . .'.[19] Boutros Boutros-Ghali, as Secretary-General of the UN (and as an African) similarly rejected the need for a new Declaration more responsive to cultural differences, since there 'is no one set of European rights, and another of African rights. . . . They belong inherently to each person, each individual, and are not conferred by, or subject to, any governmental authority. There is not one law for one

---

[13] Inter Press Serv., 9/19/97, 1997 WL 13256668.

[14] See e.g. Kishore Mahbubani, *Can Asians Think?* 57–80 (1998).

[15] Mary Robinson, 'The Universal Declaration of Human Rights: a living document,' at Symposium on Human Rights in the Asia-Pacific Region, at United Nations University, Tokyo, 27 Jan. 1998. www.unhchr.ch/htm/menu2/3/a980127.htm.    [16] Ibid. at 3.

[17] Ibid. at 4.    [18] Ibid. at 6.

[19] Cumaraswamy, 'The Universal Declaration of Human Rights: is it Universal?', 18 Human Rights LJ 477 (1997); 58–9 *The Review,* Int'l Comm. of Jurists, 118 (1997). See also Bertrand G. Ramcharan, 'The Universality of Human Rights', *The Review*, ibid. at 105 (1997).

continent, and one for another. And there should be only one single standard—a universal standard—for judging human rights violations'.[20]

Despite the distractions offered by this linking of a new emphasis on human responsibilities with a curbing of human rights, it should be recognized that responsibilities and rights are not inherently inimical. Chapter 5 has argued that individual liberty is not equivalent to absence of social responsibility. Most persons do not deny the need for community standards and welcome social efforts to remove obstacles that block personal choice and individual potential. For example, prohibition of racial discrimination in hiring should pose no problem for advocates of personal freedom. Neither should the defenders of free speech cavil at the regulation of radio and television to ensure greater content diversity. Only an unthinking individualist would oppose communitarian protections against the ravages of racial prejudice or the totalizing effect of mass culture, both of which restrict the options available to individuals.

## 2. DISCURSIVE REQUISITE/DEMOCRATIC ENTITLEMENT

Nevertheless, in the nature of things, 'freedom to' and 'freedom from' often do pose adversarial claims. On one side, property owners, seeking relief, demand freedom from taxes that deprive them of the fruits of their labours. On the other, unpropertied families demand 'freedom to' access a system of free, publicly supported, technologically sophisticated, education that requires revenue generated by high property taxes. Some degree of conflict is likely. In the international community, the 'north–south dialogue' features comparable claims and counterclaims. In any sophisticated, liberal community, this kind of conflict is played out in forums of civil discourse, where participants give voice to the various interests they represent.

It may be true that some of this discourse only reflects the participants' raw self-interest. But it can also serve another function, advancing the search for social consensus through principled reasoning and appeals to moral instinct. In this it succeeds more often than cynics admit. Persons without school-age children do complain about high taxes but, for the most part, they also support free, quality education. At the international level, too, dissonant distributive rights-based claims increasingly are negotiated in discursive negotiating forums, where good-faith efforts are made at deploying principled logic and moral reasoning. How else can one explain the support of states like Russia, Canada, Norway, and Iceland, with large frozen wastelands, for measures to halt global warming?

Discourse, of course, only enables a process of adjustment to operate; it does not conduce to any particular outcome. Principled reasoning and moral

[20] 18 Human Rights LJ 478 (1997).

intuition may help the discourse, but cannot promise a perfect allocation. Such formulas as 'from each according to abilities, to each according to need'[21] have proven their inadequacy, being either too inflexible to work or too flexible to be of much use. Instead, only a contingent, existential equilibrium may be achievable, and that only through an open process of discursive politics. Since such a process cannot be validated objectively by the perfect equilibration of its outcomes, it must be validated by its legitimacy.[22]

Many local and national forums exist to assist in the negotiating of contingent political equilibrium. The degree to which such negotiations are able to manifest their legitimacy powerfully affects the compliance pull of their allocational outcomes. As James Madison observed in *Federalist no. 10*, the search for pragmatic equilibrium to resolve distributive issues among 'various and interfering interests forms the principal task of modern legislation, and involves the spirit of party and faction in the ordinary operations of the government'.[23] This is equally true at the international level. It is only through the fraught process of open discourse that global and regional forums of governance can hope to attain and sustain belief in the integrity of their allocational choices. This makes critical the legitimacy of those purporting to represent the various discursive interests.[24]

All too evidently, international law and institutions are not as perfected in meeting this test as are many of their constitutional counterparts in liberal democracies; yet international regimes, too, must focus increasingly on promoting and perfecting their manifest legitimacy, because allocation of goods and balancing of rights is ever more becoming their business.

Much remains to be done. International regimes, even as they became more powerful, have remained stubbornly the exclusive domain of bureaucrats and diplomats. That global forums and institutions, despite this evident 'democratic deficit', remain almost exclusively the domain of states attests to the continuing potency of the Vattelian idea. As more power flows to international organizations with responsibilities for trade, disarmament, global warming, and disease-control, the discourse is still limited to diplomats and bureaucrats whose democratic legitimacy is a thin veneer.

The textbook solution to this would be world governance through directly elected representatives. Since this is not about to happen, a second-best approach is to ensure that those who speak in global discourse themselves represent democratically elected governments. That way, the outcomes of diplomatic discourse may at least claim to manifest the valid consensus of all

---

[21] Karl Marx, *Critique of the Gotha Programme* (1875). The quote may also be attributed to Louis Blanc, *Organisation du Travail* (1840), or to Morelly, *Le Code de la Nature* (1755). Bartlett's *Familiar Quotations* 563(a) (15th edn., 1980).

[22] See Thomas M. Franck, *The Power of Legitimacy Among Nations* (1990).

[23] Quoted and analysed in Charles A. Beard, *An Economic Interpretation of the Constitution of the United States* 156 (1961).

[24] See Thomas M. Franck, *Fairness in International Law and Institutions* (1995).

those at interest. Fortunately, the global system, of late, has begun to make some progress towards such secondary democratic legitimation.

To recapitulate: governance involves allocational choices. International governance seeks equilibrium between self-interested claims of persons, groups, and states, as well as between claims of 'freedom from' and 'freedom to'. To be effective, the process by which decisions are reached must be seen to be either impartially judicial or politically discursive. To be genuinely discursive, the discourse must give true voice to freely expressed interests of the *polis*. Realizing this, international institutions have begun to take an active interest in fostering their member governments' democratic legitimacy.

## 3. THE ETYMOLOGY OF DEMOCRACY

'Democracy', as the word's etymology suggests, is about people's role in governance. Specifically, democracy is about people's right to participate, and the terms of their participation, in the discourse leading to the formation of social values that inform political choices and then manifest themselves in public policies and actions. It is about both a civil society and a civic culture; about the structure, function, and legitimacy of the most basic and also the most exalted levels of voter participation in direct and representative governance. It is about the role of individuals in the common enterprise of choosing among competing visions of a shared future.

That there is a growing public and intergovernmental consensus regarding this right to participate is evident in the common standards by which each government's legitimacy is now assessed by various regional and global institutions. That standard does not demand conformity to some one-size-fits-all model of democracy. Rather, it measures the extent to which members of a *polis* actually consent to whatever process is used to consult and govern them.

Although this democratic entitlement, just emerging as a commonly accepted personal right, does not endorse any particular mode of popular participation, it does envisage the freely derived consent of people to the mode by which they participate in self-governance. For example, it is possible to argue that, at its present state of consciousness, the international *polis* is content to be governed by institutions in which they participate only indirectly through diplomats accredited by national governments, so long as those governments, at least, are directly and fairly accountable to the respective national electorates.

This emphasis on accountability is not some ancient Greek tradition validated by lengthy history and practice. The participatory rights of racial minorities, the unpropertied, and of women were recognized in Europe, India, Japan, and the Americas only a few generations ago. Elsewhere, universal suffrage came even more recently. Only in the last decade of the twentieth century did it attain the status of a universally recognized individual right.

Today, almost all governments seem to want to be seen as freely and fairly elected by an electorate constituted in accordance with the principles of universality and equality. Moreover, to be regarded as legitimate by the international system, each state's process of consultation must perpetually be revalidated by the consent of those being governed: at a minimum by each citizenry's willing participation in the electoral process. At the core of democracy's international systemic definition, then, is not any one particular global model of democratic consultation but, rather, a broad right of all persons to be consulted in a way they consider meaningful.

### 4. THE NORMATIVITY OF DEMOCRACY

The evolution of a principled legal basis for the democratic entitlement, although accelerating after 1986, received its first impetus in the United Nations Charter. Article 73, although dealing only with decolonization, requires member states to 'develop self-government, to take due account of the political aspirations of the peoples, and to assist them in the progressive development of their free political institutions'. Although the intent of this obligation was to influence colonial powers, not political societies in general, it did have an impact beyond the colonies. After all, if democratic participation ('self-government') was to be the required norm for Africa, India, and the Caribbean, how could it be irrelevant to totalitarian Eastern Europe and other nations which, although self-governing, allowed no meaningful popular self-expression and participation? Even if the original impetus for codifying the right to self-determination had only been to rouse the public consciences of America, Britain, the Netherlands, France, and Belgium—where vaunted democratic traditions could be contrasted embarrassingly with the same societies' authoritarian colonial traditions—the implications of that essentially successful appeal could not be limited to one place and time.

Decolonization thus was an effective appeal to the colonizers' conscience. The 1970 UN General Assembly Declaration on Friendly Relations proclaimed a duty to give all adults in each colony the 'political status freely determined' by them.[25] Most colonial regimes, after some initial resistance, felt morally (and sometimes forcefully) compelled to heed that summons. For two decades, only the two Western European dictatorships—Portugal and Spain—held out. Elsewhere, change occurred quickly through a mixed strategy of induced guilt, appeal to democratic solidarity, and, when unavoidable, mass insurgency. By 1950, Britain and, thereafter, most other colonial powers, found it increasingly

---

[25] Declaration on Principles of International Law concerning Friendly Relations and Co-operation among States in accordance with the Charter of the United Nations, Annex to GA Res. 2625, 25 UN GAOR Supp. no. 28 at 121, UN Doc. A/8028 (1970), reprinted in 9 ILM 1292 (1970).

difficult in theory and practice to reconcile their democratic governance at home with the colonial regimes they had established abroad. Thus, they began to transform colonies into what they hoped would be adaptions of their own metropolitan democracy.

Sometimes a recognizable form of democracy did take root, as in India, the Philippines, and Botswana. More often, hurried decolonization produced indigenous authoritarian or totalitarian systems of governance under cover of rapid social and economic modernization and the preservation of national unity. Even before the collapse of European communism, however, these touted 'Asian' or 'African' approaches to guided governance began to self-destruct.

The international system has played a significant role in that transformation. Stung by the increasingly embarrassing contradiction between self-determination and democracy, the community of states—including third-world autocracies—felt constrained to participate in the project of defining universal rights, including political freedoms, in such a way as to make them as applicable to independent states as to colonies. Thus, in particular, the logic of a campaign to end apartheid in South Africa, an independent state and founding member of the UN, required a rhetorical shift from the former emphasis on self-determination in colonies to a new demand for universal participatory democracy in all states.

This more universal concept of democracy as a right of all peoples first appears in the Universal Declaration of Human Rights, adopted by the General Assembly on 10 December 1948. It specifies a universal right to freedom of opinion and expression (article 19), to peaceful assembly and association (article 20), and to 'periodic and genuine election which shall be by universal and equal suffrage and shall be held by secret vote or by equivalent free voting procedures' (article 21).[26] Being a mere resolution of the General Assembly, it had no binding effect, making it easy for many blatant dictatorships to pay hypocritical homage to its high principles. Nevertheless, over time the Declaration has achieved a deep historic resonance.

Two decades later, many of the Declaration's concepts reappeared as fixed legal obligations in the Covenant on Civil and Political Rights.[27] This landmark treaty, with 140 state parties as of August 1998,[28] spells out specific rights to freedom of thought (article 18) and of association (article 22). It provides that everyone 'shall have the right to freedom of expression' and that 'this right shall include freedom to seek, receive, and impart information and ideas of all kinds . . .' (article 19(2)).[29] It also guarantees periodic and genuine elections

---

[26] Universal Declaration of Human Rights, GA Res. 217A(III), UN Doc. A/810 at 71 (1948).

[27] International Covenant on Civil and Political Rights, 16 December 1966, 999 UNTS 171, reprinted in 6 ILM 368 (1967). Entered into force 3 Jan. 1976. [Hereafter ICCPR.]

[28] *Multilateral Treaties Deposited with the Secretary-General*, Status as at 5 Aug. 1998, ST/LEG/SER.E.

[29] The enumerated entitlements to freedom of expression, however, could only muster general support after being qualified by a clause permitting the imposition of temporary restrictions where 'necessary . . . [f]or the protection of . . . public order . . ., or of public health or morals . . . .' ICCPR, *supra* n. 27, art. 19(3).

by universal and equal suffrage and secret ballot.[30] While these now became legal 'rights', the strictures of the Cold War still inhibited their implementation.

The collapse of communism took down with it the one-party ideology of Africa, the *caudillismo* of Latin America, and the 'guided democracy' of parts of Asia. This opened the way for a transformation in thinking about human rights, beginning in the late 1980s, on a scale comparable to that following the collapse of the Axis powers in 1945. The results were evident in Manila, Moscow, and Rio, but as well in the UN compounds in New York and Geneva. The General Assembly, in 1991, by overwhelming assent, adopted a resolution for 'enhancing the effectiveness of the principle of periodic and general elections'.[31] It stated nations' collective 'conviction that periodic and genuine elections are a necessary and indispensable element of sustained efforts to protect the rights and interests of the governed and that, as a matter of practical experience, the right of everyone to take part in the government of his or her country is a crucial factor in the effective enjoyment by all of a wide range of other human rights and fundamental freedoms, embracing political, economic, social and cultural rights'.[32] The resolution adds 'that determining the will of the people requires an electoral process that provides an equal opportunity for all citizens to become candidates and put forward their political views, individually and in co-operation with others . . .'.[33]

These agreed normative underpinnings for a global democratic entitlement have been further developed at the regional level by the European states, together with Canada and the United States. The Conference on Security and Co-operation in Europe (CSCE)[34]—now the Organization on Security and Co-operation in Europe (OSCE)—recently joined unanimously in spelling out the contents of the new right to participate in free and open elections. At a meeting in Copenhagen in June 1990, participants affirmed that 'democracy is an inherent element of the rule of law' and recognized 'the importance of pluralism with regard to political organizations'.[35] Among the 'inalienable rights of all human beings', they decided, is individual and universal participation in 'free elections that will be held at reasonable intervals by secret ballot or by equivalent free voting procedure, under conditions which ensure in practice the free expression of the opinion of the electors in the choice of their representatives'. Also on the list of recognized entitlements is a government 'representative in character, in which the executive is accountable to the elected

---

[30] Ibid. art. 25(b).    [31] GA Res. 45/150 of 21 Feb. 1991.    [32] Ibid. para. 2.
[33] Ibid. para. 3. See also Resolution 46/137 of 17 Dec. 1991.
[34] Conference on Security and Co-operation in Europe, Final Act, 1 Aug. 1975, 73 Dep't St. Bull. 323 (1975), reprinted in 14 ILM 1292 (1975).
[35] Conference on Security and Co-operation in Europe, Document of the Copenhagen Meeting of the Conference on the Human Dimension, 29 June 1990, reprinted in 29 ILM 1305, 1308, para. 3 (1990) [hereafter Copenhagen Document].

legislature or the electorate'; and political parties which are clearly separate from the state.[36] To give effect to these principles, the thirty-five member-states made recognition of the democratic entitlement by governments the condition precedent to recognition of every regime's right to govern. They declared that 'the will of the people, freely and fairly expressed through periodic and genuine elections, is the basis of the authority and legitimacy of all government'.[37]

The Copenhagen Document further affirmed that all citizens have the right to expect 'free elections at reasonable intervals, as established by law'; a national legislature in which at least one chamber's membership is 'freely contested in a popular vote'; a system of universal and equal adult suffrage; a secret ballot or its equivalent; free, nondiscriminatory candidature for office; freedom to form political parties that compete 'on a basis of equal treatment before the law and by the authorities'; fair and free campaigning; 'no legal or administrative obstacle' to media access, which must be available 'on a non-discriminatory basis for all political groupings and individuals wishing to participate in the electoral process'; and that the 'candidates who obtain the necessary number of votes required by law are duly installed in office and are permitted to remain in office until their term expires or is otherwise' terminated in accordance with law.[38]

This was an entirely unprecedented initiative by North Atlantic and European nations to endorse and define a popular right of individuals to participate in liberal electoral democracy.[39] The state parties went on to commend the growing practice of involving foreign observers in national elections. The Copenhagen participants invited 'observers from any other CSCE participating States and any appropriate private institutions and organizations who may wish to do so to observe the course of their national election proceedings, to the extent permitted by law', and pledged to 'endeavour to facilitate similar access for election proceedings held below the national level'.[40]

Later in 1990, the leaders of the member-states meeting in Paris, declared 'a new era of democracy, peace and unity'.[41] Unanimously, they endorsed a Charter, which commits them 'to build, consolidate and strengthen democracy as the only system of government of our nations'.[42] It restates the older entitlement to free expression but adds the right of every individual, without discrimination, 'to participate in free and fair elections',[43] backed by the governments' pledge to 'co-operate and support each other with the aim of making democratic gains irreversible'.[44] Although the Charter is not a treaty, its language is weighted with legal terminology and is self-consciously norm-

---

[36] Ibid. at 1309, para. 5.      [37] Ibid. at 1309, para. 6.      38 Ibid. at 1310, para. 7.

[39] Thomas Buergenthal, 'The Copenhagen CSCE Meeting: A New Public Order for Europe', 11 Hum. Rts. LJ 217, 221–2 (1990).

[40] Copenhagen Document, *supra* n. 35, at 1310, para. 8.

[41] Conference on Security and Co-operation in Europe, Charter of Paris for a New Europe and Supplementary Document to Give Effect to Certain Provisions of the Charter, 21 Nov. 1990, Preamble, *reprinted in* 30 ILM 190, 193 (1991).

[42] Ibid. at 193.      [43] Ibid. at 194.      [44] Ibid. at 195.

creating. In particular, it builds on the assumption that electoral democracy is owed not only by each government to its own people, but also by each member-state to the whole OSCE community.

All this activity to create global and regional norms embodying democratic participatory rights has been accompanied, albeit at a slower pace, by efforts to establish global and regional machinery for actually implementing the new rules and meeting the newly aroused expectations.

## 5. MONITORING COMPLIANCE WITH THE DEMOCRATIC ENTITLEMENT

Monitoring is the logical first step towards securing compliance. As we have seen, the effective international and regional monitoring of states' compliance with human rights norms is of quite recent origin and has only just begun to be implemented in earnest. Paradoxically, although the democratic entitlement is the most recent human right to win global recognition, it has one of the longest monitoring track records, having begun in the 1950s as a controversial feature of the UN's supervision of decolonization. Right from the start, states responsible for colonial and trust territories were required to submit periodic reports to a committee of the UN General Assembly or to the Trusteeship Council detailing progress towards self-determination. In most instances, this meant reporting on progress in each colony towards democratic self-government. These activities, and reports on them by the 'administering powers', were subjected to close scrutiny by UN committees.

The committees did more than study reports; they also sent abroad missions of inspection. These observed key colonial parliamentary elections and plebiscites to ensure fairness and openness as former dependencies made their way towards independence.[45] When the colonial era drew to a close, the significance

---

[45] Beginning in May 1956, the UN Trusteeship Council sent monitors to the plebiscite in which the people of British Togoland chose to join Ghana. Report of the United Nations Plebiscite Commissioner for the Trust Territory of Togoland under British Administration, UN Doc. T/1258 and Add.1 (1956). It monitored the pre-independence plebiscites in the British Cameroons in Nov. 1959 and Feb. 1961. See GA Res. 1350, 13 UN GAOR Supp. no. 18A, at 2, UN Doc. A/4090/Add.1 (1959) (whether the Northern Cameroons wished 'to be part of the Northern Region of Nigeria when the Federation of Nigeria becomes independent'); GA Res. 1352, 14 UN GAOR Supp. no. 16, at 26, UN Doc. A/4354 (1959) (whether the Southern Cameroons wished to achieve independence by 'joining the independent Federation of Nigeria or the independent Republic of Cameroons'); GA Res. 1473, ibid. at 38 (putting the questions posed in the GA Res. 1352 plebiscite before the Northern Cameroons); see also Report of the United Nations Commissioner for the Supervision of the Plebiscites in the Southern and Northern Parts of the Trust Territory of the Cameroons under United Kingdom Administration, UN Doc. T/1556 and app. (1961). Similarly, following the Nov. 1959 violence between the Hutu and Tutsi tribes in what was then Belgian-administered Ruanda-Urundi, the United Nations supervised a pre-independence election and referendum that determined the separation of the linked indigenous kingdoms and the future of the monarchy. GA Res. 1579, 15 UN GAOR Supp. no. 16, at 34 (elections), UN Doc. A/4684 (1960); GA Res. 1605, 15 UN GAOR Supp. no. 16A, at 8, UN Doc. A/4684/Add.1 (1961) (referendum).

of the UN's election-monitoring role, instead of declining, actually increased, because the last cases of decolonization were among the most difficult. In these instances, a United Nations 'honest broker' role proved indispensable. A remarkable example is UNTAG, the United Nations' transitional administration, that acted as midwife in the birth of an independent Namibia. Created by the Security Council, UNTAG supervised both the final months of South African administration and, in November 1989, conducted the crucial elections that preceded independence. Deploying more than seven thousand military and civilian personnel at a cost of $373 million, it took responsibility for maintaining peace, overseeing South Africa's military withdrawal, and assisting in the drafting of a new constitution. It helped achieve the rapid repeal of discriminatory legislation left over from South African administration, implemented a political amnesty, oversaw the return of political refugees, and was instrumental in keeping the election peaceful and fair.[46]

In 1961, the United Nations assisted New Zealand, the administering authority, in conducting a plebiscite in Western Samoa that endorsed a draft constitution and a form of association with the former trustee. GA Res. 1569, 15 UN GAOR Supp. no. 16, ibid. at 33 (whether the inhabitants of the Territory accepted 'the Constitution adopted by the Constitutional Convention on 28 October 1960' and endorsed 'that on 1 January 1962 Western Samoa should become an independent State on the basis of that Constitution'); see also Report of United Nations Commissioner for the Supervision of the Plebiscite in Western Samoa, UN Doc. T/1564 and Add.1 (1961). On 17 June 1975, the United Nations observed the vote in which residents of the Northern Mariana Islands endorsed a loose form of political confederation with the United States. Report of the United Nations Visiting Mission to Observe the Plebiscite in the Northern Mariana Islands, Trust Territory of the Pacific Islands, 43 UN TCOR Supp. no. 2, at 24, UN Doc. T/1771 (1976). And, at various times in the 1980s, it supervised plebiscites in the rest of the US Pacific Islands Trust that determined the future status of those several archipelagos. See Report of the United Nations Visiting Mission to Observe the Plebiscite in the Federated States of Micronesia, Trust Territory of the Pacific Islands, 51 UN TCOR Supp. no. 1, at 14, UN Doc. T/1860 (1984) (21 June 1983 plebiscite for the islands of Truk, Yap, Kosrae and Ponape); Report of the United Nations Visiting Mission to Observe the Plebiscite in the Marshall Islands, Trust Territory of the Pacific Islands, ibid. (no. 2) at 12–13, UN Doc. T/1865 (1984) (7 Sept. 1983 plebiscite); Report of the United Nations Visiting Mission to Observe the Plebiscite in Palau, Trust Territory of the Pacific Islands, 53 UN TCOR Supp. no. 2, at 14, UN Doc. T/1885 (1986) (21 Feb. 1986 plebiscite).

The United Nations also oversaw key elections in non-Trusteeship colonies. Its observers were present at the referendum establishing a new constitution for the Cook Islands in 1965. GA Res. 2005, 19 UN GAOR Supp. no. 15, at 7, UN Doc. A/5815 (1965); Report of the United Nations Representatives for the Supervision of the Elections in the Cook Islands, UN Doc. A/5962 and Corr.1 (1965). Observers were also present at the pre-independence referendum and elections in Spanish Equatorial Guinea in 1968. GA Res. 2355, 22 UN GAOR Supp. no. 16, at 54, UN Doc. A/6716 (1967); United Nations Mission for the Supervision of the Referendum and the Elections in Equatorial Guinea, UN Doc. A/7200/Add.4, Anns. V, VI (1968). Independence was formally achieved on 12 October 1968. The United Nations undertook similar monitoring of the referendum on the future status of West New Guinea (West Irian) from 14 July–2 August 1969. GA Res. 1752, 17 UN GAOR Supp. no. 17, at 70, UN Doc. A/5217 (1962); Report of the Secretary-General regarding the Act of Self-determination in West Irian, UN Doc. A/7641 (1969). The United Nations also monitored the November 1980 elections conducted in the New Hebrides under French and British administration, which led to the creation of independent Vanuatu. GA Res. 34/10, 34 UN GAOR Supp. no. 46, at 199, UN Doc. A/34/46; Report of the United Nations Mission to Observe the Elections in the New Hebrides, UN Doc. A/34/852 (1979).

[46] 'Namibia, Independence at Last', UN Chron., June 1990, at 4. Namibia formally achieved independence on 21 March 1990, ibid.

Slightly later, buoyed by UNTAG's success, similar election monitoring and transitional roles were authorized by the UN Security Council for the Western Sahara,[47] Cambodia,[48] Mozambique,[49] Nicaragua, and Haiti,[50] this despite the fact that all but the first of these were already fully independent states. The UN role in each instance was justified as necessary to end a conflict by recourse to a democratic consultation with the population. In some instances, the UN in effect supervised the government in the period leading up to elections; in others it limited its activity to securing peaceful and fair campaigning and reasonable honesty at the polls.

The collapse of totalitarian regimes around the world created a demand by independent states to legitimate their new and as-yet fragile democracy by global monitoring of their elections. By 1991, the General Assembly was emboldened, with only four dissents, to establish a formal procedure—later supported by a division of the Secretariat—to help independent states requesting electoral assistance, an authorization since regularly re-endorsed.[51]

Electoral assistance—now also provided by non-governmental as well as intergovernmental institutions[52]—is an important tool for achieving compliance with agreed electoral norms. So, too, is the procedure for international institutional review of state conduct affecting the right of persons to meaningful participation in the larger democratic process. 'Participation' presupposes far more than mere voting, embracing a broad range of expressive freedoms. Here the ICCPR has proven useful. As we saw in Chapter 8, the states party to the Covenant are legally obliged to 'undertake to submit [periodic] reports on the measures they have adopted which give effect to the rights recognized [in the Covenant] and on the progress made in the enjoyment of those rights'.[53] Among the explicitly protected rights are those pertaining to speech, assembly, and candidature for public office. The reports on state compliance with these obligations are scrutinized by the Human Rights Committee of independent experts. The reporting state's representatives are cross-examined. The Committee reports its findings to the other state parties and to the United Nations Economic and Social Council.[54] Although many states are tardy in their reporting, this international monitoring of what had but recently been

---

[47] S/Res/690 (1991) of 29 Apr. 1991.

[48] S/Res/826 (1993) of 20 Nov. 1993, and resolutions cited therein.

[49] S/Res/797 (1992) of 16 Dec. 1993.

[50] S/Res/637, 44 UN SCOR (Res. & Dec.) at 19, UN Doc. S/INF/45 (1989); GA Res. 45/2 (12 Oct. 1990).

[51] GA Res. 46/137 of 17 Dec. 1991. See also GA Res. 52/119 and 52/129 of 12 Dec. 1997.

[52] The leading example of non-governmental electoral assistance is IDEA, the Institute for Democracy and Electoral Assistance, established in Stockholm, Sweden.

[53] ICCPR, *supra* n. 27, art. 40(1).

[54] For a discussion of this procedure see D. McGoldrick, *The Human Rights Committee* 62–119 (1991).

among the most intimate attributes of sovereignty is no longer seriously questioned.

The Committee has been active in overseeing compliance with ICCPR's articles 18, 19, and 22, which deal with free expression and association. Its monitoring is a refinement of the older practices of UN committees monitoring colonial self-determination but today's Committee of Experts applies a much better developed set of democratic norms in a more methodical fashion. It has been critical, for example, of compliance by Uganda and Zanzibar[55] and has posed searching questions to representatives of Mali[56] and Jamaica.[57] In monitoring the openness of states' political processes, the experts are aided by an extensive non-governmental human rights network.

As we have observed in Chapter 8, the ICCPR's optional procedures permit states[58] and individuals[59] to lodge specific complaints of non-compliance. All petitions brought under the individual complaint procedure are drawn to the Committee's attention by the United Nations Secretary-General.[60] Some have dealt with denials of the democratic entitlement.[61] On that basis, the Committee found Uruguay's former military regime in violation of article 19(2) of the Covenant when it denied a petitioner the right freely to engage in political and trade union activities.[62] In *Perdoma and DeLanza v. Uruguay*,[63] the complainants alleged that they had been detained on account of 'subversive association' based on their political views and connections. The Committee found that there was no evidence to substantiate the charges of subversion and concluded that the arrest, detention, and trial of the petitioners had not been justified on any of the grounds permitted in the Covenant's article 19(3).[64]

The Human Rights Committee has also monitored compliance with article 25 on electoral rights and, under the Optional Protocol, has examined a small number of petitions regarding the conduct of elections. In reviewing two citizens' complaints against the military regime of Uruguay, the Committee concluded that they had been arbitrarily deprived of protected rights by

[55] Report of the Human Rights Committee, 36 UN GAOR Supp. (no. 40) at 42–3, UN Doc. A/36/40 (1981).                                                                 [56] Ibid. at 50–1.

[57] Ibid. at 56–7.

[58] ICCPR, *supra* n. 27, art. 41. For a discussion of this procedure see McGoldrick, *supra* n. 54, at 120–246.

[59] ICCPR, ibid., Optional Protocol, *opened for signature* 19 Dec. 1966, art. 1, 999 UNTS 302; see also McGoldrick, ibid. at 127.

[60] Human Rights Committee, Provisional Rules of Procedure, Rule 78(1), UN Doc. CCPR/C/3/Rev.2 (1989). See Report of the Human Rights Committee, 44 UN GAOR Supp. no. 40, at 179–82, UN Doc. A/44/40 (1989).                                     [61] McGoldrick, *supra* n. 54, at 127.

[62] *Alba Pietroroia v. Uruguay*, Communication R.10/44, 1981 Report, *supra* n. 55, at 153–9.

[63] Report of the Human Rights Committee, 35 UN GAOR Supp. (no. 40) at 111, UN Doc. A/35/40 (1980).

[64] Ibid. See also *Grille Motta v. Uruguay*, Communication R.2/11, 1980 Report, ibid. at 132; *Weinberg Weisz v. Uruguay*, Communication R.7/28, 1981 Report, *supra* n. 55, at 114; *Hertzberg v. Finland*, Communication R.14/61, Report of the Human Rights Committee, 37 UN GAOR Supp. no. 40 at 161, UN Doc. A/37/40 (1982).

decrees banning their political party and by being prevented from running for office.[65]

Another venue for implementing the democratic entitlement is via the inter-governmental Human Rights Commission and the office of the United Nations Secretary-General. At the request of the former, the latter has appointed special representatives to report on several governments' alleged gross violations of political and other freedoms. In one instance, the Secretary-General's repre-sentative eventually persuaded the parties to El Salvador's decade-long civil war to accept the creation of a UN Observer Group (ONUSAL) which successfully organized and supervised free elections that led to the completion of the peace process and the restoration of democracy.[66]

Regional organizations, applying regional laws through regional institutions, have also supervised new democratic entitlements. These have previously been identified in Chapter 8. The outstanding example is the European Convention for the Protection of Human Rights and Fundamental Freedoms. Its article 10, para-graph 1, provides: 'Everyone has the right to freedom of expression. This right shall include freedom to hold opinions and to receive and impart information and ideas without interference by public authority and regardless of frontiers.'[67]

Paragraph 2 of article 10 does permit derogation in the form of:

restrictions . . . necessary in a democratic society, in the interests of national security, territorial integrity or public safety, for the prevention of disorder or crime, for the protection of health or morals, for the protection of the reputation or rights of others, for preventing the disclosure of information received in confidence, or for maintaining the authority and impartiality of the judiciary.

States' implementation of both this rule and its exceptions is monitored by the European Human Rights Court.[68] As noted in Chapter 8, this Court, previously aided by the European Rights Commission, has become an effective fulcrum, balancing competing rights claims of individuals with those of society or of other individuals. The Court has weighed freedom of the press against a defendant's right to an impartial trial.[69] It has drawn boundaries between free

---

[65] Case 34/1979, 1981 Report, *supra* n. 55, at 130; Case 44/1979, ibid., Annex XVI, at 153.

[66] Central America: Efforts Towards Peace: Report of the Secretary-General, UN Doc. S/22494 and corr.1. (1991); see also NY Times, 13 Aug. 1991, at A8, col. 3. See further Letters dated 8 Jan. and 12 April 1991 from the Secretary-General to President Cristiani (of El Salvador) concerning UN observation of the March 1991 elections in El Salvador and concerning constitutional reform, reprinted in *United Nations and El Salvador: 1990–1995, UN Bluebook Series* vol. IV at 132, 133 (1995); Report of the Secretary-General on ONUSAL and First Report of the ONUSAL Human Rights Division, A/45/1055 (1991); Report of the Secretary-General A/50/517, p. 5, part V (1995).

[67] European Convention for the Protection of Human Rights and Fundamental Freedoms, 4 Nov. 1950, 213 UNTS 221, Europ. TS no. 5 (entered into force 3 Sept. 1953) [hereafter European Convention].

[68] Ibid. at art. 19, establishing the European Commission on Human Rights and the European Court of Human Rights. See also arts. 20–55.

[69] *The Sunday Times Case*, 30 Eur. Ct. HR (ser. A) (1978).

expression and obscenity[70] and sought a principled equilibrium between a free press and the laws of libel and slander.[71] In so doing, it has made far more specific—hence legitimate—the Council of Europe's system of norms pertaining to expressive rights, just when that regime is rapidly expanding to include the newly freed but democratically inexperienced nations of Eastern Europe. In a controversial 1998 decision, the Court found that Turkey, by banning its Communist Party, had violated article 11 of the European Convention. 'Democracy', the judges insisted, 'is without doubt a fundamental feature of the European public order.'[72]

Progress is being made, albeit more slowly, in the inter-American regional system. The American Convention on Human Rights,[73] also previously discussed in Chapter 8, provides an elaborate textual basis for protecting freedom of thought and expression (article 13), the right of assembly (article 15), and freedom of association (article 16). Monitoring and enforcement is performed by the Inter-American Commission (articles 34 and 64(1)) and the Inter-American Court (articles 33, 62, and 64). As of December 1996, twenty-five states—not including the United States—adhere to the Convention and seventeen accept the Court's compulsory jurisdiction.[74]

## 6. ENFORCING DEMOCRACY

Monitoring may establish that violations have occurred: but then what? An obstacle to making the democratic entitlement effective is the lack of graduated and flexible responses to a state's gross and prolonged violations. At present, the choice for collective action too often is limited: either to take military action or to do nothing. Military enforcement raises the spectre of colonialism and war. The international system needs less draconian responses to violations of the democratic entitlement. It also must ensure that the last-chance deployment of military means to enforce democracy occurs only in circumstances that do not constitute disguised colonialism. The General Assembly has emphasized this in the resolution demanding 'Respect for the principle of national sovereignty and non-interference in the internal affairs of States in their electoral processes'.[75]

To achieve the latter objective—uncoupling military rescue of democracy

---

[70] *Handyside Case*, 24 Eur. Ct. HR (ser. A) (1976); *Case of Muller and Others*, 133 Eur. Ct. HR (ser. A) (1988).        [71] *Lingens Case*, 103 Eur. Ct. HR (ser. A) (1986).

[72] Case of United Communist Party of Turkey and Others v. Turkey, Judgment, 133/1996/752/951, 30 January 1998, para. 45.

[73] American Convention on Human Rights, 22 Nov. 1969, OEA/Ser.K/XVI.1.1, doc. 70, rev.1, corr.1 (1970), reprinted in 1 *The Inter-American System*, pt. II at 51 (F.V. Garcia-Amador ed., 1983), 9 ILM 673 (1970) (entered into force 18 July 1978) [hereafter American Convention].

[74] Christina M. Cerna, 'International Law and the Protection of Human Rights in the International System', 19 Hous. J. Int'l L. 731, 737–8 (1997).

[75] GA Res. 52/119 of 12 Dec. 1997.

from old-fashioned military interventionism—there have been determined efforts to establish the principle that recourse to military force is impermissible unless it has been authorized by the Security Council or, perhaps in extreme emergencies, *ad interim* by a regional organization. Against the background of two centuries of unilateral military intervention by imperial powers into the affairs of smaller, weaker states it is understandable that any military intervention, even to protect or restore democracy, is regarded with suspicion.[76]

Nevertheless, the international and regional systems have gone some distance towards legitimating such interventions *provided* the case for the need to use force is made to, and accepted by, a representative jury of governments, and not by any, possibly self-interested, regime acting on its own. Such jurying is imperfectly, yet best, performed by the UN Security Council, sometimes in co-operation with a regional organization.

The Council is the most effective instrument for multilateralizing a decision to intervene forcefully on the side of democracy in a civil conflict. Although the Council is obliged by article 2(7) of the Charter not to intervene in matters which are 'essentially within the domestic jurisdiction' of a state, it is released from that constraint if it finds that a government's suspension of democracy constitutes a threat to international peace and security requiring collective measures under the Charter's chapter 7. International law does not, however, permit any state, or any regional organization, to take the enforcement of the democratic entitlement exclusively into its own hands.

If the Security Council decides on collective action against a usurper regime, it has various calibrated means at its disposal: to impose diplomatic, economic and military sanctions, to embargo an offending state's tourism, exports and participation in international cultural and sports activities, and, if all this fails, to authorize UN member-states or a regional organization to deploy force to restore a legitimate regime.

In recent years there have been examples of the collective use of each of these measures. In 1993, the Council utilized its broad enforcement powers under chapter 7 of the Charter to impose a fuel and arms embargo on the junta in Haiti after its overthrow of the elected government of President Aristide,[77] and to authorize its members to enforce it militarily.[78] One year later, the Council authorized members to invade Haiti and restore its democratic regime.[79] After a coup overthrew the elected government of Sierra Leone in 1997, the Security Council, after the failure of diplomatic and economic pressure, authorized an

---

[76] Thus, the General Assembly of the UN regularly couples its calls for free and fair elections with a restatement of the need to respect 'for the principles of national sovereignty and non-interference in the internal affairs of States in their electoral process.' See e.g. GA Res. 52/119 of 12 Dec. 1997.

[77] SC Res. 841, UN SCOR, 48th Sess., 3238 mtg., at 120, UN Doc. S/RES/841 (1993).

[78] SC Res. 875, UN SCOR, 48th Sess., 3293 mtg., at 125, UN Doc. S/RES/875 (1993).

[79] SC Res. 940, UN SCOR, 49th Sess., 3414 mtg., at 51, UN Doc. S/RES/940 (1994). See Domingo E. Acevedo, 'The Haitian Crisis and the OAS Response: A Test of Effectiveness in Protecting Democracy,' in *Enforcing Restraint: Collective Intervention in Internal Conflicts, infra* n. 86, at 119.

armed intervention by the West African regional organization, ECOWAS, utilizing ECOMOG, its military component.[80] This led to the restoration of the legitimate government, a move 'welcomed' by the Council.[81]

Involving a regional organization in the enforcement of the democratic entitlement tends to legitimate an intervention by multilateralizing the decision to intervene, provided the regional system is not merely camouflage for the interests of one powerful member. Article 2(b) of the Charter of the Organization of American States, with 35 members[82] the oldest of the regional groupings, authorizes it 'to promote and consolidate representative democracy'. Although long maintaining a policy of non-intervention, its OAS General Assembly in 1991 passed a resolution on Representative Democracy,[83] giving its Council of Ministers authority to intervene against any state in which democratic process is interrupted.[84] On several subsequent occasions, these powers have been threatened or invoked: in 1991 against the Haiti junta, and against coups in Peru in 1992, in Guatemala in 1993, and in Paraguay in 1996.[85] These procedures were enhanced in 1997 by amendment of the OAS Charter to allow suspension of a member whose legitimate government is unconstitutionally overthrown.[86]

Thus, the international system has begun to assume a degree of collective responsibility for restoring democracy in states where it has been lost. Clearly, loss of democratic process is no longer purely a matter within one state's domestic jurisdiction. This is acknowledged by the October 1991 Document of the Moscow Meeting of the CSCE's Conference on the Human Dimension, representing most of Europe, the US, and Canada, which reaffirmed 'that issues relating to human rights, fundamental freedoms, democracy and the rule of law are of international concern, as respect for these rights and freedoms constitutes one of the foundations of the international order'. The participating states 'categorically and irrevocably declare[d] that the commitments undertaken in the field of the human dimension of the CSCE are matters of direct and legitimate concern to all participating States and do not belong exclusively to

[80] SC Res. 1132, 52nd Sess., 3822 mtg., UN Doc. S/RES/1132 (1997); SC Res. 1162, 53rd Sess., 3872 mtg., UN Doc. S/RES/1162 (1998); SC Res. 1171, 53rd Sess., 3889 mtg., UN Doc. S/RES/1171 (1998). See also Report of the Secretary-General on the Situation in Sierra Leone, UN Doc. S/1997/811 (1997). [81] S/RES/1171, ibid.

[82] Aida L. Levin, 'The Organization of American States and the United Nations', in *Regionalism and the United Nations* 147, 149 (Berhanykun Andemicael ed., 1979).

[83] OEA/Ser.P/XX1.0.2/AG/Res.1080 (1991).

[84] Ibid. paras. 1, 2. See also Protocol of Amendment to the OAS Charter ('Protocol of Washington') adopted 14 Dec. 1992, 33 ILM 1005 (1994).

[85] See Resolution on Solidarity with the People of Haiti, OAS Permanent Council OEA/Ser.G/CP/Res. 489, Doc. 720 (1987). See also Resolution on Democracy in Nicaragua, OEA/Ser.F/II.21, Doc. 8, Rev. 2 (1989). See also Thomas W. Lippman, 'Joint Effort Heads Off Coup Threat in Paraguay', Wash. Post, 26 Apr. 1996, at A30.

[86] Protocol of Amendment of the Charter of the OAS, adopted 14 Dec. 1992. 33 ILM 1005 (1994). See also *Enforcing Restraint: Collective Intervention in Internal Conflict* (Lori F. Damrosch ed., 1993) and the case studies therein.

the internal affairs of the State concerned'.[87] In Part II of the Moscow Document, the members pledge that, in accordance with the Charter of the United Nations, in case of overthrow or attempted overthrow of a legitimately elected government of a participating State by undemocratic means, they will continue to support vigorously the legitimate organs of that State upholding human rights, democracy and the rule of law, recognizing their common commitment to countering any attempt to curb these basic values.[88]

The Moscow Document, by introducing a system of mediation, also enhances the range of options available to prevent and reverse violations of democratic rule. Paragraphs 3–16 envisage a 'resource' of experts, from which mediators may be selected to advise when any six CSCE member-states make a complaint against another member alleging a default in complying with the 'human dimension' established by the Document.

## 7. WHEN DEMOCRACY IS NOT ENOUGH

Although the international system has made progress in promoting and protecting people's democratic entitlement, democracy alone cannot be the sole guarantor of persons' rights, much less of a stable balancing of rights. Majoritarian electoral politics are important, but not sufficient, to guarantee individual rights and freedoms or to weigh competing entitlements. Democracy cannot promise to protect individuals or groups against the oppression of a majority. In the words of US Supreme Court Justice Stevens, something more than democracy is necessary to guard 'the individual's right to make certain unusually important decisions that will affect his own, or his family's destiny' and protect 'the abiding interest in individual liberty that makes certain state intrusions on the citizen's right to decide how he will live his own life intolerable'.[89]

Judge Rosalyn Higgins has remarked that, just as national law functions to balance individual with communitarian rights, so 'it is the function of international law to reconcile these elements when they occur across State boundaries'.[90] But *what* law; and *how* made? Although equilibration through discourse is a necessary element in a rights-based regime, law made by parliamentary majorities may not always suffice to ensure the survival of a peaceful, consensual society in times of stress. It is not only kings and dictators, but also elected

---

[87] Conference on Security and Co-operation in Europe, Document of the Moscow Meeting of the Conference on the Human Dimension of the CSCE, 3 Oct. 1991, Preamble, at 2 (unofficial text of the US delegation), reprinted in 30 ILM 1670 (1991) [hereafter Moscow Document].

[88] Moscow Document, ibid. at 9, para. 17.

[89] Stevens, J. (dissenting) in *Bowers v. Hardwick*, 478 US 186, 217 (quoting *Fitzgerald v. Porter Memorial Hospital*, 523 F.2d 716, 719–20 (7th Cir. 1975)).

[90] Rosalyn Higgins, 'The Taking of Property by the State', 176 *Recueil des Cours* 259, 274 (1982-III).

legislatures that have been known to infringe on personal freedoms of conscience and expression, restrict affective choices, and deprive the weak of allocational equality.

In mature liberal democracies, electoral majoritarianism tends to be mitigated by entrenched constitutional guarantees watched over by an independent judiciary applying historically deep-rooted principles. In such a society, 'the rule of law' may even, at times, contradict democratic legislative or executive processes, becoming the best defence of liberty and equality against wayward effects of democracy.

For the international system of governance to reach maturity, its newly vigorous emphasis on democracy must be balanced by counter-majoritarian incidents of the 'rule of law'. Of this there are already vestiges, including the independent tribunals and commissions of experts discussed in chapter eight, augmented by the body of normative rights protections developed since World War II and a notion of *jus cogens*.

The Vienna Convention on the Law of Treaties defines *jus cogens* as 'a preemptory norm of general international law. . . accepted by the international community of States as a whole as a norm from which no derogation is permitted and which can be modified only by a subsequent norm of general international law having the same character'.[91] A study of *jus cogens* by Lauri Hannikainen concludes that there is 'a great deal of evidence' of 'the existence of peremptory obligations to respect human rights'.[92] These 'trumping norms' may be seen as intimaters of emerging universal constitutionalism.

Together these elements constitute the early vital signs of an emerging global consensus around 'morally pluralistic constitutional democracy'.[93] The emerging international human rights regime, both its juridical and political institutions, is beginning to conform to this consensus.

## 8. CONCLUSIONS

The emergence of a globally recognized set of norms or laws that vouchsafe the rights of individuals to be 'let alone' autonomously to develop their identities, has raised questions of fairness and justice. An examination of these claims compels us to consider two forms of responsibility that emerge as concomitants to the rights being accorded individuals. The first pertains to persons' and

---

[91] Vienna Convention on the Law of Treaties, article 53. UN Doc. A/Conf.39/27 (1969). 8 ILM 679 (1969). Entered into force 27 January 1980.

[92] Lauri Hannikainen, *Peremptory Norms (Jus Cogens) in International Law: Historical Development, Criteria, Present Status* 425 (1988). The author concludes: 'In my view there is no doubt that contemporary international law has reached a stage in which it has the prerequisites for the existence of peremptory obligations upon States to respect basic human rights.' Ibid. at 429.

[93] Fleming, *supra* n. 2, at 12.

governments' responsibility to ameliorate the consequences of historic biases that force some to compete on an unlevel playing field. The second pertains to responsibility for balancing the rights of individuals with those of the state and of ethnic, religious, and other groups or minorities.

Both in national and international regimes, there is need to balance 'freedom from' with 'freedom to', to achieve what is perceived as a fair allocation of social goods, and to resolve competing claims among the parts of the rights triad. This requires a legitimate system of political discourse and electoral decision-making, as well as a principled adjudicatory and administrative process for applying rules and principles lodged in fundamental normative instruments, in deeply rooted custom or *jus cogens*, or in laws enunciated in the political arena. Liberal democracies already have these components in place, although none has yet perfected its own domestic system. The international community now appears ready to emulate this aspiration and to embark on the road to its fulfilment.

# 11

## *Summing Up*

There are two things which I can do very well: one is an introduction to any literary work, stating what it is to contain, and how it should be executed in the most perfect manner; the other is a conclusion, shewing from various causes why the execution has not been equal to what the author promised to himself and to the public.

1 Boswell's *Life of Johnson* (Powell rev., Hill ed.) p. 46

There is much in this work that cannot satisfactorily be summarized in brief conclusions. What matters is to have presented evidence from which each reader can tease personal conclusions. To offer a set-piece summation is to preempt the reader's autonomy and subvert his or her individual rights. It may also tempt busy persons to read only what seems to be a distilled essence of the matter in a few handy pages. That would compound a misrepresentation. This, in truth, is only the pedestrian destination of an adventuresome journey.

Despite these cautions and misgivings, here are some final thoughts derived from the contemplation of human identity in the age of individualism, an epoch that challenges older, entrenched communitarian values and institutions.

The contemporary human condition—modern sensibilities, advanced technologies, urbanization, and proliferating sophistication—has created fissures in the façade of communitarian identity.

I hope I have not overstated.

Persons still identify themselves by their membership in collectivities: the tribe, nation, state, religion, class, culture, and language. History and myth still inform individuals' sense of who they are. Elites retain formidable power to ensure that individuals conform to the community's received wisdoms. Even the rapidly evolving international system still tries to limit participation, as Vattel long ago ordained, to traditional, sovereign states. A cold crust still covers much of the planet.

But, in this cold, brittle crust deep fissures are appearing. Deep inside these one sees signs of tectonic change. Most notably, persons are beginning to define themselves as autonomous *individuals*. Gradually, this is surfacing: in national and international law and in a new social consciousness. Some persons are beginning to assert individual human rights in practice, pursuing their entitlements in political fora and judicial tribunals. Persons are even insinuating themselves into corridors of international diplomacy, where laws and policies are made.

While individuals increasingly claim a right to self-determine the contours of their own identities, this does not necessarily challenge frontally the older communitarian affiliations. It may, however, undermine the claim of those societies to be the sole, natural, and ineluctable building blocks of everyone's identity. Those claims stand exposed as based on bad genetics, faulty ethnography, and myths. Modern individualists may still choose to participate in traditional tribal rituals, play the single-minded patriot, embrace a parent's religion, or dance to kinfolk music. But they are also likely to insist that their choice manifests subjective preference, not some imposed, inescapable mandate of god, nature, or history.

More and more this insistence on autonomous personhood is buttressed by law, both national and international, which continually widens the space for private choice in matters of belief and conscience, gender and sexuality, education and career: matters that were traditionally regulated by communitarian controls.

While this transformation is not everywhere proceeding at a uniform rate, it is nevertheless profoundly pandemic, propelled by forces that transcend territorial, cultural, linguistic, religious, and ethnographic boundaries. Although these new personal freedoms were realized first in some Western societies, there is nothing inherently Western about the desire of persons to make private choices in matters of intimate importance.

There are discernible commonalities in the way freedom of conscience came to assert itself in countries such as England, the US, and Sweden. Such commonalities are also evident across other categories of emancipation from the strict conformity that communitarian societies long demanded of individuals in choosing their beliefs, name, career, gender, domicile, and other aspects of identity. Individualism has proved contagious, spreading under propitious circumstances of industrialization, economic development, the emergence of an urban middle class, universal and higher education, political democratization, and revolutions in personal access to information and communications. These exogenous factors, over time, are universally replicable and the human rights they tend, however incidentally, to foster are increasingly supported by the laws and mores of an emerging international system.

A demand for personal emancipation is now also beginning to surface in many non-Western communities. In some places, these demands are still being repressed by those who benefit most from the status quo, but their repression differs from earlier eras mainly in that the preponderance of international opinion now more often mobilizes on the side of victims. When England's Queen Mary I burned early Anglicans for their views on transubstantiation, most of Europe was behind her. Today, the UN Security Council manifests a different ethos. An example typical of present-day thinking is a recent unanimous resolution demanding an end to the Afghani regime's 'discrimination against girls and women and other violations of human rights' and its adherence to prevailing 'international norms and standards . . .'.[1]

Despite communitarian cant, the emergence of individualism has not, as its inevitable concomitant, engendered personal alienation, anomie, or social atomization. On the contrary, occurring at a time of exponential growth in communications facility and technology, individualism has enabled the formation of new, voluntary, even virtual, communities of persons unlimited by the previous boundaries of proximity, genetics, and language. Increasingly, as the rapid proliferation of non-governmental international organizations demonstrates, traditional communitarian societies are coming to accommodate the inevitable reality of individual choice in constructing personal identities around multiple layers of freely selected affinities and newly constituted, often transnational, communities of shared interest.

This tendency frees individuals to engage their energy in voluntary co-operation and enterprise, thereby helping to construct a more effective and responsible system of mixed private and public governance. It need not threaten the continuing viability of older social communities (the ethnie, tribe, nation, and state) so long as these do not force membership on unwilling individuals and freely permit exit. Rather, the new realities of social interaction, conflict resolution, economic, scientific, and cultural development, transnational ecological and resource management, instantaneous mass communications, unlimited information storage and retrieval: all these combine to point to the evolution of a complex, multilevel, vibrant new civil culture and civic society that slips the surly bonds of territoriality.

At the international level, since the end of World War II, an elaborate system of rules and procedures has come to afford protection for persons' lives, liberty, personal security, privacy, conscience, and equality of opportunity. It purports to protect individuals' freedom of speech, movement, choice of language, and participation in politics and other forms of association. It aims to protect persons against arbitrary arrest or punishment. These norms are intended to shield individuals even against their own governments: a concept hitherto virtually unknown in international law and state practice.

While these new rules are still defied here and there, now and then, their implementation has become institutional, systematic, and routine. Examples include the European, Inter-American, and African Human Rights Courts, the Human Rights Committee of the Covenant on Civil and Political Rights and the special rapporteurs appointed at the instance of the UN Human Rights Commission. These and other innovative mechanisms now frequently exert pressure on governments to conform to standards which, half a century ago, were unthinkable. Hundreds of complaints by persons against their own

---

[1] S/RES/1214 (1998), para. 12.

governments are now routinely processed in this fashion and the resultant findings tend to be implemented by complaisant national governments.

Remarkable is not the occasional instance of recalcitrance but the high degree of compliance this new regime has secured. In just a few years, the way a state treats its own citizens has gone from a jealously protected matter of national sovereignty—the 1945 Nuremberg Tribunal's statutory powers, typically, were carefully drafted to exclude acts committed by Germany against its own Jewish citizens—to one entirely appropriate for international condemnation and, in egregious cases (South Africa, Southern Rhodesia, Haiti, and Kosovo) even for international enforcement measures.

From the practices of a broad range of international and regional rights-protecting regimes it can be surmised that individuals are now generally accepted as rights-holders and as claimants. There also appears to be general recognition that personal rights are to be protected not only by national but also by international law and institutions. Most remarkably, there is now widespread recognition that the various forms of assistance to governments provided by intergovernmental institutions—security, fiscal stability, and development aid—can and should be conditioned on the recipients' compliance with fundamental human rights norms.

These developments are not cost free. Understaffed, pro-bono legal services with inadequate resources are struggling to provide complainants with the skilled services needed to make effective use of the new remedies. Equally, governments, especially those of small and poor countries, are finding it hard to keep up with the proliferating requirements for detailed (and duplicative) periodic reports on their compliance with the new regimes protecting persons' civil and political rights, the rights of women and children, and freedom from torture.

Nevertheless, the burgeoning canon of individual rights has begun to crack open the previously encrusted Vattelian system, transforming formerly unchallenged concepts of state sovereignty and curbing the long-established powers of society to compel individuals to conform even to its most repressive practices. Almost everywhere, persons are gaining in the struggle to construct their personal identities through autonomous choice among ever-expanding options.

This emerging triumph of individualism, while still contingent, has alarmed traditional defenders of communitarian values. Not all are appeased by evidence that autonomous individuals actually militate towards new, freely chosen social affiliations and responsibilities. Some critics consider the greatest danger to arise not from individual anomie but from the very idea of personal affiliative choice itself. In particular, some particularist groups, long engaged in struggle with what they perceive as the homogenizing power of the state, have now also joined the battle against corrosive individualism.

We thus are seeing the emergence of a rights triad—individual, state, and group—locked in a precarious and stressed balance.

Group-rights advocates increasingly position themselves in aggressive opposition to prevailing notions of individual rights, even as they try to deconstruct established multi-ethnic states. While not all religious, ethnic, racial, cultural, or linguistic groups are outright secessionists, many demand autonomous control over culture, education, religion, family law, land-ownership, and inheritance. Most particularist movements seek power to enforce communitarian values, rules, and policies, sometimes in outright opposition both to the state above, and the individual below. The most illiberal set out to deny basic freedoms to their members and to stop or punish individuals who seek to renounce their group affiliation.

More generally, individualism is criticized by the more militant group-rights advocates as a siren call to abandon historically, ethnically, and culturally validated identities in exchange for a ticket of admission to the undifferentiated and meaningless mass culture of our day.

It is not necessary to accept this characterization. But it is difficult to deny the current force of groups' demands for parity with the state and the individual in a new triad of rights claimants. Yet it is hard to foresee how such a triad would apportion rights in practice, or how it would adjust and accommodate incompatible claims to self-realization. Nevertheless, it is becoming conventional wisdom that the claims of the individual, the group, and the state must coexist in some reasonable balance.

The search for such a balance begins with acceptance of the rule that each of the three categories of claimants must be able to enjoy those rights essential to its survival. This *survival principle*, easily stated but difficult to apply, calls for practical subsidiary principles. Three are discernible from evidence of state practice: local option, assisted exodus, and the subordination of particularism. Local option facilitates the synchronization of different systems of law to accommodate different identities within a common political space: for example, one matrimonial law for Hindus, another for Muslims. Assisted exodus artificially creates a discrete territorial basis for treating autonomous or federated groups differently within a loose common polity. In its worst manifestation it becomes ethnic cleansing. The subordination of particularism, undoubtedly the most complicated of the principles of adjustment, asserts the individual's residual moral supremacy when rival claims among the triad cannot be otherwise adjusted. This trumping power of fundamental human rights has already been manifested by the international system against deviant regimes, most dramatically those of South Africa, Rhodesia, Yugoslavia, and Afghanistan.

Practice, however, is not the only authority. The priority of personal rights in international practice is also supported by moral intuition, which argues the priority of persons. Among the triad of rights-claimants, only the individual is a natural construct. Both the state and the group, by contrast, are formed by historic–social conditions, their existence subjectively certified by the recognition of others. In this sense, the inherent rights of persons are prior to, and differ in kind from, the acquired rights of groups and states. Persons' claim to rights emanates from the undeconstructible objective fact of personage and not from such contingent conditions as those of state sovereignty or group cohesion. From this it follows that personal rights have a strong moral claim to priority over the rights of states and groups: at least in situations of conflict not otherwise resolvable by clear guidance from normative law or political negotiations.

Priority, however, is not predominance. The common interest of the components of the triad is in preserving the balance necessary to enable each part effectively to interrogate the others. The international system increasingly recognizes and facilitates that balance as a good in itself.

The age of individualism, by recognizing what US Supreme Court Justice Brandeis has characterized as the right, above all others, of persons 'to be let alone' has powered a rising tide of social and economic development by unleashing private initiative. While this rising tide has lifted most boats, the right to be left alone tends to benefit those already most favoured by social rank, intelligence, family cohesion, and education. Leaving alone the poor and incapacitated accords them little or no share in progress. The benefits of being left alone thus must be balanced by social commitment to equalizing the conditions of those left behind.

While this sort of responsibility is increasingly acknowledged by the civil communities of states, it is as yet much less evident at the international level. The recent emphasis on universal, personal rights has not as yet been matched by commitment to universal social responsibility. This has aggravated the gap between those benefiting the most from new freedoms and those least advantaged. Although that gap is mitigated within most states by remedial measures, such measures are only inadequately deployed, if at all, at the global level.

Not surprisingly, efforts are already underway to link 'freedom from' with 'freedom to'. Efforts led by Fr. Hans Küng and former President Jimmy Carter link the commitment to individuality and freedom with individual responsibility for creating a just social order. Unfortunately, some of this nascent momentum has been exploited by communitarians and authoritarians to attack more generally the recent advances in recognition of personal rights and to revive the charge that individualism represents a narrowly Western value. These efforts have been rebuffed vigorously by, among many others, the UN Human Rights Commissioner and former Irish President Mary Robinson and UN Secretary-General Kofi Annan.

Despite these diversions, there is apparent a large potential symbiosis between personal rights and responsibilities. Individual rights flourish when the many, not just an elite, recognize them to serve their own interests. That is most likely to occur when all ensure equal opportunities for each.

Ensuring equality of opportunity without the stifling requirement of equal outcomes requires more delicate balancing. Such a balance can be hypothesized by social philosophy. But in an age rightly distrustful of philosopher-kings, its implementation must be left by default, to the discourse of democratic politics. It is in the political forum that the search is conducted for an optimum balance between the social and economic claims of advantaged and deprived persons.

Why politics? Whereas disputes regarding personal rights to freedom of conscience or freedom from torture may frequently be resolved by adjudication, disputes regarding redistributive rights—levels and allocation of the tax burdens to support public schools, for example—tend to be referred to the political forum because they are of such general importance, pitting not one individual against a government or another individual but the many against many, and because general normative texts tend not to be very helpful in their resolution. This makes it essential that the political process by which such important social allocations are made be generally accepted as democratic and legitimate.

All too evidently, international political institutions fall far short of this democratic legitimacy. International regimes, even as they become increasingly involved in managing and allocating global resources, remain stubbornly the domain of bureaucrats and diplomats. The former represent no one; and although the latter purport to speak for governments, they are unelected. So are some of the regimes they represent.

Little, realistically, is about to be done about instituting direct popular representation in international institutions of governance. Something is being done, however, to ensure that those who speak in global discourse, at least do represent governments that, themselves, have been chosen democratically. To the extent these efforts are beginning to arouse in citizens an expectation of democratic participation in their national level of governance, the international system's legitimacy, too, is fortified. Of late, that international system has made impressive, if still tentative, progress towards promoting such a global democratic entitlement. While the world's population may still for a time have to abide governance by diplomats, they are at least being assured of a right to choose the governments that appoint them.

The emergence of an internationally recognized right of democracy may be the most important manifestation of the age of individualism. The secret ballot, after all, is each person's ultimate medium of self-expression. As an international norm, however, it began as a by-product of the UN Charter's requirement (in article 73) that colonies be assisted towards democratic self-government. Gradually, the rules and procedures conceived for decolonization became loosely applicable everywhere. Both the Universal Declaration of Human Rights and the Covenant on Civil and Political Rights now oblige states to conduct free, fair, and secret elections at regular intervals by universal and equal suffrage. With the collapse of communism and *caudillismo*, the legal texts began to be realized in practice, reinforced by UN, Inter-American, African, and European regional machinery for assisting, monitoring, and even conducting democratic elections. It is now accepted that what had previously been the most cherished prerogative of sovereignty has become subject to international and regional law and standards, which, in a few egregious instances, have even been enforced by collective measures (Haiti, Sierra Leone, Guatemala, Paraguay).

Despite such progress, the democratic legitimacy of burgeoning global regimes is far from perfected and is at best only indirectly validated. Even were it to be perfected, however, democracy could not be the whole answer to protecting individual rights. While democratic politics can play a leading role in making many allocational decisions, it is less suited to protecting the rights of individuals and minorities against conformist pressures. As in mature democracies, so too the international system must continue to protect counter-majoritarian rights of persons through judicial and quasi-judicial institutions giving effect to the rule of law. There must be judicial institutions and experts willing to say 'no' to governments, whatever the status of their democratic mandate.

We have the building blocks. A new democratic impulse, together with growing respect for individual rights and an awakening sense of international social responsibility; together these can build foundations of universal constitutional democracy.

# Index